Culture and Customs of South Africa

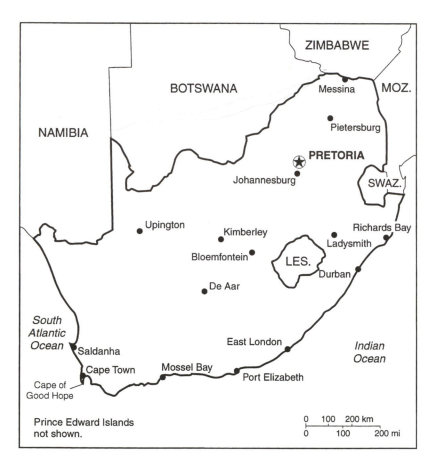

ZIMBABWE

BOTSWANA

MOZ.

Messina

NAMIBIA

Pietersburg

PRETORIA

Johannesburg

SWAZ.

Upington

Kimberley

Richards Bay

Ladysmith

Bloemfontein

LES.

De Aar

Durban

South
Atlantic
Ocean

East London

Indian
Ocean

Saldanha

Cape Town

Mossel Bay

Port Elizabeth

Cape of
Good Hope

Prince Edward Islands
not shown.

0   100   200 km

0   100   200 mi

South Africa

Culture and Customs of South Africa

FUNSO AFOLAYAN

Culture and Customs of Africa
Toyin Falola, Series Editor

GREENWOOD PRESS
Westport, Connecticut • London

Library of Congress Cataloging-in-Publication Data

Afolayan, Funso S.
  Culture and customs of South Africa / Funso Afolayan.
    p. cm. — (Culture and customs of Africa, ISSN 1530–8367)
  Includes bibliographical references and index.
  ISBN 0–313–32018–7 (alk. paper)
    1. Ethnology—South Africa. 2. Material culture—South Africa. 3. South Africa—History. 4. South Africa—Politics and government. 5. South Africa—Social life and customs. I. Title. II. Series.
GN656.A36 2004
306'.0968—dc22   2003060058

British Library Cataloguing in Publication Data is available.

Library of Congress Catalog Card Number: 2003060058
ISBN: 0–313–32018–7
ISSN: 1530–8367

First published in 2004

Greenwood Press, 88 Post Road West, Westport, CT 06881
An imprint of Greenwood Publishing Group, Inc.
www.greenwood.com

Printed in the United States of America

The paper used in this book complies with the
Permanent Paper Standard issued by the National
Information Standards Organization (Z39.48–1984).

10 9 8 7 6 5 4 3 2 1

For
Abimbọla
Nkosikazi—Iyawo mi ọwọn

Contents

Series Foreword

AFRICA is a vast continent, the second largest, after Asia. It is four times the size of the United States, excluding Alaska. It is the cradle of human civilization. A diverse continent, Africa has more than fifty countries with a population of over 700 million people who speak over 1,000 languages. Ecological and cultural differences vary from one region to another. As an old continent, Africa is one of the richest in culture and customs, and its contributions to world civilization are impressive indeed.

Africans regard culture as essential to their lives and future development. Culture embodies their philosophy, worldview, behavior patterns, arts, and institutions. The books in this series intend to capture the comprehensiveness of African culture and customs, dwelling on such important aspects as religion, worldview, literature, media, art, housing, architecture, cuisine, traditional dress, gender, marriage, family, lifestyles, social customs, music, and dance.

The uses and definitions of "culture" vary, reflecting its prestigious association with civilization and social status, its restriction to attitude and behavior, its globalization, and the debates surrounding issues of tradition, modernity, and postmodernity. The participating authors have chosen a comprehensive meaning of culture while not ignoring the alternative uses of the term.

Each volume in the series focuses on a single country, and the format is uniform. The first chapter presents a historical overview, in addition to information on geography, economy, and politics. Each volume then proceeds to examine the various aspects of culture and customs. The series highlights the mechanisms for the transmission of tradition and culture across generations:

the significance of orality, traditions, kinship rites, and family property distribution; the rise of print culture; and the impact of educational institutions. The series also explores the intersections between local, regional, national, and global bases for identity and social relations. While the volumes are organized nationally, they pay attention to ethnicity and language groups and the links between Africa and the wider world.

The books in the series capture the elements of continuity and change in culture and customs. Custom is not represented as static or as a museum artifact, but as a dynamic phenomenon. Furthermore, the authors recognize the current challenges to traditional wisdom, which include gender relations; the negotiation of local identities in relation to the state; the significance of struggles for power at national and local levels and their impact on cultural traditions and community-based forms of authority; and the tensions between agrarian and industrial/manufacturing/oil-based economic modes of production.

Africa is a continent of great changes, instigated mainly by Africans but also through influences from other continents. The rise of youth culture, the penetration of the global media, and the challenges to generational stability are some of the components of modern changes explored in the series. The ways in which traditional (non-Western and nonimitative) African cultural forms continue to survive and thrive, that is, how they have taken advantage of the market system to enhance their influence and reproductions also receive attention.

Through the books in this series, readers can see their own cultures in a different perspective, understand the habits of Africans, and educate themselves about the customs and cultures of other countries and people. The hope is that readers will come to respect the cultures of others and see them not as inferior or superior to theirs, but merely as different. Africa has always been important to Europe and the United States, essentially as a source of labor, raw materials, and markets. Blacks are in Europe and the americas as part of the African diaspora, a migration that took place primarily due to the slave trade. Recent African migrants increasingly swell their number and visibility. It is important to understand the history of the diaspora and the new migrants, as well as the roots of the culture and customs of the places from where they come. It is equally important to understand others in order to be able to interact successfully in a world that keeps shrinking. The accessible nature of the books in this series will contribute to this understanding and enhance the quality of human interaction in a new millennium.

Toyin Falola
The University of Texas at Austin

Preface

SOUTH AFRICA is, in many ways, Africa's oldest and newest nation. In 1910, it gained its independence from British rule as the Union of South Africa, the first state in Africa to break loose from European colonial domination. The vast majority of the other African states would not secure their independence for another four decades. However, for the peoples of South Africa, the 1910 independence was a highly constricted one. It gave autonomy and power to the white minority, but denied liberty and equality to the majority of the population till the last decade of the twentieth century. The end of apartheid and the establishment of a nonracial, nonsexist, and multiparty democracy in 1994 finally brought freedom to all the inhabitants of the country. April 27, the date of the first epochal democratic elections in South African history, became South Africa's Freedom Day, marking its birth as Africa's newest nation.

The newness of South Africa poses a major methodological problem for any attempt to study the culture and customs of its peoples. Anthropologists have long abandoned the idea of the static and unchanging society. All human societies are cultures in transition. For South Africa, this is even more so. Since 1994, this newest of the African states has been going through a period of rapid transformations. Rescuing and rebuilding this nation from the ravages of colonialism and of the apartheid years is a work in progress. While we are still studying to understand what the nation has been and where it is coming from, we as yet do not know where it is going or what it is going to become. It is in recognition of this reality that I have adopted a sociohistorical approach in this study. The present is still too new, too fluid, and too much in a state of flux, that to understand it one must do so within the framework of the past.

Diversity is a word that should have a place of honor in the South African lexicon. The most racially diverse in Africa, the "rainbow people of God," as Archbishop Desmond Tutu puts it, South Africa is also one of the most ethnically, culturally, and linguistically varied on the continent. Besides its various Khoisan- and Bantu-speaking African groups, it is home to the most populous communities of Asians and Europeans in Africa. This diversity has remained a crucial and a salient element of its history and society, and it is fully taken into consideration in this reference. However, no attempt is made to cover every aspect of the culture and customs of each and every one of its many peoples and groups. Such a comprehensive and indeed encyclopedic exploration, even if desirable, is impossible within the scope and purpose of this volume. Thus, I have been selective and deliberate, hopefully not arbitrary, in the range of issues and topics explored in the series parameters, influenced by my assessment of their relative importance and by the nature and extent of the available information. The bibliographical essay at the end of the book provides extensive additional sources for those interested in more profound explorations of the issues examined in this volume.

With regards to terminology and orthography, a little explanation is in order. As a result of its linguistic diversity and its history of racial and group antagonisms, language was used by the dominant white minority to denigrate and marginalize the other racial groups in the country. To avoid or minimize confusion, I have used more acceptable and less subjective terms, where appropriate and where such exist. For examples, I have used Khoikhoi instead of Hottentots; San instead of Bushmen; Khoisans, when referring to all the autochthonous groups; and Afrikaners instead of Boers, except where historical accuracy demands otherwise. More problematic is finding a commonly acceptable term to refer collectively to the Bantu-speaking peoples. In this respect, I have avoided the use of *kaffir* (Arabic for "infidel") and natives, two of the many derogatory terms used by whites to describe black people for many centuries. Depending on the context and the time period referred to I have used the terms "blacks," "Bantu," and "Africans," while acknowledging these facts: first, that the term "Bantu" was not (until recently) used by whites as a badge of honor to describe Africans; and second, that all racial groups in South Africa can legitimately claim to be Africans as citizens of South Africa. For want of a more acceptable alternative, the term "colored" is used to refer to Malay and other mixed-race peoples. Its continuing rejection as a racist terminology by those it purports to describe explains why it is not capitalized in this volume.

Acknowledgments

AFTER studying and teaching South African history and culture for many years, writing this book was for me a voyage of exploration and of discovery. My journey was made easier as a result of seminal works already done on South Africa by other scholars, to whom my necessarily attenuated notes may not be enough to reveal the extent of my indebtedness. Notable among such pioneer scholars are David Hammond-Tooke, Peter Magubane, Lorna Marshall, Leonard Thompson, Sandra Klopper, Anitra Nettleton, Eleanor Preston-Whyte, Percival Kirby, Franco Frescura, Hans Fransen, Michael Chapman, Keyan and Ruth Tomaselli, Lee Switzer, Veit Erlmann, David Chidester, Muff Anderson, Charles Ambler, and David Coplan, to mention just a few. My research work in South Africa was facilitated by the friendship and hospitality of many scholars as well as by others, most of whom space will not permit me to name. Notable among these are Gabriel and Gloria Francis, Dorothy Masugu, Dennis Philip, Tunde Lawuyi, Teboho Moja, Sean Fields, Gideon Khabela, Nomvinbi Meriwether, Jan Shabangu, and Philip Nkabinde.

I remain indebted to the series editor, Dr. Toyin Falola, for his advice and support at different stages of this project. Ms. Wendi Schnaufer, my editor at Greenwood Press, deserves a medal for her incredible patience and professionalism as she tactfully nudged me on to finish up the project. Thanks to Jennifer Beard for expertly copyediting the volume. I am also grateful to Jane Davis, Lyn Graybill, Helen and Russell Mason, Akin Akinade, Janet Bergman ("reporting live from Durban"), Meg Curtin, and Jennifer Beard, for making available to me photographs and other relevant materials in their possession.

All the photographs not specifically ascribed are mine. The University of New Hampshire at Durham, through its College of Liberal Arts' Faculty Scholars Program, its Center for the Humanities, its Center for International Education, its Office of Sponsored Research, and its Department of History, was immeasurably helpful in granting me a semester study leave to work on the project and in sponsoring research trips to South Africa.

Finally to my soul mate, Abimbola, and my T-kids, Tobi, Tomi, Tolu, and Tinu, for their understanding and support, but even more for ensuring that love and peace prevailed at the home front, I owe more gratitude than I can hope to express here. The birth of the new South Africa in 1994 was a miracle, obtained after decades of intense struggle and at a high cost. I have been privileged to live to see that transformation and to join in its celebration. I hope my readers will find as much pleasure in perusing this book as I did in writing it.

Chronology

c. 1–3 million years	Early Stone Age; *Australopithecus africanus; Homo erectus* in Southern Africa.
c. 30,000–100,000 B.C.	Middle Stone Age; *Homo sapiens* in Southern Africa.
15–30,000 B.C.	Late Stone Age; earliest known example of rock art; San hunter-gatherers and related groups in southern Africa.
c. 2500–A.D. 200	Livestock domestication; Khoikhoi herders move into South Africa.
A.D. 300	Iron-using Bantu-speaking mixed farmers begin to move into South Africa.
500–700	Early Iron Age in the eastern Cape; Lydenberg terra-cotta heads.
1300–1500	Sotho-Tswana settlements on the interior plateau; Nguni settlements in the southeastern coastal and highland regions.
1487	Portuguese explorers, led by Bartholomew Dias round the Cape of Southern Africa in a storm.
1497	Vasco da Gama rounds the Cape to complete the European much-sought-for Atlantic sea route to India.
1510	Francisco d'Almeida, viceroy of Portuguese India, and 57 of his men killed by the Khoikhoi at the Table Bay.

1652	The Dutch East India Company, under the command of Jan van Riebeeck, obtains land from the Khoikhoi to establish a refreshment station at the Cape.
1658	First two shiploads of slaves from Angola and West Africa transform the Cape into a slave society, setting the stage for importation of more slaves from Indonesia, Ceylon, and Madagascar.
1659–77	Khoikhoi resistance wars against the gradually expanding and land-appropriating Dutch settlers.
1688	About 200 Huguenots, fleeing from religious persecution, arrive from France and settle around Franschboek at the Cape.
1713	Khoikhoi population decimated by smallpox brought to the Cape aboard a Dutch ship returning from Batavia.
1779–80	First in a series of nine Xhosa-White Frontier Wars.
1793	Lombard Bank, the first bank in the country, opens at the Cape.
1795	Britain seizes the Cape from the Dutch to forestall its takeover by Napoleonic France.
1800	*African Advertiser* and the *Cape Town Gazette* are first published.
1802	Lady Anne Bernard returns to England from the Cape.
1803	The Dutch (Batavian Republic) regain the Cape Colony.
1806	Britain reconquers the Cape Colony.
1816–28	*Mfecane;* Shaka creates the Zulu kingdom.
1820	5000 British settlers arrive in the Cape Colony.
1824	The Sotho leader, Moshoeshoe, establishes his capital at Thaba Bosiu.
1828	The Zulu king, Shaka, assassinated in a palace coup led by his half-brother, Dingane, who succeeds him as *inkosi.*
1829	South African College (forerunner of the University of Cape Town) opens.

1834–35	The British order the emancipation of slaves in the Cape Colony, triggering off the onset of the Boer Great Trek.
1835	Xhosa paramount chief, Hintsa, murdered by the British; five thousand Afrikaners and their colored servants begin their protest emigration from the Cape into the interior, in what will be known as the Great Trek.
1837	*Voortrekkers* defeat Mzilikazi's Ndebele, forcing them to cross the Limpopo into modern Zimbabwe.
1838	The Zulu king, Dingane, orders the massacre of Piet Retief's *voortrekker* party; Zulu army defeated by an Afrikaner commando at the Battle of Blood River.
1843	Britain annexes Natal, which was founded by *voortrekkers* as the Republic of Natalia in 1838.
1850–54	Britain recognizes the independence of the Afrikaner republics of Transvaal and the Orange Free State.
1856–57	The Xhosa prophetically induced cattle-killing leads to famine and the death of thousands.
1858	Lesotho defeats the Orange Free State.
1859	Bible in Xhosa.
1865–67	Orange Free State defeats Lesotho.
1866	Afrikaans premier University of Stellebosch opens.
1867	Diamond mining begins in Griqualand West.
1868	Britain annexes Basutoland (Lesotho).
1873	South African College became University of Cape Town.
1876	The Pedi defeat the South African Republic.
1878	The Zulu defeat and wipe out a British regiment at the battle of Isandlwana.
1879	British and colonial forces defeat the Zulu.
1883	Bible in Zulu; Olive Schreiner, *The Story of an African Farm*.
1885	Haggard, *King Solomon's Mines*.

1886	Gold mining begins on the Witwatersrand; Johannesburg founded.
1887	Britain annexes Zululand; King Dinuzulu deported to the desolate island of St. Helena.
1890	Cecil Rhodes becomes Cape prime minister.
1893–94	Mohandas K. Gandhi arrives in South Africa; Natal Indian Congress founded.
1896–98	Rinderpest epidemic destroys large numbers of cattle.
1897	Enoch Sontonga writes *Nkosi sikelel 'iAfrika,* a Christian hymn which soon becomes a liberation movement anthem.
1898	Transvaal forces conquer the Venda, thus completing the white conquest of all the African populations of southern Africa.
1899–1902	The South African or Anglo-Boer War; Afrikaner republics come under British rule.
1902	Rhodes dies; Johannesburg *Rand Daily Mail* starts publication.
1904–7	63,397 Chinese workers imported to work in the mines.
1906	Bambatha Zulu rebellion against poll tax savagely suppressed.
1907	Sir James Percy FitzPatrick, *Jack of the Bushveld.*
1910	Union of South Africa established (31 May), with Louis Botha as first prime minister and Jan Smuts as deputy.
1912	South African Native National Congress formed with John Dube as first president; later becomes African National Congress (ANC).
1913	Natives Land Act limits African land ownership to designated reserves, constituting roughly 7 percent of all South African land; the enactments of a series of segregation laws begins.
1914	The New National Party (NP) founded; Gandhi returns to India.

1916	South African Native College (Fort Hare) established; Sol Plaatje, *Native Life in South Africa.*
1917	Anglo American Corporation of South Africa founded.
1918	Afrikaner Broederbond founded to promote Afrikaner nationalism.
1919	Industrial and Commercial Workers' Union (ICU) founded; South Africa receives League of Nations' mandate over South West Africa (later Namibia).
1921	Massacre of Israelites religionists at Bulhoek by the South African Police; Communist Party of South Africa formed.
1922	White workers strike and seizure of Johannesburg crushed by government troops.
1924	Roy Campbell, *The Flaming Terrapin.*
1925	Afrikaans replaces Dutch as official language.
1927	Immorality Act prohibits sexual relations between whites and others.
1928	Kirstenbosch Botanical Garden and University of South Africa founded.
1930	White women receive the franchise to vote.
1936	First edition of Afrikaans Bible; Africans are removed from Cape voters' roll.
1938	Centenary celebration of the Great Trek; first stone of the Voortrekker Monument laid.
1939–45	South Africa participates in World War II on the side of the Allied Powers.
1946	70,000 to 100,000 gold-mine workers strike crushed by government troops; Peter Abrahams, *Mine Boy.*
1948	The Afrikaner National Party wins elections and begins to implement its policy of apartheid; Alan Paton, *Cry the Beloved Country* published, soon becomes the most famous South African novel.
1949–53	Series of legislations enacted into law institutionalizing and enforcing racial segregation in all areas of South

African life: Prohibition of Mixed Marriages Act; Group
Areas Act; Immorality Act; Population Registration Act;
Suppression of Communism Act; Bantu Education Act.

1951   *Drum*, a weekly magazine, begins publication; Doris
                Lessing, *This Was the Old Chief's Country.*

1954   Federation of South African Women formed; Peter
                Abrahams, *Tell Freedom.*

1955   South African Congress of Trade Union formed; Con-
                gress of the People adopts Freedom Charter as the blue-
                print for the formation of a multiracial and democratic
                South Africa; Ritter, *Shaka Zulu.*

1956   Coloreds removed from the Cape common voters' roll;
                156 activists on trial for treason; Huddleston, *Naught
                for Your Comfort.*

1958   Laurens van der Post, *The Lost World of the Kalahari.*

1959   Pan Africanist Congress (PAC) formed by Robert
                Sobukwe; *King Kong* musical, featuring Miriam
                Makeba, Hugh Masekela, Thandi Klaasen, and penny-
                whistler and child prodigy, Lemmy "Special" Mabaso
                (the Kwela kid) and a hundred other talents, opens;
                Mphahlele, *Down Second Avenue*

1960   White representation of Africans in Parliament termi-
                nated; police kill 67 antipass demonstrators at
                Sharpville; ANC, PAC, Communist Party, and other
                resistance groups banned.

1961   Zulu Chief and ANC president, Albert Luthuli,
                receives Nobel Peace Prize; South Africa becomes a
                republic and leaves the British Commonwealth; Lauren
                Van der Post, *The Heart of the Hunter.*

1962   La Guma, *A Walk in the Night;* Luthuli, *Let My People
                Go;* Van Wyk Louw, *Tristia.*

1964   The Armaments Corporation of South Africa
                (ARMSCOR) established; Nelson Mandela, Walter
                Sizulu, Govan Mbeki, and others sentenced to life
                imprisonment at the Rivonia Trial; Wibur Smith, *When
                the Lion Feeds.*

1966	Hendrick F. Verwoerd, South African prime minister since 1958, is stabbed to death by a demented white-man in the House of Assembly; B. J. Vorster becomes prime minister; District Six, the life and soul of Cape Town, declared a White only area.
1966–68	Lesotho, Botswana, and Swaziland become independent.
1969	Steve Biko forms the South African Students' Organization; Eugene Marais, *The Soul of the Ape.*
1971	Oswald Mtshali's *Sounds of a Cowhide Drum.*
1974	*Ipi Tombi,* commercially popular African musical opens; Market Theatre, Johannesburg; Gordimer, *The Conservationist* (cowinner of the UK Booker Prize).
1975–76	Mozambique and Angola win their armed struggle for independence from Portugal; South African Defence Force troops invade Angola; Mangosuthu Buthulezi revives the Inkatha movement.
1976–77	Protest by Soweto school children against the compulsory learning of Afrikaans spread throughout the country, resulting in clashes with the police and the death of nearly 600 people.
1977	Steve Biko, leader of the Black Consciousness Movement, arrested and tortured to death by the police; United Nations imposes compulsory arms embargo against South Africa; Bessie Head, *The Collector of Treasures.*
1978	Pan Africanist Congress leader Robert Sobkwe dies; Botha succeeds Vorster as prime minister and launches total onslaught against enemies of apartheid; Essop, *The Hajj and Other Stories.*
1979	Gordimer, *Burger's Daughter;* Kunene, *Emperor Shaka the Great;* André Brink, *A Dry White Season;* Matshoba, *Call Me Not a Man.*
1980–81	Coetzee, *Waiting for the Barbarians;* Paton, *Towards the Mountain;* Gordimer, *July's People;* Serote, *To Every Birth Its Blood.*

1981–88   South African Defence Forces invade Angola and carry
                 out hit-and-run raids and acts of sabotage against
                 Lesotho, Mozambique, Zimbabwe, and Zambia;
                 Umkhonto, the ANC armed wing, attacks the main
                 South African military base at Voortrekkerhoogte and
                 its nuclear plant at Koeberg.

1983   J. M. Coetzee, *Life and Times of Michael K;* Fugard,
                 'Master' Harold and the Boys.

1984–86   Township revolts spread from Sharpville to East Rand,
                 Soweto and other black South African townships; gov-
                 ernment intensifies violent suppression of resistance;
                 Desmund Tutu, the Archbishop of Cape Town, and
                 head of the Anglican Church in Southern Africa,
                 awarded Nobel Peace Prize; Breytenbach, *The True
                 Confessions of an Albino Terrorist.*

1985   Botha declares state of emergency; first contact between
                 the government and imprisoned and exiled ANC lead-
                 ers; Joseph Lelyveld, *Move Your Shadow: South Africa,
                 Black and White,* wins the Pulitzer Prize.

1986   Pass laws repealed; thousands detained; the media
                 prohibited from covering or reporting unrests;
                 Commonwealth-appointed Eminent Persons' Group
                 Mission recommends tougher sanctions against South
                 Africa; the U.S. Congress rejects President Ronald
                 Reagan's policy of constructive engagement with
                 apartheid South Africa, overturning his veto to pass the
                 Comprehensive Anti-Apartheid Act, which imposes
                 sanctions on South Africa; Ngema, *Sarafina.*

1987   Gordimer, *A Sport of Nature;* Culture in Another South
                 Africa Conference, Amsterdam.

1989   F. W. de Klerk replaces Botha as National Party leader,
                 and soon as president; Walter Sisulu and seven other
                 long-term political prisoners freed.

1990–91   De Klerk unbans the ANC, PAC, SACP, and other
                 opposition groups; Mandela released unconditionally
                 after 27 years in prison; Namibia becomes independent;
                 ANC suspends armed struggle; Rian Malan, *My Trai-
                 tor's Heart* (1990); Jeanne Goosen, *Ons is Nie Almal So
                 Nie* (1990).

1991   Continuing repeal of all racial and segregationist laws;
                        Mandela is elected ANC president; nineteen parties
                        from all races attend Convention for a Democratic
                        South Africa (Codesa); Nadine Gordimer wins Nobel
                        Prize for Literature.

1992   Whites-only referendum approves government reform
                        process; continuing tension and rivalry between sup-
                        porters of the ANC and those of Buthulezi-led
                        Inkatha results in the massacre of 46 ANC supporters
                        at Boipatong and threatens the negotiation process;
                        four million workers support ANC-COSATU–
                        sponsored stay away strike; tough negotiations results
                        in a Record of Understanding and a formula for power
                        sharing in the new government of national unity;
                        South Africa attends the Olympics after thirty-two
                        years of absence.

1993   European Economic Community lifts sanctions; de
                        Klerk announces the dismantling of South Africa's six
                        nuclear weapons; Chris Hani, leading ANC and Com-
                        munist Party member, assassinated by two right-wing
                        Conservative Party members; Parliament approves an
                        interim constitution providing for a nonracial, non-
                        sexist, and multiparty democracy and a Bill of Rights
                        in a unitary South Africa; Mandela and de Klerk
                        receive the Nobel Peace Prize; Mark Behr, *A Smell of
                        Apples.*

1994   South Africa hands over Walvis Bay to Namibia; the
                        ANC wins the first nonracial election (April 27–30);
                        Nelson Mandela is sworn in as president (May 10) and
                        forms a government of National Unity; South Africa
                        rejoins the British Commonwealth and UNESCO,
                        reclaims its seat in the United Nations' General Assem-
                        bly, and is welcomed into the Organization of African
                        Unity and the Non-Aligned Movement; Mandela, *Long
                        Walk to Freedom.*

1995   Death penalty is ruled unconstitutional; Truth and
                        Reconciliation Commission (TRC) established, chaired
                        by Archibishop Desmond Tutu; Commission for the
                        Restitution of Land Rights inaugurated; South African
                        Springbok rugby team wins World Cup.

1996   Bafana Bafana, the national soccer team, wins the
               Africa Cup of Nations, and qualifies for the World
               Cup; Mandela signs constitution at Sharpville.

1997   Constitution takes effect; Winnie Mandela reelected as
               ANC Women's League president; de Klerk resigns as
               NP leader and retires from active politics; Thabo Mbeki
               succeeds Mandela as ANC president; Zakes Mda, *Ways
               of Dying.*

1998   President Bill Clinton makes state visit to South Africa;
               South Africa sends troops into Lesotho to quell a mili-
               tary uprising against the government; the TRC submits
               its report; Conference of the Non-Aligned Movement,
               ICC, Durban.

1999   ANC wins second nonracial nationwide elections;
               Thabo Mbeki becomes president, with Jacob Zuma as
               deputy president; F. W. de Klerk, *The Last Trek—A New
               Beginning;* J. M. Coetzee, *Disgrace,* wins the 1999
               Booker Prize; Commonwealth Heads of Government
               Meeting, ICC, Durban.

2000   XIII International AIDS Conference, July 7–14, ICC-
               Durban.

2001   United Nations World Conference Against Racism,
               Racial Discrimination, Xenophobia, and Related Intol-
               erance, August-September, ICC-Durban.

2002   UN World/Earth Summit on Sustainable Develop-
               ment, August 26 to September 4, Johannesburg.

2003   J. M. Coetzee wins the 2003 Nobel Prize for Literature.

1

Land and People

The Republic of South Africa occupies the southernmost part of the African continent. Covering a land area of over 470,000 square miles, one-seventh the area of the United States, and roughly twice the size of Texas, South Africa is one of the largest and certainly the most industrialized states in Africa. With a heterogeneous population of approximately 45 million people possessing the bulk of the region's minerals, the best and largest of its arable lands, its major cities, its best ports, its most productive industries, and its most developed communication systems, South Africa is the most dominant country in southern Africa. With its huge mines drawing hundreds of thousands of workers annually from as far away as Zambia, Zimbabwe, Malawi, and Mozambique, and dominating both the export and import trades of virtually all its neighbors, South Africa is also the economic hub and powerhouse of southern Africa.

Containing the largest community of whites in Africa south of the Sahara, South Africa was the last African country to be freed from minority white domination. The country of South Africa came into being on May 31, 1910, with the union of four previously self-governing British dependencies, namely the Cape, Natal, Orange Free State, and Transvaal provinces. In 1948, the ruling government of South Africa officially adopted the policy of apartheid, racial separation or separate development, to govern the relations between the different races inhabiting the country. On May 31, 1961, in the face of mounting criticism of its racist policies, South Africa formally broke its relations with the British Commonwealth of Nations by proclaiming itself a republic. Thereafter and for the next three decades, South Africa remained a pariah state, a shadow from behind which it could not emerge, until the formal abrogation of apartheid laws during the early 1990s and the introduction of multiracial democracy on April 27, 1994.

THE LAND

Key Features

Situated latitudinally between 22 percent south to 3 percent south, and longitudinally between 17 percent east and 33 percent east, South Africa covers a total area of 470,689 square miles (1,219,080 square kilometers). Bounded in the southwest by the Atlantic Ocean and in the southeast by the Indian Ocean, South Africa shares boundaries with Namibia in the northwest, with Botswana and Zimbabwe in the north, and with Swaziland and Mozambique in the northeast. The independent country of Lesotho is entirely surrounded by South African territory and is located in the southeastern part of the republic.

The location of South Africa at the southern tip of the African continent has had a profound influence on its historical geography, giving it a number of distinctive features.[1] First, since only a tiny fraction of its northeastern extreme falls within the tropic, South Africa is Africa's only truly temperate country. Second, a combination of latitude and elevation has resulted in the emergence of a wide range of natural environments unmatched anywhere on the continent. Third, South Africa's generally low latitude has meant that only a small variation can be discerned between its summer and winter daylight periods. For instance, in Cape Town, at the peak of the country's summer (December 22) the maximum hours of sunshine is 14.25, while it receives the maximum of 9.53 hours of sunshine at the peak of its winter months (June 22). Fourth, composed of some of the oldest rocks on the planet as well as some of the recently formed ones, South Africa contains a wide range of strategically important minerals, making the country one of the most endowed regions on earth, with major consequences for its social history.

Fifth, for millennia South Africa was separated from other regions of the world. Overland, it was separated from Europe by great distance and by physical barriers such as the Sahara Desert and the equatorial forest. By sea, thousands of miles of ocean water ensured its continuing isolation until the voyages of discoveries of the late fifteenth century. This great isolation by land and by sea combined effectively to cut it off from the main currents of world history and civilizations. Sixth, and in spite of its geographical isolation, South Africa's location at the junction of two of the world's great oceans, Indian and Atlantic, assigns to the country considerable strategic importance. It is to this historical position as the halfway house between the peoples and states of the East and those of the Europeans to the West that South Africa owes its origin as a modern state, with the establishment of the first European settlement at the Cape in 1652.

Seventh, this strategic location between the East and the West accounts for the peopling of South Africa by migrant groups from other parts of Africa as well as from Europe and Asia. Eighth, the strategic importance (especially to Europe) of its location and, later, its fabulously rich mineral wealth would result in a continuing influx of Europeans that would ensure, even at the peak of European rule, that South Africa's white population would be larger than the white settler populations of all other sub-Saharan African countries put together. Ninth, South Africa's cultural pluralism is further reinforced and consolidated by the mosaic-like divisions of traditional regions associated with its various racial groups.

Tenth, for over half a century, and most especially from 1948, the political geography of South Africa was dominated by the social and political doctrine of apartheid or separate development along racial lines, a pernicious ideology of racial domination that bequeathed to South Africa a legacy of racism, violence, and oppression, out of whose shadows the country is now struggling to escape. Finally, South Africa's enormous resources and industrial development have made it the most industrialized and the only developed country in Africa, concealing the gross inequality between its rich white minority and its poor black majority populations, another major legacy of its tortuous history. Many of the foregoing features will be further explored in the discussions that follow.

Physical Features

South Africa is a country of strikingly beautiful and varied landscape, with a wide variety of climatic zones that range from the Kalahari Desert in the northwest to the dramatic mountain range in the southeast, and from the Mediterranean coastal ridges in the south central region to the rolling prairie savanna grassland of the central plateau and the north. Its splendid scenery, spectacular mountain ranges, rich game reserves, well-tended national parks, and amiable climate have combined to make South Africa a major tourist destination, most especially since the demise of apartheid and the advent of majority rule in 1994. As a whole, the topography of South Africa can be divided into two major physiographic provinces: the interior plateau and the marginal strips of low lands between the plateau and the coast. Separating the two areas is the great escarpment of its eastern and southwestern regions. The most extensive of the two regions is the saucer-shaped upland Central Plateau. On the whole, the plateau is an elevated flat land, with rolling, softly undulating, often steep-sided, flat-topped hills known as *tafelberge* (table

High-rise hotels and office buildings in the Indian Ocean port city of Durban, Kwa-Zulu Natal. Durban, with its pleasant climate and alluring beaches, is the most popular conference destination in South Africa.

mountains) and conspicuous boulder-strewn knobs rising from its surface. The plateau is also traversed by narrow river valleys and ridged at its rims by a hilly topography. At its center it is about 2,000 feet (600 meters), while on its rims it reaches elevations in excess of 5,000 feet (1,500 meters). In its interior it consists of a series of rolling grasslands or *velds* (Afrikaans for fields), the largest subregion of which is the highveld, with much of its surface lying above 5,000 feet (1,500 meters), resulting in pleasantly cold winters and frequently cool, untropical summers. The highveld, regarded as the body of the plateau, extends from the Western Cape Province through the Free State to the Northern Province, rising into a series of rock formations known as the Witwatersrand (meaning Ridges of White Waters in Afrikaans, and commonly shortened to Rand). The significance of the Rand lies in the fact that, apart from serving as a watershed for numerous rivers, its ridge is the site of the world's largest gold deposits and of South Africa's leading industrial city, Johannesburg. North of the highveld is a dry savanna subregion, known as the Bushveld, which has open grassland and scattered trees and bushes. Like the Rand, the Bushveld is a virtual treasure-house of minerals. Extending over an area of 350 by 150 kilometers, the Bushveld is one of the largest and best-known layered volcanic complexes in the world, containing extensive deposits

Street scene in Melrose lined with jacaranda trees ablaze with their lilac blossoms. Though constituting only 1 percent of the earth land area, South Africa is home to 10 percent of all its flowering plants. twenty-four thousand plant species have been identified so far in South Africa. The Cape Peninsula alone is home to 2,600 indigenous species. (Jane Davis)

of platinum and chromium and sizeable deposits of copper, fluorspar, gold, nickel, and iron.

On the outer edge of the plateau, where the elevation descends to sea level from its crests, is the Great Escarpment, a semicircle of highlands paralleling South Africa's eastern and southern coastline, stretching over 1,400 miles and standing as the most conspicuous and continuous topographical feature in the country. Viewed from below, the Great Escarpment gives an appearance of a mountain range and, even though geomorphologically it is a single unit, each section has its own local name. The escarpment reaches its highest peaks in the Drakensberg Mountains in KwaZulu-Natal and the Eastern Cape provinces.

The highest points in South Africa are the Mont-aux-Sources (3,299 meters), Champagne Castle (3,376 meters), and Giant's Castle (3,313 meters). Thabana-Ntlengana, the highest point on the subcontinent at 3,482 meters, is situated neither on the escarpment itself nor in South Africa, but on an obscure plateau in the country of Lesotho, also known as the Mountain Kingdom. In many places the ruggedness of the escarpment poses a formidable barrier to communication. For instance, the 250 kilometer stretch of the Natal Drakensberg, to the north of Mont-aux-Sources, is traversed by only a single jeep track. Thus, the major discernable gap in the escarpment, located to the north of Beaufort West, became the main route of communication between Cape Town and the interior. In the great wall of the Natal Drakensberg, the escarpment attains its most majestic form with its mass of castellated buttresses, deep amphitheaters, and fully undercut vertical face carps, making it one of the finest sights of scenic beauty and spectacular grandeur on the African continent.[2]

Animal Kingdom

The open and undulating relief and congenial climate combine to make South Africa home for an extremely dense population and wide variety of animals. The abundance of wild fruit trees provides food for a fairly large number of birds and animals. Among the birds to be found are grey louries, hornbills, shrikes, flycatchers, and rollers, most especially in the northern grasslands. Raptors, black Korhan, blue crane, and guinea-fowl are found all over the savanna grassland, while the purple-crested louries and green pigeons are common only in the coastal grassland. The cold waters of the western coast are home to penguins, many of which also breed on the adjacent offshore islands. Though South Africa is poor in forests, those limited forests are a magical world for birds such as the Knysna lourie, the Cape parrot, the sugar-bird, and the rameron pigeon. Ostriches, indigenous to the region, were once very common, but much hunting has drastically decimated their population and reduced their commercial importance. Today they are raised on many farms in the Western and Eastern Cape provinces for their feathers. Another large bird found in the country is the bustard.

Reptiles are also numerous. The coastal rivers of KwaZulu-Natal are natural homes to a wide variety of crocodiles. Croc meal is among the many notable wild game tourist delicacies in the region. A wide variety of snake

The ostrich, "king of the birds," at Oudtshoorn, Western Cape. Fuelled largely by Victorian and Edwardian fashion demands, Oudtshoorn's dry and hot Karoo climate and pebble-strewn loamy soil turned it into the world's leading center of ostrich farming in the late nineteenth century. (Jane Davis)

broods can be found all across the country. Most notable of these are the puff adders, cobras, tree snakes, and the mambas, many of which are poisonous.

The lack of fresh water has not meant the absence of fish. Numerous species, most notably the yellowfish and the babel, flourish in the shallow rivers, burrowing into the mud at the onset of the dry season, from which they emerge at the beginning of the rains. Offshore fishing also provides numerous edible fishes, most especially in the coastal waters along the country's west coast and that of Namibia. The most lucrative catches are the stockfish, redfish, sole, snoek, silverfish, pilchard, rock lobster, and important migratory fishes, such as the Cape salmon (*geelbek*), cob, salmon bass, and kabeljou. Most of these catches are sold fresh, canned, or frozen for the local and regional markets. Meal and oil made from pilchard, *maasbanker,* and other fishes are used as animal feeds or as edible oils and fats for humans. The Cape shore is home to numerous game fish, such as tunny, red steenbras, and yellowtail. Rock oysters are common on the northeastern coastal bays, and numerous sharks live off the KwaZulu-Natal, where they are kept off the many popular beaches by specially designed shark dragnets.

Similarly, and for millennia, large numbers of animals have ranged across the savannah grassveld and coastal forests of South Africa. Among the large animals still found in South Africa are lion, elephant, buffalo, rhino, leopard, cheetah, hippo, giraffe, zebra, kudu, waterbuck, oryx, warthog, and many others, most of which inhabit the Bushveld savanna. The hot, dry Nama-Karoo low grassland is home to the bat-eared fox, the saddle-backed jackal, the meercat, and the ground squirrel. The Orange-Vaal-Pongola river basins of the central plateau are home to the black wildebeest, blesbok, and eland. The semango monkey (an endangered species), the bush pig, bushbock, and the delicate blue duiker are to be found in the high rainfall forests of the eastern escarpment and the eastern seaboards. Though all these animals can still be found in many parts of South Africa, over the last two centuries and especially with the arrival of Europeans, vigorous and indiscriminate hunting and poaching have led to the extinction of many species, the near extinction of others, and the drastic decimation in the population of the surviving ones, many of which have been driven into the mountain ranges, the desert frontiers, and the eastern Northern Transvaal. Many of the popular species, most especially the Big Five (lion, elephant, giraffe, rhino, and hippo), which once ranged freely and in abundance over the entire country for millennia, are mainly found in the many national parks that now adorn the country.

Parks and Games Reserves

The most extensive of the parks is the Kruger National Park, which occupies an area of 8,000 square miles on the frontier with Mozambique. With its subtropical climate, the park is home to the principal animals of South Africa, namely lions, leopards, cheetahs, wildcats, jackals, elephants, hippopotamuses, baboons, and different types of antelopes. The zebra, which once grazed in large numbers on the grasslands of the Central Plateau, is now almost extinct, and can be found only in certain parts of the Kruger Park. The Hluhluwe Game Reserve in northern KwaZulu-Natal is home to the last remaining herds of white, as well as black, rhinoceros. The Kalahari National Park is home to thousands of gemsboke, one of the most beautiful antelopes found in South Africa; springboks, cheetahs, and hyenas can be found there as well. The rugged mountains of KwaZulu-Natal and the Drakensberg are homes to baboons, jackals, hyenas, wilddogs, wildcats, and monkeys. The Addo Elephant National Park, north of Port Elizabeth, is home to small remnants of elephant herds. The bontebok, an almost extinct antelope, is today preserved mainly in the Bontebok National Park, east of Cape Town. The only gazelle found in South Africa is the springbok, which appears on the national emblem. A glimpse of the wide variety and the wealth of animal life in pre-European South Africa can be seen in the antelopes, a characteristic

Zebra, impala, and a wildebeest and her calf (just minutes old). Kruger National Park, Mpumalanga. South Africa is home to two zebra species. South Africa's commitment to conservation is evident in its nearly 600 game reserves, parks, and wilderness areas. (Helen and Russell Mason)

example of the South African fauna, whose many species include impalas, heartbeests, kudus, rietboks, oribis, and klipspringers, in addition to others already mentioned.

THE PEOPLE

South Africa, with its 2002 population estimate of 45.5 million people, is one of the most racially and ethnically complex societies in the world. It is made up of five major groups. The first and the earliest inhabitants of the country are the Khoisan, also known (albeit derogatorily) as Bushmen and Hottentots. The next group to arrive in the region are the Bantu-speaking Africans, who can be divided into a number of fairly distinct ethnic groups. Largest are the Nguni—made up of the Zulu, Swazi, Ndebele, Pondo, Thembu, and Xhosa, who constitute more than two-thirds of the population—and the Sotho and Tswana. The third group to arrive are the European or white peoples, whose settlement in the region from the mid-seventeenth century onward signaled a new era in race relations and in socio-political domination in Southern Africa. Intensified and sustained sexual interactions between the white settlers and other resident groups resulted in the emergence of the colored population. The final group is made up of Asians, mostly Indians, who were first brought into the country during the mid-nineteenth century.[3]

Population: Trends and Statistics

A mid-2002 estimate put the ethnic composition of the population at 78.04 percent Africans (blacks); 10.02 percent Europeans (whites); 8.62 percent coloreds; and 2.47 percent Asian, in a total population of 45,454,211. The overall growth rate of the population declined from 2.9 percent in the 1980s to 2.4 percent in 1995, though the rates varied from one racial group to the next: 2.6 percent for blacks, 2.2 percent for coloreds, 1.9 percent for Asians, and 1.0 percent for whites. The population is widely expected to double by the year 2025. In 2000, life expectancy at birth was 49.6 years for males and 52.1 years for females, with life expectancy for black males being nine years less than for white males, according to the *World Health Organization* (WHO) *Report.* Though women outnumber men (51.2 to 48.8 percent) in the general population, men outnumber women in the five provinces with significant male employment in farming, manufactures, and mining. Consequently, in most of the rural areas and former homelands like QwaQwa and KwaZulu, where labor policies have drawn men away to urban enclaves, the population of women is often over 55 percent. In 1995, the overall fertility rate was 4.1 births per adult female, while the crude birth rate was 27.1 births per 1,000 people, with 12 percent of all births being to women age 19 or younger. Infant mortality rate was 45.8 deaths per 1,000 live births, while the average annual death rate for the total population was 7.6 per 1,000. In 1995, the median age was estimated at 19.2 years, with 37 percent of all South Africans being 15 years or younger, while only 13 percent were above the age of 50. The sharp disparities in the racial groupings is evident in the fact that while 52 percent of blacks were under age 19, only 31 percent of whites were.

The overall population density was 34.4 persons per square kilometers in 1995, with extremely uneven distribution. The eastern half of the country, home to the nation's minerals and its best agricultural lands, is more densely populated than the arid western section. Consequently, more than two-thirds of the population live in the wetter eastern third of the country and in the Southern Cape. Until 1994, the most densely populated parts of the country were the homelands, with an average density in excess of 300 persons per square kilometers. In the Gauteng—the Johannesburg, Pretoria, Witwatersrand cluster—7 million people constitute 17 percent of the national population, but live on less than 2 percent of the land. The Gauteng is thus the most highly urbanized province (96 percent) followed by the Western Cape (86 percent), and the Northern Cape (73 percent); at the other end of this spectrum, the Northern Province is only 9 percent urban. Johannesburg, with a metropolitan population of over 2 million, is the country's largest city; Cape Town, the legislative capital, with 2.3 million, is next, with the inclusion of its surrounding areas; the port city of Durban has 1.1 million; and Pretoria, the country's administrative capital, has approximately 1 million people. Other major cities are Port Elizabeth, a leading industrial city, and Kimberley, situated within the nucleus of the nation's diamond industry.[4]

Europeans are widely spread geographically, though 80 percent of them live in the cities. More than 60 percent of Africans still live in the rural areas; an increasing number can be found in the large, sprawling black townships and squatter settlements ringing the major urban centers, many of which, for decades, thanks to apartheid laws, were forbidden cities to almost all but the white population and those working for them. Africans constitute the majority in all the provinces except the Western Cape, the only province with a white demographic domination. The colored population is found mainly in the Cape, while Asians are concentrated largely in KwaZulu-Natal and the Witwatersrand.

Ethnic Groups and Languages

Like the other countries of Africa, South Africa, as a territorial unit, came into being, for the most part, as a result of lines arbitrarily drawn on the map of Africa by European imperialists during the scramble for and partition of Africa during the closing decades of the nineteenth century. The arbitrary nature of this state creation led to the incorporation of diverse ethnic groups within its confines. Some like the Zulu and the Xhosa, with their clearly defined territories, were incorporated entirely within the new nation. Others like the Tswana, Swazi, Sotho, Ndebele, and Venda found themselves segmented into different countries.

The Khoisan (San, Khoikhoi, and Related Groups)

The earliest known people to live in South Africa were the San (derogatively described by Europeans as Bushmen). They were the remnants of an earlier population that had roamed the grassveld and shrublands of southern African plateau and mountain ranges for millennia. It is not certain how early the San began living in this region, but archaeological records indicate that the San and their ancestors were in southern Africa for the best part of the last 10,000 years. The San lived by hunting, fishing, and gathering and traveled in small, isolated groups, which resulted in the emergence of a wide variety of highly differentiated dialectal groups. The Khoikhoi, a pastoralist group, arrived in the South African region approximately 2,000 years ago.

Most scholars believe that the Khoikhoi were originally San, but ceased to be San when they shed their scavenging and gathering existence and became pastoralists. Together the two groups are known as Khoisan. With the Khoikhoi's mastery of stockbreeding, through which they kept cattle, sheep, and goats, they fanned out in migratory bands from the area of present day Zimbabwe to the plateau grassveld of South Africa, hedging the preexisting San into the mountain ranges of the Drakensberg and the arid landscapes of the Kalahari, areas especially suitable for livestock breeding. By the time of the European advent in the late fifteenth century, the Khoikhoi were already established in the western and southern coastal areas and the interior regions of South Africa. Hence they were responsible for welcoming the newcomers, trading with them, supplying them with provisions, revealing to them the lay of the land, and eventually granting them the land on which they later decided to settle. Over the centuries, a combination of factors resulted in the near extinction of the Khoisan groups in South Africa. The most decisive was the catastrophic smallpox epidemics of the early eighteenth century, which combined with the cultural pressure of the Bantu migrants and the military depredation of the European settlers to spell the demise of the Khoisan in South Africa. Today, hardly any pure members of the Khoikhoi group can be found within the South African republic.

A handful of surviving San bands have held on precariously in places like Twee Rivieren in the Cape Province and Lake Chrissie in the Transvaal. The majority of the San are now found in the desert and semidesert regions of the Kalahari in Namibia, where they have survived as the Nama and Herero, two groups decimated almost to the point of extinction during the brief period of German imperialism at the beginning of the twentieth century. Though the Khoisan have ceased to be a major force in modern southern Africa, they contributed substantially, first, to the early development of European settlement at the Cape and, second, to the cultural evolution of the Cape colored population in South Africa. Substantial elements of the Khoisan language are retained in the language of the Griqua of Western Cape, while the click sounds common to many of the Bantu languages are clear indications of continuing Khoisan linguistic impact.

The Nguni: Zulu, Swazi, Xhosa, and Related Peoples

The Nguni constitute approximately two-thirds of the black population of South Africa. They can be divided into three major subgroups: the Northern Nguni, the Southern Nguni, and the Ndebele. The Zulu, with an estimated population of 8 million, are the largest ethnic group in South Africa. The

Zulu emerged as a major group in southern Africa toward the end of the eighteenth century, when they constituted themselves into a number of Nguni-speaking chiefdoms north of the Tugela River. Early in the nineteenth century, the various warring chiefdoms were forged into a powerful state through the military leadership of Shaka, whose adoption of new fighting strategies enabled him to expand ruthlessly and consolidate the new state. Shaka's epic-making career set in motion the series of demographic, military, and political revolutions collectively known as *mfecane* (Nguni word for crushing), a state formation movement that dramatically transformed the states and societies of southern Africa during much of the nineteenth century. These military efforts also led to the emergence of the Zulu, hitherto a small and largely insignificant group, as the most dominant indigenous polity and demographic group in South Africa. Though the Zulu empire weakened and fragmented after Shaka's death, the amaZulu's sense of cultural and ethnic identities survived to become a major rallying point in South African politics most especially during the 1980s and early 1990s, when the various African groups jostled to inherit the mantle of power in the imminent postapartheid state.

Like the Zulu, the Swazi, with an estimated population of 1.6 million, constitute the other major Northern Nguni group, though more than one-half of the population lives in Swaziland. Like their Zulu kinsmen, the Swazi were organized into a number of closely related patrilineal chiefdoms until the late eighteenth century when, under the rule of Ngwane I, they were brought together to resist the expanding state of the Mthethwa, ruled by Dingiswayo. The death of Dingiswayo at the hand of the Ndwandwe pressured Ngwane and his people to withdraw to the mountainous region that later became the center of the new Swazi kingdom. Through adroit diplomacy Ngwane I was able to maintain the independence of his kingdom, successfully resisting incorporation into the Zulu kingdom through a careful cultivation of peaceful relations with Shaka and his successors.

To prevent the area from falling into the clutch of the Afrikaners, the British annexed the Swazi kingdom in 1903, and it became a British High Commission territory in 1907. After resisting successive attempts by South Africa to annex and incorporate it, Swaziland became independent under the rule of King Sobhuza II in 1968. During the 1960s the Swazi-inhabited land within the South African republic was delineated as the KaNgwane self-governing homeland, with a population of approximately 400,000 people. The majority of the South African Swazi are today found within the Mpumalanga province situated to the west of Swaziland.

The Xhosa and their closely related kinsmen, the Pondo, Thembu, and Mfengu, number nearly 6 million and are concentrated in the Eastern Cape

Province. Their language, isiXhosa, is closely related to Zulu. The Xhosa appear to have been the earliest of the Bantu migrants to reach the area of present-day South Africa and thus the first to come into direct contact with the Khoisan as well as with the European settlers that began to push into the South African interior from the second half of the seventeenth century onwards. The Xhosa's superior material culture, most especially their possession of metallurgy, gave them decisive military advantages over the preexisting Khoisan groups, most of whom they either eliminated, enslaved, or assimilated, though not before the Khoisan had left a permanent imprint on the language of their conquerors. IsiXhosa has more than a dozen click sounds assimilated from the Khoisan speakers, a clear indication of a long period of mutually beneficial acculturation between the two groups. The gradual acculturation and progressive incorporation of the Khoisans into Xhosa communities resulted in the emergence of an extremely diverse society.

In regard to the economy, the Xhosa combined animal husbandry with farming and hunting. Settlements were usually sited on the numerous ridges overlooking the many rivers in the area, such as the Fish, Keiskama, Buffalo, and the Kei rivers. Cattle were at the heart of Xhosa economy, serving as the store of wealth, the symbol of status and power, and the means of exchange. Cattle served other important functions: bridal payments, pack animals, and as the major means of transportation. The most important crops grown were corn, sorghum, and tobacco. Iron smithy and woodcarving were important traditional occupations. As the first Bantu groups to come into direct contact with Europeans, the Xhosa welcomed European missionaries and educators into their territory, with the result that by the beginning of the twentieth century a core of western-educated elite began to emerge and dominate the nationalist and postapartheid politics of South Africa. Nelson Mandela, his successor, Thabo Mbeki, and many of the leading contemporary South African black politicians are of Xhosa origins. During the apartheid era, and in apparent acknowledgement of the size and diversity of the group, the South African government recognized two groups of Xhosa, delineating them into two independent homelands: the Ciskei, for the Gcaleka Xhosa; and the Transkei, for the Ngika Xhosa.

Ndebele

The majority of the Ndebele live in Zimbabwe, where they number nearly 1.7 million and are known as Matabele; 300,000 of them live in Botswana; while approximately 800,000 of them are in the Northern Province of South Africa, which is directly adjacent to Zimbabwe. Though isiNdebele belongs to the Nguni language family, it has been strongly influenced by Sotho, causing some scholars to classify it with the Sesotho language groups. The *mfecane* had far-reaching consequences on the Ndebele. Powerful warriors emerged among them who subjugated smaller chiefdoms and assimilated them into Ndebele society. The most notable of these was Mzilikazi, who fled with thousands of his supporters and their war booties from Shaka in 1817 to the present area of Zimbabwe, where he established the foundation of the Ndebele state. As a result of the *mfecane,* many of the Ndebele dispersed throughout much of Natal and the Transvaal, where they repeatedly clashed with the *voortrekkers* (Boer pioneers) around the present area of Pretoria. The clashes continued until the end of the nineteenth century, when Paul Kruger, the Afrikaner leader, jailed or executed many of the Ndebele's leaders, dispossessed them of their lands, and reduced many of the survivors to indentured servitude under Afrikaner farmers. Under apartheid most Ndebele found themselves assigned officially to either the Sesotho-speaking homeland of Lebowa or the KwaNdebele homeland in southern Transvaal. Most of the Ndebele population, however, could not survive in these generally barren and overcrowded homelands. By the mid-1980s, close to 500,000 Ndebele people were living in the urban centers and other regions of South Africa.

The Sotho

Estimated at 7 million, the Sotho constitutes the second largest African language group in South Africa. Three million Sotho and other closely related groups live outside of South Africa, the majority of whom are in Lesotho. The Sotho can be subdivided into three heterogenous groups. The first of these are the Northern Sotho groups, of whom the Pedi are the most populous. The Pedi were responsible for the assimilation of the northern Ndebele groups. The Pedi (or BaPedi) society arose out of a confederation of small chiefdoms that had been established sometimes before the seventeenth century in what later became the northern Transvaal. Defeated early in the nineteenth century by the armies of Mzilikazi, they revived under the leadership of Sekwati. Thereafter, they repeatedly clashed with the *voortrekkers* during the later half of the nineteenth century.

Another important subgroup of the Northern Nguni are the Lobedu, a group closely related to the Shona of Zimbabwe, but displaying striking linguistic similarities to the Sotho. The Lobedu have attracted considerable anthropological interest because of their unique political system, which is headed by a woman ruler, Mujaji, the Rain Queen. As the focus of power and authority in the state, she is considered a sacred being, with the very basis of her power resting, not on military might, but on her ability to make rain. The South Sotho are made up of a diverse group of peoples numbering close to 3.6 million. Of these, 1.6 million live in Lesotho, while the remaining 2 million live in the Eastern Cape, the Free State, and KwaZulu-Natal, the three

provinces surrounding the country of Lesotho. The many chiefdoms constituting the South Sotho were brought together under a single political
umbrella during the reign of Moshoeshoe I in the 1830s, largely in response
to the displacements occasioned by the *mfecane*. The close ties that some of
the Sotho groups had established with various San groups led to the incorporation of many click sounds in their languages, distinguishing them from the
North Sotho. The Fokeng and the Tlokwa are among the other major groups
of the South Sotho.

Tswana

The Tswana (BaTswana) emerged as a heterogeneous group out of the integration of a diverse group of peoples, the most notable of which were the
Tlhaping, the Rolong, the Hurutshe, the Kwena, the Koni, and others. Also
known as western Sotho, their language, Setswana, is a close cousin to Sesotho,
and the two are mutually intelligible for the most part. There are 4 million
Tswana in southern Africa: 1 million of these live in the independent country
of Botswana, while the remaining 3 million live in the Northern and Northwest provinces of South Africa. Though the Tswana culture is similar to that of
closely related Sotho groups, their societies are more highly stratified, and are
especially noted for their complex legal systems, which involved a hierarchy of
courts and mediators as well as draconic punishment for the guilty. Tswana
farmers often establish mutually beneficial patron-client relations with the
Khoisan, receiving wild game meat and animal pelts in exchange for cattle.
During the era of apartheid, nearly half of the Tswana in South Africa were
assigned to the independent homeland of Bophuthatswana. This homeland,
in spite of the rich mineral wealth within its area, remained desperately poor.
The result was that the majority of the Tswana population had to turn to
migrant labor in the mines and the urban centers of South Africa for their
livelihood.

Tsonga

Though the Tsonga share a number of cultural similarities with the Nguni,
their language sets them apart as a distinct group. Made up of a diverse population, there are 1.5 million of them in South Africa, where they form part
of a continuum with other Tsonga and Tsonga-related peoples in Mozambique and Zimbabwe, who number more than 4.5 million. Traditionally, the
Tsonga lived mainly by fishing. A few raised goats and kept chicken, and
farming was also important. Their tsetse fly–infested coastal lowland habitat
made cattle raising uncommon. By the eighteenth century, most Tsonga were
organized into several small and independent chiefdoms in which inheritance
by brothers, rather than sons, was a defining feature of the social system, a

practice common in many Central African societies but rare among other South African groups. During the *mfecane* upheaval of the nineteenth century, a large portion of the Tsonga population came under the military sway of Soshangane, a Zulu warrior who set in motion the process of the integration of the Shangaan, Thonga, Tonga, and other smaller groups of Nguni and Sotho elements that collectively became known as the Shangaan-Tsonga group.

Venda

The last and the smallest of the four major African groups are the Venda, who number approximately 600,000. They appear to have originated from the Great Lakes region of East Africa. Migrating in a series of waves, they were already settled south of the Limpopo River by the sixteenth century, where they met and assimilated the local population. The Venda's southward push was held in check by the Tsonga, who were similarly moving westward from Mozambique. Though the Tshivenda vocabulary is similar to Sesotho, its grammatical structure is closely related to Shona, the dominant language of Zimbabwe. Similarly, Venda culture is an eclectic incorporation of East African, Central African, Nguni, and Sotho elements. As with many East African peoples the consumption of pork is considered a taboo, a prohibition not common in southern Africa. In addition, like the Sotho and the Xhosa, though unlike some other Nguni groups, they practice male circumcision. Again unlike most African languages, the Venda language has no known dialects. The Venda became adept in the practice of terrace agriculture, which uniquely enabled them to draw and retain most of the 700,000 people assigned to their nominally independent homeland under the apartheid regime. The limited success recorded in agriculture, however, could not prevent 70 percent of its men from eventually working as migrant laborers in other parts of South Africa. The maintenance of a sharp distinction between the ruling group and the common people was another feature of the sociopolitical system.

Whites

There are roughly 5 million whites (mainly of European ancestry) in South Africa, making up close to 13 percent of the population. Of these, 3 million are Afrikaans-speaking (Afrikaners). These are the descendants of Dutch immigrants, whose Cape version of the Dutch language evolved to be known as Afrikaans. The remaining 2 million are largely English speaking, though there are sizeable populations who speak Portuguese, German, Greek, Italian, and Dutch as well.

Afrikaners

The Afrikaners were the first whites to settle in South Africa. Originally from the Netherlands, they arrived in 1652 to establish a refreshment post at the Cape meant to service the commercial, dietary, and marine needs of the trading ships of the Dutch East India Company. Five years later the company released some of the officials from their obligations by giving them the freedom to farm on their own account and produce victuals for the passing trading ships. The arrival in 1688 of a small group of French Huguenots who were fleeing religious persecution in France infused new blood and swelled the settlers' numbers. Though the new arrivals were subsequently and completely absorbed by the preexisting Dutch community, they were responsible for pioneering South Africa's wine industry, today one of the world's best. Long distance and effective separation from Europe coupled with successful expansion and consolidation of their settlement led to a major revolution in the consciousness of the settlers. They ceased to regard themselves as tenuous colonial interlopers and began instead to view themselves like their contemporary Americans on the other side of the globe, as pioneer adventurers engaged in the noble task of carving a new and permanent home for themselves and their children, out of the wilderness and barbarism of an untamed continent.

Farming and husbandry were the two most important occupations of these early pioneers. Struggle over the control of the limited produce market often led to conflict with the Cape governors. In the course of one of these conflicts, an early eighteenth-century Cape governor, Willem Adriaan van der Stel (1699–1707), used the term *boer* (a vulgar Dutch word for farmer) to abuse the farmers. Instead of shaking off the insult, the farmers promptly adopted the term as a badge of honor and began to use it to address themselves. Soon the two terms, Boer and Afrikaner, became interchangeable.[5]

The nineteenth century saw the influx of more European immigrants, mostly Dutch and Germans; the most sizeable of these was the group of legionnaires and other individuals who arrived from Germany in large numbers, settling around East London on the eastern frontier between 1848 and 1858. The concerted attempt made by the British to anglicize the 26,000 strong Afrikaner population failed, but not before it had provoked a series of reactions that culminated in the Great Trek, in which groups of Afrikaners abandoned the Cape to the British and migrated north into the South African interior to establish independent republics for themselves. The struggle over who would control South Africa was not resolved until the Anglo-Boer War (1899–1902) finally brought the Afrikaners and their republics under British rule.

Though independence from British rule was achieved in 1910, the heyday of Afrikaner dominance did not begin until 1948, with the ascendancy of the Afrikaner nationalist party and the formal institutionalization of apartheid as the official policy of government and racial relations in South Africa. An important element in the development of Afrikaner racial and covenantal mindset is their close identity with the Dutch Reformed Church, and their consciousness of themselves as a chosen people, covenanted to each other and to their God. Over the years, Afrikaners took delight in emphasizing their status as God's chosen people, their reputed indomitable pioneering spirit, their sense of nationalism and individualism, and their pious commitment to their church and their national leaders.[6]

English-Speaking South African Whites

In 1620, two English sailors hoisted the English flag at the Cape, ostensibly annexing the strategic point for their sovereign, King James I. The sovereign, however, appeared not to have been much impressed, as England did nothing to concretize its claim to the region. In 1699, an English ship, *Fidelity*, put three crewmembers ashore in what would later become Port Natal (later Durban), to trade for ivory. The ship never returned for the crew; and nothing came of this attempt. It was not until 1795, when the British annexed the Cape, that an English-speaking community became established in South Africa.

By 1803, when the Dutch government in Holland recovered the Cape, the number of English had grown to about 80. In the 1820s, as part of the British attempt to protect their newly acquired Cape Colony from frequent attacks and incursion from the Xhosa, groups of migrants were brought from England, Ireland, Scotland, and Wales to settle on the eastern frontiers. In spite of the harsh conditions of the frontiers, the new settlers managed to develop into a hardy group of pioneers who valued religion and education. Many schools, and later a university, were established. In addition, a number of churches, mainly Anglican, Methodist, and Presbyterian, were founded while English missionaries were given every incentive to promote Anglican Christianity among the indigenous groups. To counter the cultural hegemony of the Afrikaners, Anglicization became a major policy of the British rulers at the Cape, resulting in much cultural efflorescence. Artists, writers, poets, journalists, craftsmen, and merchants soon transformed the various port settlements into major cities such as Port Elizabeth, East London, and Durban, all of which became thriving centers of learning and of English culture. Two companies of English soldiers stationed in Port Natal in 1843 introduced English plays and the game of cricket. The great rush for riches that came with the discovery of diamonds (1867) and gold (1886) resulted in large-scale British immigration into the interior regions of the Orange Free State and the Transvaal.

Other European Groups: Portuguese, Greeks, and Jews

Beside the Afrikaans and English-speaking peoples, other European groups contributed in various ways toward enriching the South African demographic and cultural mosaic. The largest of these was the 49,000 Portuguese immigrants who came mostly from Angola and Mozambique after the discovery of diamonds and gold. South Africa was also the recipient of thousands of Portuguese refugees who fled following the collapse of Portuguese imperialism in Angola and Mozambique during the mid-1970s. The Portuguese were noted early for their great proficiency in the production and retailing of vegetables and fruits. Many of them also worked as teachers, doctors, lawyers, and artisans.

There is a thriving, if small, Greek community in South Africa. In 1880, 11 Greek sailors jumped ship in Port Elizabeth to establish the nucleus of a Greek community, estimated at 13,000 in 1994. Several Greek churches, schools, and cultural associations can be found in the main urban centers, most especially in the Witwatersrand area, where at least three Greek newspapers are published.

South Africa is also home to a relatively cohesive community of 130,000 Jews. Jewish connections with South Africa date to very early days. Beside the Jewish astronomers, mapmakers, and navigators who assisted the Portuguese in their explorations, Jewish capital was invested in the Dutch East India Company, and men of Jewish origin were among the pioneer settlers at the Cape. The first Hebrew congregation was established at the Cape in 1841, Port Elizabeth in 1862, and Johannesburg in 1887. Over the years the Jews made considerable contributions to the economic, civic, and cultural life of South Africa. Names like Mosenthal and Oppenheimer became internationally famous in finance and industry. They were also in the forefront of major developments in art, science, literature, and the Afrikaans language.

Asians

Indians

There are roughly over 1 million people of Asian ancestry in South Africa, all of whom—with the exception of approximately 20,000—are of Indian origin. The advent of Indians in South Africa was connected with the demand by European farmers in the Natal colony for the recruitment of Indian laborers to work their newly established sugar plantations. After much

Indian women protesting against the continuing practices of racism and the caste system, Durban. The occasion was the United Nations' World Conference Against Racism, Racial Discrimination, Xenophobia, and Related Intolerance, held in Durban, August/September 2001.

pressure, the British agreed to the request. The first barge of 330 laborers from Madras arrived in Durban aboard the *Truro* on November 16, 1860. Indentured to serve from three to five years, they were given the option at the end of their first contracts of renewing their contracts, returning to India at the expense of the government, or receiving an allotment of crown land equivalent in value to the cost of a return passage. The majority opted to remain. They received their land allotment and took up other gainful occupations in the expanding colonial economy. Other groups of Indians arrived during the 1870s, and quickly established themselves as traders and merchants in the colony. These were known as passenger Indians because they paid for their own passage and were neither obligated nor inclined to return to India. The different circumstances of their arrival in the country created class division between the two groups. Since the passenger Indians, the majority of whom were Muslims, were generally wealthier and came from northern and central India, they were given citizenship rights and were not subjected to the laws and deprivations suffered by those usually poorer Hindus who came as indentured servants or slaves.

Official government policy in regard to Indians was that most of them would have to be repatriated back to India. It was not until South Africa became a republic in 1961 that Indians were finally and officially accepted as permanent, though not equal, members of the South African community. Subjected to various forms of racial and economic discrimination and prohibited, during the nineteenth century, from living in the Orange Free State, the majority of the Indians live within a 150 kilometer radius of Durban, where they constitute the largest Indian community outside of Asia. The rest can be found in Gauteng and the Cape Provinces, where they are concentrated in the suburbs of Lenasia (Johannesburg), Laudium (Pretoria), and Rylands (Cape Town). The Indian community in South Africa is fairly heterogeneous as distinctions in religion and language are especially marked. Though most Indians speak English as their first language, 70 percent of them are Hindu, a few of whom still speak Tamil, Telugu, Hindustani, Gujarati, and sometimes Afrikaans as their second or third language. Roughly 20 percent are Muslims and speak Urdu and Gujarati. Approximately 8 percent are Christians, and quite a few are adherents of other religions.

Chinese

The shortage of black mineworkers that followed the Anglo-Boer war caused the government to approve the recruitment of Chinese laborers in 1902. By 1906, there were 50,000 Chinese immigrants, mainly from the Province of Shantung, working in the Witwatersrand. As the recruitment of black workers improved, it became possible to repatriate the majority of the Chinese workers between 1908 and 1910. The next influx of Chinese began in the 1920s and was associated with improved trade relations between South Africa and the Republic of China. Most of the new immigrants were from a higher social background in China. They came to South Africa in response to the business opportunities generated by the expansion of the mining industries, serving as technocrats and industrialists in the South African economy. By the early 1990s, there were roughly 12,000 Chinese living in South Africa. While most of the South African-born Chinese speak both English and Afrikaans, Chinese dialects such as Hakka or Cantonese are widely spoken at home and among other Chinese. Since they came before the 1949 communist revolution in China, the majority of them are Roman Catholics and Baptists and are concentrated in the major urban centers, such as Johannesburg, Port Elizabeth, Pretoria, Cape Town, East London, Durban, Kimberley, and other towns.

Colored

There are roughly 3.2 million South Africans of mixed-race identity, known collectively as colored in apartheid terminology. This term is not particularly acceptable to the people to whom it is applied, and hence it is not usually capitalized, but one for which we as yet have no viable alternative. The colored community developed from years of intermingling between the slave population, the Khoisan, Asians, and Europeans, most especially at the Cape. Their antiquity dates back to the beginning of the Cape settlement itself. Few European women came to settle at the Cape. Consequently, a great deal of sexual activities between the European settlers and masters and their Khoisan and female servants and Malaysian female slaves began to lay the foundation for the emergence of a whole new race in South Africa. Visiting sailors also had free access to the Cape female slaves to satisfy their sexual appetites, in the process fathering many children of mixed-race identity. Similarly on the burgher plantations, where the number of men always exceeded that of women, Boers freely had sexual relations with their female slaves on the farm, kept Khoikhoi mistresses, and often patronized urban female slaves and colored prostitutes, thus swelling the number of out-of-wedlock children of mixed-race identity. As part of the solution to the marriage challenge, the company brought a large number of Malayan women to serve as wives to the settlers, thus adding a Malayan cultural element to the new community.

The majority of the colored people (85 percent) live in the Western Cape and Northern Cape provinces, while the rest can be found in parts of KwaZulu-Natal and other provinces. Eighty-three percent of the colored population speak Afrikaans, while the rest speak English as their first language. As a result of their genetic kinship with the Afrikaners, the Cape colored were closely associated with the Afrikaner population, though this did not save them from the many indignities they had to suffer under apartheid, such as evictions from homes and neighborhoods desired by whites. For awhile they enjoyed the franchise in the British-ruled Cape Colony, but with the onset of apartheid the nationalist government, in a most despicable act of constitutional gerrymandering, soon eliminated even this limited privilege.[7] The colored dilemma and uneasiness with black majority rule became quite The colors have always occupied an ambiguous position in the scheme of things in South Africa. Their kinship relations with whites gave them access to some jobs in the civil service and industries that were denied to other Africans. However, their close association with whites during the apartheid era and after, and most especially the distancing of many of their more conservative leaders from the revolutionary aspirations of the ANC have made them an object of suspicion in the eyes of the oppressed black majority. The colored dilemma and uneasiness with black majority rule became quite apparent during the 1994 election when the colored community of the Western Cape voted by a solid majority to give the Nationalist Party its only provincial victory.

Official Languages

During the apartheid era, English and Afrikaans were the only official languages of South Africa. Both were taught as compulsory subjects in all schools and to all population groups. With the end of apartheid and the onset of majority rule in 1994, nine other languages were added to the mix of official languages to make 11. The nine new ones are isiZulu, isiXhosa, isiNdebele, Sepedi, Sesotho, Setswana, siSwati, Tshivenda, and Xitsonga, all of them spoken over a wide area of the country. These nine languages are all Bantu languages, all of which appeared to have developed from a branch of the Niger-Congo language family, spoken over a wide area of western, central, eastern, and southern Africa. 14.4 percent and 8 percent of the population speak Afrikaans and English as their mother tongues. The figures for isiZulu, isiXhosa, and Sepedi, are 22.9, 17.9, and 9.2 respectively. All official languages are accorded parity and equity of treatment in government language use. The 1996 South African Constitution guarantees everyone the right to use and be instructed in the language of his or her choice, wherever this is practicable.

NOTES

1. For a fuller discussion of these features see the chapter, H. J. De Blij and Peter O. Muller, "South Africa: Crossing the Rubicon," in *Geography, Regions and Concepts* (New York: John Wiley & Sons, 1992), 440–49.

2. *South Africa, 1989–90: Official Yearbook of the Republic of South Africa* (Pretoria: Bureau for Information, Department of Foreign Affairs, 1989/90), 2–9; *South Africa: Country Study* (Washington, D.C.: Federal Research Division, Library of Congress, 2000); *South Africa Yearbook 2001/02* (Pretoria: Government Communication and Information System, 2002); and J. P. Jessop, "Ecological Setting," in W. D. Hammond-Tooke, ed., *The Bantu-Speaking Peoples of Southern Africa* (London and Boston: Routledge & Kegan Paul, 1974), 46–49.

3. The main sources for the information in this chapter are *South Africa, 1989–90: Official Yearbook; South Africa, 1993; South Africa: Country Study* (2000); *South Africa Yearbook 2001/02;* and Hammond-Tooke, ed., *The Bantu-Speaking Peoples of Southern Africa.*

4. For the details of these statistics see: *Official Yearbook; South Africa: Country Study* (2000); *South Africa Yearbook 2001/02; South Africa Survey, 2000/01* (Johannesburg: South African Institute of Race Relations, 2001), 45–50; and *African South of the Sahara 2003* (London and New York: Europa Publications, 2003), 982–88.

5. *South Africa, 1989–90: Official Yearbook,* 68.

6. See Allister Sparks, *The Mind of South Africa* (New York: Ballatine Books, 1990) and Donald Harman Akenson, *God's Peoples: Covenant and Land in South Africa, Israel, and Ulster* (Ithaca, N.Y., and London: Cornell University Press, 1992).

7. Rodney Davenport and Christopher Sanders, *South Africa: A Modern History* (New York: St. Martin's Press, 2000), 379–83, 395–96.

2

History and Political Economy

HISTORY

The First South Africans: From Hunter-Gatherers to Pastoralists

Evidence provided by archaeologists and physical anthropologists has shown that South Africa was at the forefront of human evolution. Fossils of the Early Man, termed *Australopithecus africanus,* found in some cave deposits in the Transvaal and the northern Cape province, have been dated to 3 million or more years before the present. Evidence of continuing human habitation over several millennia has also come to light with the unearthing in the Klasies River Mouth in the Eastern Cape province of some of the earliest fossils discovered anywhere in the world associated with the modern *Homo sapiens* and dated to more than 50,000 years ago. Over the centuries, successive waves of migrants have moved into the region. As these groups adapted themselves to the different climate, topography, and animals living in their respective territories, a wide variety of cultures emerged in the region.

The first people to be established in the region were apparently the ancestors of the San, who the early white settlers derogatively described as Bushmen. They were hunter-gatherers who lived mostly by hunting, fishing, fruit gathering, and insect collection. They were generally small in stature and had light brown or olive skins. They appeared to the first European visitors as firm and hardy, neat and delicate, young and innocent, and modest yet unreserved. From approximately 2,000 years ago the San differentiated into several groups and adapted themselves to the varied ecological zones in the region. The various groups spoke distinctive but distantly related languages, all of which had strong click sounds that are difficult to render in the modern

Western alphabets, but elements of which later became incorporated into the linguistic equipment of succeeding groups in the region. The San lived in bands that numbered between 20 and 80 people and were centered on the nuclear family. Mobile and nomadic, they lived in caves and temporary camps moving from one watering, foraging, and hunting zone to another depending on the vicissitudes of the climate and food supply.

Since wealth accumulation was not a feature of the San existence, there was a high degree of equality and egalitarianism. Class formation was alien to this society. The main division was gender, in the area of labor. The men were in charge of hunting, while the women, in addition to child care, had primary responsibility for collecting edible plants and insects, the main source of food supply for the community. To meet their basic material needs, they fashioned numerous tools from wood, stone, and bones, transforming animal skins into clothes and wood into musical instruments, bows, and arrows. To increase the deadly efficiency of their rudimentary weaponry, they smeared their arrow tips with poisons extracted from snake venoms, insects, and plants.

Khoikhoi and the Advent of Pastoralism

The last few centuries before the Common Era witnessed the advent of another group in the South African area. These were the people Europeans called derogatively Hottentots, but who called themselves Khoikhoi, meaning men of men, probably to distinguish themselves from the hunter-gatherers already domiciled in the region. Originating from the dry grasslands of the northern Kalahari Desert in Botswana, the Khoikhoi spread rapidly into present day Namibia and South Africa's Western Cape province. Like the San, the Khoikhoi hunted animals and gathered fruits, using bows and arrows, spears and traps. The two groups also looked quite similar in appearance and spoke closely related click-sound languages. These striking similarities have led many scholars to conclude that the Khoikhoi were probably and originally a branch of the San hunter-gatherers, whose way of life became transformed through the addition of pastoralism sometime in the last few centuries before the Common Era. When, from, and where the Khoikhoi adopted pastoralism is not very clear, though many scholars believe they originally obtained cattle from Bantu-speaking farmers to the north.

Pastoralism provided the Khoikhoi with a regular supply of meat, soured milk, and butter. This resulted in a remarkable improvement in their diet, vis-à-vis the San, making them slightly taller than their San distant kinsmen. With a more steady source of food supply the Khoikhoi could live in more settled communities and much larger settlements than the San, even though they still moved their cattle from season to season, and between mountains and valleys in search of grazing fields. To store their milk, butter, and melted fat, the Khoikhoi made hard, baked-clay pots and fashioned leak-proof pots out of reeds. Cattle became useful for transportation and as pack oxen. They also became a measure of wealth and a valuable medium of exchange. Unlike the San ethos of egalitarianism, accumulation became a feature of Khoikhoi life as increasing importance and status were attached to livestock possession. Since men controlled the livestock, they assumed a position of dominance over women, unknown in San societies. Disputes over cattle ownership or the control of grazing fields were settled by chiefs who presided over clans or groups of clans.

Mutual interests dictated the nature of the relationships between the San and the Khoikhoi. Relations were sometimes hostile, in the form of cattle raids, but more often friendly, with the San obtaining cattle meat from the Khoikhoi in exchange for wild game and fruit. Considerable intermixing also occurred between the two groups. San herded cattle for Khoikhoi owners in return for milk or sometimes adopted pastoralism to become Khoikhoi, while Khoikhoi who had lost their cattle to drought or disease often adopted a hunting-gathering life style. Intermarriages were also common between the two groups, and, even though the San were initially more numerous, in time the economic advantages of the Khoikhoi soon swung the demographic balance in their favor, making them the most dominant of the two groups. The striking similarities and frequent intermingling between the two have led historians to coin the joint-name, Khoisan, for all the click-sound language speakers of southern Africa.

Bantu Expansion, Metallurgy, and the Onset of Mixed Agriculture

Following closely on the heels of the Khoisan pastoralists were the speakers of the branch of the Niger-Congo family of languages later known as Bantu. The first, original, or proto-Bantu language was spoken in the Nigeria-Cameroon borderland some four or five thousand years ago. Responding to a variety of economic, ecological, and demographic pressures, the proto-Bantu speakers emigrated from their original homeland. Over the centuries, these proto-Bantu speakers gradually but effectively infiltrated and colonized new lands while differentiating themselves into well over six hundred linguistic and cultural groups. Fanning out in two directions, one group moved southward into equatorial Africa where they adapted to a forest ecology; the other group moved east toward the great lake regions and then south along the eastern-southern African coast, where they adapted to a grassland ecology. What was unique about these new migrant groups, dramatically distinguishing them from preexisting Khoisan groups, was that in addition to owning cattle and sheep they grew cereal crops and possessed tools and weapons made with iron.

By the early centuries of the Common Era, these Bantu-speaking farmers, or more accurately agro-pastoralists, were spreading rapidly over much of the wetter and more arable eastern wooded valleys and coastal plains of South Africa. In this region, depending on the varying local climate and natural resources, they practiced mixed farming as they gathered wild plants and fruits; fished in the rivers and in coastal waters; hunted a wide range of animals; kept cattle, goats, and sheep; and planted millets, sorghum, melons, gourds, and peas. Sedentary or living in semipermanent villages, these migrants with dark brown pigmentation and robust physiques had, by the time of the European advent, become the most dominant group on the southern African subcontinent and the ancestors of the vast majority of the people of present-day South Africa. Their more stable and nutritious diet led to population increase and the establishment of longer-lasting settlements and to stronger and more complex sociopolitical organizations. In the early period of their contact, relations between the Khoisan and the Bantu farmers appeared to have been generally cordial and mutually beneficial. In many cases the Khoisan welcomed these mixed farmers, showed them the environment, taught them medicinal secrets, exchanged wild game and nuts for crops and cattle, and served as herders. They also provided them with women to sustain their practice of polygyny, an essential in an agricultural society where the possession of many children and control over several women meant more labor supply for herding and crop cultivation. In the long run, however, the clear economic and social advantages of the iron-using and increasingly more populous farmers soon tilted the balance of power in their favor, resulting in the gradual assimilation, displacement, or elimination of the Khoisans.

Among the triumphant mixed farmers, control over cattle and trading goods resulted in a marked differentiation of wealth and status and the emergence of small-scale polities, marked by a gendered division of labor and a highly patriarchal sociopolitical organization. By the eighteenth century, two major sociocultural and linguistic groups emerged. The first of these were the Sotho-Tswana speakers, located in the interior plateau and in the present North West, Northern Province, Mpumalanga, and the Free State. The other groups were the Nguni-speaking groups, the most notable of which were the Xhosa and Zulu, situated in the region between the Drakensberg and the Indian Ocean, now the KwaZulu-Natal and the Eastern Cape. Though considerable and complex interactions occurred between these groups, as well as between the preexisting Khoisan communities, the political system remained characterized by a high degree of segmentation and a centralized megastate did not emerge in the region until the era of revolutionary state formation associated with Shaka Zulu and the *mfecane* in the early nineteenth century.

The White Invaders

1652 is etched into the South African historical memory as the year of the establishment of the first European settlement at the Cape. The story of this settlement, however, dates back to the fifteenth century and is closely connected with the beginning of the European voyages of discovery. Thwarted in their overland routes by the powerful Islamic empires of Asia and unable to dislodge the Arabs from their control of the Mediterranean Sea routes, European nations led by Portugal began to look for alternative routes that would take them to Asia, the major source of much needed spices and other goods. By the end of the fifteenth century, these efforts began to yield some fruits. In 1487, Batholomew Dias, in the course of a trip to India, was driven by an Atlantic storm past the Cape of South Africa to the Mossel Bay. In reporting his discovery to his sovereign, Diaz named the new cape the Cape of Storm, but the King of Portugal promptly reversed the decision, calling the new cape the Cape of Good Hope. Benefiting from the experiences of others who had sailed the route before him, Vasco da Gama rounded the Cape in 1497 and eventually reached India before sailing back to Lisbon. This began a new era in world history with major consequences for all the continents of the world in the succeeding centuries.

Table Bay at the Cape of Good Hope became a strategic stopping and victualizing point for ships in the course of their long journey from Europe to Asia. For the next 150 years, the Khoikhoi willingly bartered cattle and sheep for copper, iron, and tobacco. Iron was used for making spears and arrows, while copper was useful for making jewelry and functioned as currency for obtaining cattle from other pastoral groups in the interior. However, before long, the sailors' demand for cattle began to outstrip what the Khoikhoi could supply without imperiling their stock of herds. In a society that saw cattle as a store of wealth and a symbol of status to be parted with only when absolutely necessary, the Khoikhoi were not keen on selling off their stock of cattle, except for the old and the infirm. In consequence, the price of cattle rose, while European sailors, in desperation, often took the law into their hands by stealing or raiding Khoikhoi cattle, thus provoking retaliatory attacks by the Khoikhoi on the next group of sailors to arrive. The instability inherent in this relationship finally prompted the Dutch, who by the seventeenth century had displaced both the Portuguese and the Spanish as the leading merchant nation in the world, to establish more stable relations with the indigenous people.

Thus, in 1652, the directors of the Dutch East India Company sent Jan van Riebeeck and his party of 90 men to establish a small, fortified station at Table Bay that would perform the specific and limited functions of supplying passing ships with fruit, vegetables, grain, and fresh water; providing temporary housing where sick sailors could recuperate; and maintaining good relations with the Khoikhoi, who were the main source of meat for the company fleets. There is no evidence that this was meant to be more than a temporary though stable refreshment and trading post. That it became permanent and assumed a new and unforeseen degree of autonomy and dynamism were due to four interlocking factors. First, to supplement the production of the company's garden and the still unreliable Khoikhoi cattle supply, the company released some of its officials from their contracts and allowed them to begin to farm and raise cattle as free burghers. Second, in 1657, a shipload of slaves from a captured Portuguese vessel from Angola arrived, providing the settlers with the much needed cheap labor to create the basic infrastructure of a colony, namely a fort, a jetty, roads, and labor to work the gardens and farms. With the arrival of more slaves, most of whom came from Indonesia, India, and Madagascar, the Cape became a slave society in every sense. Between 1652 and 1807, the year of the British abolition of the oversea slave trade, nearly 60,000 slaves were imported into the Cape Colony. Third, more groups of immigrants began to swell the population of the settlers. Notable among these was a group of 200 protestant refugees fleeing from persecution in France. Finally, as the settlers expanded inland, they intruded on the lands of the pastoralists, who soon began to clash violently with the settlers as they were progressively dispossessed of their land and stock holdings.

Khoisan resistance to the Dutch encroachment provoked a series of wars and continued until the end of the eighteenth century, but superior military technology gave the settlers the upper hand. From 1715 onwards, the burghers organized civilian commandos, obtained arms from the company, and carried out an extermination campaign against the resisting indigenous population. They treated those resisting like vermin, killing off the adults and capturing the children and the cattle as booties of conquest. Landless and cattleless, Khoisan survivors had little choice but to accept their degradation in status to various forms of tenancy and servitude under the settler farmers. A few daring ones moved to the arid and mountainous Kalahari Desert and other barren regions not desired by farmers to carry on a precarious existence.

With the breeds of cattle they obtained from the Khoikhoi, and others they later imported, the settlers soon became owners of great herds of cattle and flocks of sheep. They followed the practice of transhumance, a practice they learned from the Khoisan. For their subsistence, the burghers lived on and hunted the massive herds of game they met in the Cape interior. In some cases, their hunting brought several species, like the blauwbok antelope and the quagga zebra to extinction while reducing others to tiny remnants. Continued overhunting and overgrazing soon produced disastrous ecological consequences for the region.

Further expansion brought the European farmers into direct contact with the amaXhosa, the southernmost vanguard of the Bantu-speaking peoples. In a series of wars that spanned nearly a century, the Xhosa stoutly resisted the white settlers' incursions with varying degrees of success, until their power was finally broken after the religion-inspired, Xhosa cattle-killing episodes of the mid-nineteenth century. At the heart of the new colony was the city of Cape Town, the seat of the VOC government of the colony, its major market and principal seaport. The new society created by the trekboers was not a self-sufficient one; they were utterly dependent on the labor of slaves and the indigenous people. Though it labeled itself Christian, it was a morally loose society in which male promiscuity with women from the subordinate classes was widely condoned. It was also a highly stratified society based on race. For the lower classes, made up of the slaves and the dispossessed Khoisan pastoralists, life was harsh, violent, brutish, nasty, and short.[1]

The *Mfecane* Revolution and the Rise of African States

During the closing decades of the eighteenth century, a combination of factors (demographic pressures, increased demands for ivory and other products of the wild, the rise of able leaders, and periodic drought and other ecological pressures) led to the intensification of state-formation activities in the South African interior, most especially among the Bantu-speaking groups who had become well-established in the region. Competition over the control of land, people, and cattle led to conflict and, in some cases, warfare as stronger chiefdoms swallowed up smaller and weaker ones, setting in motion a process of political centralization unheard of in the region before the eighteenth century. By the beginning of the nineteenth century, five major polities had emerged in the hinterland of Delagoa Bay and Natal. These were the Mabhudu, Ndwandwe, Mthethwa, Thulare (Bapedi), and Ngwaketse kingdoms. The struggle for dominance among these states produced violent eruptions in which the states of Mthethwa, under Dingiswayo, and Ndwandwe, under Zwide, emerged triumphant. During the second decade of the 1800s, the power of Mthethwa was broken by the Ndwandwe. It was at this point that Shaka, the ruler of the then small chiefdom of the Zulu and at one time a general in Dingiswayo's army, came into the fray. After keeping himself out of much of the conflict between the superpowers in the region, he had sufficient force to confront and finally defeat the victorious amaNdwadwe in 1819. Thereafter, the kingdom of Shaka Zulu became the dominant power in the region.

Shaka is no doubt the most controversial figure in South African history, revered by many for his military prowess and political sagacity, and reviled by others for his bloodthirstiness. He was certainly a highly gifted, talented, and visionary leader, whose excesses were to a great extent the byproduct of the ruthlessness and competitiveness that were the hallmarks of his time. His most important innovations were based on preexisting traditions. His military regiments, the *impis,* were based on the Nguni age-grade associations, whose military role he strengthened by transforming them into a standing army. Armed with the short stabbing spear (*assegai*), the *impis* fought bare-footed to ensure speed and agility. Conquered or subordinate chiefdoms were incorporated, though their rulers were permitted to retain their positions pro-vided they remain untiring in their loyalty and payment of cattle and other tributes to Shaka. A new and integrating sense of nationalism was promoted as every inhabitant, no matter his or her origin, became a Zulu, speaking the Zulu dialect, the language of the kingdom. By the 1820s, the Zulu kingdom had become predatory, and Shaka's military ruthlessness and incessant war-fare occasioned considerable instability and tension in the kingdom, culmi-nating in his assassination in 1828.

Shaka's death was not the end of trouble for the region. The maelstrom that he had unleashed reverberated with far-reaching consequences until the end of the century, creating widespread havoc, upheaval, the rise and fall of many states, demographic hemorrhage, destruction of settlements, neglect of farm-ing, decimation of livestock, famine, and human carnage. Three notable new states emerged in the region beside the Zulu: the Ndebele, created by Mzi-likazi, a general in Shaka's army who fled north with his cattle (after spurning an order from Shaka to surrender them to him), conquering all the peoples and groups along his path and acquiring their herds; the Swazi, founded by Sobhuza; and the Sotho, established on the flat-topped Thaba Bosiu moun-tain fortress by Moshoeshoe. All these states incorporated displaced elements from various ethno-linguistic groups to create new polities in the region. For the Nguni, this was the time of the *mfecane,* which means crushing, a time of much destruction and great suffering in which many thousands died violent deaths and many more were displaced while war-induced famine and starva-tion apparently drove some to cannibalism. In their destitution, many of the displaced poured into the Cape colony in search of work and subsistence. Finally, the denuding of the population of the South African highveld pre-sented the European invaders, who from the 1830s onward began to push inland, with an unprecedented opportunity for territorial conquest and political domination.[2]

The British Advent and the Afrikaner Great Trek

In 1795, the British seized control of the Cape in order to prevent this strategically important land, the stepping-stone to Asia, from falling into the hands of revolutionary France, which had recently established its control over the Batavian Republic, as the Dutch state was then called. In 1802, Britain and France signed the Peace of Amiens, which resulted in a temporary truce between the two countries. Consequently, Britain returned the Cape to the Dutch, only to recapture it again three years later with the resumption of hostility with Napoleon. The Vienna Settlement of 1815, which followed the final defeat of Napoleon, eventually confirmed British sovereignty over the Cape Colony. Though initially the British showed very little interest in the complex and anarchic society they had acquired beyond the Cape peninsula, a combination of internal and external pressures eventually demanded a more proactive approach.

The first impetus for change occurred in 1820, when in response to growing unemployment and social unrest in Britain, the British government set aside 50,000 pounds to relocate and resettle some of the marginalized and deprived of British society. The first batch of 5,000 migrants (out of about 80,000 who had applied), made up of carefully selected men, women, and children, mostly from the lower middle classes and mostly artisans, arrived in 1820 with a mandate to settle on and tame the land on the Cape eastern frontier, west of the Fish River, that had been seized from the Xhosa by the British imperial army. The arrival of these settlers and others who followed them from Britain had far-reaching consequences on Cape colonial society. Unlike earlier European immigrants, they refused to assimilate themselves into the Dutch-dominated settler society and culture. Instead they strove to maintain their distinctive language, traditions, and religious beliefs, introducing new complexities into an already complicated society.

To further complicate matters, a combination of the forces of protestant evangelicalism, humanitarian abolitionism, and the dictates of industrial capitalism caused the British Parliament to unilaterally abolish the slave trade in 1807. In 1828 the British passed Ordinance 50, which abolished the pass laws and freed the Khoikhoi and other free blacks to sell their labor wherever they wished in the colony. Six years later, in 1834, Britain abolished slavery in all its colonies. In the Cape civil service, British officials began to replace Boers, while English began to take the place of Dutch in education and in the courts. Naturally, these changes were considered intolerable by the Boers, since they threatened the racial order of their society.

Thus, from the end of 1835, disillusioned bands of *voortrekkers* (pioneers) with their wives, children, and livestock struck north in their ox wagons, determined to escape British control in their search for freedom and a land they could truly call their own. This was the Great Trek, the most momentous and the most celebrated event in Afrikaner history, which saw the emigration of about 6000 Boer farmers; this number represented 10 percent of the Cape white population at the time, from the Cape across the Orange River to the highveld plateau south and north of the Vaal River, as far north as the Limpopo River, westward to the edge of the Kalahari Desert, and as far east as subtropical Natal. In many of these places the *voortrekkers* ran into the vortex of cataclysmic wars already unleashed by the *mfecane*. Many of the pioneers perished, but enough survived to eventually establish a series of independent Afrikaner republics that coalesced into the Orange Free State and the South African Republic (the Transvaal) by the middle of the nineteenth century. In 1843, the British annexed Natal, making it their second colony in the region. Attempts made between 1859 and 1877 to unite the four polities into a single colony under the British failed.

The Mineral Revolution and the Road to Apartheid

The discovery of the world's richest diamond fields in Kimberley (1867) and its richest gold fields in the Witwatersrand (1886) rejuvenated British imperial interests and designs in the region. South Africa became a magnet to fortune hunters, who flooded into the region by the thousands to try their luck at the fabulous, yet to be tapped wealth of this land. The struggle over who would control the world's richest mineral fields pitched the Boer Republics against the British and the two European groups against the Griqua, Tswana, and other African groups, all of whom began to lay claim to the mineral-bearing regions. The battle for control was fierce and protracted with many twists and turns that eventually culminated in the Anglo-Boer War of 1899–1902. Though the British won, the cost of the war for both sides was very high: 26,000 Boer women and children died in British concentration camps; 6,000 Boer commandos out of a total of 35,000 perished in the battles; the British casualties were put at 21,942 out of an army of 500,000 men; while the cost to the British tax payers was 191 million pounds. All of South Africa, including the nonsettler territories of Basutoland and Bechuanaland, came under direct British rule.

In 1906–7 as part of the attempt to rehabilitate and assuage the defeated and still-disgruntled Afrikaners, the British granted their two former republics self-government. On May 31, 1910, the four self-governing republics came together to form the Union of South Africa, with a unitary constitution that gave little concession to state rights but guaranteed the equality of the two official languages. The new constitution also favored the countryside in the delimitation of voting districts, while retaining political power in the hands of white men, who constituted 93 percent of the electorate. White women and all non-whites were disenfranchised except in the Cape Province, where the preexisting limited franchise rights of qualified coloreds and blacks were retained, permitting them to elect whites to represent their interests, since nonwhites were prohibited from sitting in Parliament.

The post-union government of South Africa was dominated by a triumverate of Afrikaner war generals: Louis Botha and Jan Smuts from the Transvaal and Barry Hertzog from the Orange Free State. Botha, the first prime minister, and Smuts who succeeded him in 1919, pursued a policy of conciliation between the two white communities and cooperation with Great Britain. Barry Hertzog was, however, opposed to the policy of reconciliation. He called for the maintenance of two streams in the white South African nation and a policy that would favor and focus more attention on the plights of the Afrikaner poor. Forced to resign his cabinet position in 1912, Hertzog formed the National Party with other dissenters from the ruling South African Party. That same year, leading members of the growing African elite, under the chairmanship of Pixley Seme, founded the South African Native National Congress (SANNC), which became the African National Congress (ANC) in 1921. In the meantime, to force African peasants into migrant labor in the mines and on white farms, the 1913 Land Act reserved 87 percent of South African land for the exclusive use of whites, who at no time constituted more than 13 percent of the population. South Africa's active participation in World War I on the side of Britain secured for it the control of German South West Africa (Namibia).

General Hertzog, who became prime minister in 1924, took steps to solve the native problem, through a policy of systematic extension of racial and spatial segregations that deprived blacks of their franchise rights in the Cape Province. The granting of the franchise to all white males in 1930 and to all white females the following year watered down the value of the few colored and black votes still retained at the Cape. The passing of the 1936 Land Act effectively eliminated the remaining black votes at the Cape. The years between the two world wars witnessed the revival of Afrikaner nationalism, which received an impetus with the formation of the Broederbond, an exclusively and rabidly racist organization meant to coordinate the Afrikaner struggle for political and economic power. The 1930s witnessed a dramatic surge in Afrikaner literary activities that climaxed in the 1938 celebration of the

Great Trek, which stirred Afrikaner nationalist feeling and increased support for the Afrikaner dominated National Party. In 1948, the Afrikaner National Party was voted into office by a narrow majority. Its victory came mainly from the support of two groups: Afrikaner farmers, who were feeling the crunch of the loss of low-cost African labor to the towns; and Afrikaner workers, many of whom were becoming unemployed and impoverished by the stiff competition offered them by low-cost African migrant workers in the mines. The Afrikaner National Party's policy of apartheid and its pledge to maintain white racial dominance in every sphere of life in South Africa were particularly attractive to these groups.

The Apartheid State

The victory of the National Party marked the beginning of a new era in the history of South Africa. The new government was headed by Daniel Malan, who was succeeded by the hard-line Johannes G. Strydom in 1954, and in 1958 by Hendrick F. Verwoerd. As the chief architect and leading ideologue of apartheid, Verwoerd, more than any other South African ruler, came to personify the new direction of South Africa. When he was assassinated in 1966 by a deranged Afrikaner shortly before delivering a major speech to Parliament, Balthazar J. Vorster became prime minister. Vorster retired in 1978 and was succeeded by Pieter W. Botha, who remained in power until he was edged out by F. W. de Klerk in 1989. De Klerk negotiated the end of apartheid and the introduction of nonracial democracy to South Africa in 1994.

Under the National Party, racial segregation—the foundations of which had already been laid in the first half of the twentieth century and especially under the rule of the triumvirate Afrikaner generals—became progressively extended through the policy of apartheid. Apartheid, which means apartness, as a doctrine of racial and political hegemony argues that each race and nation should be kept entirely apart, socially and territorially, and allowed to develop along its own inherent and unique cultural lines. For the majority of the African population the areas envisaged for their separate development were the scattered and poverty-stricken Native Reserves that collectively constituted about 13 percent of the entire national territory. Between 1948 and 1968 a series of closely related laws and measures were devised to restructure South African society to conform totally to the dictates of the apartheid ideology. The 1949 Mixed Marriages Act forbade interracial marriages while the Immorality Acts of 1950 banned sexual relations between whites and blacks and later between whites and coloreds. The 1950 Population Acts provided for the classification and registration of the entire population on the basis of

An Indian mother and daughter pose beside the statue of Gandhi in downtown Pietermaritzburg in 2002. A few blocks away is the train station where Gandhi, as a young Indian lawyer newly arrived from London, was thrown out of the train in 1893 for riding, as a colored, in the first-class section reserved only for the exclusive use of whites.

race. That same year the practice of urban segregation was given legal teeth through the passing of the Group Areas Act, which designated particular residential areas for specific races in the towns. Existing laws reserving categories of work (skilled work for whites, non-skilled for nonwhites) were further strengthened. Petty apartheid or race segregation in public places, such as trains, buses, post offices, elevators, church halls, sidewalks, hospitals, and beaches, was introduced to all the places where it had not been practiced before.

Signs such as White Only became the ubiquitous symbols of the new order all over the country. The Separate Amenities Act ruled that amenities provided for the different races need not be of equal standard. The Separate Representation of Voters Acts of 1951 and 1955 formally abrogated the Cape Colored franchise, while the Bantu Self-Government Act of 1959 provided for the setting up of new political institutions in the black homelands that effectively terminated their citizenship rights in South Africa, where only whites could own and exercise citizenship rights. The 1959 Extension of University Education Act prohibited the admissions of nonwhites to universities such as those of Cape Town and the Witwatersrand that had been previously opened to them. In 1968, multiracial political organizations were made illegal.

Enforcement of these myriad laws brought considerable anguish and suffering to the African population and to some extent to Asians and coloreds as well. In essence, achieving the goals of apartheid required that South Africa become a police state in which terror, police brutality, and violent repression became the order of the day. A 1962 General Law Amendment Act gave the government the power to arrest and sentence, without jury trial, to various penalties from isolation to death, any person found guilty of furthering or encouraging undesirable social and economic change. This sweeping power was further reinforced by the Terrorism Act of 1967, made retroactive to 1962, which authorized arrests without warrants, solitary confinement, indefinite detention, mass trial, and mass sentencing of persons and groups perceived by the apartheid government to constitute a threat to national security.[3]

Dismantling the Leviathan: From Ghandi and Sobukwe to Biko and Mandela

Beside periodic and spasmodic episodes of peasant and rural revolts, such as the Bambetta Rebellion of 1906, and religious or millenarian uprisings such as the Enoch Mgijima Church of Israel's 1921 clash with the police that left 200 of the Israelites dead, resistance against colonial domination and white oppression centered around a number of African and Asian political movements. One of the earliest of these was the Natal Indian Congress, organized by Mohandas K. Gandhi in 1894 to fight against residential and commercial discriminations against Indians in Natal. Though the method of nonviolent resistance that the Indians introduced to South Africa achieved very little for them; it became a powerful moral weapon evoked again and again with far-reaching consequences and remarkable successes in the struggle against apartheid in South Africa, for independence in India during the 1930s and 1940s, and for civil rights in the United States during the 1950s and 1960s. In 1952 the ANC, in alliance with the South African Indian Congress (SAIC) and other resistance groups, launched a campaign of nonviolent resistance against discriminatory laws in the course of which 10,000 Africans courted arrest.

The apartheid government's mindless repression of these nonviolent efforts produced increased militancy in the African nationalist camp leading to the formation of more radical organizations like the Pan-Africanist Congress

(PAC). Formed in 1959 and led by Robert Sobukwe, the PAC led a major demonstration against the government in March 1960 at Sharpeville, in the course of which 67 unarmed demonstrators were shot dead by the police. The brutality of this suppression brought the apartheid regime under an unprecedented wave of international condemnation, while its economy suffered a direct hit with a net outflow of foreign investment capital. In defiance of widespread calls for its international isolation, South Africa declared itself a republic and withdrew from the British Commonwealth of Nations in October 1960. To deal with the continuing demonstrations over the Sharpeville massacre, the government banned both the ANC and the PAC. In response, both groups went underground and abandoned nonviolence. The ANC established a military wing, Umkhonto we Sizwe (MK-Spear of the Nation), under the leadership of Nelson Mandela, with the express objective of forcing the government to the negotiating table through a carefully executed program of sabotage attacks on government properties, while minimizing civilian casualties. These efforts achieved little. With its enormous power and resources, the apartheid state was able to absorb the shock of the sabotage attacks and the attendant economic impact. In 1964 Mandela and several other nationalist leaders were sentenced to life imprisonment and tossed into jail, where most of them languished for the next three decades and where they remained the focus of internal and international opposition to apartheid.

With the leading nationalists dead, in jail, under house arrest, or in exile, the 1960s and the early 1970s were years of relative peace and prosperity for South Africa. The economy boomed while the government took steps to replace explicit racism with a program of granting separate nationalities to Africans as the main rationale for denying them citizenship and civil rights in South Africa. Beginning in the mid-1950s and continuing until the early 1980s, nearly 3.5 million Africans and thousands of coloreds and Asians were stripped of their South African citizenship, forcibly removed from their locations or black spots, such as Orlando or Sophiatown and other designated or reclassified white areas, and relocated to government-constituted homelands based on ethnicity. South Africa granted independence to the Transkei (Xhosa) in 1976, Bophuthatswana in 1977, Venda in 1979, and Ciskei (Xhosa) in 1981. All these states remained financially dependent on South Africa and no other country apart from South Africa recognized their independence. Though Africans mounted strong resistance to these efforts to denaturalize them and turn them into pass-carrying aliens in their own country, these drastic measures were carried out with ruthless precision and unscrupulous efficiency by the security police whose powers were massively expanded during these years.

Soweto and the Demise of the Apartheid State

Within South Africa, resistance against apartheid continued. Quiescence on the political front did not mean nationalistic acquiescence. The 1960s and 1970s were a time of major literary efflorescence as black and white writers, journalists, novelists, playwrights, and commentators brought a strong liberationist message to the South African reading public. Renegade church leaders such as Trevor Huddleston of the Anglican Church and Beyers Naude of the Dutch Reformed Church began to question the compatibility of apartheid and the Christian faith. Black theaters, music, and magazines became vehicles of criticism, dialogue, and confrontation with the South African dilemmas: apartheid and the apartheid state. In addition, the remorseless pressure of industrial capitalism compelled the government to ease restrictions on job reservations on the basis of race, thus opening up many skilled and semiskilled positions for blacks whose growing confidence found expression in the formation of militant trade unions and a spate of crippling strikes during the 1970s.

Similarly, the government attempt to control and tame the minds of young Africans through a program of inferior and limited education backfired, producing widespread frustration among Africans, which eventually led to the emergence of the Black Consciousness Movement (BCM). Led by Steve Biko, the BCM aimed at infusing in the black community a new sense of pride in themselves as black people, and in their religion, culture, and ways of life. The efforts bore fruit, especially among the young. On June 16, 1976, thousands of black school children in the Johannesburg suburban black township of Soweto took to the street to protest, among other things, the use of Afrikaans, the language of their oppressor, as the medium of instruction in all black South African schools. Violent police repression caused the riots to spread rapidly to many other black urban areas. By the time the dust settled, more than 600 people, many of them under seventeen, had been killed.

Soweto was a watershed in South African history; thereafter things would never be the same again. Though not quite obvious at the time because of the government's apparent success at repressing the revolt, Soweto marked the beginning of the end of the apartheid order. In 1977, Steve Biko was arrested and tortured to death by the police. All antiapartheid groups were outlawed. In June 1980, riots erupted in Cape Town leaving 40 people dead. The opposition, led by Oliver Tambo of the ANC in exile and by clergymen Desmond Tutu and Allan Boesak of the United Democratic Front (UDF) within the country, put the apartheid government and society under pressure. Sabotage attacks masterminded by exiles from without were supplemented by regular antigovernment rallies and insurrection from within. With the ANC calling on its supporters to make South Africa ungovernable, unrest escalated as children abandoned their schools and workers joined in to keep the apartheid

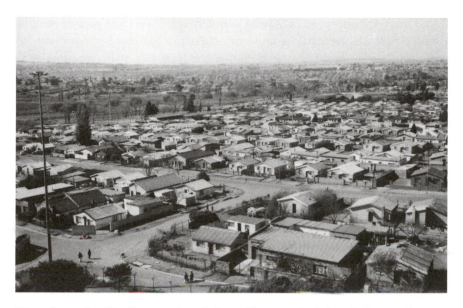

View from the Sir Earnest Openheimer Tower and Cultural Center, Soweto, Guatang, 2002.

society permanently in ferment. Funeral processions of slain demonstrators, which had become a daily occurrence, were transformed into antigovernment rallies and became occasions for more police killings.

In the meantime, the economy plummeted as South Africa came under increasing international political, economic, and military isolation and sanctions, through sport boycotts, visa restrictions, credit denial, and crippling outflow of investment capital, putting the prosperity of the privileged white minority in jeopardy. The defeat of the South African army, with its demoralized soldiers and outdated Mirage fighters, at Cuito Cuanavale in 1988, at the hand of the more resolute Cuban and Angolan forces, armed with modern Russian-made MiGs, showed the biting impact of arms embargo. The collapse of communism in Eastern Europe and Russia exploded the myth of South Africa serving as a bastion of capitalism against the forces of communism in southern Africa. The efforts of Prime Minister P. W. Botha to reform the racist state, end some of the more intrusive elements of apartheid, carry out some constitutional changes to allow Asians and coloreds some political participation, though without loosening overall white political and economic control, could not arrest the plunge towards cataclysm. These reforms were, by this time, simply too little and too late.

By 1989, a state of stalemate was reached in which savage government repression through the demonstration of overwhelming fire power, mass arrests, torture, and assassination could not defeat the forces of resistance, while the opposition forces, having virtually achieved their goal of making South Africa ungovernable, could not unseat the apartheid government.[4] A fortuitous stroke in 1989 caused Botha, the fearsome arch repressor, nicknamed the Great Crocodile, to be shoved aside. F. W. de Klerk assumed the leadership of the National Party and of the government. An astute conservative, a mild-mannered conciliator, a brilliant lawyer from a younger generation of Afrikaners, de Klerk was determined to seize the initiatives from the opposition by sacrificing overall white political dominance while protecting their position and economic status in the country. In his first speech to Parliament on February 2, 1990, the new president surprised everyone when he announced the unbanning of the ANC, the PAC, the Communist Party, and all other proscribed antiapartheid organizations, and the impending release of all political prisoners including Nelson Mandela. Nine days later, Mandela walked out of prison, after 27 years in the apartheid dungeon: tall, grey-haired but dignified, carrying in his pocket, or so it seemed, the promise and the hope of a new South Africa.

Months of chaotic and bloody negotiations followed, during which the loyalists and other nostalgic beneficiaries of the apartheid system did everything possible to derail the transition. The main battle line for succession was drawn between the ANC, led by Mandela, and the Zulu-dominated Inkatha Freedom Movement, led by Mongoshutu Butholezi, who received tactical support from various extremist Afrikaner right groups. However, in the end, sanity prevailed. Elections for South Africa's first multiracial government were held on April 27, 1994. The ANC won an overwhelming majority, though less than the two-thirds that would have allowed it to unilaterally write the new South African constitution. Mandela became president, while de Klerk, leader of the National Party, became one of the two vice presidents.

For the new South Africa, the challenges are many. The most immediate among these is the establishment of a stable political order and the ending of the endemic culture of violence and urban crime that is largely the byproducts of decades of apartheid repression; the need to grapple with the problems of rural poverty and urban unemployment; urgent attention to the problems of youths who abandoned schools during the 1970s and 1980s to fight for freedom and who now find themselves frustrated, angry, and without the skills to function in and benefit from the new South Africa. A cursory look at the history of South Africa since 1994 shows that progress is being made. Notable among these signs of progress are: the setting up of the Truth and Reconciliation Commission led by Archbishop Desmond Tutu; the drafting and adoption of a new constitution; the gradual dissipation of irredentist demands from white and black separatist groups; the successful carrying out of the second multiparty and multiracial elections in 1999; and the smooth transition from Mandela to Thabo Mbeki. All these, coupled with the peace and stability that has permitted the holding of several major international conferences in South Africa, and the country's booming and expanding tourist industry are all indicative of the rapid progress already made toward the realization of the dream of forging a new society in this historically troubled but richly endowed region of the African continent.[5]

EDUCATION

In traditional African societies, most especially before the advent of the Europeans, adults had the direct responsibility for transmitting the cultural values and skills of the group to the young. In many Nguni-speaking societies, membership in highly regimented age-groups became one of the principal means for the acquisition of basic knowledge and vital skills connected with the civic, religious, military, and political affairs of the community. Through close interactions within the family, women learned the basic domestic and agricultural skills necessary for the survival of the family and the group. When the Europeans came to the Cape in the eighteenth century, they brought with them their own system of education. Initially, the emphasis was on religious instruction since the first schools were established and run by the Dutch Reformed Church, whose commitment was to conversion and confirmation for which literacy was considered important. Itinerant teachers (*meesters*) taught basic literacy and numerical skills in the rural areas. The advent of the London Missionary society in 1799 led to the establishment of several British mission schools.

Throughout the nineteenth century, Afrikaners remained resentful of the English education system, considering the language and curriculum a threat both to their language and their Afrikaner values. Consequently, most of them refused to enroll their children in British or government-sponsored schools with the result that by 1877, while some 60 percent of school-age children in British-dominated Natal and 49 percent in the Cape Colony were enrolled in school, only 12 percent in the Afrikaner dominated Orange Free State and 8 percent in the Transvaal were in schools. The decision of the government toward the end of the century to accord equal recognition to Afrikaans as a language of instruction in the public schools, increased school enrollment in the Afrikaner republics.

The institutionalization of apartheid in 1948 led to the promulgation of the Bantu Education Act of 1953, which widened the educational gaps between the races. The act prescribed an inferior form of education for blacks, since according to its chief architect and later prime minister, Hendrik Verwoerd, there was no sense in providing blacks with skills and training for which they would find no opportunities in life since there was no place for them in the white-dominated South Africa, "above the level of certain labor," to use his well-quoted phrase. By the 1970s, the government was spending on black education only one-tenth of what was being spent on white education. Resentment over the inferior facilities, teachers, and textbooks provided for black schools coupled with the tension over the enforced use of Afrikaans as the language of instruction in black schools exploded into a major student revolt in the Johannesburg township of Soweto in June 1976, in which more than 600 people died. Thereafter many black South African youths abandoned the schools to join the liberation struggle in exile or from within South Africa, with a battle cry of "liberation before education." Resolved to make South Africa ungovernable, schools became objects of vandalism and arsonist attacks, and administrators and teachers who did not join the protests found it difficult to continue to maintain normal school activities.

The end of the apartheid policies in the early 1990s inaugurated a new era in South African educational history. Desegregation became the norm as state schools began, from 1991, to admit pupils from all races. In 1995, free and compulsory education for all population groups between the ages of 7 and 16 became mandatory. In 1995, there were a total of 20,780 primary and secondary schools in South Africa, out of which 477 were private. In 1996, 94 percent (93 male and 95 female) of pupils in the relevant age-group were enrolled in primary schools, while the figure for secondary schools was 51 percent (46 male and 57 female), making a total enrollment figure of over eleven million pupils, no doubt an impressive achievement within a short period after the demise of apartheid. In 1999, there were 21 universities and 15 *technikons* in the country. *Technikons* are tertiary educational institutions providing technical and commercial vocational training. The largest of these institutions is the University of South Africa (Unisa), an open concept, long-distance learning system with a 2001 enrollment figure of 170,000 students. In 1999/2000 the government allocated 21.4 percent of its budget to education, an indication of the high priority given to education in the creation of the new South Africa. Nevertheless, the challenges are enormous. The literacy rate for whites is 93 percent, while for blacks it is 32 percent. The legacy of decades of neglect, inferior facilities, lack of qualified teachers, the need to rehabilitate and reeducate generations of youths who abandoned schools in the name of the struggle, the challenges of racial integration, curricula reform, and the challenge of providing qualitative and accessible education to everyone, promises to tax to the utmost the will and the resources of the post-apartheid South African government and people.

School children pose for a quick photo shot in front of a war memorial, downtown, Pietermaritzburg. The turbulent history of South Africa has ensured that whatever else the country may be lacking, memorials to war heroes, especially Afrikaner and British dead, are abundant.

THE ECONOMY

Pre-Capitalist Economy

Before the nineteenth century, South Africa was not perceived by Europeans to be a land of riches. Unlike West and East Africa, no minerals or valuable cash crops were known to flourish there. It is not surprising that for nearly 200 years after the Europeans stumbled onto the Cape, no serious effort was made either to settle in or possess the region as they tried to do in the Congo-Angola region and along the Swahili coast of East Africa. Throughout this period and for long after, the main usefulness of the Cape was first as a convenient stopping point and a source of fresh food supply for European ships in the course of their long journey from Europe to East Africa and Asia. When the Dutch East India Company landed its first set of settlers at the Cape in 1652, their principal commission was to make available to the merchant ships produce obtained through trade with the Khoikhoi or through domestic farming by the settlers themselves. Thereafter and for the next two centuries agriculture was the dominant sector of the economy of the new colony. As a result of South Africa's diverse climate and relief forms, a wide variety of crops continue to be grown.

Fishing

Both fishing and forestry contribute modestly to the economy. The extensive Atlantic and Indian Ocean waters around South Africa's coasts are rich with fish and other marine life. Since the nineteenth century, fishing fleets from many nations have explored and continued to exploit the fishing grounds of South Africa. The fishing industry expanded rapidly after the Second World War. To check overfishing, the government has adopted a number of stringent conservation measures to regulate fishing and marketing within a 200 nautical mile radius of the South African coastal waters. The wide range of fish caught within the South African offshore waters includes the Cape hakes (*stockvisse*), Cape horse mackerel (*maasbanker*), South African pilchard, whitehead's round herring, the South African anchovy, snoek (barracouta), silver scabbardfish, chub mackerel, the Cape rock lobster, and the Cape Hope squid. Other marine resources landed include mollusks, mullet, oysters, seaweed, abalone, mussels, guano, and seals.

Mining

By the end of the nineteenth century, mining had outstripped agriculture as the dominant sector of the South African economy. South Africa is undoubtedly one of the world's leading mineral producers. It is also one of the oldest: archaeological research confirms that mining in the South African region dates to about 40,000 years ago. Early search efforts for minerals made by European settlers at the Cape remained unsuccessful until the discovery of copper in the Cape Province in the mid-nineteenth century. Mining, however, continued to be peripheral to the economy until the late nineteenth century when the chance discovery of diamonds in 1867 and of gold in 1886 inaugurated a new era in South Africa's history. These discoveries transformed South Africa from a poor, backward agricultural economy to a rich, industrialized, urbanized, modern economy. Diamonds and gold took South Africa from being an economic backwater to Africa's leading industrial state and a major center of international capital and investment. South Africa's minerals are exported to over 100 countries. The wealth derived from these minerals provided South Africa with the resources to develop the most extensive and the most advanced transportation and communication systems in Africa. Minerals remained the leading foreign exchange earner for the country until the mid-twentieth century, when mining was outstripped by manufacturing.

If there is any country that is synonymous with gold in the world, it is South Africa. It is the world's leading producer of gold; an achievement it has maintained unchallenged for more than a century. In 1970, gold production reached a record 1,000 metric tons. Thereafter production declined, and eventually stabilized during the mid-1980s at an annual production volume of over 600 tons of gold per year. But even then South Africa was still supplying close to 40 percent of the world output, a fabulous achievement. Ninety-eight percent of South Africa's gold comes from the Witwatersrand basin in the center of South Africa's central plateau. The 1990s was a time of pressure for the international gold industry and market, resulting in a sharp decline in prices. By 1997 gold prices were at an alarmingly low level, creating considerable stress for the South African gold industries. Several mining companies folded up, while many workers were laid off as steps were taken to revamp the industries through mergers and consolidations.

The instability in the world-market price for gold stimulated the development of other valuable mineral industries and in this South Africa has been well served. During the early part of the twentieth century, it was the leading producer of gem diamonds. Today it is the world's fifth leading producer. South Africa has a flourishing diamond-cutting industry that receives first priority in the processing of raw or rough diamonds. Being the hardest substance known to man, diamond is widely used for drilling and for the manufacture of high abrasives. South Africa is also Africa's leading producer of coal and iron ore. Coal has overtaken diamonds as the country's second most valuable exports. In addition, the absence of petroleum in marketable quantity has made coal especially valuable as the country's leading source of energy, generating 84 percent of the country's energy requirements, mainly in the form of electricity, but also as liquid gas. South Africa is the world's fourth leading supplier of coal, and the world's sixth leading supplier of iron. Similarly, South Africa is the world's leading producer and exporter of aluminosilicate (38 percent of the total world supply), chromium (55 percent), manganese (82 percent), platinum-group metals (69 percent), vanadium (33 percent). In addition, it has the largest world-known deposits of all these minerals as well as of gold, diamonds, and fluorspar, and it is among the four leading producers of asbestos, lead, nickel, phosphate rock, titanium minerals, uranium, vermiculite, zinc, and zirconium minerals. Many of these minerals are exceptionally rare, extremely valuable, and extraordinarily costly. All the world's major minerals are found in South Africa in economic quantities, with the exceptions of petroleum and bauxite.

As a result of the biting effect of economic sanctions imposed during the peak of the apartheid era, the South African authorities expended a considerable sum of energy prospecting for oil within the South African frontiers and underneath its ocean waters. The effort finally yielded fruit. In February 1985, after 20 years of intensive search for petroleum deposits, the government-owned Southern Oil Exploration Corporation (SOEKOR) announced the discovery of oil offshore at Mossel Bay, off the south coast of the Cape Province, with a daily output potential of 2,600 barrels of light crude oil. More significant were the natural gas reserves estimated at 30,000 million cubic meters.[6]

Manufacturing

Unlike other countries of Africa, the manufacturing industry is the largest sector of the South African economy. In 1998, the manufacturing sector employed 1,385,000 workers, an equivalent of 14.7 percent of the employed labor force. Of this number, over half are black, less than one-quarter are white, and the remainder are colored or Asian. In 1999 manufacturing contributed an estimated 18.2 percent of the Gross Domestic Product (GDP). Prior to the development of mining, there was little manufacturing going on in southern Africa. This was due largely to the sparse nature of the population, and the absence of many major urban centers with markets large enough to attract manufacturing entrepreneurs. Though the mining industry provided capital to industrialization, it did not initially stimulate more than its small-scale tertiary industries. But the wealth generated by mining was so great that there was very little incentive to invest anywhere else, as mining was allowed to swallow up all available capital, labor, and enterprise. In addition, the mining industry's policy of favoring cheap imports did not augur well for the protection of local industries.

It was not until the 1920s, when the government began to adopt a program of actively protecting local industries, that South African manufacturing experienced a new lease of life. South Africa's experience during the First and Second World Wars revealed the difficulty of relying on imports to meet local needs while at the same time stimulating the development of local industries to service the requirements of the Allied powers whose own industries had either been hampered by the war or were simply compelled to focus mainly on war munitions production. The establishment of one heavy industry after another, such as that of the Iron and Steel Corporation of South Africa (ISCOR) in 1928, led to a rapid expansion in industrial output and its contribution to the national economy.

Initially the majority of South Africa's factories were sited at the main entry ports to the country, namely Cape Town, Port Elizabeth, and Durban. With the growing population of the mining enclave of the Witwatersrand, factories began to be situated there as well. The end result is that more than 75 percent of the country's net industrial output comes from these four industrial areas while the rest of the country remains largely underdeveloped industrially.

Four major groups of industries can be identified. The first and probably the earliest to develop were the food, drink, and tobacco industries, responsible for processing South Africa's produce for both domestic consumption and export. The end of apartheid and the lifting of sanctions stimulated a rapid expansion in South Africa's wine industry output and export. In 1999, 40 percent of its 130 million liters went to the United Kingdom, and much of the remainder went to other African countries. The next group is the textile industry. These were already well-established before the Second World War and have continued to meet a substantial portion (60 percent) of the country's textile requirements.

The third group is comprised of the chemical industries, which began in South Africa with the manufacturing of explosives for gold mining operations. The Modderfontein factory, near Johannesburg is one of the largest makers of explosives and fertilizer in the world. The final and the most rapidly expanding group centers around the iron, steel, and engineering industries. With employment of an estimated 500,000 workers this is the largest sector of the industrial establishment. Begun as a supportive industry for the maintenance of the mines, this sector has taken on a life of its own, especially with the establishment of ISCOR which began to produce pig iron and steel from iron ores and quickly dominated this industrial sector.

An array of manufacturing engineering complexes also developed, producing domestic hardware, rolling railway stocks, motor vehicle components, and to some extent aircraft and ships. In 1992, the transport equipment industry produced 93,600 commercial vehicles and 206,600 passenger cars, with the majority of the cars containing at least 66 percent local content. Servicing all these is a well-developed industrial and financial infrastructure made up of an efficient transportation system, a well-developed and secure power supply, a functioning and efficient telephone system, a program of water resource conservation and development, and a sophisticated, stable, well-regulated financial and monetary structure. Equally important to the development of these industries has been the availability of a cheap labor supply. A major impact of industrialization has been the drawing away of large numbers of Africans from traditional rural subsistence economy and from all the countries of southern Africa to the ever-expanding urban and market-oriented industrial economy dominated by white capital and white managerial skills. Though the acute shortage of skilled manpower has opened new opportunities for qualified coloreds, Asians and blacks, the entrenched decades-old inequities in job positions and gross income disparities between whites, who had priority in pay and skilled jobs, and blacks, who held the

A middle-class family with their car, dog, and house in the Florida Lake suburb of Johannesburg. First from right is their maid. The end of apartheid has opened up new opportunities for blacks and other previously disadvantaged groups.

lowest jobs and received the poorest pay, remain with coloreds and Asians hanging precariously somewhere in between.[7]

SUBSISTENCE AND THE POLITICAL ECONOMY

Agriculture is the main traditional form of subsistence among all South African groups. In almost every case, women are the agriculturists, with men performing the heavy work of clearing the virgin land or breaking up the soil for sowing. Small boys assist their mothers to scare away birds from the sprouting grains or ripening crops. Work parties, made up of neighbors, are periodically engaged to take care of the more arduous task of plowing, ridging, and harvesting. Operating in rotation from farm to farm and lavished with beer, working in parties is usually an exciting and convivial engagement. The country's differing landforms and variable climates have resulted in the emergence of many soil types. The Pedi, for instance, recognizes seven soil types, with each being suited for different crops or for grazing. Summer is the season of rain for most of the region, and the best watered, most fertile, most wooded land is the southeastern region of the country. In the mountainous Drakensberg and other places, the uplands are used for grazing, while the valleys are reduced to cultivation. Traditionally, land is owned by the community rather than by the individuals. Chiefs acting on behalf of their people allocate land to those in need who thereafter exercise all rights of ownership as long as the allotted portion remains in use. Each wife receives at least one field from her husband for her own exclusive use. Unallocated or abandoned lands belong to the entire community and are available to be used for hunting, gathering, grazing, and watering.

Digging sticks or wooden hoes, made of very hard wood, hardened in the fire, were widely used by the Nguni. The introduction of the iron hoe, made up of an iron blade with a pointed tang which is inserted or wedged through the head of a wooden haft, was a great improvement. Axes are also used to fell trees and chop wood, while the adoption of the plough dramatically improved the efficiency of indigenous agricultural practices. Different groups practice crop rotation, mixed cropping, shifting cultivation, and land fallowing to varying degrees. For a long time the most staple crop was sorghum; but this has now been displaced in importance by maize. A wide variety of beans, sweet potatoes, groundnuts, tobacco, and Indian hemps are grown. Different types of pumpkins and gourds are grown for food when young and green and, when ripened are used as shells to be converted into containers to hold milk, oil, medicine, water, snuff, and food. Harvested crops are stored in grain pits, a bell-shaped cavity situated in the cattle enclosure, covered with flat stones, sealed with cow dung, and hidden from view through a loose layer of soil, as among the Nguni and Venda; or in enormous woven baskets or termite-proofed granaries, as among the Sotho and the Hlubi, and Nguni with very close ties to the Sotho. Rain-making ceremonies and other rituals are performed by the chief and other specialists to avert drought and famine, control insect pests, deter intruders, and ensure fertility and good yield.

Though agriculture is the chief means of subsistence, the most prestigious occupation for the people is pastoralism and the premier status is marked by cattle possession. Even among the Venda and the Tsonga, where diseases spread by the virulent tsetse fly and other factors make cattle keeping difficult, they are still kept wherever practicable. For the Nguni and the Sotho-Tswana, cattle are equated with life and their uses are many. They are a source of food, in the form of milk, butter, blood, and, occasionally, meat. Their skins are translated into clothing, bags, shields, ropes, and other objects. Their horns are transformed into medicinal, chemical, and other receptacles. Even their dung, besides serving as good fertilizers for the soil, is not discarded; instead it is converted into cement to plaster and beautify walls and floors when moist, and into fuel for fire, when dry. In many places, oxen serve as beasts of burden, and are increasingly used in recent years for plowing. Competitive races between specially trained, unmounted oxen are also a popular pastime; oxen that distinguish themselves in this sport are commemorated in folklore long after their death.

For the man, cattle are his measure of value, his principal investment stocks, his future guarantee, and his social security. To be cattleless is to be a man of no substance, little value, and no future; it is to be no man. Hence the Bantu's intense interest in and major preoccupation with cattle; a Bantu herder could instantly name each of his cattle, even when they could be numbered in hundreds, distinguishing each one by age, sex, color, shape of horns, and other peculiar features, sometimes evincing even more personal intimacy and bonding than with their children.

Songs, folktales, and riddles are connected with the herds and the principal bull of each herd is regularly lavished with evocative praises by the owner. As the premier store of values and future guarantees, cattle are rarely slaughtered for food or for sacrifice, except in exceptionally important occasions, or when they are too sick or too old to survive. Cattle theft is considered a major crime, and cattle raiding is a major cause of warfare between groups. As a popular Tswana song states: *Kgomo modimo wa mogae, modimo wa nko e meets; kgomo leotlanya dithsaba, o bolaile banna ba le bantsi,* meaning "Cow, God of the home, God with a moist nose; cow that makes the tribe fight, you have killed many men."[8]

Men have the exclusive prerogative for the care and management of cattle. Herding and milking are carried out by young boys working with or under the supervision of men. The most important part of a homestead is the cattle kraal, made up of a central enclosure of stout poles within which the cattle are kept at night. As the most sacred space in the homestead, the kraal is the site where cattle are killed for sacrifices; where men hold important meetings and adjudicate cases and pass sentences; where visitors are received; where men are buried, wrapped in the skin of freshly killed ox. Women are not permitted to enter the kraal unless they belong to the family and mostly when bringing food, and even then are strictly forbidden from entering when menstruating, to avoid polluting the herd and bringing misfortune. Goats and sheep are also widely kept. Though usually kraaled and herded separately from cattle, they fulfill the same function, providing milk and meat, and are also used for the payment of *lobola* as well as for sacrifices. No one, however, lavishes praise on them and there is hardly any reluctance in slaughtering them for food. Fowl are kept mainly for food and for sacrifices. Dogs are used mainly for hunting, another occupation dominated by men.

The rich and varied game of South Africa made hunting a popular sport and an important source of food. Skins, horns, and sinew obtained from game animals are converted into clothing, drum covers, bags, bow strings, and ropes, especially among the Sotho and among others not rich in cattle-holdings such as the Tsonga and the Venda. Hunting methods varied from collectively herding the game into V-shaped fences leading to pitfalls or covered pits, set with sharp-pointed wooden stakes, to the use of rope and net traps. Spears, axes, bows, and arrows were also used. The creation of many game reserves and the prohibition against the unauthorized killing, trade, and export of certain species have resulted in the official regulation of hunting and the transformation of the indigenous hunting culture without abolishing it.

GOVERNMENT AND POLITICS

On May 31, 1910, South Africa gained its independence from British rule as a unitary state. Half a century later, on May 31, 1961, under a new constitution passed by the South African Parliament, it became a republic, ruled by a government headed by a prime minister who was responsible to a white-only parliament. A few coloreds and blacks who met certain literacy and property qualifications could elect a few whites to represent them in parliament. By 1968, even this token franchise for nonwhites had been abolished. A constitutional reform in 1984 abolished the office of the prime minister, vested full executive authority in the office of the president, and created a tricameral parliament made up of a dominant white chamber and two subordinate chambers elected by coloreds and Asians. Blacks, who constitute 75 percent of the population, had no representation. Multiparty negotiations, which began in January 1991, resulted in the country's first multiracial elections on April 27, 1994, which brought the ANC led by Nelson Mandela to power. The new Constitution of the Republic of South Africa, 1996, took effect as the supreme law of the land on February 4, 1997.

The new postapartheid government is constituted of three tiers—executive, legislative, and judiciary—and operates at three levels—national, provincial, and local. The three tiers and levels are separate, distinct, interdependent, and interrelated. Legislative authority is vested in the bicameral parliament, made up of the National Assembly and the National Council of Provinces (NCOP). The Upper Chamber of the National Assembly consists of between 350 and 400 members elected to a five-year term through a system of proportional party, national, and provincial representations. There are more than 50 political parties in the country. In the 1999 national election, the ANC secured 266 seats, the Democratic Party gained 38, the Inkatha Freedom Party (IFP) secured 34, the New National Party (NNP) won 28, the United Democratic Movement (UDM) obtained 14, the African Christian Democratic Party had 6, and the remaining 14 seats were shared by 7 other smaller parties in proportion to the percentage of the national votes secured by each of them.

Executive power is vested in the president who is elected to a five-year term by the National Assembly from among its members. Usually the party with the largest number of parliamentary seats produces the president. When no party wins a clear majority, a coalition or alliance of parties will produce the president and form the government. As head of state and head of government, the president exercises his power through his deputy president and a cabinet of ministers and deputy ministers, whom he or she appoints (and can dismiss) from among members of the National Assembly. The president can select no more than two ministers from outside the National Assembly. Judicial power is vested in the Supreme Court, whose members are appointed to a seven-year term by the president on the advice of the Justice Service Commission (JSC). The Constitutional Court (CC) is empowered to interpret, protect, and enforce strict adherence to the principles of the constitution, as well as resolve constitutional disputes between the different tiers and levels of government. Presided over by a president and deputy president, it is made up of 11 judges, all of whom must be citizens of South Africa, who are appointed by the president on the advice of the JSC. The CC also guards the fundamental rights and freedoms of individuals guaranteed in Chapter Two of the 1996 constitution.

For administrative purposes, South Africa is divided into nine provinces and organized into 284 municipalities. Of the municipalities, six are metropolitan, namely Tshwane, Johannesburg, Ekurhuleni, Durban, Cape Town, and Nelson Mandela; 231 are local; while 47 are district municipalities. Each municipality is ruled by a council charged with primary responsibility for local, rural, or urban service delivery and integrated planning and development. Each province can adopt its own constitution, though none of these may override the federal constitution. Provincial legislatures consist of between 30 and 80 members, elected by proportional representation. The provincial government is headed by a premier who is elected by the provincial legislatures from among their own ranks and who rules through an executive council. The constitution recognizes the institution, status, and role of traditional leaders; in 2000, parliament established the Commission for the Promotion and Protection of the Rights of Cultural, Religious, and Linguistic Communities. The Commission was also charged with the responsibility for promoting values and programs that will develop peace, tolerance, and national unity among the various South African groups and communities.[9]

NOTES

1. On the early history of South Africa see Leonard Thompson, *A History of South Africa* (New Haven: Yale University Press, 1995), 1–69; Robert Ross, *A Concise History of South Africa* (Cambridge: Cambridge University Press, 1999), 1–53; and

Roger B. Beck, *The History of South Africa* (Westport, Conn.: Greenwood Press, 2000), 9–40.

2. On the mfecane and its aftermath in southern Africa see Funso Afolayan, "The Mfecane and South Africa," in Toyin Falola, ed., *Africa, Vol. 1: African History before 1885* (Durham, N.C.: Carolina Academic Press, 2000), 359–84; J.D. Omer-Cooper, *The Zulu Aftermath* (Evanston, Ill.: Northwestern University Press, 1966); Carolyn Hamilton, *Terrific Majesty: The Powers of Shaka Zulu and the Limits of Historical Invention* (Cambridge, Mass.: Harvard University Press, 1998).

3. On the mineral revolution, Afrikaner nationalism, and the rise of apartheid in South Africa see William H. Worger, *South Africa's City of Diamonds: Mine Workers and Monopoly Capitalism in Kimberley, 1867–1895* (New Haven and London: Yale University Press, 1987); Saul Debow, *Racial Segregation and the Origins of Apartheid in South Africa, 1919 –1936* (London: Macmillan Press, 1989); and Dunbar T. Moodie, *The Rise of Afrikanerdom: Power, Apartheid and Afrikaner Civil Religion* (Berkeley and London: University of California Press, 1975).

4. William Beinert, *Twentieth-Century South Africa* (Oxford: Oxford University Press, 1994), 250.

5. For the end of apartheid and the establishment of democratic rule see F. W. de Klerk, *The Last Trek—A New Beginning, The Autobiography* (New York: St. Martin's Press, 1999); Tom Lodge, *Black Politics in South Africa since 1945* (London and New York: Longman, 1993); Nelson Mandela, *Long Walk to Freedom: The Autobiography of Nelson Mandela* (London: Little Brown & Company, 1994), Martin Murray, *The Revolution Deferred: The Painful Birth of Post-Apartheid South Africa* (London and New York: Verso, 1994); Alister Sparks, *Tomorrow Is Another Country: The Inside Story of South Africa's Road to Change* (New York: Hill and Wang, 1990) 215–41 and Funso Afolayan, "The Rise and Fall of Apartheid," in Falola, *Africa, vol. 4: The End of Colonial Rule, Nationalism and Decolonization* (Durham, N.C.: Carolina Academic Press, 2002) 427–61.

6. For more comprehensive information on the mineral resources of South Africa, and the major sources for this section, see: *South Africa, 1989–90: Official Yearbook of the Republic of South Africa* (Pretoria: Bureau for Information, Department of Foreign Affairs, 1989/90), 317–38; *South Africa, 1993: Official Yearbook of the Republic of South Africa* (Pretoria: South African Publication Service, 1993), 127–44; *South Africa: A Country Study* (Washington, D.C.: Library of Congress, 1997), 205–14; *South Africa Yearbook 2001/02* (Pretoria: Government Communication and Information System, 2002), 409–33; L. Flynn, *Studded with Diamonds and Paved with Gold-mines, Mining Companies and Human Rights in South Africa* (London: Bloomsbury Press, 1992); B. Cairncross and R. Dixon, eds., *Minerals of South Africa* (Johannesburg: Geographical Society of South Africa, 1995); and *South Africa Minerals Yearbook, 1997* (Wits: Minerals and Energy Policy Center, 1997).

7. On industrialization in South Africa, past and present, see: *South Africa, 1989–90: Official Yearbook*, 407–46; *South Africa: A Country Study*, 222–38; D. Hobart Houghton, "South Africa: The Economy," in *Encyclopedia Americana* (Danbury, Conn.: Grolier Incorporated, 1999), vol. 25, 268–72; and B. Fine and

Z. Rustomjee, *The Political Economy of South Africa: From Minerals-Energy Complex to Industrialization* (Johannesburg: Witwatersrand University Press, 1996).

8. Quoted in Margaret Shaw, "Material Culture," in Hammond-Tooke, ed., *The Bantu-Speaking Peoples of Southern Africa*, 95.

9. On government and politics in post-1994 South Africa, see: *South Africa Year-book 2001/02*, 299–325; H. Klug, *Constituting Democracy: Law, Globalism and South Africa's Political Reconstruction* (Cambridge: Cambridge University Press, 2000); T. Lodge, *South African Politics since 1994* (Cape Town: David Philip, 1999); and D. Wood, *Rainbow Nation Revisited: South Africa's Decade of Democracy* (London: Andre Deutsch, 2000).

3

Religion and Worldview

Religion is a central aspect of life, culture, and society in South Africa. For the Khoisan as well as for the Bantu-speaking peoples and groups, religion is a pervasive element of sociocultural existence. The advent of European traders, settlers, and colonizers from the late fifteenth century onwards prepared the way for the advent of new religious traditions in the region, namely Christianity from Europe and Islam and Hinduism from Asia. The racial and linguistic diversities of South African society are clearly reflected in the wide variety of religious traditions and practices prevalent in the region. It is through religion that the worldviews and attitudes toward life of the various peoples and groups of South Africa are best exemplified and given cosmic and concrete expression. In South Africa, the role of religion has been especially decisive. Within the locus of the country's tumultuous history, religion has remained entangled in the social, economic, and political relations of power, relations that within the South African context privileged a small minority while dehumanizing and precluding the overwhelming majority from the realization of their full human potential and empowerment. For members of the ruling minority, religion became the basis for the rationalization of their political and racial dominance as well as the legitimization for their displacement and dispossession of the indigenous population. On the other hand, members of the oppressed and disempowered majority took steps to invoke, appropriate, create, subvert, and invert religious ideas, symbols, and practices to promote their struggle for liberation from social, economic, and political domination.

KHOISAN RELIGIONS

Khoisan religious beliefs vary from one group to the other. Nevertheless, certain commonalities can be established between them. At the center of Khoisan religion is the belief in a supreme God, known as Tsui or //Goab, or as //gangwan!an!a (big big god) and by other names, who presides over the affairs of men. As creator and the deity who alone causes the sun to rise daily and the rain to fall regularly in its season, he is responsible for life. In direct opposition to this greater and good God who lives in the east is a lesser and evil one who lives in the west, known as //Gaunab, or //gangwa matse (small god), who uses his independent and superhuman power to bring sickness, misfortune, and death. Among the /Xam of the Northern Cape, this cosmic dualism of the coexistence of the forces of good and evil is combined in the personality of a being called /Kaggen or cagn, who is at the same time a creator god as well as a trickster deity, powerful and often benevolent, but sometimes malevolent, malicious, mischievous, and even stupid. The widespread representation of the eland, an animal created by and special to /Kaggen, in Khoisan rock paintings is indicative of the veneration accorded this capricious deity. Many tales are told of /Kaggen's picturesque adventures, often trying to trick hunters to pave the way for the escape of the eland, his favorite creature. Early European writers' equation of the /Kaggen with the Christian devil is indicative of their pejorative attitude toward the San, and their limited understanding of their beliefs.

Death, Ancestors, and the Hereafter

Khoisan beliefs about death vary widely. For some, at a person's death, his or her spirit ascends into the sky where it becomes a star. For others, the sight of a shooting star is indicative of a death occurring in the human community. Some Southern San speak of a great hole in the bowels of the earth, which serves as the abode of dead people and animals. For many Kalahari groups, the dead's final destination is the great God's house in the sky. However, while the nature of the terrain of the departed remains uncertain, the reality of their continuing influence in the life of the living remains beyond question. Thus, for most Khoisan communities, while Tsui//Goab was the archprotector, the earthly fates of individuals are believed to reside in the hands of Heitsi-Eibib, the ancestor-hero, whose numerous adventures—including his many deaths and resurrections—are widely celebrated in Khoisan folklore and religion. Khoisan habitats are punctuated here and there by the many graves of Heitsi-Eibib made up of piles of stones or cairns. Situated beside pathways and at river crossings, these graves are sites of veneration at which individuals can stop to meditate and add more stones as offerings for good fortune in their life endeavors. The *//gagwasi,* the spirit of the dead, are not held responsible for all deaths. People who die peacefully after a long and good life are said to have been eaten up by heaven, *n/ a m a* (literally heaven ate him or her). On the other hand, serious illnesses, violent or premature deaths, and accidents are considered to be the works of the *//gagwasi.*

Khoisan thoughts and worldviews are preserved in and transmitted through numerous myths and tales that are widely cherished and fondly told. Among the most popular is the creation story, which speaks of two creations. In the first creation, animals were not distinguishable from the first humans, who had developed very little in the areas of culture and customs to be considered significantly different from other mammalian creatures. During this preculture phase people and animals lived in a single large village led by the elephant, K'au, and his wife, Chu!ko, in which a wide variety of animal characters, such as the jackal, dung beetle, python, bustard, praying mantis, and others play notable roles that are still recollected in many stories. In many of these stories, the praying mantis, represented as a trickster deity, features as a central character. It was the second creation that liberated man and gave him the ability to acquire more refined culture, manners, and social codes, thus dramatically separating himself from the animals.

The Healing Ritual Dance of the San

The Khoisans are well known for their ritual dances. Especially for the Kalahari San, ritual dances provide an unusually effective means of social healing and communal bonding. At the core of this ritual is a supernatural potency called *n/um.* For the San, the word *n/um* has a wide range of meanings. It is used in different contexts to refer to medicine, energy, power, special skill, menstrual blood, sorcery, and many other things. In relation to the healing dance, the *n/um* is a substance lying at the pit of the stomach of healers or *n/um kausi,* meaning medicine owners, and is activated through healing dances. The healing dance usually begins after sunset. To start, a fire is lit. Women sit around the fire clapping their hands and singing highly evocative and powerful medicine songs. Next the healers, usually men, begin to dance in response to and around the women. As a rule the women tend the fire and do the singing while the men do the dancing and enter into a healing trance. Occasionally, a woman or two joins the dance, and even more exceptionally a woman healer emerges to enter into a trance. Even though women rarely serve as healers, their strong, sustained singing remains crucial, since without it the *n/um* cannot boil and the men cannot achieve a healing trance state. The first few hours are usually relaxed and low key. Then, the women intensify their beautifully complex melodies and intricate rhythms as they sing songs without words; meanwhile, the men dance and beat a circular path in the sand several inches deep, displaying rapid, intricate, graceful body movements. As they dance, the *n/um* within their bellies begins to heat up, reaching a boiling state that surges through the spinal cord and explodes in the brain. Overwhelmed with enormous sacred power the healer's legs begin to tremble, his chest begins to heave, and his senses are flooded with strange visions. Temporarily disoriented and shaking vigorously, the healer begins to run around, sometimes walking through fire and handling live coals with impunity.

The onset of a trance state is evident in the glassy stares, intense footwork, and heavy breathing of the dancer. As his sweat begins to ooze profusely, the other men call on the women: *gu tsiu, gu tsiu,* meaning pick it up, pick it up. In response the women raise their voices and intensify their singing, as one healer after another falls into a trance. Still unsteady, the healer moves from one person to the next laying his vibrating hands on the chest and back of the supplicants, inducing supernatural protection and healing. A seriously sick person can receive an hour or more of attention from one or several healers working in relays or simultaneously, in the course of which his or her bare back, chest, forehead, legs, and arms are robed with the magical sweat cascading from the healers' inner *n/um.* The process of healing usually involves pulling sicknesses from the body of the sick; seeing, speaking to, and arguing with *//gagwasi;* and making herbal and dietary prescriptions and prohibitions. The ritual dance usually lasts all night long, though on special occasions dances have been known to last without interruption through the next day and till the morning of the third day.

The ritual dances and especially the trance states bridge the gap between the world of the living and the world of spirits. It provides access to the lesser deities, nameless shades, and ancestral spirits who cause sicknesses through the invisible and mystical arrows they shoot into their victims. Through the dance-induced healing trance, the healers obtain the means of transcending the limits of human nature and crossing the frontiers of the human and natural worlds. Through it they obtain the power to chase away malicious and marauding spirits, to travel in the spirit to distant lands to watch over and cure relatives and other supplicants, to ascend into the sky to appease capricious forces, and to ensure the reordering of man's moral and social order. For the San healers, achieving altered states of consciousness opened the door to the acquisition of spiritual knowledge and healing power that would otherwise have been inaccessible. Healing dances occur on the average once a month or more frequently depending on the season, the size of the band, and other circumstances of the group. They are not just religious rituals for they also serve the social function of providing the group with the opportunity for socializing, bonding, festivity, letting off steam, and celebrating life and existence in the hard and arid land of the Kalahari Desert. The discovery of many prehistoric San rock paintings, with their many scenes of ecstatic dancing, trance states, healing performances, and images of power, confirm the antiquity and continuing resilience of this extraordinarily effective method of social and spiritual engineering among the Khoisan-speaking peoples of South Africa.[1]

BANTU RELIGIOUS TRADITIONS

As in the case of the Khoisan, it is difficult to speak of Bantu religion; it is more appropriate to say Bantu religions. There are as many religions as there are Bantu groups. However, the common ethnolinguistic origins of the various Bantu groups have ensured that the commonalities in their religious traditions outweigh the differences. In this section we will focus on these commonalities, while simultaneously recognizing the differences and the peculiarities of each religious tradition.[2]

The Supreme Being

At the center of Bantu religions is the belief in the existence of a high god, who as the lord of the universe is the ultimate divinity, perceived as eternal, omnipotent, omnipresent, and omniscient. Though he is the overarching deity in all the religious traditions, he is considered too remote, transcendent, inaccessible, and well beyond human understanding and manipulation. Thus, the high god has no special altar or temple, and no special class of priests or priestesses dedicated to him. Unlike other lesser deities and spirits, the high god has no prayer, worship, or sacrifice directed to him, since he is not in a position to either demand, receive, or respond to them. The major attribute of this high god is his perception as the creator, the one who brought the universe into being. Different groups call him by different names, depending on the nature of their conception of him. For the Xhosa he is known as umDali or uQamatha. The Sotho and Tswana call him Modimo, while the Venda refer to him as the Raluvhimba. The Tsonga speak of two deities. The first, known as Ntumbuluko (Nature), is attributed with the creation of the world. The second, referred to as Tilo, an impersonal force and deity of the sky, is presented as the author of life and death with the power to send or withhold storms and rain, as well as to inflict children with convulsions. He could, however, be propitiated to send rain in times of drought through the wetting of graves of twins, unusual beings considered sacred and special to him. Among the Zulu he is Unkulunkulu, the great, great one, and

Inkosi Yezulu, chief of the sky. For the Zulu, creation was an act of the God of the Sky, a father god who also has a special name, Umvelinqangi, meaning the first to emerge, the first ancestor, and the first of the twins, the other twin being the earth. At death, ancestors return to the earth, which is the mother; only in exceptional circumstances do ancestors return to live with Umvelin-qangi. Unlike the ancestors, the high god is not a focus of ritual; he is rarely, if ever, invoked for help in times of crisis. He is a god at bay, a *deus otiosus*, who after his original creative acts, has remained disconnected from, remote to, and uninterested in man's present mundane and cosmic preoccupations. However, he remains important as a mythical reference point to explain the origins of man and the universe.[3]

Myths Conceptualizing the Origins and Nature of the Social Order

Among the Bantu, as with most African peoples, myth is a powerful means of conceptualizing, articulating, and transmitting cosmic realities and world-views. There are three groups of creation stories. First are those that present the creation of man, *abantu* (meaning the people) as the joint act of the God of the Sky and the mother earth. For the Zulu, man emerged out of a bed of reeds. Similar creation stories are found among the Swazi, Mpondo, Tsonga, and Sotho. Second, among the Mpondo, Sotho, Tswana, Venda, and Tsonga, the first human beings emerged from a hole in the ground. For the Tsonga the hole was from a rock at Lowe, on the surface of which the first ancestors left their prehistoric footprints permanently engraved. The Lovedu and the Venda also associate Khuzwane with the many footprints found on certain rocks in their lands. Third, especially among the Pedi, a Northern Sotho group, the high god Kgobe created the world while his son, Kgobeane, fash-ioned human beings like a potter molding jars from clay.

Other myths grapple with some of the most perennial questions facing the human race. One attempts to explain the origin of death by relating it to an original breakdown in communication between the human and the spiritual worlds. In this well-known story of the chameleon and the lizard, the high god sent the chameleon to carry a message of immortality to man. But the chameleon in its characteristic way dallied, unnecessarily delaying the deliv-ery of its message. In the meantime, for reasons not always indicated, the high god changed his mind and subsequently dispatched the more agile lizard with a second message, a message of death, which was swiftly and directly deliv-ered, thus ensuring that human beings would thenceforth have to die. By the time the chameleon arrived, it was too late. However, all hope was not lost: communication with the spirit world can still be restored through ritual sacrifices, while eternal life can be obtained through entering at death into the status and abode of the ancestors.

Myths are not static means of representing an unchanging and timeless world of ideas and events; indeed they are dynamic means of creatively and resourcefully conceptualizing the social and political orders in their three dimensional forms: past, present, and future. The past is as important as the present, while the present is not perceived as a slave to the past. Myths provide the discourse through which an understanding of present conditions can be gained in terms of the primordial past. For example, a Zulu creation myth of the mid-nineteenth century relates how the high god in creating human beings, not only made them male and female, but also made them black and white. To the whites he assigned the waters or the sea as their abode and also gave them clothing and guns. To the blacks he gave the land and the right to carry spears. Whatever the antiquity of this myth, in its present form it is clearly a creative articulation of the observable oppositions—black and white, land and sea, spears and guns—that characterized the Zulu world of the nineteenth century. By connecting and subsuming these oppositions under the direct prerogative of the high god, the Zulu could explain the origin of the contemporary order, an order out of joint because the white man, not content with his divine destiny, has left the sea to lay claim to what is not his and dispossess the black man of his divinely validated possession, land. Order can only be restored if the white man returns back to where he rightly belongs, the sea and the unknown worlds within or beyond it. The significance and popularity of such myths among the dispossessed and disempowered Africans can hardly be overestimated.

Another myth that attempts to explain the origin of the black man's subordination to white rule in South Africa offers the premise that even though both black and white people emerged from a bed of reeds, the black people were the first to depart from this bed to establish themselves in the world, leaving the white people behind. However, the white people turned this to their own advantage, by staying longer on the bed of reeds and taking their time to acquire wisdom, develop laws, and master science and technology, with which they were eventually able to subjugate the black people. The import of this myth, besides establishing the antiquity and seniority of black people in Africa, is to show that white dominance is not a product of magic or good luck, but the result of patient endurance and hard work. The implication is that, if the black man would also take time to return to the ancients and learn the necessary creative wisdom, he too would gain access to the knowledge and power that has made the white man great, come to par with him, and thus liberate himself from his present scientific, economic, and political subordination. Thus myths are not mere esoteric accounts referring only to ancient and primordial events, with little or no relevance to contemporary realities. They are neither fixed in time nor in space; they are flexible and versatile enough to be creatively adopted and adapted to provide answers to current problems, shed lights on current predicaments, and address fundamental social conditions that are inherent in the expanding, complex, and conflicting nature of human economic and political interactions characteristic of southern Africa in the nineteenth and twentieth centuries.[4]

Nature Spirits

Beside and below the high god are local and nature spirits. These spirits are usually associated with and are products of the reflections of the people on the awesome effect of notable geographical features such as mountains, rivers, caves, groves, and vegetation, and on the power and majesty of important natural phenomena such as rain, drought, storm, lightning, flood, and the seasons. Unlike the high god, one can hardly generalize about the nature spirits since, as free spirits, they vary in their peculiarities and uniqueness from one group to the other. The Venda have the most developed belief in nature spirits in that the spirits of dead chiefs are believed to inhabit certain groves. Other spirits, not directly associated with any particular lineage, are believed to inhabit the mountains and rivers. Often represented as foreigners and as dismembered monstrosities, these spirits are considered generally dangerous and a chance meeting with any of them can prove lethal to an unwary traveler. However, the majority of the local spirits are associated with rivers and lakes, not a surprising development in a region of water scarcity where the reality and threat of impending drought is a continuing challenge. Lake Fundudzi, in the Venda country, is believed to be home to the ancestral spirits of the guardians of the lake. The large pool below the Phiphidi Falls is believed to be home to the spirits of the Nguni autochthones, the sound of whose dancing motion under the water can be heard by visitors to the pool. The belief in nature spirits is less developed among the Nguni, but some Xhosa groups speak of people of the river (*abantu bomlambo*) who inhabit the deep pools and who, as invisible night marauders, inflict illness, blindness, mental derangement, and other harms on their victims. Except in Pondoland, the *abantu bomlambo* are not considered to be *amathongo,* or clan ancestors, though they are sometimes associated with them. Instead they are referred to as *amatshologu,* meaning an evil manifestation of the ancestral spirits. Sometimes represented as crocodiles and snakes, offerings of maize, sorghum, and tobacco are made to them and they are believed to play active roles in the initiation of diviners, teaching them the secrets of the deeps.

The Zulu are noted for their belief in a nature goddess, Nomkhubulwana, the Princess of Heaven. She is believed to possess the mastery of beer making, cropping, harvesting, and all other useful arts, which she teaches to those who please her. As the personification of spring, she holds the secret of rain, which she can withhold at will in her displeasure. Propitiating her involves trans-vestitism and a role reversal in the course of which young unmarried women put on men's attire and perform functions normally taboo for women, such as herding and milking cows, thus trespassing on the privileged prerogatives of men. Aspects of these seasonal rituals involve the women and the girls going naked and singing lewd songs, while the men and boys are not permit-ted to participate and must be completely hidden from sight. Similar rituals of role reversal, associated with privileged access to cattle and sexual obscen-ity are practiced among the Thembu, Bhaca, and Tsonga. The significance of Nomkhubulwana lies in the fact that she is a female deity, an uncommon phenomenon in the region, and a personification of the spring, an apotheosis rare among the Bantu. Among the notable and extant nature spirits or demigods of the Sotho-Tswana are Lôwê, Tintibane, Matsieng, and Thobêga, who are presented as deified, preexisting autochthones who inhabit the woods, groves, and mountains of the region and to whom sacrifices of corn, meat, and wine are made. The caves or groves inhabited by these spirits are usually covered with dense forests with impenetrable undergrowth made eerie by the presence of huge gliding snakes and other creatures making horrid noises and rendering the space out of bounds to all except the keepers and priests.[5]

Ancestral Rituals

The high god as well as the nature and local spirits, though central to the structure of Bantu beliefs, are in practice peripheral to daily social and politi-cal preoccupations. They are important for providing answers to questions related to the origins of man and of society and of other awe-inspiring natu-ral phenomena. But the mainsprings of man's sociocultural existence and of his personal problems do not stem from his relation with his natural environ-ment; rather, they are rooted in his relationships with his fellow human beings. The norms and values underpinning the mechanism of social rela-tions and of conflict resolution are everywhere affirmed through appeals to superhuman authority, an authority conceptualized and personified among the Bantu by superempirical beings known as the ancestors. These entities are known by different names, such as *amadlozi* or *amathongo* among the Zulu, *shikwembu* among the Tsonga, *vadimo* or *zwidajani* among the Lobedu, *midzimo* among the Venda, and *badimo* among the Tswana, Pedi, and South Sotho. The ancestors are the spirits of the dead members of the lineage or family who as the living dead continue to show interest in and exercise influence over the lives and affairs of surviving relatives.

Though it is generally believed that every dead person achieves immortality at death, not all become ancestors. The fate of children who die in infancy and of young, unmarried people who die without having had a child remains unclear. Those who die taboo deaths and those for whom the necessary funerary rites are not performed become ghosts (*setshosa*), remaining restless in their graves and continually haunting the lives and homes of their descendants. The significant ancestors can be from either the paternal or maternal sides of the family, though as a rule male ancestors tend to predominate, except among the Venda and Tsonga, where both feature prominently in rituals. Ancestors are usually referred to in the plural; when an individual ancestor is singled out for mention it is often because ritual has revealed that that particular ancestor is at the root of a particular affliction or misfortune that has befallen his surviving descendants. As such, the ritual sacrifice and discourse must be addressed to that particular communicating ancestor to restore harmony between the human and the spirit worlds.

Ancestral ritual fulfills many functions. First it provides one answer, among others, for the causes of affliction. By attributing to the ancestors the power to chastise their descendants for acts of disobedience, illnesses and misfortune can be explained through references to the displeasures of an ancestral spirit. Second, by giving the lineage head the prerogative to carry out the rituals of restoration and healing, ancestral beliefs symbolically and ritually validate the jural authority and rights of the homestead elders and senior men over the productive power of younger men and the reproductive power of younger women. Third, by demanding, compelling, and providing the strategies for individuals to be restored to a state of harmony with the ancestors and focusing on the dire consequences of violating the ritual rule of conduct they represent, ancestral religion affirms the spiritual dimension and social norms and values of the community or homestead. In emphasizing this validating role of ancestral ritual, we must, however, be careful not to perceive ancestor religion as just a force of conservation, in which out-of-date elders attempt to stifle the young in an insidious attempt to maintain and preserve anachronistic customs and beliefs. Like other elements of Bantu religion, ancestral beliefs have served and continue to serve as a dynamic force of continuity and change, of stability and transformation. In nineteenth and twentieth century South Africa, the values, norms, and practices of ancestral religions were effectively mobilized and creatively adopted, adapted, and deployed by Africans as a strategy of resistance to European cultural and political domination that came to malign and threatened to destroy and displace those beliefs.

Fourth, ancestral beliefs provide an understanding of life after life that effectively dissolves death and mitigates it of the effectiveness of its forlorn sense of finality and total loss. For most Bantu groups, man is composed of two elements. The first is the physical body known variously as *mele, mmele,* or *nama* (flesh). The second element is the invisible or incorporeal spirit, known as *moea* (wind) and *seriti* (shadow). Venda and Pedi religions define a tripartite conception for man in which the soul, known as *moya* (literally wind or breath), is a third element and the indispensable life principle inter-twining the spirit and the body. The soul, which the Zulu call *idlozi* or *ithongo,* cannot die; only the body does. Thus, death is not the end; it is a change of status. To die is not to dissolve into nothingness; it is to be trans-formed into an ancestor, an infinitely more powerful and more permanent state to aspire and look forward to. The death of a loved one is mourned, but the loss is not perceived as permanent. A year or so later, the period of mourn-ing and other funerary rites conclude in the festive and communal ritual of *ukubuyisa idlozi* (Zulu), meaning the bringing home of the ancestors. This final ritual symbolically and effectively evokes and welcomes back from the underworld (located under the earth or in the sky or beyond the horizon) and into the homestead and the house the spirit of the recently departed, who will, along with the *amakhosi* (the group of ancestors), henceforth assume the new and enhanced status of the spiritual guardian of his or her descendants.[6]

Witchcraft, Sorcery, and the Symbolisms of Evil

The provenance of evil is not considered the sole province of the ancestors. Ancestors are not generally perceived as being evil. They can afflict their descendants, but they do so only as a matter of course, a kind of last resort, and usually in response to gross violations and trespasses committed by the living. So it is the living and not the living dead who are held directly respon-sible for the offense that has resulted in illness or misfortune. Ancestors pro-vide perspective through affliction, which alerts their descendants to the existence of disequilibrium in the delicate but necessary balance between the natural human world and the world of the spirits. The Bantu live in a world that recognizes a duality between a state of affairs considered right, moral, normal, and safe, and another, perceived as wrong, immoral, abnormal, and unsafe. A state of negative imbalance between the natural and the social world produces misfortunes of all kinds, ranging from sickness to drought. A prin-cipal object of religious ritual is to restore society to a state of equilibrium in which a good relationship is established and maintained between humans, as well as between humans and their ancestors, forces of nature, and the gods. Religion and witchcraft provide the means for explaining and thus coming to terms with misfortune and evil in the world.

The concept of chance has very minimal application in Bantu worldview. With the exception of minor sickness and death from old age, every misfortune is attributed to the machinations and works of external agents. Two groups of external agents are usually identified. The first are the ancestors, who as loving parents send misfortune as an explicit chastisement for breaches of religious and kinship obligations by their erring and recalcitrant descendants. In this case, the afflicted rather than the afflicter is held responsible for bringing the misfortune upon him or herself through negligence; the ancestors remain blameless and are not perceived as originators of evil. On the other hand, where a diviner diagnoses misfortune at the hands of witches and sorcerers, the victim is held blameless; he or she is a target of malevolence by humans using superhuman power to cause affliction. Unlike ancestral spirits, witches and sorcerers (or wizards) are perceived as agents of evil propelled by hate, envy, malice, and an evil personality to wreak harm and violence on innocent victims. While ancestrally sent sicknesses are bad, they are not evil and are usually curable; witchcraft/sorcery-induced sicknesses are explicitly directed to both harm and kill.

Witchcraft and sorcery beliefs serve as means of resolving interpersonal conflict as well as of acquiring, retaining, and expressing power in the competition for social and political advantages. The recent spate of witchcraft accusation that swept through parts of post 1994 South African society attests to the survival and resilience of these apparently primordial beliefs, especially in the atmosphere of social stress characteristic of postapartheid South Africa.[7]

Sacred Specialists: Herbalists, Priests, and Diviners

Having a belief system that provides relatively satisfying explanations for evils and misfortunes is one thing; providing the strategies and means of coping with and warding off the evil is another. The work of restoration and healing is the prerogative of three classes of specialists. The first of these is the diviner, who diagnoses the cause or causes of any misfortune. The second is the lineage head, who, as the genealogically senior male member of the descent group, is the only one who can invoke the ancestral spirits during any ritual. In some cases, his younger brother or another elder so designated can represent and officiate on his behalf. Among the Mpondo, an elderly uterine sister of the homestead head past the childbearing age can also officiate as the priestess of her lineage. Among the Lobedu, every sister is a potential priestess, and different sisters are called upon to officiate at different rituals. The third is the herbalist, known among the Zulu as *inyanga yokwelapha,* who administers medicines derived from plants and animals. While herbalists may invoke ancestral spirits in their works, they operate basically as medical experts possessed of an array of knowledge and technique to ensure healing. Known variously by different names, *ixhwele* among the Xhosa, *nyanga* among the Tsonga, *ngaka* among the Sotho, and *nanga* among the Venda, herbalists often inherit their knowledge and skills, even though these can also be learned through apprenticeship and training.[8]

Diviners are by far the most important religious functionaries. Known variously as *igqira* among the Xhosa, *isangoma* among the Zulu, or *ngaka* among the Sotho-Tswana, the diviner possesses great religious knowledge, power, and prestige. The diviner's sole prerogative in discerning the causes of misfortune and sickness sets him or her apart in the gallery of ritual specialists among the Bantu. Though there are male diviners, by far the greater majority of Nguni diviners are women. In apartheid South Africa, with the limited access to health care provided for Africans, the indigenous sacred specialists assumed new significance in that they offered social, psychological, and physical healing in a crisis-ridden society. Resort to traditional therapeutic methods of healing also became a form of resistance to European and Western domination, which for years condemned traditional healing practices without any serious or sincere attempt to either understand or acknowledge their therapeutic potentials. This process involved a medicalization and psychologicalization of sacred specialists to make them more responsive and competitive in the changing and turbulent health-care market of South Africa. It is not uncommon today to find the shops of *izinyanga* (plural) and *isangoma* in urban centers, where they receive and consult with patients and dispense their medicine.[9]

Rites of Passage: Life Transitions

Rituals and celebration mark transitions that are considered both crucial and dangerous, such as those from and to the other world. These rituals involve the active participation of women who assume central roles, such as *umdlezane* (mother of birth) and *umfelokazi* (mother of death) among the Zulu. At the birth of a child, the new mother is placed under ritual restraints and restrictions for approximately ten days. During this period, she must remain in seclusion and only in the company of married women, since her recent association with new life has put her in a state of ritual pollution that could endanger men, cattle, and crops. The period of confinement is ended with an ancestral ritual of sacrifice that signifies the entry of the child into the world and its incorporation into the father's patrilineage. The mother is also purified and reincorporated into the homestead but effectively transfers her rights over the child to the father's jural and patriarchal authority.

Like birth, a death in the family creates a dangerous condition of pollution requiring ritual action to mark and facilitate the transition of the dead into the world of the living dead. In this ritual, women also play the cardinal roles. Among the Zulu, only married women can handle, prepare, and deliver the corpse, like a newborn child from the womb, through the doorway of the hut to the men of the homestead. Role reversal is also characteristic of funerary rituals. This involves women washing the corpse with their left hands, wearing their dresses inside out, walking backwards out of the hut to mark the extraordinarily dangerous reversal of life and status characteristic of death and the passage of the deceased into the reversed world of the ancestors. The world of mourning is one in which night is day, white is black, up is down, and the bitter tastes sweet. A woman, usually the senior or great wife of the departed, assumes the role of the principal mourner in a funerary ritual, observing certain rituals and prohibitions such as refraining from sexual relations. At the end of her year-long period of mourning, she will be ritually purified and readied to enter either into marriage with a brother of the deceased or journey back to her parents' village. It is also at this point that the final rite of the funerary ritual will take place. Known as *ukubuyisa* (the bringing home of the ancestor), the rite marks the formal incorporation of the deceased into the world of the ancestors, and the purification and reincorporation of the principal mourner into the normal life of the homestead.

In addition to rituals marking the entrance into and departure from this world, there are initiation practices directed at preparing the young, male and female, for their future roles in adult society. Though there are differences in emphasis and details, the broad outline of an initiation ritual is basically the same. Nearly all of them involve three stages. For boys, first comes the phase of separation during which the initiates are secluded in the bush outside the village for nearly a month, engaged in dancing, singing, and other technical chores under the supervision of senior men or women. Thereafter, the transition phase takes the initiates to the chief's court, where they are circumcised and kept secluded in special lodges to heal while learning the myths, songs, dances, rituals, and ethical norms and values of the society. The final phase involves a ceremonial coming out that marks the reincorporation of the initiates into their new statuses as adults who can now participate in the public and political activities that were traditionally the prerogatives of men.

Female initiation is usually shorter and less elaborate. Known as *bojale* among the Tswana, it also involves the three ritual phases of separation, transition, and reincorporation, though the emphasis in role instruction is on the domestic sphere, and the main objective is to prepare young girls for success as wives and mothers. Like the boys, the girls' change in status and transition into adulthood is symbolically inscribed in their body through the ritual of circumcision. Other rituals are carried out to ensure the fertility of the land and to affirm the authority of the rulers. In a land of limited water supply and desert-like conditions, rainmaking rituals assume a major communal and political significance. Among the Lovedu, chiefs such as Mujaji, the Rain Queen, became responsible for ensuring, through rituals, regular rainfall, good crop, abundant harvest, and the stability of their realms.

European domination and the impact of Christian missionary activities did much to weaken and undermine the traditional basis of many South African rituals, but they have somehow managed to survive, even if in many cases, in attenuated forms. The apartheid regime's emphasis on creating pockets of semi-independent African homelands contributed to this survival by reinforcing the authority of the old order over the new. More significantly, in response to the racial denigration and oppression of the apartheid era, many of the already abandoned or extant traditional rituals such as those associated with initiation into adulthood have been revived and restored in recent years as veritable symbols of African cultural identity, group mobilization, and resistance in the face of white racial and political domination. The Shaka Day celebration, the Zulu Reed Ceremony (for girls), the Inkatha Cultural Association, and others among the Zulu are indicative of the concerted efforts being made in modern, postapartheid South Africa to revive, adopt, adapt, and deploy past practices as instruments of sociocultural inculcation. These are also means of political mobilization in a democratic South Africa, in which ethnic identity has to compete with other variables such as race, class, and gender in the struggle for hegemony and access to resources and power.

CHRISTIANITY

Cape of Good Hope: The Advent of a New Religion

In 1488, Bartholomew Dias, a Portuguese navigator, was the first European (along with his crew) to reach the South African coast where he erected a limestone pillar, or *padrao,* bearing a Christian cross and a Portuguese coat of arms, in the eastern Cape.[10] This ritual act marks the advent of Christianity in South Africa, and points to the subsequent history of the country in which religion, race, politics, and commerce remain closely and intricately intertwined. The establishment of a refreshment post at the Cape by the

Dutch East India Company in 1652, marked the beginning of a more permanent Christian presence in South Africa. Article XIII of the Company Charter clearly connects religious and commercial interests when it states that the new Dutch venture at the Cape is aimed at creating a settlement in which "the name of Christ may be extended, and the interests of the Company promoted."[11] However, this express commitment to proselytization notwithstanding, the Company and its officials showed very little interest in missionary efforts aside from setting up literacy instructions for their slaves; even this was done haphazardly and halfheartedly, because of uncertainties regarding the status of baptized slaves. This situation changed in the nineteenth century with the arrival of more missionary groups from Britain, France, Germany, the Americas, and the Scandinavian countries, who were more aggressive in their proselytizing efforts and less encumbered by close association with the Company's political and commercial interests.

Nearly all of the missions subscribed to the validity of the colonial enterprise, rationalizing and calling for European military and political subjugation of the heathens as a way to open up these blighted lands to the easy penetration of Christianity and civilization. From their perspectives, Christianization was one puzzle in the jigsaw of a civilizing mission that also included trade, literacy, industry, and the extraction and exploitation of indigenous labor. In that worldview, the velvet dress, the bonny hat, the square houses, the ploughs, the hammers, and the saws were all elements and tools of the new Christian and invariably European lifestyle considered to be good for Africans.

One dominant theme of this cross-cultural discourse was the belief among the missionaries that Africans had no concept of religion or of the existence of a supreme being. However, in the face of African-sustained resistance to Christian conversion and in the light of the missionaries' engagement with the practitioners of indigenous beliefs, the sweeping denial of African religions could not stand. Compelled to recognize that Africa was not a religious vacuum, a *tabula rasa* for easy Christian conversion, but instead a land teeming with competing beliefs and a plethora of deities and spirits, the missionaries dismissed such belief systems as superstitious, anachronistic, and false. They proclaimed the superiority, universality, totalitarianism, and exclusiveness of their Christian God and religion as opposed to the more pluralistic, adaptive, and accommodative African religious worldview.

However, in spite of the benefits offered by connections to the missions, the predominant African response to the missionary evangelical efforts during the nineteenth century was one of resistance. Though African rulers were often willing to welcome the missionaries, they were not oblivious to the fact that the new and alien visitors were the vanguard of a foreign political power determined to eventually supersede them. Rulers wanted friendship and trade, not conversion. Taking a cue from the rulers, the people remained loyal to the homestead, the chiefdom, and their ancestral religions. The progressive destruction of independent African states during the closing decades of the nineteenth century, by forces of European political and commercial imperialism, opened the floodgate for large-scale, mass conversion to Christianity in much of South Africa. Many of the missionaries became active agents as informants, instigators, fighters, and collaborators in the European conquest of African states. The advent and proliferation of several Christian groups, sects, and denominations made the twentieth century the golden age of Christianity in South Africa. By 1996, 80 percent of all South Africans, 76 percent blacks, 93 percent whites, 89 percent coloreds, and 12 percent Asians claimed to be Christians. The major denominations are: the Nederduitse Gereformeerde Churches (NGK), clumsily translated Dutch Reformed Church; Roman Catholic; Methodist; Anglican; Lutheran; Presbyterian; United Congregational; Apostolic Faith; Baptist; and a wide variety of African indigenous churches.

The Dutch Reformed Church

The NGK, the first to be established in South Africa, consists of four independent churches that are historically related. It established its first congregation in 1665 at the Cape and held its first synod in Cape Town in 1824. Following the Afrikaner's Great Trek of the 1830s, three new churches were organized by the *voortrekkers,* increasing the number of organized NGK churches to four. Various attempts made since the mid-nineteenth century to unite the four churches proved abortive until 1962 when the NGK churches finally came together to form a general synod with responsibility for general policy. Even though it is the church of most whites and most especially Afrikaner South Africans, the NGK has more colored adherents than whites. It is also perceived as the prime inspiration and validator of apartheid. Women play only a limited role in the church and cannot serve as ministers, though a law of 1982 allows them to be elected as deacons.

Roman Catholic Church

The arrival of Catholicism in South Africa can be dated to 1486, when Bartholomew Dias erected a cross on Santa Cruz Island in Algoa Bay. Thirteen years later, Vasco da Gama erected a similar cross and celebrated mass with his shipmates at Mossel Bay. In 1838, Father Patrick Raymond Griffith arrived as the first resident bishop. His tenure witnessed a rapid growth in the

Catholic Church in South Africa. By the time of his death in 1862, the Catholic population had grown from 700 in 1838 to 20,000. Under Griffith and the bishops who succeeded him, new stations were opened in Grahamstown, Port Elizabeth, Durban, Pretoria, Bloemfontein, and other places. To aid its evangelical efforts, the church established schools and institutes to provide literacy, agricultural, industrial, and theological training for its members and others interested in tapping into the reservoir of knowledge offered by the West. During the apartheid years the Catholic Church remained resentful of the policy and programs of the National Party government, most especially their use of legislative power to nationalize and capture all mission schools to propagate their own brand of protestant religion with its emphasis on racial separation and inferior education for blacks, Asians, and coloreds. As of 2000, 9 percent of all South Africans were Catholic. The sect has over 2,500 churches, over 1,000 priests, over 200 religious brothers, 5,000 sisters, 336 church schools with 87,000 pupils, 80 hostels, 20 orphanages, 38 hospitals, 75 dispensaries, and over 150 theological and other training institutions.

Methodism and Anglicanism

In terms of membership, the Methodist Church of South Africa ranks as the third largest denomination in South Africa after the African Independent Churches and the NGK. The church made remarkable progress among the Xhosa for whom its focus on rural and the urban areas as well as its avowed condemnation of racism in church and state affairs gained it many converts. Methodist missionaries published the first Xhosa grammar in 1834 and the first Xhosa Bible in 1859. The Methodists are also noted for their active interest in and engagement with black education, through an array of educational institutions that they established all over the country, to provide quality education to children of all races in South Africa.

Like the Methodists, there are two churches in South Africa that grew out of the Anglican Church. The oldest of these is the Church of England in South Africa. It held its first service in April 1749, but made little impact beyond the Cape, until the arrival of the 1820 British settlers rejuvenated its flagging strength and its focus on expansion. In 1870 the church broke in two with the emergence of the Church of the Province of South Africa. The new church prospered at the expense of the old, expanding its reach to other parts of South Africa, most especially through the promotion of black education. And, even though the large African mission group remained loyal to the Church of England, the church lost the bulk of its assets to the Church of the Province in 1910. With its 100,000 members and limited resources, the Church of England in South Africa has remained faithful to its Protestant, reform, and evangelical traditions.

AFRICAN INITIATED CHURCHES

The Ethiopian Churches

The largest and the fastest growing churches in South Africa are the group of African Initiated Churches generally referred to as African Independent Churches. From the name, the most common feature of these churches is that they are African inspired, African led, African membership-dominated, and African-centered churches. These churches can be grouped into two. The first are the Ethiopian churches that began to emerge toward the end of the nineteenth century. Disenchanted with the sectarian conflict, doctrinal disputes, racial segregation, and capitalist orientation that characterized the protestant mission churches, black Christian leaders began to form their own churches. The reluctance of the white-led protestant missions to appoint Africans to leadership positions in their churches, even when these Africans were as educated or even more educated than their white counterparts, was particularly galling to black Christians. Their feelings of resentment became more acute especially from the 1880s and 1890s onwards as other avenues of advancements began to close quite quickly through government policies of land appropriation, racial segregation, job reservation, and heavy taxation. African Christians felt the need to assert African leadership and equality with whites in church affairs, often as a first step toward asserting African equality and autonomy in economic and political affairs. For this reason, the Ethiopian churches were welcomed by African nationalists as partners in the struggle for African independence from white rule.

For similar reasons, and in spite of their concentration on the ostensibly religious business of teaching, preaching, and industry, the Ethiopian churches were viewed with misgivings and suspicions as veritable threats to white political control. By providing an unusually successful model of African initiatives, autonomy, and leadership, they became a source of inspiration to later-day African nationalists who strove to bring about the same change in state affairs. With over five million members, the African Independent Churches command the largest number of followers in South Africa. While providing ample room for the affirmation of African autonomous religious identity, the Ethiopian churches have remained quite close theologically and liturgically to their parent mission churches, most especially the Methodist, Presbyterian, and Congregational churches.

Worshippers at a Sunday evening meeting on the grounds of a primary school yard in Soweto. Note the leopard leather headbands of the men and beaded hats of the women, symbolizing African culture. The African Independent Churches (AIC) are among the most widespread religious movements in South Africa. There are more than 500 AIC congregations in Soweto alone.

The Zionists or Apostolic Churches

The second group of independent churches is the Zionist or Apostolic church. These are made up of the Pentecostal, charismatic, and millenarian movements which placed special emphasis on the gifts and workings of the Holy Spirit, speaking in tongues, and faith healing. Many of these are products of American Pentecostal missionary endeavors of the early 1900s, and have maintained their connections with that source. Usually centered around a charismatic prophet-healer, these churches are noted for the bright uniforms worn by their members, their use of long robes, sticks, drums, water, and other symbols. Their elaborate administrative and organizational structures provided important leadership outlets for blacks denied such opportunities in colonial and apartheid South Africa. Though the Zionist churches can be found all over South Africa, they appear to be concentrated in the urban areas, where their fervent singing, drumming, dancing, and spirit possession provide a means of emotional release and moral anchor in the midst of the frustrations and uncertainties characteristic of life in twentieth-century

Religious devotees walking barefoot on a Good Friday weekend. (Jane Davis)

South Africa. Over 900 independent churches are situated in the urban complex of Soweto alone. The churches are generally small in size, though a few can boast a membership of half a million or more. Two of the most notable of the larger ones are the Zion Christian Church (ZCC), established by Engenas Lekganyane in 1910, and the Ihanda lamaNazaretha (Nazareth Baptist Church), founded by the Zulu prophet, Isaiah Shembe. By creatively blending Christianity with African beliefs, the independent churches allow the Africans to practice Christianity in a way that is neither culture-bound nor Eurocentric in that it can be made amenable, responsive, and translatable to the beliefs and practices of other cultures.[12]

HINDUISM

Two groups of Indians came to South Africa in the nineteenth century. Between 1860 and 1911, when the recruitment of indentured laborers ended, 150,000 Indians came to work and eventually settle in South Africa. Of this number, over 80 percent were Hindu, 12 percent were Muslims, and 5 percent were Christians. These early Indian workers found ways to carry on their Hindu religion through private prayers, offerings, and services, though they were usually too poor to support the public display of their religious beliefs through the construction of temples and support of a priestly class. The financial support that would provide the Hindu population and religion with the means for the visible display of its beliefs would be provided by the second group of Indian immigrants who began to arrive in South Africa toward the end of the nineteenth century. Known as passenger Indians, because they paid their own fares unlike their predecessors who had their return fares paid by the government, they came to South Africa as traders, merchants, and entrepreneurs. Though most of these free immigrants were Gujarati Muslims, some of them were higher-caste Hindus, a few of whom came from the priestly class.

From 1867 onward, Hindu temples began to dot the landscape of South Africa, spreading gradually from Durban to Pietermaritzburg, Port Elizabeth, Johannesburg, and Pretoria. The most impressive of these is the ornate, futuristic, marble-floored Temple of Understanding in Chatsworth. Designed by the Austrian architect, Hannes Raudner, laid out in the shape of a lotus flower, surrounded by a moat and a lush ornamental garden, and built by the International Society for Krishna Consciousness, it remains a major tourist attraction. Unlike in India, where it provides a unifying framework, the caste system does not feature prominently in the practice of Hinduism in South Africa. Collectively despised and persecuted by the South African government, the Hindu community of South Africa had enough trouble contending with officially imposed racial and political oppression to allow caste-related concerns to weaken the unity of their commitment to struggle against political injustice.

For most Hindus in South Africa, religious life is centered on rituals in the home, services and offerings at the temples, and the careful observance of an annual calendar of sacred festivals. The daily domestic rituals involve the lighting of a sacred lamp, the erection of flag pole, chanting of hymns and recitations from the sacred books (*sandyopasaha*) to illustrate the triumph of light over darkness and of good over evil, and drawing moral lessons to inspire and guide the Hindu in his daily and domestic lives. At the communal level, the most important festival is the Deepavali, which begins with the lighting of a lamp for the Goddess of Light, to symbolize the inevitable triumph of good over evil in human and cosmic affairs. With Hindu religious rituals so intimately integrated into household relations and affairs, the refusal of the South African government to recognize Hindu marriage practices, such as polygamy, was particularly unsettling to the Hindu community. Widespread Indian protest, especially among women, culminated in the nonviolent protest led by Mahatma Gandhi against discriminatory laws in 1913. Gandhi's principle of *satyagraha* (meaning keep to the truth) and its concomitant strategy of the superiority of using love, spiritual convictions, and nonviolent means to resist injustice became a model for civil rights leaders in the United States, as well as for nationalist leaders in Africa, Asia, and other parts of the world, even long after the violent death of its architect in 1947.[13]

ISLAM

There are roughly 400,000 Muslims in South Africa, constituting slightly less than 2 percent of the population. The Muslim population originated from three groups. The first set of Muslims came as slaves from Indonesia, Malaya, India, Ceylon, Madagascar, and the East African coast. A 1770 law at the Cape, which made the selling and buying of Christian slaves illegal, caused slave owners to take steps to prevent the conversion of their slaves.

A mosque in Durban, Kwa-Zulu Natal, 2001. Durban is home to the largest Muslim community in South Africa.

Denied the benefits offered by Christianity, the slaves turned to the alternative source of religious and spiritual nourishment offered by Islam. The net result was a dramatic increase in the number of Muslim slaves at the Cape, and an enduring interest in the Islamic religion that would aid the growth of the faith. By the time of the abolition of slavery in South Africa in 1838, two-thirds of Cape Town's non-European population was Muslim. The second group of Muslims in South Africa were those who came as prisoners and political exiles to the Cape. The most celebrated of these was Shaykh Yusuf, an Indonesian of noble origin from Makassar who had led a guerrilla campaign against Dutch rule in Indonesia.

The third group of Muslims came from Company convicts. Between 1653 and 1767, approximately 1,000 convicts were brought from Indonesia to the Cape. Becoming free blacks after serving their sentence, these former convicts contributed to the establishment of Islam at the Cape. The fourth group of Muslims came from the passenger Indians, the majority of whom were Muslims. Usually made up of well-to-do, enterprising traders and other professionals, they provided the material resources and the elite leadership for Muslims as well as for the Indian resistance movements of the late nineteenth and early twentieth centuries.

Conflict over festival practices and funerary rites involving the issues of religion, law, and public health pitched the Cape Muslim community against the government in a series of show-downs and face-offs during the closing decades of the nineteenth century. For the most part, however, Muslims in South Africa accommodated themselves to their minority status, maintaining their loyalty to the government for as long as their practice of the basic tenets of their religion was not hampered. The establishment of apartheid in 1948, with its many discriminatory laws that did not spare the Muslims of any of the indignities suffered by the black majority, began to draw Muslims into the ranks of the African nationalists.[14]

JUDAISM

There were practicing Jews among the Portuguese explorers and early settlers in South Africa, but these appeared to have practiced their faith in private until 1841 when the first Jewish congregation was organized at the Cape of Good Hope, with the significantly punning name of Tikvath Israel (Hope of Israel). Eight years later, in 1849, the first synagogue was consecrated and opened for public worship, servicing the needs of approximately 60 families that constituted the Jewish community at the Cape. Though new congregations were organized in response to increased Jewish migration, the number of adherents remained small until the discovery of diamonds and gold came to accelerate the pace of Jewish (indeed all) migrations to South Africa. Thus between 1880 and 1914, the Jewish population in South Africa increased from 4,000 to 40,000. Fifty percent of the new arrivals settled in the gold-mining city of Johannesburg, which became the largest center of Jewish life. In response to the boom in the ostrich feather industry stimulated by the demands of the European fashion market at the end of the nineteenth century, many ostrich farm settlements became centers of Jewish life in South Africa. One of these, Oudtshoorn, became known as the Jerusalem of South Africa. Fifty percent of the 127,000 Jews in South Africa are still found in Johannesburg.

Though the Jews of South Africa came from a wide variety of backgrounds—such as Britain, Germany, Netherlands, and many other nations—the majority were of Lithuanian ancestry. Though they came in search of economic opportunities, these Lithuanian immigrants were also fleeing the political domination and anti-Semitic persecutions to which they had been subjected under Tsarist and Socialist Russian rules. Jews, most especially those of European ancestry, have occupied important positions in South Africa as successful mining capitalists, prosperous merchants, and leading civic leaders. Many, however, were at the lowest reach of the European society; for instance, the extreme poverty of many Lithuanian Jews often resulted in a life of illegal liquor trading and prostitution.

For decades before 1948, leaders of the Jewish community in South Africa, most especially the socialists among them, remained opposed to and at best skeptical about the Zionist movement to establish a Jewish homeland in Palestine; rather, they were focused on building a Jewish community that would be firmly and permanently based in South Africa. Nevertheless, Zionism also gained widespread support and established several associations in South Africa. These divisions started to blur, however, in the face of growing and sometimes virulent anti-Semitism that came to dominate the press, as well as political and public discourse in South Africa before 1948. During the 1930s and 1940s, the government took practical and legislative measures to severely restrict the immigration of Jews to South Africa, citing reasons of unassimilability. Paradoxically, from 1948 onwards, the National Party Government of D. F. Malan began to ease these restrictions to admit Jews into the privileged circle of the white minority ruling class with its racist apartheid ideology. As in other parts of the world, Jewish life in South Africa remains centered on the Torah or written law, the precepts of the oral law, and commitment to the *halakha* or the observance of rituals and ethical duties. Most Jews are adherents of the Orthodox Jewish tradition, which from 1986 had been organized as the Union of Orthodox Synagogues of South Africa. Approximately 20 percent of the Jewish population follows the Reformed or

Progressive movement, while several ultra-orthodox groups have remained active in the urban areas, thus increasing Jewish diversity in the country.[15]

CONCLUDING REMARKS ON RELIGION, POLITICS, AND SOCIETY

Religion has remained important in the history, politics, and culture of South Africa. For the African majority, religion was a pervasive, sociopolitical force infusing all aspects of life and existence. For the white minority who came to dominate the economic and political life of the country in the last three and a half centuries, religion provided the vocabulary for group divisions, for defining the doctrine of apartheid, and for justifying racial and political dominations. Europeans, with their Christian civilization, felt superior to the *kaffir* (Arabic word for unbeliever), whose illiteracy, lost state, and uncivilized habits made them justifiable objects of white conversion efforts and racial domination. Blacks were to be ruled, deprived, dispossessed, and dominated not because they were blacks as such, but more because they were heathens. The Hamitic hypothesis, which presented blacks as descendants of Ham, cursed by God, in the Hebrew and Christian scriptures, to serve the children of Shem, and similar myths of scientific racism, found sympathetic ears in South Africa. The Afrikaner-dominated Dutch reformed churches were the leading proponent of religion as an ideology of racial and political domination. The English-speaking Anglicans and Methodist churches also gave measured supports to apartheid since they were not willing to jeopardize their dependence on mining and industrial capital funding from Britain. All these churches reinforced the class structure of South Africa by preaching a gospel of subservience and loyalty to constituted authority—whether it be political, mining, industrial, or religious—while remaining generally oblivious to the iniquities and inequities of the apartheid system and society. Similarly, by insisting that women be restricted to their divinely ordained duties of home, family, and children cares, the Afrikaner and English-speaking churches cooperated with the state in changing and subverting African patterns of marriage and gender relations. With the new emphasis on the cult of domesticity and as a result of being denied leadership positions in church and state, women lost the power and influence that the payment of bride-wealth (*lobola*) and their domination of the agricultural spheres had traditionally conferred on them.

Nevertheless, in the struggle against European colonialism, apartheid, and racial oppression in South Africa, religion came to play a prominent part. Nearly all the leaders of the early African nationalist groups, like the SANNC (later ANC), were products of mission education. For many of them, religion became a major source of inspiration, through which they were able to develop an ideology or even a theology of liberation that was creatively and effectively deployed in the struggle against the evils of racism and oppression in South Africa. Mandela still remembers with fondness his first white missionary teachers who gave him his name Nelson and contributed to the shaping of his positive attitudes toward white people generally in spite of the racism of many with whom he had to deal. Even within the rank of NGK there were a few, unfortunately too few, like Dr. Beyers Naude, who came to question the compatibility of apartheid and the Christian faith, causing a crack in the white orthodox monolith. Desmond Tutu, the 1984 Nobel Peace Laureate, used the relative inviolability of his position as the Anglican Archbishop of Cape Town to lead a nonviolent but active protest against the injustices of the apartheid order. In 1994, Desmond Tutu became the chairman of the Truth and Reconciliation Commission, an assignment signaling that religion would continue to play an active role in the quest for reconciliation and healing in postapartheid South Africa.[16]

NOTES

1. On the healing dance and the religious system of the Khoisan and the main sources for the discussion in this section, see Richard B. Lee, *The Dobe !Kung* (New York: Holt, Rinehart and Winston, 1979), 103–18; Lorna J. Marshall, *The !Kung of Nyae Nyae* (Cambridge, Mass.: Harvard University Press, 1976); Marshall, *Nyae Nyae !Kung, Beliefs and Rites* (Cambridge, Mass.: Peabody Museum Monographs, Harvard University, 1999); and David Chidester, *Religions of South Africa* (London and New York: Routledge, 1992).

2. On Bantu religions of South Africa and the sources for the discussion in this section, see Chidester, *Religions of South Africa* 3–34; W. D. Hammond-Tooke, ed., *The Bantu-Speaking Peoples of Southern Africa* (London and Boston: Routledge and Kegan Paul, 1975), 318–66; Janet Hodgson, *The God of the Xhosa* (Cape Town: Oxford University Press, 1982); and Thomas Lawson, *Religions of Africa: Traditions in Transformation* (San Francisco: HarperCollins, 1985).

3. On the concept of the Supreme God among the various South African peoples, see Irving Hexham, "Lord of the Sky, King of the Earth: Zulu Traditional Religion and Belief in the Sky God," *Sciences Religieuses/Studies in Religion,* 1981, 10, 273–78; and Janet Hodgson, *The God of the Xhosa* (Cape Town: Oxford University Press, 1982).

4. Details of the myths discussed briefly in this section can be found in Henry Callaway, *The Religious System of the Amazulu* (London: Folklore Society, 1884); Dominique Zahan, *The Religion, Spirituality and Thought of Traditional Africa* (Chicago: University of Chicago Press, 1979); and Chidester, *Religions of South Africa,* 6–9.

5. On nature spirits, see W. D. Hammond-Tooke, "World-view I: A System of Beliefs," in Hammond-Tooke, ed., *The Bantu-Speaking Peoples of Southern Africa* (London and Boston: Routledge and Kegan Paul, 1974), 318–43.

6. On ancestor ritual, see: Chidester, *Religions of South Africa*, 9–13; H. Kuckertz, ed., *Ancestor Religion in Southern Africa* (Cacadu: Lumko Missiological Institute, 1981); and D. Hammond-Tooke, *The Roots of Black South Africa* (Johannesburg: Jonathan Ball Publishers, 1993), 149–67.

7. On witchcraft and the problem of evil, see Hammond-Tooke, "World-view I," 335–39; *The Roots,* 169–83; and Chidester, *Religions of South Africa,* 13–17.

8. On ritual specialists and the search for health, see Hammond-Tooke, *The Roots,* 185–97; D. Hammond-Tooke, *Rituals and Medicine: Traditional Healing in South Africa* (Johannesburg: A. D. Donker, 1989); and H. Ngubane, *Body and Mind in Zulu Medicine* (London: Academic Press, 1977).

9. On the continuing relevance and resilience of traditional healing practices in modern South Africa, see N. Arden, *African Spirits Speak: A White Woman's Journey into the Healing Tradition of the Sangoma* (Rochester, Vt.: Destiny Books, 1999); S. Campbell, *Called to Heal: Traditional Healing Meets Modern Medicine in Southern Africa* (Halfway House: Zebra Press, 1998); and M. V. Gumede, *Traditional Healers: A Medical Perspectives* (Johannesburg: Skotaville, 1990).

10. On the story of Christianity in South Africa and the main sources for this section, see Chidester, *Religions of South Africa*, 35–147; Peter Hinchliff, *The Anglican Church in South Africa* (London: Darton, Longman, and Todd, 1963); B. A. Pauw, "The Influence of Christianity," in Hammond-Tooke, *The Bantu-Speaking Peoples,* 415–40; Martin Prozesky, *Christianity in South Africa* (Johannesburg: Southern Book Publishers, 1990); and Richard Elphick and Rodney Davenport, *Christianity in South Africa: A Political, Social, and Cultural History* (Berkeley and Los Angeles: University of California Press, 1997).

11. The quotation is from J. Du Plessis, *A History of Christian Missions in South Africa* (London: Longmans Green; reprinted, Cape Town: Struik, 1965), 21.

12. On the African Independent Churches in South Africa, see Chidester, *Religions in South Africa,* 112–47; Bengt G. M. Sundkler, *Bantu Prophets in South Africa* (Oxford: Oxford University Press, 1961); Martin West, *Bishops and Prophets in a Black City: African Independent Churches in Soweto, Johannesburg* (Cape Town: David Philip, 1975); G. C. Oosthuizen, ed., *Religion Alive: Studies in the New Movements and Indigenous Churches in Southern Africa* (Johannesburg: Hodder & Stoughton, 1986); and Robert Edgar, *Because They Chose the Plan of God: The Story of the Bulhoek Massacre* (Johannesburg: Ravan Press, 1988).

13. On Hinduism and religions among the Indians of South Africa see Chidester, *Religions of South Africa,* 168–75; Hilda Kuper, *Indian People in Natal* (Westport, Conn.: Greenwood Press, 1974), 186–216; and C. Kyppusami, *Religions, Practices and Customs of South African Indians* (Durban: Sunray, 1983). On Gandhi, see M. Swan, *Gandhi: The South African Experience* (Johannesburg: Ravan Press, 1985).

14. On Islam in South Africa, see: Frank R. Bradlow and Margaret Cairns, *The Early Cape Muslims* (Cape Town: A. A. Balkema, 1978); Suliman E. Dangor, *A Crit-*

ical Biography of Shaykh Yusuf (Durban: University of Durban-Westville, 1982); A. Davids, *The Mosques of Bo-Kaap: A Social History of Islam at the Cape* (Athlone, Cape: South African Institute of Arabic and Islamic Research, 1980); and Chidester, *Religions of South Africa,* 158–68.

15. On Judaism in South Africa, see Chidester, *Religions of South Africa,* 168–82; Gustav Saron and Louis Hotz, eds., *The Jews in South Africa: A History* (Cape Town: Oxford University Press, 1955); and Gideon Shimon, *Jews and Zionism: The South African Experience, 1910–1967* (Cape Town: Oxford University Press, 1980).

16. See Desmond Tutu, *No Future without Forgiveness* (London: Rider Books, 1999).

4

Literature

Literature, oral or written, is at the heart of South African life, culture, and society. Informed by tradition, history, geography, economics, and politics, literature has been at the center of the quest for identity, autonomy, freedom, and empowerment in South Africa. The sheer volume, variety, and richness of literary works in all genres attest to the vibrancy and significance of literature in the development of this frontier society of Africa. The enriching though often conflicting diversity of literature, society, and rival nationalisms in South Africa—as defined by the variables of race, class, and gender—is most easily understood and underscored as a centripetal force of history working toward its emergence. Using a chronological as well as a thematic approach, this chapter will examine the distinctive though interrelated literary traditions that have developed in South Africa in the last five centuries.

ORAL LITERATURE

Literacy, the art of reading and writing, came to South Africa with the Europeans and was formally consolidated with the establishment of the Dutch settlement on Table Bay in 1652. Europeans did not, however, introduce literature to the region. Before 1652, and long after, the indigenous peoples of South Africa gave expression to their creative and intuitive imagination through the medium of oral tradition. Transmitted by word of mouth from one generation to another, oral traditions are the means through which nonliterate societies conceptualize, preserve, and transmit their empirical and cosmic realities. Oral traditions are not just rote recitations; they are performances. In this regard, context is as important as content. Though oral tradition invariably refers to and draws its inspiration, models, and archetypes from the past, its recitation or performance is a present event.

The earliest inhabitants of South Africa about whom we have information are the Khoisans. We must turn to them in order to begin to learn the lost and fading voices of African oral literature. In stories, songs, and rock paintings, the San left behind impressive records of their life, culture, and society. Among the San, songs, chants, and poems are the most popular form of literary expression. In terms of structure, subject, and style, these poems can be classified into different categories, namely panegyric, lyric, elegy, religious verse, and others. Other important forms of literary expression are the fictional and nonfictional prose narratives, proverbs, and riddles.

For the San, songs are a prominent part of religious life. Usually associated with animals, these sacred songs are featured in healing dance rituals where they are sung and danced to by choirs of girls and women in order to induce a trancelike state in the men-healers who are thereby empowered to draw sicknesses out of the afflicted. They also feature in hunting and rain dances to ensure a good hunt as well as regular rainfall in the perennially arid land of the San. In a society without priests, the invocation of spirits through sacred songs is a spontaneous event that can be carried out by any individual as the need arises. Living in a harsh and climatically challenging environment, San songs and stories are filled with allusions and anecdotes dealing with the scarcity and sparseness of the San life. In the often-quoted classic, "Prayer to the Young Moon," the sheer necessity of food is poignantly brought out through fast-paced invocations, intense repetitions, and parallelisms.[1]

In the Khoi-Khoi poem, "Hymn to Tsui-Xgoa [the Supreme God]," published in 1864, we find a prayer for rain, life, and sustenance. "Let stream to earth the thundercloud," the supplicant cries, asking for rain so that his or her people and their "flocks" may live. This is a desperate and desolate cry for divine intervention, provision, and abundance in a land of dryness and scarcity from a people who have experienced nothing but dispossession and injustice from waves of hostile, alien invaders.[2]

It is important to note that these poems were recorded during the middle of the nineteenth century, at a time when the Khoisans were on the verge of extinction. Centuries of cultural and demographic assimilation by the various Bantu groups and over two centuries of extirpating wars with Europeans decimated the Khoisan population and almost eliminated them as a distinct and major cultural group in southern Africa. Deprived of their cattle by Trekboer farmers and commodores and dispossessed of their lands by these and other more powerful interlocutors, the surviving Khoisans who tried to maintain their cultural integrity had to content themselves with a precarious existence in the arid and desolate lands of the Kalahari Desert and in other barren,

rugged terrains of southern Africa. Khoisan perspectives on European imperialism, with all its dehumanizing, dislocating, and destructive consequences,
found expressions in powerful and highly evocative, if mournful, poetry.
With elegiac resonance, poignancy, and passion, laced with powerful images
and intense metaphor, these poems speak of broken groups, broken families,
broken promises, and broken hopes.

Equally important, though probably less complex and more readily accessible, were the prose narratives of the Khoisan peoples. Storytelling by specialist elders and even more so by nonspecialists was a popular communal
pastime. Though the actual stories are usually loaded with meanings and messages to be disseminated to all listeners, the convivial storytelling sessions
were important occasions for social intercourse and group bonding. As with
many other African groups, the !Kung word for story includes within its com-
pass a wide range of narratives—fictional or factual, formal or informal, cosmic or empirical, natural or divine—that feature tales of supernatural beings,
animal parables, hunting, and historical recollections told with varying structures, content, and purpose. Some of these stories deal with cosmological
themes. They speak of a time when God walked on earth and feasted with
humans. They recollect a time before time, when the earth was inhabited by
half-human and half-animal beings and when all animals were still people.
Hunting stories explore and celebrate the once-upon-a-time abundance of
the fauna, the skill of the hunter, the origin and secret of hunting, and the
character of certain popular games such as the eland and the springbok. Others lament the contemporary dreariness of the hunting field, the decimation
of the fauna, and the decline of hunting culture, which spelled the cultural
doom of the hunter-gatherer societies. As in many other societies in Africa,
these stories deal with such fundamental issues of existence as the origin,
nature, and functions of life; death; man; animals; sex; hunting and gathering; pastoralism; and many other aspects of daily life.

At the center of many of these stories is the San trickster-deity, the mantis,
who became for the San the symbol of the Supreme Being with its ubiquitous, mysterious, multi-legged, hovering, unpredictable ways. Mischievous
and incorrigible in many of the stories, the mantis became the great, manip-
ulative author of confusion and disorder, with its love for lurking in dark and
shadowy places. Like the mantis, other animals had stories, duties, and peculiar qualities attributed to them. At the top is the eland, the ever-abundant
source of food supply even in dry times, with its perfect shape, graceful poise,
and intrinsic beauty, a clear demonstration of the completeness of divine creation. In the wily hyena, with its lopsided walk and prowling gaze, the living
reality of evil and the need for eternal vigilance to keep the forces of darkness
at bay are conceptualized in fascinating stories. Others are the hamerkop bird

with its extrasensory perception; the lynx with its love of light; and the striped mouse, usually presented as a visible reminder of the diversity of life and consciousness. Through these stories, whether fanciful or cosmological, the San explore the origin, nature, and consequences of good and evil, truth and falsehood, between humans themselves as well as between humans and other forces of life such as nature, animals, and spirits.[3]

For the Khoisan, a man's life is embedded in his story, in the same way as a group's existence is a function of its own peculiar story. Without a story, a man or group has no life, no identity, no focus or loci of reference and self-definition. To be without a story is to become lost, perplexed, and forlorn in the world. The destruction of the Khoisan's way of life, his conquest, dispossession, and assimilation by alien cultures and groups began the process of the erasing of his memory and story, thus setting the stage for the gradual but eventual death of his culture. This idea of the centrality of the story to the existence and survival of the Khoisan way of life is brought out eloquently in many San narratives of the nineteenth century, testifying to the acute homesicknesses, passionate longing, and moving lamentation for a dying culture that had become the lot of the San by this period.[4]

Bantu Oral Literature

Stories and Folklore

As with the Khoisan, the Bantu-speaking peoples of South Africa also conceptualized, preserved, and transmitted their culture through the means of oral tradition. In narrative prose, myths and legends, animal and human stories, and tales of chiefs and of ordinary people, as well as in proverbs, aphorisms, riddles, songs, lyrics, and praise poems, Africans gave concrete and artistic expressions to their deepest feelings and to their creative and intuitive imaginations. Different forms of oral literature are deployed to account for the perennial issues of fear and conflict between and betwixt clans and cultural groups, to celebrate the achievements and deplore the failures of individuals and groups, and to transmit wisdom and values considered vital to conduct and harmonious relations. In symbolic and idiomatic languages, they explore the fundamental issues of life, such as love and hostility; courage and resourcefulness; beauty and ugliness; justice and retribution; order and chaos; and the triumph of good over evil. Women, particularly grandmothers, are usually the storytellers motivated by a definite mandate to educate and instruct the young and old alike in the ways and lores of the group. Meant to also entertain, most especially after a long day of work, stories are best told or performed in the more relaxed and calm atmosphere of the evenings, the time of the spirits.

In addition to stories about humans and animals, there are stories about monstrous beings whose grotesqueness is surpassed only by their stupidity, which allows men to always triumph over them in spite of their apparent superhuman powers. Presented as half-human and half-beast, often with physical deformities and living on land or in the deep and dark recesses of large waters, the ogres or monsters, known as *dimo* (Sotho) or *zimu* (Nguni), are human-eaters who can run faster than the winds. Stories between humans and animals are generally and surprisingly devoid of conflict. Instead the animals feature as aids and helpers to humans in times of need, especially so in dire need. In one story, a mouse pressures a group of men to flay off its skin and use it as a charm to neutralize the dangers of a nearby well-known sorcerer named Ngangezulu (as-great-as-the-heavens).[5]

Poetry and Songs

Beyond the prose narratives, Africans also express their emotional and aesthetic experiences through poetry. Two forms can be identified. The first is the lyric and dramatic poem, made up of various kinds of songs. In the second category are praise poems. The lyric—a short poem that is sung—is apparently one of the most common forms of literary expression among the indigenous peoples of South Africa. For each song, there is usually a leader and a chorus. The leader sings the important words in the songs, while the chorus repeats some of the leader's words or responds with rousing though often meaningless monosyllabic ejaculations such as "Ye ha he," "fe la la," "ho ho ho," etc. Sung on formal and informal occasions, during periods of merriment and festivity, and to mark rites of passages such as births, initiations, marriages, deaths, and title-taking, a wide variety of these songs can be identified. Among the most widespread are love songs, hunting songs, war songs, work songs, satires, children's game songs, and lullabies. Love songs are usually sung by women to give expression to their feelings on a wide range of subjects.[6]

Praise poems are regarded in most African societies as the highest form of literary expression. This may be due largely to their association with a society's strongest personages, rulers, nobles, and others who seem to have loomed larger than their society. Praise poems are sung or chanted to evoke, affirm, and celebrate the essential qualities of nations, states, ethnic groups, clans, individuals, animals, and even inanimate objects. Full of epithets, highly evocative and figurative, moving and emotionally charged, laced with similes and metaphoric resonance, their recitation, or more appropriately, performance is always a major event. Composed and recited by highly respected specialists groomed in the history and tradition of the community, the mastery of the praise poem is not the sole prerogative of the professional

praise poet. All young adults and men in particular, are expected to be knowledgeable about and able to recite the praise poems of their immediate clans
and families.

It is in praise of chiefs and notable historical personages that the praise
poem is usually at its finest, its most evocative, and its most powerful. Among
the Bantu of South Africa, a chief is a chief because of his birth into a chiefly
family, but he is also a chief by the will of the people. Through praise poetry,
the power and legitimacy, duties and obligations, and relevance and resilience
of chieftaincy are validated and acknowledged. But praise poetry should not
be viewed as an arcane survivor from the past with little or no relevance to
contemporary society. By simultaneously eulogizing the achievements and
critiquing the failures and flaws of powerful kings and leaders, these poems
provide models of acceptable conduct. Similarly, through praise poetry, communal solidarity and group identities are defined, redefined, reinforced, and
affirmed. The praise poet occupies an important position in the life of the
community as he adopts and adapts the praises to celebrate and censure the
kingship. Numerous poems celebrate the greatness, terror, and memory of
Shaka, king of the Zulu, and undoubtedly, the most famous, feared, and
reviled of all the pre-twentieth-century South African rulers.[7]

WRITTEN LITERATURE

Emergence of African Written Literatures

The development of written literary forms among the African peoples was
closely associated with the activities of the Christian missionaries. Their commitment to converting Africans to the religion of the Book required literacy
education as well as the reduction of the indigenous languages to writing. By
the middle of the nineteenth century, full translations of the Bible began to
appear with the publications of the Setswana Bible in 1857, Xhosa in 1859,
Southern Sotho in 1881, and Zulu in 1883. The remarkable nature of this
achievement can be seen in the fact that an Afrikaner Bible did not appear
until well into the twentieth century. Only the missions, however, were
actively interested and engaged in educating Africans. Consequently, the earliest educated African elite were predominantly products of missionary education. The Xhosa were also the first group to become actively engaged with
the missionaries, most especially those of the Glasgow Missionary Society,
whose representatives soon translated the Xhosa language into writing. Thus,
the emergence of written literatures among the indigenous peoples cannot be
separated from the history of the European imperial and missionary enterprise. It is indeed part of the story of the frontiers, characterized by the clash

of arms, military conquest, land dispossession, demographic dislocation, cultural transformation, and political domination.

African responses and resistances to this contest of power found expression in the Christianized but eloquently memorable voices of Ntsikana and Makanna. Ntsikana's "Great Hymn," recorded in 1828 by the missionary John Philip, though Christian in content, was African in meaning and medium. Composed like the indigenous praise poem, it celebrated the greatness, power, goodness, and justice of God in the midst of European dispossession, violence, and injustice. Another pioneering voice from this era was that of the warrior-prophet Makanna, whose millenarianism and military, verbal, and apocalyptic resistance to the British was captured and preserved for us in Pringle's "Makanna's Gathering." Captured and imprisoned by the British on Robben Island, Makanna drowned attempting to escape. His dramatic story and eloquent speech, as recorded by Pringle, portray the British as unwanted meddlers in affairs that do not concern them and of which they know little. Inspired by the activities and, most especially, the words of Ntsikana and Makanna, new generations of the African educated elite completed the transition of indigenous literature from tradition to modernity. Notable among these early pioneers was Tiyo Soga, who translated John Bunyan's *Pilgrim's Progress* (*Uhambo lo Mhambi*) into Xhosa. This translation had an influence on the promotion of Xhosa literacy that rivaled that of the translated Xhosa Bible. Another notable disciple was J. T. Jabavu, a politician, writer, and editor. His periodical, *Invo,* became a vehicle for the expression of African Christian liberal ideas. Soga's example was followed by the translation of *Pilgrim's Progress* into Zulu by J. W. Colenso under the title of *Ukuhamba KwesiHambi* in 1883. A Southern Sotho translation appeared in 1896 as *Leeto la Mokeresete.* This was followed by Robert Moffat's Setswana *Loeto Iwa go Mokeresete* in 1909.

The first half of the twentieth century witnessed some major developments in indigenous written literature. Among the Xhosa the leaders were S. E. K. Mqhayi, H. M. Ndawo, G. B. Sinxo, and J. J. R. Jolobe. The most notable of these was Mqhayi, whose three novels, four volumes of poetry, two biographies, as well as other essays and translations, gave him the reputation of being the father of modern Xhosa literature. His poem, *Nkosi sikelel'-iAfrika* (God Bless Africa), subsequently became the ANC anthem, giving him a lasting reputation. Jolobe also became well known. His two novels, one play, three collections of poetry, four translations, many school readers, and numerous essays gained him several national literary awards. His translations included Booker T. Washington's *Ukuphakama ubusuku ebukhokeni* (*Up from Slavery,* 1951) and H. Rider Haggard's *Lmigodi Kakumkani Usolomon* (*King Solomon's Mines,* 1958).

Among the Sotho, the national idealism and didacticism that infused early Xhosa writings were also evident in the works of Thomas Mofolo, whose first novel, *Moeti wa botjhabela* (*The Traveler to the East*, 1907), showed the unmistakable influence of *Pilgrim's Progress*, with its religious themes of virtue and sin, light and darkness. Mofolo's fame, however, came from his third work, *Chaka*, a historical novel, written probably in 1909 though not published until 1925. *Chaka*'s stylistic grandeur, poetic prose, creative intermingling of history and fantasy, myth and legend, militarism and heroism, fabled tales of man and monster, and tragic outcome have combined to establish it as a literary epic and a classic of early African written literature. *Chaka*'s success appears to have inspired others to focus on cultural heroes in novels, poems, and plays based on extant folktales and praise poems, kept reasonably close to accepted national history. J. L. Dube's *Insila kaShaka* (Shaka's Bodyguard) published in 1930, set the stage for this phase of written literature. Others in this genre followed in rapid succession. Among these are R. R. R. Dhlomo's *UDingane* (Shaka's Half-Brother, Assassinator, and Successor) in 1936, *UShaka* (1937), *UMpande* (1938), and *UCetshwayo* (1952). All are historical novels focused on notable kings of the Zulu. Similarly, among the Tsonga and the Venda, the didacticism evident in earlier works can be seen in pioneering works such as C. T. D. Marivate's *Sasavona*, T. N. Maumela's *Elelwani* (1954), E. S. Madima's *A si ene* (1958) and Majara's southern Sotho *Mmakotulo* (1953). Centered on female characters, these novels explore the stress and tension of the intersections of such subjects as virtue, morality, parental authority, love and forced marriage, migration and urbanization, and the clash between tradition and modernity in twentieth-century South Africa.[8]

Afrikaner Literature

Perennially on the frontier of history and geography, early Afrikaner writers were preoccupied with the task of defining a new identity for their emerging society and giving literary expressions to their frontier experience. Confronted with the hazards of a new climate, embroiled relentlessly in expansionist wars with the indigenous groups and later with the British, and subjected to multiple personal and national misfortunes, Afrikaner pioneers wrote poems that were generally sad and elegiac. In the wake of the Anglo-Boer War (1899–1902), Jan F. E. Celliers lamented the destruction (by the British, of course) of the Afrikaners' idyllic way of life, while celebrating the heroism of his people. The themes of personal and national suffering came together in the melancholic poems of J. D. du Toit (1877–1953). Similarly, C. Louis Leipoldt (1880–1947) used colloquial Afrikaans to vent to his bitterness at the suffering of his people, while celebrating the glory of nature with its beautiful cascades of colors, shapes, and scents. Tormented by the bitter memory of the war, the suffering of man, the certainty of death, and the apparent indifference of God, Eugene N. Marais (1871–1936) produced the first major poem in Afrikaans, *Winternag* (1905), in which the exuberance of nature gives way to sadness, and joyousness gives way to doom.

The streak of agnosticism, hinted at in the agonizing poems of Marais, took center stage in the works of A. G. Visser and Toon van den Heever, whose poems marked a shift away from preoccupation with the Anglo-Boer war. The new poets were concerned not only with national and religious themes, but also with human emotions and thoughts in all their ramifications. Elisabeth Eybers added a female dimension to the story by exploring, through her poetry, the world of women, from childhood to old age. World War II witnessed the advent of a new generation of poets noted for the use of new themes, methods, and striking metaphors. The leadership of this group belonged to J. J. Opperman (1914–85), whose epic, *Joernaul van Jarik* (1949), uses allusion and meticulous construction to explore the issues of man's responsibility, guilt, and purpose in life. The surrealist imagery and poignant eroticism of Ingrid Jonker (1934–65) found full flowering in the poetry of Breyten Breytenbach, whose years in exile and in prison turned out to be the most productive of his career as he employed the thoughts of Zen Buddhism to explore the themes of longing and nostalgia for his fatherland.[9]

The turbulent decades of the 1970s and 1980s witnessed the emergence of a whole new generation of poets, among whom many of the most prominent voices belong to women, in whose hands poetry becomes a vehicle for social and political commentary and, sometimes, dissent. Notable among the female voices were Sheila Cussons, Wilma Stockenstrom, Antijie Krog, and Lina Spies. Other poets like J. C. Steyn, Merwe Scholtz, and T. T. Cloete consciously, with subtlety and boldness, exploited the grammar of the Afrikaans to explore the themes of love, nature, and man's place in the universe. In the hands of these writers as well as with others, such as Andre Brink, Henriette Grove, Hennie Aucamp, the narrator or speaker becomes the most active agent in a literature of self-consciousness, intertextuality, identity crisis, and a critical exposé of South African troubled society. Similarly, colored poets, such as V. Peterson (1914–87) and P. J. Philander (b. 1921) using white or standard Afrikaans, and others like Peter Blum, using the spoken Afrikaans dialect, address the social and political conditions of the colored population.

As with poetry, early Afrikaans prose writers were inspired by the protracted struggle of the Afrikaner people for autonomy and independence from British imperial control. This struggle for identity and self-actualization resulted in the Great Trek of the 1830s and ultimately reached its climax in the Anglo-Boer war at the end of the nineteenth century. The need to resist Anglicization resulted in the attempt to manufacture an Afrikaner national identity from words, through the conscious adoption of Afrikaans, a colloquial Dutch or kitchen language, spoken among the poorer classes and servants of the Afrikaners. In the hands of ardent Afrikaner patriots such as Rev. S. J. du Toit, Afrikaans was given respectability and deployed as the Afrikaner national language in the struggle for the domination of South Africa. Through newspaper publishing, books, pamphlets, essays, the production of standard dictionaries, grammars, schoolbooks, and Bible translations, literature in Afrikaans became part of a sustained and conscious effort to define, establish, and consolidate a distinct sociocultural identity for the Afrikaner people. Much of the early prose was meant to entertain as well as educate. Among the early pioneers were C. J. Langenhoven, Jochem van Bruggen, D. F. Malherbe, J. van Melle, and C. H. Kuhn, who explored the themes of poverty and depression, wisdom and foolishness, nature and man, the eternal cycle of birth and death, the tension between morality and politics, and the clash between the young and the old, as well as between tradition and modernity.

The major breakthrough came with the Sestigers (the writers of the sixties), who did for Afrikaner prose what the Dertigers (writers of the thirties) had done for poetry. Andre Brink (b.1935), in a series of novels, began to gradually move away from the reluctance of earlier writers to become engaged in social and political issues through the production of committed works that attempt to grapple with the intractable dilemma confronting the Afrikaner people and their racist ideology in a world of postcolonial freedom and liberalization. Other committed works included Steyn's *Dagboek va 'n verraaier* (1987), a searching exploration of the troubled state of mind of the Afrikaner intellectual. Similarly, in *Die swerfjare van Poppie Nongena* (1978), Elsa Joubert offers the reader a critical chronicle of the suffering and struggle of a black woman and her family under the terror of the apartheid government influx control. The military struggle between South Africa and its neighbors during the 1970s and 1980s resulted in the development of a new genre known as border literature, written by demobilized soldiers, among the most notable of whom are Koos Prinsloo (*Jonkmanskas,* 1982) and Etienne van Heerden (*My Kubban,* 1983).

Afrikaner writers used drama to explore some of the most enduring themes of their history, but the genre is less developed than Afrikaner poetry and prose. Celliers and C. J. Langenhoven wrote didactic plays and farcical comedies to explore many of the issues connected with the Anglo-Boer war and its consequences on the Afrikaner people. During the 1920s, works by J. F. W. Grosskopf and C. Louis Leipoldt explored the themes of poverty, love, witchcraft, and religion to inaugurate the beginning of serious social drama. The one-act play, *Alle paaie gaan na Rome,* by Uys Krige, one of the outstanding poets of the 1930s, is a brilliant affirmation of the triumph of love over hate and destruction. Krige's translations of *Twelfth Night* (1967) and *King Lear* (1971) into Afrikaans also introduced Shakespeare into the Afrikaner stage. The endless struggle against time, old age, and death is the subject of Bartho Smith's *Christine* (1971), while Andre Brink's plays *Die verhoor* (1970) and *Die rebelle* (1970) are significant explorations of the theme of revolt against authority. Adam Small's *Kanna hy ko hystoe* (1965) uses poetic drama and powerful characterization to explore the violent and tragic world of the colored population in apartheid South Africa, making the play one of the most notable in Afrikaans. The subjects of race relations, guilt, the overwhelming power of evil, and its capacity to triumph over good are hauntingly explored in the works of Chris Barnard and P. G. du Pleissis.[10]

South African Literature in English

As with literary writings in Afrikaans and other African languages, literature in the English language is also closely associated with the imperial enterprise. Five categories of literary output in English can be identified: nonfiction, novels, short stories, poetry, and drama. Since the English, unlike the Dutch, were not established in South Africa until the time of the Napoleonic wars (1795–1815), much of the early writings in English or by English writers were in the form of travel tales, adventure stories, diaries, reports, and other nonfiction forms of writings. In 1814, Britain bought the Cape Colony from Holland for two million pounds. Thereafter, Britain took upon itself the task of consolidating and extending its gains while taming and civilizing the indigenous inhabitants as well as the Boer settlers, who were perceived as being no less wild, uncouth, and in need of civilization.

Travel Accounts

English visitors and travelers to the Cape saw it as part of their mission to contribute to the realization of these imperial objectives. All the writers, whether English, French, German, or Dutch, looked at Africans from the perspective of Europeans. They wrote on the landscape, the climate, the flora, and the fauna. They commented freely on the customs and practices of the people. Africans were presented as being part of the landscape, as homogenized groups, with little or no distinct identity; they were generalized together, labeled with stereotypes, and presented as typecasts ripe for and amenable to the colonizing and civilizing influence of the traveler's country and culture. The most memorable and shrewd account of Cape society can be found in *The Letters and Journal of Lady Anne Bernard* (1750–1825). Lady Anne's noble birth and good connections (she was an intimate friend of the Prince of Wales) secured her husband an appointment as colonial secretary to the Governor of the Cape colony. Since the Governor's wife did not accompany him to the Cape, Anne Bernard became the official first lady in Cape Town, a vantage point that gave her the opportunity to entertain many visitors while moving within the elite circles of power brokers at the Cape. Her many letters to her friends—most notably Henry Dundas, the secretary of war—revealed her passion, perspicacity, patronizing humanism, and her sympathy for the victims of European imperial domination. With vigor and candor, as well as with sentimental naivety and deep insight, she called for reforms of colonial policies that would treat the locals with humanity and fairness, and protect them from the rapacity of the Dutch.[11]

The Novel

Until the 1880s very few English novels were written in or about South Africa. The mineral revolution of the late nineteenth century and its accomplished industrialization and massive immigration from Europe and the Americas resulted in a renaissance of literary activity. Novels focused on rural and urban lives, customs and cultures of the African peoples, the impact of the mineral revolution and European imperialism on the indigenous population, and a multitude of other subjects were published from the 1880s onward. The first English novel to receive widespread acclaim was Olive Schreiner's *The Story of an African Farm* (1883). Set on a lonely Karoo farm, which gave it an exotic slant for its English readers, and written with pathos and authenticity, the book represents a startling protest against the oppression of women and against the hypocrisies of South African and other societies of the time. The young heroine of the book, Lyndall, a free spirit, spurns her mysterious lover, rejects marriage, and instead opts to have an illegitimate child. The author's views on feminism and marriage, her espousal of the freedom of women, and her defense of illegitimacy were clearly ahead of her time.[12]

Very little of lasting significance was produced before World War I. The advent of Sarah Gertrude Millin (1889–1968) marks a turning point in the writing of the English novel in South Africa. Under her the writers' commitment to addressing social issues through literary forms became a pivotal concern. The color question with the attendant concern over miscegenation received insightful and sensitive handling in a series of fascinating though at times tendentious novels (17 in all) that appeared between 1919 and 1965. The most notable of these was *God's Step-Children*. Published in 1924 as part of Millin's "Trilogy on the Coloured Race," it is the story of a white priest, the

Reverend Andrew Flood, who dissociates himself from his fellow whites to live with *kaffirs* and Hottentots, with unwholesome results for everyone. Though the story ends in desolation and rejection for Flood, the theme of whites seeking rapprochement with other groups is clearly prophetic of the future of South Africa. Other notable novels of protest and social concerns include Pauline Smith, *The Beadle* (1926), W. C. Scully, *The Harrow* (1921), and the first two novels in English by black South Africans, Dhlomo's *African Tragedy* (1929), and Solomon Plaatjie's *Mhudi* (1930).

The polygenesis of South African society has made the theme of racial interaction a popular subject of literary expressions. One of the first to take a stab at this sensitive issue was William Plomer in his *Turbott Wolfe* (1925); this daring and energetic exploration of a white-black love-lust triangle provoked shock and resentment among whites at the time. Racial themes were also at the center of Alan Paton's justly famous novel, *Cry the Beloved the Country* (1948). Written and published just before the formal institutionalization of apartheid, it documents the story of an individual black man, Reverend Stephen Khumalo, and of black men in general, suffering in the urbanized and white-dominated cities of South Africa. Somber and moving, elegant and episodic (like most pioneering South African novels), its daring critique of injustice, its call for love instead of hate, its message of comfort and hope in the midst of desolation, and of faith and trust instead of fear have combined to make it a classic of twentieth-century literature and the most widely read novel about South Africa.

Other novels informed by racial themes include Paton's *Too Late the Phalarope* (1953), *Ah, But Your Land Is Beautiful* (1981), Peter Abrahams, *Mine Boy* and *Tell Freedom* (1954), and works by Harry Bloom, Doris Lessing, Alex la Guma, Bessie Head, and others. Other writers who have profitably explored and creatively exploited racial themes are J. M. Coetzee, whose *The Life and Times of Michael K* won the Booker Prize in 1983, and Joseph Lelyveld, whose nonfiction account of South Africa in the turbulent years of black uprising (*Move Your Shadow: South Africa, Black and White*) won the Pulitzer Prize in 1986. Jeanne Goosen, whose award-winning novella, *Ons is Nie Almal So Nie* (1990), challenges the hegemonic dominance of the apparently monolithic racialism of Afrikaner volk culture, affirming, albeit implicitly and pathetically, the essential humanity of many white folks, by asserting that "not all of us are like that" (meaning racists). Nadine Gordimer, noted for her gift of short story writing, has established a solid reputation for herself through a series of impressive, brilliantly evocative, artistically delicate, intricately structured, authentic novels. Like J. M. Coetzee, Alan Paton, Andre Brink, Rian Malan, and other white South African writers who attempted to live up to their commitment to justice, racial equality, engagement with blacks, and support for liberal, communist, or Africanist reforms and transformation, Gordimer imbues her novels and short stories with the tension, the uncertain idealism, and the agonizing sense of the unscalable limitations of cultural and racial givens of her historical context. Awarded the Nobel Prize for Literature in 1991, Gordimer's career evokes the unresolved conflicts and contradictions of white writers as members of a privileged elite struggling to gain acceptance as representatives and spokespersons of the oppressed and victimized people of South Africa.[13]

Short Stories

Unlike the novel, the short story genre developed early and quickly in South Africa. In form and structure, the short story is more closely related to oral tradition. Like oral tradition, the storytellers are often characters in the stories, using the medium of the story to reveal much about themselves and the world in which they live. The short story also appears to be more amenable to the unsettled life, general illiteracy, and relative primitiveness characteristic of the white pioneers' frontier experience in South Africa. For black South African writers and others living under the stifling shadow of apartheid oppression, the short story genre comes in handy. As one observer noted, such writers did not have the luxury and the ease to organize their lives into writing novels, and are compelled to use the short story as a short cut to prose and as a means of offloading some burdens from one's chest in the quickest possible time.[14] More pointedly, and as Njabulo Ndebele aptly puts it, "it is the literature of the powerless," released in cascades of thoughts and which can only provide no more than vignettes of experiences, spectacular flashes, perfunctory details, provocative indictments, and tantalizing glimpses of their disempowerment.[15]

Experiences on the veld provided the material for most of the stories in collections by James Fitzpatrick, *The Outspan* (1897), W. C. Scully, *Kafir Stories* (1895), and Ernest Glanville, who published such collections of animal adventure stories as *Claw and Fang* (1923) and *The Yellow-Maned Lion,* published in 1925. That same year, Pauline Smith's collection, *The Little Karoo,* was published. The stories reveal her "strange, austere, tender, and ruthless talent," to quote the perceptive words of Arnold Bennet, who wrote the introduction to the book. The introductory story, "The Pain," is a poignant and picturesque portrayal of the rural Afrikaner. The story presents such a person as an isolated, poor, jaundiced illiterate with an uncanny passion for independence, an unbridled love for tradition, attachment to the land, and an etiolated sense of biblical destiny. With all their underlying tension and tragedies, the stories established for Smith a worldwide reputation. In the hands of Herman Charles Bosman, whose seminal collection, *Mafeking Road,* made its debut in 1947, the short story became the means for a major onslaught against all forms of bigotry plaguing South African society. A man of considerable talent and intense pathos, Bosman brought new freshness to the South African literary scene, though many of his short stories were not published in his lifetime. Doris Lessing, whose career parallels Gordimer's in many ways, published *This Was the Old Chief's Country* (1951) which contains "A Sunrise on the Veld," a story written with such delicacy, evocativeness, and sensitivity that it has become a classic of South African short fiction. Nadine Gordimer, probably the most prolific and most renowned contemporary short story writer from South Africa, has published several volumes of short stories focused on a wide range of subjects, from women and sexuality to political tensions and animal stories. Ahmed Essop's *The Hajj and Other Stories* (1978), focuses on the tensions and crises of life in the Fordsburg Indian community and is written with an incisive humor that brings an Indian perspective to short story writing in South Africa.

Poetry

The first South African writer in English to establish himself as a leading poet was Thomas Pringle (1789–1834). Born in Scotland, crippled by a childhood accident, and forced to depart from South Africa in unsavory circumstances, Pringles's poems offered an informed though at times indifferent perspective on fundamental and recurring concerns of the fractured South African society, such as exile, alienation, miscegenation, oppression, and resistance. His most famous poem, "Afar in the Desert," reveals his attraction to the South African environment with all its fascination, virginity, and exoticism. The poem also shows his troubled sensibility, divided mind, passionate longing, alienating experience, and his struggle to identify himself with the new country of South Africa.[16]

The early twentieth century was dominated by the poems of Carey Slater, whose *Footpaths Thro' the Veld, and Other Songs and Idylls of South Africa* (1905) evokes and celebrates the adventurous and picturesque in South African life. The 1940s and 1950s were dominated by a new generation of poets whose unusual consciousness of the tension and paradoxes of the dynamism and divisions of South African society found expressions in often satirical poems that evoke the beauty of the continent and the unrelenting resilience of its peoples. Two notable voices from this era are William Plomer (1903–73), and Roy Campbell (1901–57). Plomer's classic poem "The Scorpion" reveals his brilliance and evocative power. Campbell, with his posturing gait and restless energy, was an early prodigy, publishing his most spectacular long poem, *The Flaming Terrapin* (1924), at the age of 24. His most anthologized poem "The Zulu Girl," published when he was 30, reveals the range and maturing of his talents.

One of the most notable black South African poets who wrote in English was H. I. E. Dhlomo. His long poem, *Valley of a Thousand Hills* (1941), gained him a wide reputation. Oswald Mtshali's anthology, *Sounds of a Cowhide Drum* (1971), brought together a large number of highly engaged poems by black writers such as Dennis Brutus, Mongone Serote, Sidney Sempamla, and Arthur Nortje. Also of significance is the anthology, *Voices from Within: Black Poetry from Southern Africa* (1982), introduced and edited by Michael Chapman and Achmat Dangor. Comprehensive and representative, it includes a wide range of selections from the mythical resonance of San's "Prayer to the Hunting Star," to the dignified and reflective poems of the pre-Sharpville era (1890–1960), the protest poems of the post-Sharpville years (1960–76), and the angry and defiant poems of the post-Soweto (1976) turbulent years. Roughly covering the period of the past one hundred years, the poems reveal successive stages of transformation and change in the methods, techniques, and subjects of black South African poetry. The extraordinary vitality, the specific relevance, and universal significance of black poetry are explored. Many of the poems creatively employ the literary devices of repetition, parallelism, and hyperbolic imagery common to traditional African oral poetry.

In the early colonial era, black poetry was dominated by mission-educated intelligentsia, many of who, like A. K. Soga, had to struggle to free themselves from the debilitating idiom and influences imposed by the missions. By the early 1930s Christian optimism had given way in the poems to confrontation with the challenges created by the sociopolitical dilemma of modern South Africa. Deprived through Bantu Education of exposure to Afro-English literary traditions, the generations of African writers growing up in South Africa from the 1950s onward eschewed imported models and techniques, opting instead for open or naked forms. Concerned with the stark realities of survival, the group of Soweto poets that includes Casey Motsisi, Njabulo Ndebele, Oswald Mtshali, Mongone Wally Serote, and Mafika Gwala adopted a literary sensibility attuned to the expression of protest and the raising of the political consciousness of their oppressed African people. Mtshali's *Sounds of a Cowhide Drum* (1971) marked a shift from mere concerns with lyrical themes to struggle poetry. With the disturbances of Soweto, the emphasis on black consciousness and race-pride gave the post-Soweto poems—such as those in Mtshali's banned collection, *Firflames* (1980)—a hard, apocalyptic tone that focuses on the horrors of the present and the certainty of a revolutionary future for South Africa.

The Playhouse Theater, with its mock Tudor façade, is Durban's major art center for the performances of ballet, opera, and drama.

Drama

The development of drama in English came later than the other genres. The first noticeable play was Stephen Black's *Love and the Hyphen* (1909). For the next few decades the drama competed with the cinema for the South African stage. The stimulus provided by World War II through official sponsorship led to the production of plays such as Madelene Masson's *Passport to Limbo* and *Home Is the Hero.* Lewis Sowden's *Kimberley Train,* first produced in 1958, also received some attention. The establishment of the National Theatre Organization led to a ferment of dramatic productions with the emergence of new playwrights such as Guy Butler, H. I. E. Dhlomo, Geraldine Aron, Fatima Dike, and Percy Mtwa. From the 1960s onward, however, the South African stage was dominated by the plays of Athol Fugard, who is widely regarded as the greatest playwright to come from South Africa. His many plays reveal his engaging sensitivity, social commitment, and penetrating insight into the tension and complexity of race relations in apartheid South Africa. Unlike many contemporary South African writers, Fugard is widely respected at home by all the races, while his works have been well-received abroad. Through the use of subtle imagery and stimulating metaphors, Fugard has perfected the fine art of successfully though danger-ously navigating the murky waters and fine lines of South African censorship. Among his notable plays are: *No-Good Friday, The Blood Knot, Boesman and Lena, Sizwe Banzi is Dead, Master Harold and the Boys,* and *My Africa! My Children!.* The 1970s also witnessed the emergence of protest drama by black South Africans as part of the thriving cultural life of the black townships. The plays in this category include Zakes Mda's *The Hill* as well as plays by Dan Maredi, Maishe Maponya, and Matsemala Manaka.

Apart from furnishing South African literature with its most popular sub-ject, the practice of apartheid stimulated ethnicity and resulted in the isola-tion of South African society and the emergence of pigmented literary traditions structured along the racial divides of the society. Perhaps with the end of apartheid—and an accompanying newfound interest in its entangled history of interconnected and shared experiences in peace and at war, as ene-mies and friends—a new self-awareness will begin to develop among South African writers and readers of their common and unique identity as South Africans rather than just as blacks or Afrikaners, thus setting the stage for the emergence of a South African national literature. Perhaps, too, this will be a literature that, while recognizing and celebrating the diverse cultural and his-torical experiences of its many peoples and groups, will become an instru-ment of nation building and national integration in the cultural and political mosaic that is the new South Africa.

NOTES

1. For the full version of the poem, see Michael Chapman, *Southern African Lit-eratures* (London and New York: Longman, 1996), 25.

2. For the full version of the poem, see Chapman and Achmat Dangor, eds., *Voices from Within: Black Poetry from Southern Africa* (Johannesburg: A. D. Donker, 1982), 21.

3. On the mantis mythology and other folktales among the San, see the many col-lections by Laurens van der Post, most especially, *A Mantis Carol* (New York: Mor-row, 1976); *A Story Like the Wind* (New York: Morrow, 1972); *The Heart of the Hunter* (New York: Morrow, 1961); *The Night of the New Moon* (London: Hogarth Press, 1970); and A. C. Jordan, *Tales from Southern Africa* (Berkeley: University of California Press, 1973).

4. Chapman, *Southern African Literatures,* 31.

5. For a fuller discussion of these stories see C. Jordan, *Towards an African Liter-ature: The Emergence of Literary Form in Xhosa* (Berkeley and Los Angeles: University of California Press, 1973), 4–15; and Jordan, *Tales from Southern Africa.*

6. Jordan, *Towards an African Literature,* 18.

7. The most popular of these poems is the epic recorded by Maziri Kunene, *Emperor Shaka the Great* (London: Heinemann, 1979).

8. For a fuller discussion of the emergence of indigenous written literature and the major sources for the discussion in this section, see Jordan, *Towards an African Literature,* 37–83; *South Africa 1989–90: The Official Yearbook of the Republic of South Africa* (Pretoria: Bureau for Information, Department of Foreign Affairs, 1989/90), 625–35; and Chapman, *Southern African Literatures,* 39–67, 202–59.

9. See Ingrid Jonker, *Selected Poems,* translated from the Afrikaans by Jack Cope and William Plomer (London: Cape, 1986); Breyten Breytenbach, *Return to Paradise* (London: Faber & Faber; Cape Town: David Philip, 1993).

10. On Afrikaner literature and the major sources for this section, see *South Africa 1989–90: The Official Yearbook of the Republic of South Africa,* 613–21; and Chapman, *Southern African Literatures,* 75–128.

11. A. M. Lewin Robinson, ed., *The Letters of Lady Anne Bernard to Henry Dundas from the Cape and Elsewhere, 1793–1803; Together with Her Journal of a Tour into the Interior and Certain Other Letters* (Cape Town: Balkema, 1973). See also Chapman, *Southern African Literatures,* 80–86.

12. On Olive Schreiner, see C. Clayton, ed., *Olive Schreiner* (New York: Twayne; London: Prentice Hall International, c. 1997); and Chapman, *Southern African Literature,* 133–44.

13. On Nadine Gordimer, see Stephen Clingman, "Writing in a Fractured Society: The Case of Nadine Gordimer," in Tim Couzens and Landeg White, eds., *Literature and Society in South Africa* (Burnt Hill, Harrow: Longman Group Limited, 1984), 161–74; and Clingman, *The Novels of Nadine Gordimer: History from the Inside* (Amherst: University of Massachusetts Press, [1992], c. 1986). On Coetzee, see T. Dovey, *The Novels of J. M. Coetzee: Lacanian Allegories* (Craighall: A. D. Donker, 1988); David Attwell, *J. M. Coetzee: South Africa and the Politics of Writing* (Berkeley: University of California Press; Cape Town: David Philip, 1993); and D. Penner, *Countries of the Mind: The Fiction of J. M. Coetzee* (New York: Greenwood Press, 1989).

14. Es'kia Mphahlele, "Black and White," *The New Statesman* (10 September 1960), 343.

15. Njabulo S. Ndebele, "The Rediscovery of the Ordinary: Some New Writings in South Africa," in *Rediscovery of the Ordinary: Essays on South African Literature and Culture* (Johannesburg: Congress of South African Writers, 1991), 46. See also Denis Hirson and Martin Trump, *The Heinemann Book of South African Short Stories from 1945 to the Present* (Oxford: Heinemann Educational/UNESCO Publishing, 1994), 1–9.

16. For this and other poems of Pringle, see: Leitch Ritchie, ed., *The Poetical Works of Thomas Pringle, with a Sketch of His Life* (London: E. Moxon, 1839); and E. Pereira and Chapman, eds., *African Poems of Thomas Pringle* (Pietermaritzburg: University of Natal Press, 1989).

5

The Media

Any attempt to understand social and political developments in South Africa in the last one hundred or more years must take the role of the media into serious consideration. The government's near complete control of radio and other forms of electronic media left the press as the only viable medium of opposition to the government. This vital and crucial role of the press ensured not only its popularity, but also brought upon it the ire of the apartheid government until the transition to a nonracial democratic order in 1994. The zeal and the effectiveness with which the nationalist party government monitored, censured, and banned newspapers and intimidated, harassed, deported, and jailed journalists while maintaining a stranglehold on all electronic media should leave no one in doubt about the government's full understanding of the significance of the press in South Africa.

NEWSPAPERS AND PERIODICALS

To fully appreciate the contemporary role of the media in South Africa, we must take account of its history. Unlike in other parts of Africa and probably in many parts of the colonial world where the press arose out of a struggle for freedom and independence from colonial domination, the press in South Africa did not develop as part of an attempt to challenge, subvert, and replace the colonial order; rather, the press developed, in most cases and for many years, as an auxiliary of the imperial state to promote and speak for the expanding commercial and financial interests of white proprietors. When the British seized the Cape in 1795, they also brought with them the first major printing press, which was used for the next 24 years to produce two official publications: the weekly *Cape Town Gazette* and *African Advertiser.* In 1824, the notable Cape printer, George Greig, mobilized and secured the interests and support of two recent arrivals at the Cape, Thomas Pringle and James Fairbairn, and of clergyman Abraham Faurie to start the bilingual *South African Commercial Advertiser.* In its prospectus, the newspaper committed itself to a nonpolitical, noncritical, and noncontroversial reporting and coverage of issues. Its primary focus would be trade and commerce, with some attention given to advertisement and the publication of literary materials.

In spite of official hostility to and apprehension at the prospect of a watchdog newspaper, the first issue of the paper appeared on January 7, 1824. After 18 issues, the paper ceased publication. It had run into trouble through its widespread publicizing of a libel action brought by the governor of the Cape, Lord Charles Somerset, against those who had accused him of corrupt practices. Greig was ordered to leave South Africa within one month. He did, but while in England he made such a strong representation to the Colonial Secretary that he was permitted to return and restart his publication. Three years later, the paper was again banned by the order of the governor for publishing an article critical of local officials. After more appeals to London, this time by Fairbairn, the paper reopened one and a half years later in October 1828. That same year the Press Ordinance of 1828, which guaranteed freedom of the press for the country and within the limits of the law, was promulgated.

The 1828 Ordinance gave anyone with the necessary money, equipment, and expertise the right to start and run a newspaper. Many responded to the opportunity. Several newspapers sprang up in the major cities and regions of South Africa. At the Cape, the early publications included *The SA Journal,* owned by Pringle and Fairbairn; and *The SA Chronicle and Mercantile Advertiser,* edited by A. Jadine. In 1830, the *De Zuid Afrikaan* was started as a Dutch language newspaper to counter the dominant influence of the *South African Commercial Advertiser.* P. A. Brand, a Dutchman of a slave-owning family, was particularly resentful of Fairbairn's liberalist and missionary commitment to the abolition of slavery and his undisguised hostility toward the Boers in his newspaper. The Afrikaner cause received a further boost in 1849 with the establishment of *Het Volksblad* by J. H. Hofmeyr, a prominent Cape Dutch community leader with a commitment to promoting the maintenance of separate racial identities as well as harmonious relations between the two white groups in South Africa.

In 1854, the Cape became self-governing and English became the sole language of its parliament. In consequence, the Dutch-speaking Boers, though constituting an overwhelming majority in the population, remained underrepresented in the legislature. During the 1870s both the *De Zuid Afrikaan* and Hofmeyr's *Volksvriend* merged to provide a more effective voice for the

Boer community and for the claims of the Dutch language. At approximately the same time the Society of True Afrikaners was established with a sworn determination "to stand for our language, our nation and our people."[1] In 1876, the Society established its newspaper, *Di Patriot,* edited by Rev. S. J. Du Toit, to promote its cause of developing and perpetuating Afrikaans, the Cape version of the Dutch language, as the instrument for creating the Afrikaner nation.

From the Cape, newspapers spread to other parts of the country, first with the establishment of *De Natalier* in Natal in 1844. Its opposition to the government in this English dominated colony did not gain it many friends and it closed shop within two years. Its place was taken in 1846 by *The Natal Witness,* which started as a bilingual paper but soon discarded its Dutch pretensions, becoming an English-only paper. *The Natal Witness* survived against all odds and all governments, eventually gaining for itself the reputation of being the oldest South African newspaper in continuous existence. The Natal English community secured another ally in 1854 with the establishment of the *Natal Mercury and Commercial Shipping Gazette,* by G. Robinson, whose son, Sir John Robinson, later became the editor of the paper as well as the first prime minister of the Natal colony. In the Orange River colony, the only newspaper of note for many years was *The Friend of the Sovereignty and Bloemfontein Gazette,* established as a bilingual weekly in 1850. With the independence of the Free State in 1854, it changed its name to *The Friend of the Free State.* In 1894, it began publishing in English only, while reaffirming its commitment to fighting for the interests of everyone without regard to race or color.

In the Transvaal, the first newspaper, *De Oude Emmigrant,* started 20 years after the Great Trek, was short lived. In 1874, Transvaal's first major newspaper appeared with the publication in Pretoria of *Die Volkstem.* It remained a Dutch language newspaper until 1922, when it began to appear in English. In 1951, three years after the formal institutionalization of apartheid, the paper closed, thus sharing the fate that befell all other Afrikaans dailies that failed to support the policies of the National Party. In Johannesburg, the first newspaper, *Diggers' News,* appeared in 1886. A year later, *The Eastern Star,* a Grahamstown paper, was relocated to the Rand, where it would live up to the expectation of its name by becoming the star of South African media, and what is today the biggest daily newspaper in the country, *The Star.* The establishment of *Cape Argus* in 1857 by the Oxford-educated MP Bryan Henry Darnell inaugurated the birth of South Africa's greatest newspaper empire. Under the ownership and control of the notable Cape government printer and MP Saul Solomon, the paper pursued a pro-African and anti-British editorial policy. Financial difficulties forced Solomon to sell his shares in the company to Francis Joseph Dormer, who he had appointed editor in 1877 and who had the financial backing of Cecil Rhodes to wrest ownership of the paper from Solomon. Thereafter, the paper jettisoned its pro-African stance and became intensely pro-British.

The establishment in 1876 of the *Cape Times,* South Africa's first daily newspaper sold at the cheap price of a penny, also began to whittle away from the popularity of *Cape Argus's.* Other nineteenth-century newspapers that managed to survive until the end of the twentieth century include *Daily News* (1854), *Daily Dispatch* (1872), and the *Diamond Fields Advertiser* (1878). Among the notable early twentieth-century newspapers was *Die Burger* (Cape Town, 1915), edited by D. F. Malan, who later became prime minister and the chief architect of apartheid. *Die Burger* remains today the oldest surviving Dutch-Afrikaans daily in the country. Another important Afrikaner paper was *Die Transvaler* (Johannesburg, 1937), under the first editorship of Dr. H. F. Verwoerd, who also became South Africa's prime minister and a leading ideologue of apartheid. Confronted with the realities of life on the frontiers, pioneer owner-editors, like Robert Godlonton of the *Grahamstown Journal,* responded by establishing a series of serviceable newspapers, the content, creativity, quality, and versatility of which formed the foundation of South Africa's indigenous press. The establishment in 1866 of the Argus Printing and Publishing Company brought to an end the era of independent editor-owners and ushered in the era of managerial newspapers.

South Africa is today the most media-saturated country in Africa, with over 5,000 locally registered newspapers, periodicals, and journals. And, in the wake of the free and open atmosphere created by the demise of apartheid and the ushering in of multiparty nonracial democracy, scores of new publications are registered every year. The newspapers and periodicals are organized into press groups, of which the major ones are the Argus Printing and Publishing Company and Times Media LTD, and the Afrikaans-language chains, Nasionale Media and Perskor. Between them, these four chains account for 95 percent of daily newspaper readers and 92 percent of Sunday weekly readers. In 1991, the English chain controlled 14 dailies and approximately 80 percent of an estimated 1.3 million readers (in terms of circulation), compared to the five dailies under the aegis of the Afrikaans-language chains.

The association of the Afrikaans language with apartheid did not attract many African readers to Afrikaans newspapers. The English newspapers did not suffer from such negative connotations. Instead their opposition to the apartheid government gained them an audience among the emerging African elite. In 1991, for instance, the *Sowetan,* a newspaper published by the Argus group and directed specifically to urban and middle-class Africans, displaced

The Star, also published by Argus, as the largest daily when it sold an unprecedented daily average of 219,415 newspapers, clearly signaling to all that the
future of the South African press rested in the hands of black readers. Only
those able to position themselves to meet the needs of the emerging African
readership market can survive in the new South Africa.

There are also more colored readers of English-language papers than of
Afrikaans ones. The Zulu-language weekly, *Ilanga,* published in Durban, was
the only independent newspaper to reach the 100,000 circulation mark with
a 1991 circulation figure of 120,676. There are over a hundred provincial
newspapers that are mostly bilingual, serving particular towns or regions,
focusing mainly on local affairs and local advertising.

Over the years and in cognizance of the power of the press in the dissemination of information and in the molding of public opinion, successive South
African governments have taken measures to bring the press under control. A
series of laws attempted to curtail the latitude of the press. The Defense Act
of 1957 forbade the publication of information considered prejudicial to the
security of the country. The Prison Act of 1959 made the publication of certain information relating to prisons and prisoners illegal. A Police Amendment Act of 1978 protected certain actions of the police from publication.
The most sweeping was the Publications Act of 1974 which prohibited the
publication of anything considered obscene, lascivious, blasphemous, or
derogatory toward any section of the community, a violation of privacy, or of
anything that had the potential to harm race relations and state security or
disturb law and order. A Media Council was set up in 1984 to adjudicate
complaints against the press. In 1992, it received 89 cases. Finally, the June
1986 emergency decree imposed the most severe restrictions to date on the
media by criminalizing the publication by local and foreign media of anything that could be interpreted as subversive or inciting. Journalists were specifically forbidden from reporting, recording, and photographing unrest
situations and security measures taken to check such situations. Ten years
after the 1976 Soweto uprising, South Africa was going through the most turbulent period of its history. Apartheid was in its death throes. And the
defenders of apartheid, under pressures from home and abroad, were becoming extremely desperate. For the South African press, these were the darkest
days.

After the 1948 victory of the Afrikaner-dominated National Party, the
English-language papers became in essence the opposition press, forcefully,
effectively, and consistently opposing objectionable policies and actions of
the government throughout the apartheid era. With the National Party in
majority control of parliament, and with the voice of the English speakers in
parliament muted and ineffectual, the English-language media became the

official opposition in South Africa, hated by the government and continually persecuted. The Afrikaans papers reflected the views of the Afrikaans-speaking community, uniformly and almost without exception supporting the National Party government. Until the late 1970s, the leading Afrikaner newspapers had notable Afrikaner politicians and cabinet ministers on their boards of directors, giving the papers the reputation of being regarded as kept presses. The few Afrikaner papers like the *Die Volkstem* that attempted to maintain a neutral stance or to oppose the National Party position died for lack of Afrikaner readership and patronage.

The history and politics of the South African newspapers have been dominated by the love-hate relationship between the apartheid government and the English-language press on the one hand and the rivalries between the antiapartheid English press and the proapartheid Afrikaans-language press on the other hand. This state of tension was further exacerbated during the 1970s and 1980s when the African struggle for liberation radically, violently, and relentlessly confronted the apartheid regime's remorseless, authoritarian, bloody repression of opposition. Even some of the leading Afrikaner presses could not escape infection by the liberation ferment in the air, becoming politically more adventurous and more assertive in their criticisms of the government. Increasingly and pathologically intolerant of opposition from whatever source, the apartheid government clamped down on offending presses and journalists. In May 1981, Allister Sparks, editor of the *Rand Daily Mail,* was summarily dismissed from his post. Sparks had offended white corporate interests and readership by the stridency of his press and by his sustained efforts to woo black readers, who at that time accounted for the majority of the paper's readership. Imperiled by financial difficulties, the *RDM* went under in April 1985. A similar fate befell Mr. Harald Pakendorf, editor of *Die Vaderland,* whose views were considered too liberal for the government and the newspaper board. In the same vein, Dr. Wimpie de Klerk, editor of the only Afrikaans Sunday paper, *Rapport,* was compelled to resign in March 1987. For the government, however, the most intractable challenge came from the relatively new press group dubbed the alternative press.[2]

THE ALTERNATIVE PRESS

The alternative press refers to those groups of newspapers, journals, and periodicals that were in the forefront of the struggle for equality and liberation in South Africa from 1960 onward. They are alternative, first, because they do not belong to what is generally termed the mainstream or establishment press, made up of the major press organizations usually affiliated with the Newspaper Press Union. Second, the fact that the alternative press received virtually no financial and logistic support from the South African state and from corporate sectors in South Africa caused them to be perceived as a separate media group in the country. Third, the emergence of the alternative press represented a new approach toward the covering of social and political news, an approach unusually critical and uncompromisingly outspoken about the apartheid state, as well as social, economic, and political conditions in South Africa. More than any other press group, the alternative brought what could be termed an African or a black perspective to the covering of news in white-dominated South Africa. By so doing it made visible inequities that were otherwise invisible and provided a medium of expression to alienated groups and individuals. Through their pens and courageous reporting, issues that the apartheid state preferred to suppress or simply forget were transformed into issues of national and international significance. By broadening the scope and parameter of public discourse and press freedom, they contributed to the revival of national consciousness that eventually ensured the demise of apartheid and the apartheid state. It is for this contribution that the alternative press is also referred to as the resistance press.

Three phases can be identified in the development of the alternative press in South Africa. The first phase began during the 1940s and continued until the mid-1970s, though its roots date back to the nineteenth century. Beginning with the establishment in 1884 of *Imvo Zabantsundu* in King William's Town by John Tengo Jabavu, a number of black presses struggled to find a niche for themselves in the troubled waters of colonial South Africa. By the 1940s, through a series of buyouts, amalgamations, and close-downs, nearly all the pro-African newspapers had disappeared. The few that managed to survive, such as *Inyaniso* (subtitled *Voice of African Youth*), *Isizwe* (*Nation*), *Africanist,* and *African Lodestar,* ministered to only a few urban activists and were generally ineffective in affecting the course of national affairs. During the 1940s and 1950s the resistance movement found an outlet in a number of nonracial and nonsectarian socialist newspapers such as *Fighting Talk* (1942–1963) and *Liberation* (1953–1959). In the face of relentless harassment and police brutality, these papers provided sustained coverage of opposition politics until the last of these publications was silenced by the apartheid state when it shut down *Spark* in 1963.

The second phase was associated with the development of the Black Consciousness Movement (BCM) during the 1970s. Through its newsletter and other irregular publications such as *Black Review, Black Viewpoint, World,* and *Weekend World* and its effective articulation of a counterhegemonic discourse emphasizing black racial pride, the BCM succeeded in raising political awareness among blacks from different walks of life. The final phase in the history of the alternative press covers the 1980s and the early 1990s. Within South

Africa, the United Democratic Front (UDF) and its affiliate organizations dominated resistance against apartheid during this final phase. To mobilize public support for its liberationist agenda the UDF courted and utilized the press, in particular the alternative press. Paradoxically, of the dozen or more resistance presses that sprouted into life and thrived vibrantly during the final years of the struggle that finally saw the demise of apartheid and the apartheid state in South Africa, only two survived into the twenty-first century. In order to survive, one of these two, the *Weekly Mail*, became foreign-owned, transforming itself into the *Mail and Guardian*. The other, the *East Cape News*, became part of a commercial venture.

The eclipse of the resistance press should not lead us to underestimate the significance of their contributions. By deepening political consciousness, manufacturing dissent, inspiring generations of activists, countering the static dominance of the established media and the state propaganda machine, and virulently questioning and militantly challenging the culture and climate of apartheid, the resistance press made major and lasting contributions to the South African miracle. Established for the specific purpose of dismantling apartheid and the apartheid state, the alternative press was rendered redundant by the demise of the two evils. Like most effective resistance journalism, the alternative press became the victim of its own success. As a rebel with a cause, having finally achieved its principal goal, there was little left than to pack up and go home.[3]

RADIO AND TELEVISION

Radio

On December 18, 1923, South Africa made its first radio broadcast under the auspices of the South African Railways. The postwar interest in radio and the growing popularity of the use of two-way-radio-telephone equipment encouraged the South African government to invite applications from enterprising groups to acquire licenses for wireless broadcast. Of the many applications it received, the government selected three groups, mostly government corporations considered reliable enough not to jeopardize national security through their radio broadcast. All individual applications were turned down. In the Witwatersrand, the Johannesburg Municipality was sidelined probably because of sympathy that some of its councilors had shown to the white miners' strikes of 1922. Instead, the Association of Scientific and Technical Societies (AS & TS), a club made of top managers from the mining and industrial establishments, won the license. In Cape Town the license went to the pro-government Cape Peninsular Publicity Association, after the Cape Town municipal government had turned down the offer. The third license went to the Durban Corporation. All three stations started broadcasting in 1924.

Enforcing the payment of listeners' license fees was a continuing challenge. Unlike the two-way-radio-telephone apparatus, the owners of the wireless receiver apparatus could not be easily identified and tracked down. Idealistic appeals to receivers to pay up their license dues yielded precious few results. Unable to accumulate capital and with limited advertisement revenue, the three stations began to accumulate losses. By the end of 1926, the Johannesburg station ceased broadcasting. In spite of pressures by the Post Master General, the government refused to take over the stations, uncertain yet of radio's economic viability and political usefulness. Instead the government sought the help of I. W. Schlesinger, a highly successful American entrepreneur who had already made his mark in the fields of South African insurance, theatre, and film. On April 1, 1927, the Schlesinger Corporation incorporated the three fledgling stations as the African Broadcasting Company. But even then, Schlesinger's efforts to apply the principles of mass production and distribution, prospering in the Americas, could not flourish in the South African social and economic climate with very limited interest in public broadcasting. Unable to break even, Schlesinger turned to the government for succor. Finally, in 1936, following the recommendation of a commission of inquiry, the government established the South African Broadcasting Corporation (SABC) in order to take over, develop, and manage all broadcasting and related services. On August 1, 1936, the SABC made its first unified national radio broadcast in English. In October 1937, it made its first national radio broadcast in Afrikaans. The period of 1948 to 1971 witnessed rapid expansion and major transformation in the SABC, with the introduction of commercial channels and the VHF/FM system, and the establishment of a national network linking all the transmitters around the country.

The SABC monopoly over radio broadcast remained unchallenged until the end of the apartheid state in 1994. By then the SABC was broadcasting 24-hour radio programming in 20 languages and four television services in seven languages. Six of the radio services are national. At the top of these are the English Radio South Africa and the Afrikaans Radio Suid-Afrika, neither of which carried commercials until 1985. Another is Radio Orion, an all-night service network that broadcasts daily from dusk to dawn. Closely related is Radio Allegro, a late-night service that broadcasts classical music. Radio Metro provides 24-hour service to blacks in the urban areas; while Radio 5 broadcasts youth-oriented programs on FM, as well as on medium and shortwave bands to different parts of the country. Among the leading commercial networks are Radio 2000 and Radio 702. Several community radio stations provide dawn-to-dusk broadcasting in different parts of the country. Most notable among these are: highveld Stereo, broadcasting from Johannesburg; Radio Good Hope from Cape Town; Radio Jacaranda from Pretoria; Radio Oranje from Bloemfontein; Radio Port Natal from Durban; Radio Algoa from Port Elizabeth; and Radio Lotus, which services the commercial interests of Indian listeners in Natal and the Transvaal. Black listeners are serviced through nine regional commercial radio stations, broadcasting specifically in Sesotho, Zulu, Xhosa, Lebowa, Setswana, Tsonga, Swazi, Ndebele, and Venda. Between 1995 and 2001, 80 community radio station licenses were granted, 36 of which had commenced broadcasting by 2001.

Radio RSA, the Voice of South Africa, established in 1966, broadcasts short wave external services from Johannesburg to different parts of the world in 12 languages, namely English, French, Portuguese, German, Dutch/Afrikaans, Spanish, Danish, Swahili, Chichewa, Lozi, and Tsonga. On the air for 216 hours a week, radio RSA offers lessons in the Afrikaans language to listeners in English, Dutch, French, and German. With over 100,000 letters a year from listeners, it is considered one of the most highly successful arms of the SABC and a veritable instrument for the dissemination of news (and propaganda during the apartheid era) about South Africa to an international audience. Catering to well over 13 million listeners daily and transmitting on more than 600 FM medium and short wave bands locally and internationally, the SABC was a major player in the struggle for liberation during the closing decades of apartheid rule. For a long time, owned and controlled by the government, it serviced, at times reluctantly but certainly, the interests of the apartheid state. With the demise of the latter, the SABC, like other institutions of the apartheid state determined to survive, has creatively repositioned itself as a veritable instrument for the building, extension, and consolidation of the gains of the South African democratic transformations.

Television

Television was a latecomer to the South African scene. Initially the South African government was reluctant to allow the introduction of television to the country. It was worried about the potential dramatic effects on white viewers of images beamed by the television regarding the conditions of the black population and instances of repressive violence by the state security units. After stoutly refusing for years to allow the introduction of television, the government finally responded positively to the recommendations of a commission chaired by Dr. P. J. Meyer, erstwhile chair of the *broederbond* and chair of the SABC Board of Control, by introducing the first one-channel television service on January 5, 1976. The station transmitted for 37 hours a week divided equally between English and Afrikaans services. Today SABC Television broadcasts in 11 languages over three channels. Channel One or TV1 transmits in English and Afrikaans; Channel Two (CCV-TV2) broadcasts in English, Northern and Southern Sotho, Tswana, Xhosa, and Zulu. And Channel Three (NNTV3) transmits documentaries, educational programs, and sports. SABC-TV transmits its programs over more than 200 stations scattered across the country. The government has been more successful than it was with radio listeners in collecting licensing fees from its more than 2.5 million licensed television viewers within South Africa. During peak hours, TV1 attracts more than 5 million viewers; TV2 is viewed by more than 3 million, and TV3 often records more than 2 million tuning in. The combination of these blocks of viewers makes South Africa one of the largest television audiences in Africa.

Introduced in 1978, commercials today account for roughly 10 percent of broadcasting time; this is bound to increase as South Africa becomes more and more engaged in the global world and as the level of literacy and the number of viewers continues to increase, particularly among the black population. Roughly half of all programs broadcast are produced in South Africa and focus on South Africa. The remaining programs are purchased from abroad or coproduced with other television programming organizations such as the BBC and some of the major American television networks. Visitors to South Africa are often surprised about the extent of the Western flavor of South African television programs. Many popular Western daytime and nighttime soap-operas and sitcoms have become common and regular features on the South African television networks. The most preferred are usually the American shows. These are a mix of sitcoms and dramas, such as *All in the Family, Maude, Magnum P.I., Starsky and Hutch, Today's FBI, Dallas,* and *The Mary Tyler Moore Show.* More recent additions include *Days of Our Lives, The Bold and the Beautiful,* and *The Young and the Restless,* among others. Oprah Winfrey's self-titled talk show is also popular.

The advent of the television and the radio had a devastating impact on the print media, which had to struggle to keep itself profitable, or at least afloat. The advent of television advertising from 1978 began to cut into the previously impregnable newspaper advertisement stronghold. The capacity of the television to convey directly to its viewers vivid and often instant visual images and to engage the viewers directly with immediate sensational drama began to woo away subscribers, who found television news more credible and more effective. To rescue themselves from the damaging assault of the electronic media and to recoup the losses due to dwindling advertising, the six major South African newspaper publishing groups came together and applied for a license to start their own television network. The government granted the license grudgingly, worried about the implications of granting the power of television broadcasting to independent groups not directly controlled or financed by the government. In October 1986, M-Net was launched as a subscription television service.[4]

THE MEDIA IN APARTHEID AND POSTAPARTHEID SOUTH AFRICA

Perennially conscious of the need not to bite the hand that feeds it, the SABC—at least until 1994—strove not to violate the trust or provoke the ire of the South African apartheid state. During the heyday of apartheid, it saw itself and was perceived by the government and the opposition as the mouthpiece of the apartheid state. In this respect, it did very little to prove its critics wrong. When, during the mid-1970s, the South African government raised the specter of a total war being waged against the South African state and society by a combination of communist and other left-wing forces within and outside the country, the SABC was instrumental in commanding the media front of this propaganda war. Though there existed no clear-cut statement as to what principles should guide the policy of the networks, sensible journalists knew better than to cross the fine line of what was considered acceptable to the ruling securocrats and the proapartheid white population. Everybody knew that blacks were to be entirely excluded from the broadcasts and programs except when featured in roles prescribed for them by the white establishment as servants, maids, mine and industrial workers, criminals, vagrants, and the like. Discerning editors, producers, and broadcasters knew that white viewers did not want to be disturbed with harrowing images or reports of appalling black conditions or of police brutalities against the enemy. Reporters, editors, and producers who were indiscreet or conscience-stricken enough to produce even moderately disturbing (to innocent white viewers) programs, like the one made by Kevin Harris on the 1976 Soweto uprising, were fired. Unfortunately for the cause of historical documentation for the future of South Africa, only a very few crossed that line. Therefore, the South African electronic media missed a very rare golden opportunity to record, for the future, momentous events taking place and transforming society during the closing decades of the apartheid era. Since South Africa was also, for the most part and for similar reasons, closed to the world press, posterity has been thereby deprived of the opportunity to know and view these momentous events beyond the attenuated fragments that managed to escape the highly efficient and ruthlessly suppressive censorship of the apartheid state.

With the end of apartheid and the advent of democratic rule in South Africa, the South African media industry has acquired a new dynamism and vibrancy that has positioned it to play a major role in the consolidation and extension of the gains of the South African miracle. With the shackles of many decades now crumbled by the new freedom and multiparty democracy, in spite of lingering suspicions among blacks (including prominent members of the ANC-led government) about the intentions of the white-dominated media establishment, South African print and electronic media is arguably one of the most respected in the world. With its newly discovered vibrancy, courage, and critical posture, the South African media—in spite of its mixed and, in most cases, tainted history—is regarded as one of the vital pillars that will help to support the gains of the South African revolution, most especially its nonracial, multiparty democracy and its uncompromising commitment to equality and the respect of human rights. With the wider continental African market now opened before it, its capacities for growth and expansion are immeasurable.

Notes

1. Elaine Potter, *The Press as Opposition: The Political Role of South African Newspapers* (Totowa, N.J.: Rowman and Littlefield, 1975), 34.

2. On the early history of the press in South Africa and the main sources for the discussion in this section see: *South Africa 1989–90: The Official Yearbook of the Republic of South Africa* (Pretoria: Bureau for Information, Department of Foreign Affairs, 1989/90), 655–72; Elaine Potter, *The Press as Opposition,* 30–49; and Keyan Tomaselli, Ruth Tomaselli, and John Muller, *The Press in South Africa* (New York: St. Martin's Press, 1987).

3. On the alternative press, and the major sources for the discussion in this section, see: Lee Switzer, *South Africa's Alternative Press: Voices of Protest and Resistance, 1880s-1960s* (Cambridge: Cambridge University Press, 1997); and Les Switzer and Mohamed Adhikari, eds., *South Africa's Resistance Press: Alternative Voices in the Last Generation under Apartheid* (Athens: Ohio Center for International Studies, 2000).

4. On the history of state broadcasting in South Africa, see *South Africa 1989–90,* 673–76; Ruth Tomaselli, Keyan Tomaselli, and John Muller, eds., *Broadcasting in South Africa* (New York: St. Martin's Press, 1989); and *South Africa Yearbook 2001/02* (Pretoria: Government Communication and Information System, 2001), 121–33.

6

Art and Architecture

The diversity of the South African society accounts for the efflorescence of a wide variety of art and architectural forms over the centuries and in different parts of the country. Distinct, well-developed, and generally autonomous artistic traditions can be identified in the region. Among the most notable of these are the San rock art tradition, Bantu visual and plastic arts, European artistic tradition, and other emerging motley forms that will be described here collectively as contemporary arts.

THE ROCK ART OF THE SAN

South Africa is generally considered to be the richest area of rock art in the world. Outside of Europe it is the most studied and, in contrast to the rock art of most of the world, it is probably the most understood. A considerable body of ethnographic literature is available on the San artists, much of which was collected during the nineteenth century and can be dated as contemporary with the last of the San painters of the Kalahari. Stretching over a wide area of southern Africa but predominant in the southwest and the southeast, some two thousand rock art sites containing nearly fifteen thousand pictures—mostly paintings—associated with the San have been identified. There are two types of rock art: engravings or petroglyphs and paintings.[1]

Carved rock art is concentrated on the interior plateau of the region and is either incised, made up of unbroken lines, or hammered through a series of small pits struck out of the rock. The greatest concentration and the finest examples of the petroglyphs are in the Free State Province especially around the Boshof and Fauresmith districts; in the Gautang Province around the

Klerksdorp, Rustenburg, and Krugersdrop districts; and in the Vryburg, Herbert, and Kimberley districts of the Cape Province. The largest number of petroglyphs at one single site are located outside of South Africa at Twyfelfontein in Namibia. Painted images are found in the rock shelters of the mountains that separate the southeastern coast of South Africa from the plateau of the interior highlands. The largest concentration is in the Drakensberg Mountains, where African rock painting reached the peak of its technical perfection, and where some of the finest examples of prehistoric art in the world can be found.

Paintings and petroglyphs seldom overlap. In the thousands of sites discovered in South Africa, less than 10 have both paintings and petroglyphs together. Unlike in Tanzania and Namibia, where the two have been found in the same region, in South Africa there is a distinct geographical separation between them. In South Africa petroglyphs are found mainly on the upper faces of small rocks and cliffs on or near the top of small hills (kopjes); while paintings are found mainly in rock shelters or the inner faces of caves. This almost complete geographical distinction between the two should not, however, lead one to conclude that the two art forms were made by two distinct races or peoples: cave-dwelling painters and hill-inhabiting engravers. We have no evidence to show that such topographical adaptation was central to the artistic development and creativity of the San hunting groups. A more plausible deduction would be that both the painters and the engravers were the same people. They did not paint on exposed rocks and cliffs because such works would not have lasted and could easily have been washed away by rain or by other corrosive agents of the weather such as the sun, wind, and sand. The corroded and often coarse surfaces of open rocks are also not very amenable to painting. Similarly, San artists did not engrave in rock shelters for the most part because the sandstone and granite content of these made them unsuitable for engraving; they lacked a weathered cortex or patina that would have allowed sufficient contrast between cut and uncut surfaces. Thus, it is reasonable to conclude that the perennially migrating San hunters were not so restricted in their geographical habitation, but instead moved from place to place while adapting their art to the different possibilities of their varying terrains.

Chronology, Subject Matter, and Style

Establishing a firm chronology for the abundant rock art of South Africa remains a continuing challenge. This is due to the fact that it is virtually impossible to date the paintings through the application of radiocarbon analysis. So far, the earliest date established for southern African rock art is from the southern Namibian desert, close to the South African northwestern frontier. In this place, a layer of organic debris containing eight fragments of painted stones (brought into the shelter from the outside and excavated by archaeologists) has been dated to about 25,000 B.C.E. Similarly, an incised rock fragment was found in a layer of organic debris at a site called Wonderwerk Cave in the Drakensberg Mountains of South Africa that has been dated to be over 10,000 years old. With regard to authorship, it is possible that some of the rock art could have been made by the pastoral Khoikhoi and in more recent years by the mixed-farming, Bantu-speaking groups. However, a close study of the subject matter, styles, and techniques of the rock art show that the overwhelming majority of them were made by the San hunter-gatherers, their ancestors, and other closely related peoples and groups, many of whom are now extinct.

With regard to the subject matters of the rock art, animals predominate and the animals most hunted have the greatest representation. Human figures are also common and are almost always shown in motion, engaged in one form of action or another, such as hunting, dancing, fighting, running, jumping, or marching. Usually associated with the human figures are objects of material culture such as bows and arrows, skin bags, digging sticks, and others. Mythological creatures, such as extinct and imaginary animals, human figures with animal-like heads, and other monstrous beings are also featured. In the final group are geometric forms, abstract shapes, undulating lines, regular or irregular rows of dots, map-like markings, and other indeterminate signs and symbols. Though common in Zimbabwe, representations of plants and trees are very rare in South African rock art. Sceneries are seldom represented, except in the few cases restricted to the Drakensberg Mountains, where they appear as meandering lines in the pictures. In many of these paintings, most especially in the Gauteng and the southern Cape Province, hand imprints made against the rock face served as a form of signature for the respective artists responsible for the paintings. A study of the distribution and sizes of these imprints shows that they are statistically and anatomically closer to Bushman than to either Khoikhoi or Bantu hands. In northern Transvaal some of the petroglyphs contain spoors or animal tracks cut into the rocks. Usually associated with pictures of relevant animals, these engraved spoors are most probably designed to instruct young boys in the art of animal track identification, knowledge vital to their survival as hunter-gatherer people.[2]

A Functional and Practical Art

What then were the purposes of the San rock art? For the San, art was a practical and utilitarian preoccupation. Art was inextricably linked with their economic and religious ways of life. Hunting was at the center of their culture and is the subject and focus of the majority of the paintings. Over the millennia, the San developed a hunting ritual requiring that before going out on a hunting expedition they first draw the outline of the targeted beast or game in the sand. Thereafter a series of ceremonies are performed in which an arrow is shot at the drawn animal. The place where the arrow strikes the pictured animal becomes the place the hunters aim to hit when they finally confront the living double of the drawn game. Every new hunt required a new drawing, since the San never reused or recopied an old drawing. Sometimes, however, they superimposed new pictures over previous ones, after defacing or, at times, without defacing them. This explains the existence of literally thousands of pictures of game animals and their hunters adorning hundreds of rock shelters and caves all over South Africa; no doubt, this is a fraction of what must have been a larger number, since many other pictures were drawn in the sand, on skins, and other perishable materials.

The rock art also appears to have been inspired by the San's religious beliefs. Some of the paintings depict the San involved in their traditional healing ritual dance. Through intense singing and clapping by women and vigorously ecstatic dancing and hyperventilation by men, certain spiritually gifted San healers are enabled to enter a trance or altered state of consciousness that causes a healing or supernatural potency (*n/um*) to boil up within them, which is then manifested through sweat, saliva, or even nasal bleeding. Impacted through a touch to the sick, the *n/um* brings recovery, restoration, and rejuvenation to the individuals as well as to the group.

Of all the animals hunted, venerated, and painted by the San, the most ubiquitous is the eland. A polychrome depiction of a herd of eland on a Drakensberg rock shelter face, with its soft, fulsome, delicately shaded colors, is ranked among the most magnificent, finest examples of rock art in the world. With its elegant poise, beautiful shades, peaceful demeanor, and abundant presence, the eland occupies a unique position in San cosmology. It is the most dominant subject of their songs, stories, music, dance, and art. It is the highest compliment to be told that one dances like an eland. A San in a trance state is said to stumble, tremble, and bleed from the nose while floating or staggering like an eland that has just been mortally wounded by a poisoned arrow. A San never kills an eland without first saying thank you to it in a dance. Asked by an interviewer about the whereabouts of /Kaggen, a Drakensberg San replied: "We don't know, but the elands do. Have you not hunted and heard his cry, when the elands suddenly start and run to his call? Where he is, elands are in droves like cattle."[3]

Even more impressive is the uniqueness of each artist's work, since the San artist never copied another artist's painting and rarely repeated one of his own in another cave. For the San, the urge to create was always more compelling than the need to decorate. Even in the final hours of their artistic glow, when the San were being hunted down like game by European interlopers determined to ensure the San's total and final extinction, they never allowed their art to become stereotypical. Remarkable rock paintings from this period depict Afrikaner pioneers with the men in floppy hats and the women in sunbonnets and long skirts firing their guns at and killing the San, who futilely though courageously responded with bows and arrows. Under the sustained and violent terror of the British sharpshooters and Afrikaner commandos, the San gradually but progressively lost their land and their lives, and witnessed almost helplessly the virtual and almost total decimation of their population and their artistic culture. Though silenced forever by the rapacious guns of European imperialists, the imagination of this race of artists continues to speak through the thousands of voices they have left behind on the rocks and cliffs of the land that was once theirs, an indelible and timeless reminder of a life, a culture, and a civilization, now irretrievably lost to humanity.

THE ART OF THE BANTU

Sculpture: Wood Carving

As in much of Africa, wood carving developed as a male activity in South Africa. Depending on local usage, demands, and specialization, a wide variety of items were carved by specialized craftsmen in different parts of South Africa. Some carvers became well known for their ability to carve figures and drums; others became proficient at making of bowls, mortars, and other containers; and some built their reputation on carving ritual and religious objects. In many places, as among the Zulu and some Northern Sotho groups, an artist could be commissioned to carve a wide variety of objects in use within his society, from spoons and bottles to elaborately decorated walking staffs and headrests. For such artists, the demands often dictated the type and range of work being produced. For most artists, differing abilities and market forces often combined to determine the quantity and quality of sculptural productions.

Among the peoples of South Africa, carved items are monoxylous, meaning carved from one piece of wood, except in the few cases where the artists have been influenced by European carpentry techniques. The wood selected for an object is determined by the intended use of the object. Stools and door posts are usually made from heavy woods, while light woods are reserved for making masks and other head gear that will have to be carried or worn. For small and precious articles such as spoons, pipes, and snuff containers, the dark heart of the wood is used because it is usually the hardest part. The main tools used in carving are axes, adzes, knives, and cutlasses. The adze is the principal tool for carving and chipping the object into shape. A wide variety of adze and knife sizes are used, depending on the size and degree of complexity of the object being carved. A gouge made up of a bent blade is often used to hollow out larger objects. Knives and chisels are used during the finishing stages to scrape down the rough spots, carve out the fine details, and to incise simple or elaborate decorations on the surface of the carved objects.

Usually wood is carved when it is still moist and is carefully monitored as it dries to ensure that it does not begin to crack. For most practitioners, wood carving was a part-time activity; nearly all depended on other occupations such as farming, hunting, and fishing for their livelihood. Carving skills are acquired while growing up within a partrilineage of carvers; occasionally, promising young carvers are sent to a reputable carver outside the patrilineage for a period of formal apprenticeship. In most societies, every male is expected to have the ability to carve simple objects such as spoons and hoe handles, while more complex items such as divination bowls and doors are the exclusive preserves of commissioned specialists.

Among the Venda, Tsonga-Shangane, Sotho, and Tswana, free-standing carved figures fulfill different functions. Foremost among these is their use as teaching aids during initiations, in the course of which the initiates are taught to understand and respect social values and sexual mores. The importance of marriage, of the individual's identification with the group, and group solidarity are also emphasized. Nearly all the groups already mentioned use standing wooden sculpture in male initiation rituals; only the Venda use them in female lodges. Among the Tswana and the Northern Sotho, the use of wooden figures of animals was quite common. Carved in many forms and of various sizes, the figures are used in various ways.

Sculptural styles can often, though not always, be distinguished from group to group. The Pedi are noted for their fully rounded naturalistic human figures, with heads covering between one-quarter and one-third of the entire body size. This style, which is also typical of other African sculptural traditions such as the Yoruba of West Africa, uses fine detailing to reveal different ages and statuses of the represented. The Tsonga-Shangane, who live in the Northern Province, are noted for their elongated figures: complete with smallish heads, spatulate hands, domed feet, head rings for males, peaked hairstyles for females, protruding buttocks, clearly demarcated genitals, chests, and breasts. Their use as didactic tools in matters of sex and marriage is affirmed by the fact that these figures always appear in pairs, one male and one female.[4] The elongated form of the Tsonga-Shangane standing figures makes them especially suited to serve as honorific markers outside the homes of important people and chiefs. These and other standing figures also feature as sentinels around fields. Finally, wooden figures are used as articulated puppets by many groups in divinatory and healing rituals.[5]

Headrests

Headrests are among the most common carved objects in South Africa. Over the centuries, artists from the various groups developed different headrest styles that became the markers for their groups. Among the Tsonga, human and animal figures are used as caryatids in which the crosspiece is supported on rods or slabs above the back of the animals. Rectangular-shaped, slab-type caryatids attached or suspended at varying angles between the base and the crosspiece are common among the Tsonga. The preferred animals are the horned variety of which the most represented is the antelope, noted for its beauty, grace, and variety. Cattle and goats are also featured. Among the Zulu and the Swazi, animals rarely feature as caryatids. Instead, two or more square-shaped legs support a heavy, rectangular crosspiece that curves slightly downward toward the center. Among the Swazi, the headrest crosspiece is usually supported by two fluted and bifurcated legs. Among all the groups the different sections of the headrests are embellished with various decorations, occasionally painted, though generally carved or incised with various forms of decorative motifs, ranging from geometric, raised-relief designs to curvilinear and interlace patterns. Years of usage and constant exposure to homestead cooking smoke have given many of the extant headrests a darkened and antique look, in addition to protecting them from insect attack.[6]

Doors, Musical Instruments, Divination Bowls, Ostrich Egg Containers, and Other Objects

Among the Venda, large monoxylous doors (*ngwenya,* meaning crocodile) are carved almost exclusively for chiefs, who use them mainly in their capitals. Similarly, large hemispheric drums (*ngoma*) decorated like the *ngwenya* doors with patterns of chevron triangles and diamonds interspersed with concentric circles serve as carved repositories of the chief's magical power to make rain. In the same vein, xylophones decorated with keys feature prominently in important court rituals. Other objects that serve as indices of power and status include divination bowls as well as finely finished and shining staffs. The longer and more intricately carved staffs are normally used by men, though women of unusual status such as healers and diviners also use them. Occasionally, the staff is engraved with designs incised along its entire stem, but generally the focus is on the top portion, which is usually carved into a human head and torso or animal figure. Among the Zulu, Swazi, and Tsonga, staffs with snakes curling up around the stem are not uncommon. Venda staff tops are often shaped in the form of a hand-claw enclosing an egg.

Divination bowls, though not owned by chiefs, also fall within the category of regal art, since their use is closely associated with the court. Mainly associated with the Venda and used by the most powerful of the diviners for the kings (kosi) of the Singo-Venda lineage, only 10 of these bowls have survived to the present. Basically, the bowl consists of a shallow hemispherical vessel, with a relatively wide flat rim enclosing the hollowed-out central section, decorated with images and symbols expressive of Venda cosmology. Images carved on the rim include animals representing particular lineages and kin groups, grinding stones and combs referring to women, spears representing men, and divining tablet (thangu) shapes indicating age and gender, as in senior or junior woman or man. Within the hollowed-out central section, images of crocodiles, snails, turtles, other liminal creatures, and symbols of chieftainship occupy the bottom. A small section of the rim is left plain to serve as the gate through which water is poured into the bowl. The zigzag decoration on the perimeter of the underside of the bowl represents the python and gives the impression of an enclosed, protected, autonomous polity.[7]

Other carved or embellished objects associated with domestic art include bowls, knives, milk-pails, mortars, snuff-containers, and plates. Among the Zulu, Swazi, and Pedi, four-legged plates with smooth inner surfaces and decorated undersides are used to serve meat. Among the Zulu, wooden vessels carved from solid wood and decorated with geometrically patterned, bold ridges and dark, shining paints are used for holding milk, water, and other liquids. Like staffs, metal knife handles and wooden or bone spoon handles are carved with finely designed abstract, animal, or human motifs. Sexual motifs also feature prominently in many of these carved objects. Breasts and the pubic triangles are conspicuously and alluringly displayed on mortars, staffs, spoons, lintels, and many other objects as symbols of virility and as an affirmation of the importance of women, marriage, and reproduction in the society.

Another object of domestic art is the ostrich eggshell water bottle, which long served as the principal water container among the San of southern Africa. Preparing an eggshell bottle involves drilling a small hole through the top, shaking out its content, and rinsing and deodorizing its interior with aromatic herbs. A small reed or grass stopper is used to secure the drilled hole. Prepared by married women, each of whom generally possess 5 to 10 of them, the eggshell bottle can hold about a liter of water. Filled with water and plugged, these eggshell bottles can be buried when there is an abundance of water and dug up months or years later in times of scarcity with their water still well preserved. Most eggshells were not decorated, but those that were appear to have been designed to ensure easy identification with and by their owners. The archaeological discovery at Boomplaas in the Cape Province of fragments of eggshells with geometric decorations dating to around 10,000 B.C.E. confirms the great antiquity of the decorated eggshell water bottles in the region. Animal and human representations have been found on eggshells unearthed at sites dated to the last few hundred years. In addition to water, eggshell bottles were also used to transport and store food, ochre, and pigment. And, in more recent centuries, some were buried with the dead.[8]

Pottery

Pottery making, usually from fired clay, is one of the cultural elements that distinguished the Bantu-speaking peoples from the preexisting Khoisan and related groups that they met in the southern African subregion. Virtually all the Bantu groups of South Africa fashioned and used a wide variety of clay vessels, usually fired but occasionally not. Similarly, under the influences of the Bantu, the various Khoisan groups also adopted the use of pottery as part of their domestic equipment. Among nearly all the groups, the making of pottery was the prerogative of women. It appears that originally the women of each family were responsible for making most of the pots used by their individual families. With the passage of time, however, specialization became the rule; before long, certain women from certain groups established solid reputations for themselves as adept potters. Pots and other associated ceramic vessels and objects became key articles of local and long-distance trade. In a society where the majority of people do not have ready access to electricity, pots are highly valuable because of their porous quality which enables them to keep water, milk, beer, and other liquids fresh and cool.

The availability of malleable clay in the region facilitated the development of pottery art. Swamps, anthills, and the banks of rivers are the major sources of supply, though in some places potters may need to travel some distances to get the clay as well as the ochre and graphite used for color decoration. Where the available clay is not entirely useable in its natural state, sand and other materials may be added as fillers. The basic tools used in pot making are simple: a piece of wood, a calabash, or a bone for scrapping and smoothing the inner and outer surfaces of the pots. For impressing or incising the decoration, a grass stem, a shell fragment, or a knife are used. With regard to the technique of pot building, the potter's wheel is not used. Instead, a flat stone, an old shard, or a revolving metal dish or lid serves as the platform base. In building the larger pot, the potter usually walks around the pot to fashion and finish it.[9]

The shapes, sizes, decorative patterns, techniques of execution, and other elements of style and types of motifs of fired pottery have been used by scholars to date and establish a wide range of stylistic affiliations, the succession of ancient cultures, the patterns of human migration, the differentiation into language groups, and the interactions and relations between the various and successive Bantu groups of southern Africa. Over the years, a wide variety of pottery styles, shapes, sizes, and colors emerged in the region. Venda pots are usually spherical with short necks that flare toward the rim. On the other hand, the Pedi, Ntwane, Khakha, and North Sotho domestic pots are hemispherical in shape with no neck. A decorative pattern of arcs and triangles is incised and burnished with red or black color around the shoulder of the pot a little below the rim. Similarly, Tsonga pots are burnished with incised decorations made up of geometric forms combining chevron and triangle designs. Zulu pots are also generally spherical in shape, without a neck. Their designs are placed lower down around the belly rather than the shoulder of the pots, with a preference for geometric patterns as well as for leaf- or shield-like motifs indicative or commemorative of Zulu-reputed militarism. Decorative colors are rarely used; instead the pots are burnished completely black.[10]

EUROPEAN ADVENT AND NEW ART FORMS

Painting

The establishment of the Dutch settlement at the Cape in 1652 introduced a new painting tradition to the region. European travelers, explorers, surveyors, scientists, civil servants, merchants, settlers, missionaries, and others sketched and painted pictures primarily for their own pleasure as well as to document the particulars of their environment and leave pictorial records of their pioneering experiences. A 1655 watercolor painting of Table Mountain that is now in the State Archives at The Hague is one of the earliest and among the most impressive of these paintings. However, it was not until the first half of the nineteenth century that South African painting came into its own as a distinct and developed artistic tradition.[11] British occupation set the stage for the advent of some British immigrant artists. Notable among these are several watercolorists: Thomas Bowler (1812–82), a mostly self-taught artist, is known for his historically valuable and romantically charming oil and water color paintings of the Cape landscapes and townscapes; and W. H. Langschmidt (1805–66) painted aesthetically pleasing portraits of peaceful Cape Town street scenes. Another is Thomas Baines (1820–75), who began his career as an apprenticed decorative house painter in England before relocating to South Africa, where he painted artistically fascinating scenes from the Kaffir wars of 1851–52 and of the Victoria Falls expedition of 1861–64. Others who left a wealth of sketchbook drawings noted for their historical value as well as for their romantic and picturesque rendering of the South African environment, rather than for their aesthetic importance, include Frederick T. I'Ons (1802–87), Abraham de Smidt (1829–1908), and H.W. Hermann (1841–1916). Under the influence of British-trained instructors, such as George Crosland Robinson (1858–1930), drawing was for a long time considered to be lower in status compared to painting, and thus not especially suitable for public exhibition. Thus these nineteenth-century lithographers and illustrators with their colored drawings, and in spite of the great realism of their works, were regarded as craftsmen rather than as artists in the strict sense of the term. Nevertheless, painters like Bowler and Charles Bell (1813–82) produced many valuable sketches that reveal their artistic talents.

In the late nineteenth and the early twentieth centuries, craftsmanship was gradually transformed into art. Among the pioneers of this new direction in the development of painting in South Africa was Jan Ernst Abraham Volschenk (1853–1936), one of the first self-taught South African–born painters who took on painting as a full-time engagement after retiring as an accountant at the age of 51. His pioneering paintings of the South African landscape, in spite of their dullness of color, reveal the artist's passion for the African landscape.[12]

A Parade of Women Artists

In any historical parade of South African artists, women would feature prominently. Among the earliest to distinguish themselves were the members of the Everard Group, a family of women artists. Two of these, Bertha Everard (1873–1965) and Ruth Everard Haden (1904–92), mother and daughter, became notable. Bertha was trained in London, and became known for the rhythmical graphic patterns of her post-impressionist paintings. Ruth studied in Paris but returned to South Africa in 1928. In the areas of figurative painting and naturalistic drawing, the Irish-born Dorothy Kay (1886–1964), who arrived in the eastern Cape in 1916, made lasting contributions. Her *Cookie, Anne Mavata* (1956) is a poignantly powerful and graphically naturalistic portrait of a black South African maid.

Two other women, Irma Stern (1894–1966) and Maggie Laubser (b. 1886), both born in South Africa but trained in Germany, are credited with introducing expressionist painting to South Africa. After a stint of nine years in Germany, Stern returned to South Africa in 1920, where she soon established herself as the most notable colorist of her time. She left behind a wide range of works, including figure and landscape paintings, still life and expressionist paintings, tempera and gouache paintings, and a few murals, sculptures, and ceramics, many of which are of high quality and great value. However, the spontaneity, arbitrariness, vibrancy, vitality, expressionism, and the personal commitment of her works were too much for the Cape Town art community of her time. Culturally isolated from the world and ignorant of the major development going on in Europe during the early decades of the twentieth century, the so-called experts rejected Stern's work. This critical disregard did not dissuade the public, who flocked to the galleries in large numbers to view her works, attracted by their vigor, sympathy, exotic nature, sensuality, expressiveness, and radicalism.

Maggie Laubser's contact with expressionism was less intense than Stern's, but under the influence and encouragement of the German expressionist, Karl Schmidt-Rottluff, she developed a passionate love for an earthly form of expressionism with a focus on the land, its people, animals, and plants. The gripping quality, distorted forms, and expressive nature of her portraits reveal the influence of German expressionism. Departing from the artistic conventions of the time, she rebelled against the dominant motif of landscape painting. Instead of focusing on the landscape, she chose to identify with its inhabitants, firmly rooting her art in her immediate environment. In this artistic guise as farm girl painter she produced insightful and penetrating portraits of wheat fields, field-workers, farmers working in or harvesting on their farms, fishermen in their cottages, dogs, cats, and other scenes taken from rural lives. In a society accustomed to associating art with paintings of landscapes, stately gabled homes, and portraits of dignitaries, Laubser's focus on elementary matters and moments and everyday lives and activities, her unusual penchant for still life as well as for animal and plant subjects, her emotional involvement with her subjects, and her personal identification with the natural world around her were both shocking and revolutionary.[13]

For local, visiting, and immigrant artists, the physical environment of South Africa with its peculiarities and striking features, created a sense of otherness that made landscape painting the dominant motif of South African art. In 1936, at the Empire Exhibition in Johannesburg, a wide variety of South African art featured prominently with the works of Roworth, Prowse, Kibel, Stern, Priller, Laubser, and other artists on display, indicating the maturing and international recognition of the works of these artists. Two years later, in 1938, a group of young artists led by Walter Battis and Gregoire Boonzaier formed the New Group. Conceived as an alternative challenge to the reactionary influence of the South African Society of Artists, the New Group organized lectures and exhibitions all over the country, bringing together, stimulating, and supporting a diverse group of budding artists and trading artwork for groceries. Under the direction of Battis, it took steps to promote art in general, maintain professional standards, and cultivate in the general public a more sophisticated interest in art. Most significantly, the New Group emphasized the rock paintings of the San hunter-gatherers as a necessary foundation in any movement to articulate and develop a specifically South African painting idiom.[14]

From the 1960s onward and in the wake of the Sharpville police shootings and the Rivonia treason trial and sentencing, South Africa became increasingly isolated from the international community. In consequence, South African art also began to be excluded from notable exhibitions. As the apartheid state became more repressive and increasingly intolerant of political opposition, the atmosphere became uncongenial for many artists, some of who went into voluntary exile. Those who remained and avoided political or obviously resistant motifs received sponsorship from the state and business corporations. Formalism, geometric abstraction, and nonfigurative paintings prevailed during these years.

Sculpture and Ceramics

The rural nature of the Dutch settlement and the primary focus on agriculture did not provide an environment conducive to the flourishing of the arts. The patronage and aesthetic taste needed for the sponsorship of a sculptural tradition were also lacking during these early decades. The beginning of European sculptural tradition in South Africa can be dated to the second half of the eighteenth century, with a special focus on religious decoration. This development was closely associated with the career of Anton Anreith (1754–1822). Born in Germany, he received his early training as an artist while growing up in Freiburg. He arrived at the Cape in 1777 and began to work for the Dutch East India Company as a simple carpenter. Before long, however, his artistic talent became evident. His first commission came in 1783, when the congregation of the Lutheran Church asked him to decorate its organ loft. More works followed. Anreith became the company's master sculpture in 1786. In 1805 he began to give art lessons, and in 1814 he became the founding principal of the free masons' technical school for the arts. Two years later, the works of his students became the subject of the first art exhibition to be held at the Cape. Among Anton's most important work is the richly carved baroque-style pulpit (1785–86) of the Lutheran Church in Cape Town. Impressed by what he had done for the Lutherans, the Dutch Reformed Church also commissioned him in 1788 to make an elegant pulpit for its own Cape church.[15]

The sculptural art scene was dominated during the first half of the twentieth century by a group of immigrant artists and foreign-trained South

Africans. Three figures stand out clearly during the 1920s: Ivan Mitford-Barberton (1896–1976), Mary Stainbank (b. 1899), and Coert Steynberg (1905–82). The work of each of these artists clearly reflects contemporary concerns as well as the growing European interest in African sculpture and sculptural themes.

Modern African Carvers

The success of Steynberg, with his many highly acclaimed monuments to heroes of Afrikaner nationalism, shows the popularity of representational art. Rural African carvers took advantage of the economic opportunity offered by the growing European interest and market for carved objects with African motifs to become actively engaged in the production of tourist art. Mission-educated Africans who had received instruction in wood carving from mission schools also began to make religious carvings to service the religious and ritual interest of their church clientele. Most notable among these was Ernest Macoba, whose 1929 yellow wood *Madonna* graced the Convent of the Holy Paraclete in Manzini, Swaziland for years. Another was Job Kekana (b. 1916) who carved a crucifix out of a jacaranda wood for the Cathederal of St. Savior, Port Elizabeth in 1956. Both artists also carved works in African motifs to feed the tourist market. However, in the face of growing African nationalist consciousness, Macoba soon rejected such artistic populism and pandering to white market clientele. He began to produce more stylized figures before moving to Paris in 1938, where, after a brief stint producing nonfigurative works, he abandoned sculpture altogether. Similarly, Kekana, who settled in Zimbabwe, continued in the naturalistic style to produce religious and secular carvings, while striving successfully to maintain a high technical standard in the face of mounting market pressures calling for mass production to service the tourist industry.

In more recent years, the enduring Western fascination with things considered primitive and thus original, as well as for things considered exotic has produced new stimulation and motivation for African artists to produce sculptural and other artistic works for the tourist industry. From the mid-1980s onward government-sponsored agencies, such as Ditike (set up by the Venda Development Corporation) and other commercial galleries in the urban centers, began to organize local and rural artists for the tourist craft market, prodding and guiding them to concentrate on particular kinds of arts considered to be hot sales for the tourist market. As artists responded by producing multiple versions of the same subjects, the underlying tension between originality and creativity on the one hand and mass production and profit on the other began to surface, as critics repeatedly deplored the commercialism that had crept into the sculpture industry to stunt innovation and cutting-edge originality. Many of these rural artists, all of whom have had to navigate the fine and often overlapping boundaries between tradition and modernity and African and Western, are beginning to receive recognition from scholars of South African art. This section will put a few of these artists, on whom we have sufficient information, in the spotlight.

Nelson Mukhuba (1925–87) grew up under the influence of the Lutheran mission at Tshakuma in the Venda country. He acquired his art training in the traditional way through apprenticeship to an elderly male relative. After working for a while as a carpenter and an electrician in Johannesburg, he returned home in 1958 and took to carving, producing wooden bowls, mortars for grinding corn, *ngoma* drums for use in the chief's courts, and wooden figures (*matano*) for use during women's initiation rituals. The opening in 1981 of a casino in the capital of the newly constituted homeland of Venda created a new market for tourist art, since the road to the new capital passed very close to Tshakuma. Taking advantage of the new opportunity, Mukhuba set up a stall along this road to sell his carvings to passing tourists and other interested parties. For many years Mukhuba distrusted and resisted requests by Ditike and other commercial galleries to help him market his sculptures. But the psychological pressures of navigating between two worlds was apparently too much for the artist. In 1987 he finally gave in by signing a sale contract with Ditike. A month later, he committed suicide.

Noria Mabasa (b. 1938), a Venda artist like Mukhuba, began her career making clay figures modeled after those used in the Venda women's initiation rites. She also received commissions from the local authorities to make clay figures to be used for the didactic purpose of instructing rural women about the importance of breast-feeding and proper hygiene. Soon, in response to a vision she claimed to have received, she began to make identically modeled freestanding figures of policemen, soldiers, businessmen, and other elements drawn from contemporary South African life. The popularity of these works with private and public collectors led the Goodman Gallery in 1986 to bring all these figures together as a unit, arranging them according to their ranks and photographing them. Brought together as a unit in the atmosphere of the political turbulence in South Africa in 1986, the figures were imbued with political meanings not originally intended by the artist. Another spiritual crisis, associated with visions from the ancestors, led Noria to abandon clay modeling. She took to wood sculpture, a revolutionary step in a society where wood carving is the exclusive prerogative of men. But no one could question the words of the ancestors whom she claimed directed her, in a most unusual way, to transgress the boundaries of gender and patriarchy so boldly. Inspired by the television coverage of a flood in Natal in 1987, she produced the large,

One form of traditional art is basket weaving. KwaZulu-Natal, 2001.

haunting sculpture *Carnage II,* infused with images of crocodiles, reptiles, sexuality, motherhood, witchcraft, and kinship, drawn from Venda ancestral and totemic traditions. Her sculpture *Ngoma Lungundu* shows a group of exhausted women dancing or swirling around a huge *domba* initiation drum. Though this image is ostensibly referring to the migratory story of the Venda folk hero, Singo, it also appears to be a questioning of the oppressiveness of male authority and control.

Not surprisingly, white sculptors have not been immune to influences from African cultural traditions. Bruce Arnott's bronze sculpture, *Numinous Beast,* reveals clear evidence of the influence of San rock arts. The works of Andries Botha are influenced by Zulu craft and building techniques, and Joanchim Schonfeldt remains indebted to the iconography of South African Bantu cosmology.[16] Finally, the end of apartheid and the attendant opening up of South Africa to the outside world has resulted in the development or rather renaissance of an unusually vibrant artistic tradition geared, though not exclusively, toward meeting the demands of the burgeoning tourist industry in the rainbow country. Old and new art forms in the production of clay pots, colorfully patterned grass baskets, painted gourd vessels, copper wirework objects, beaded necklaces and bracelets, and an assortments of bead-coated sticks, bottles, toys, and other containers proliferated. The production of these art forms is dominated by women, who in turn are inspired by the need

Ndebele wall murals, Lisedi Cultural Village. Note the typically bold, brightly colored, stylized geometric designs. (Jennifer Beard)

to generate additional income to support their largely female-headed rural households of industrial and modern South Africa. Ndebele women especially have received considerable tourist attention for using dazzling colors and a wide variety of geometric and organic designs to lavishly decorate their clothes, household goods, and the walls of their homes, probably to give visible expression to their claims to an exclusive and authentic cultural identity, an identity violently and insidiously threatened in the apartheid- and white-dominated South Africa before 1994.[17]

INDIGENOUS ARCHITECTURE

Khoisan Architecture

The Khoisans, the earliest inhabitants of South Africa, were also its first architects. As hunters and fruit gatherers, the Khoisans roamed as bands over the extensive and apparently sparsely populated terrain of South Africa, following its abundance of game. In these early days, they appear to have lived in caves and rock shelters. After clearing these shelters of erosion sediments and cleaning them enough to make them accessible and habitable, these nomadic inhabitants adapted, without the use of much labor or material, their rudimentary shelters and overhangs to suit their housing needs. Occasionally, the rock shelters or caves were covered at the mouth with stones or stone slabs or wooden doors fashioned from reeds, plants, or grass tied together with ropes. The San left behind them on the surfaces of many of the rock shelters they inhabited spectacular and fascinating paintings, many of which have become world famous for their beauty and artistic, aesthetic, and historical values. Rock shelters were especially suitable for the rainy season. During the dry summer months, or in places where natural rock shelters were neither abundant nor available, temporary shelters were erected. San huts were made up of branches of trees and saplings set in a circle approximately five feet in diameter and planted in the ground with the top ends bent inward and bound together by grass ropes, back fibers, or a coating of mud to form a central apex, giving the appearance of a beehive-shaped framework. The whole framework was then interlaced horizontally with smaller branches, which were in turn covered with a layer or layers of rough grass thatch, fastened together and tied to the beehive framework by a network of reed ropes. To prevent the thatch from being blown or torn away by windy weather, chunks of wood were laid on the top of the hut.

Another structure designed and built by the San consists of a single, stiff reed mat arched in a semicircle between two posts planted in the ground to create an open-ended tunnel shelter. To shield the shelter from the elements, another mat was attached as a half-arch alcove to cover one end of the tunnel, adding to the shelter a degree of privacy. The two standing posts guarding the two sides of the shelter served as racks for bows and arrows, leather bags, musical instruments, and other possessions. The alcove shelter was especially suited to a nomadic way of life because of the durability of the mats and the ease with which the reed-mat shelter could be dismantled, rolled up, carried along, and reerected at the next site of settlement.

The building style, size of opening, and care of the shelter varies with the weather. During the rainy season, the opening of the hut is usually leeward and away from the direction of the wind. Among the Khoisan, women are primarily responsible for building design and construction. They also cut and arrange the tree branches and the grasses. Selecting the site of the camp is the prerogative of the chief, who signifies his choice of a location by depositing his personal effects on the spot where his own hut is to be built. Thereafter his followers select the sites for their huts. A village is usually established around a central tree, which serves as a social and political anchor for the group. The site of this tree is where the chief kindles the first fire, which is then used to light the fire of the other members of the camp. This site also serves as the meeting place for the men and the dancing space for the group, and separates the hut of the chief and his brother from those of the other members of the group, who are usually settled in a semicircle on the opposite side of the tree.

Like the San, Khoikhoi pastoralists also developed a style of building appropriate to their nomadic lifestyle. As befitting a people always on the move in search of green pasture, their shelters are usually light in weight, small in volume, portable, easily dismantled, easily erected, and carried by oxen. Their huts are similar to those of the San, except that they are larger in scale, more sophisticated in style, and often more durable in form. A typical hut consists of between 20 and 60 debarked tree branches or undressed saplings planted vertically in the ground to a depth of one foot, in a circle of between 10 and 15 feet in diameter. The planted saplings are then slanted inward and radially to a central crown, where they are bound together by ropes or mud or cow dung to create a hemispherical framework. The vertical saplings are braced by hoops of horizontal saplings that diminish in size as they advance to the apex of the dome. The crossing points between the horizontal and vertical saplings are fastened together with reed ropes or reusable leather thongs. Thereafter, the whole framework is covered with reed mats made by women from the stem of cypress plants woven together with bark fibers. The women sometimes dye the mats by placing bundles of reeds in a mixture of dried clay dung and goat urine.

Reeds used for mats are found mainly in riverbeds and swamps. The thicker and softer ones, known as *matjiesgoed,* are preferred to the thinner and harder ones, known as *biesies.* The reeds are usually picked individually, then bundled together and allowed to dry for a few months, during the course of which they change from being dark green to golden yellow. Once dry, the reeds are soaked overnight, sorted into lengths, and then woven through the use of an awl and the patterned alternation of the reed ends. The addition of successive and overlapping layers of rush mats results in the creation of a beehive-shaped hut capable of withstanding both the rainy season, when the rush becomes swollen and watertight, and the dry season, when it contracts to allow breezes to permeate. The increasing aridity of the Kalahari and the Khoisan homeland has resulted in the scarcity of reeds, with the resultant effect that the Khoisan hemispherical structures, in many places, are now covered with tree barks, flattened cooking oil and paraffin tins, plastic waterproof membrane, and corrugated iron roofing sheets.[18]

Bantu Architecture

Available evidence shows that the first Bantu-speaking peoples of South Africa all built beehive-shaped dwellings, though the structures vary from one group to the other. Two types of beehive shelters appear to have been common among them. The major difference between the two is mainly but not solely in the treatment of the crown or apex of the roof. The first one, which is common among the Tswana, the Southern Sotho, and the Thembu, consists of a circle of upright saplings bent over and brought radially to meet or cross at the apex, giving the appearance of a cone-like, beehive-shaped structure. Thereafter, the vertical sapling structure is braced and strengthened by horizontal concentric hoops parallel to the ground and diminishing in diameter as it ascends the frame to the apex. For the Sotho, where the saplings meet at the apex, they are bound together with a stout ring to create a pointed apex. Among the Xhosa, the crown is more rounded since the saplings overlap at the top. In many cases, a tunnel entrance of about half a meter in height is created through a series of arches, which extends the hut into a sparrow pot form.

The second type of Bantu architecture that has made the Zulu famous, and is also common among some Natal and Cape Nguni groups and the Swazi, consists of a circle of upright saplings planted into the ground and bent into an arch spanning from one side of the circle to the other. As these series of semicircular arches increase in size toward the center of the frame, they are crossed at right angles by a second series of more closely spaced sets of semicircular arches that also diminish in size as the circle reaches its two extremities. Among the Swazi, the second sapling dome is not as closely set as it is among the Zulu. At every point at which the two overarching sapling frames cross, they are bound together tightly by means of woven grass or reed ropes. The next stage is to cover the resultant framework (*izintungo* in Zulu) with thatched grass. This can be done in a number of different ways. One method is to place grass mats over the crown of the frame in varying layers while binding them with ropes to the arched saplings. Thereafter, the matted frame is thatched over with grass sewn into the frame by a network of woven grass ropes or slender branches, with the finished hut resembling a gigantic hair net. In other cases, the grass thatch is sewn first onto the frame with plaited grass ropes, after which the matted grass is placed over the crown of the frame. In most cases, the lower base of the frame closest to the ground is surrounded by a thick grass rope, which will be securely fastened to the frame at a distance of about three to four feet from the ground. To this baseline or *umphetho,* other grass ropes (*izintambo*) are attached at intervals of six inches that stretch vertically in a concave to the apex. Thereafter, a series of closely spaced ropes parallel to the ground are knotted to the upright ropes or *izintambo* wherever they cross. This step completes the thatch as it encircles the frame in a series of diminishing concentric loops running from the base to the apex.

The Zulu knowledge of the nature and limitations of the wide range of materials available to them has led to a high degree of specialization in which seven different types of grass are used for the beehive hut construction, with each grass adapted to perform the specific function for which it was perceived to be most suited. The resultant hut, with its concentric rope design and finial finish, is unusually picturesque, exceptionally fascinating to the eyes, and one of the finest examples of indigenous architecture in southern Africa. In almost every case, the men are responsible for erecting the sapling framework, while grass matting and thatching are the prerogatives of women. Preparing the floor involves first scooping it out to create a slightly hollowed space, which is then overlaid with flat stone slabs covered with mud and smoothed out by a large pebble. To give a highly polished and hardened finish, a mixture of clay and cow dung, and sometimes that of ox blood and fat, are smeared on the floor.

A typical Zulu hut is divided into two sections, with the man's side to the right as one enters and the woman's side to the left. A circular depression with a raised moulded rim forms the hearth, situated about a third of the way between the entrance and the rear of the hut. Shallow depressions around the hearth serve as pot rests for the round-bottomed cooking pots. To the rear of the hut and opposite the doorway is a raised platform or curved, molded-clay ridge, known as *umsamo,* under which powerful medicine was buried when the hut was being constructed, and which serves as a storage space for cooking utensils and other household materials. Because the kaal houses the most prestigious possession—cattle—and provides the space for the storage of harvested maize, it is the most sacred space in the homestead and is solely under the domain of men, who alone qualify to be buried within its sacral space. Women and children are buried outside the kraal. A stone slab-lined, calabash-shaped pit, sunk beneath the floor of the kraal, plastered with cow dung and clay, serves as the granary for maize.[19]

The Corbelled Stone Houses

Among the Tswana and the Southern Sotho, Phetla, Phuthi, and Ghoya groups, corbelled stone huts, known as *lifala* or *libopi,* were built. These are beehive-shaped huts built from boulders of spherical dolerite or untrimmed slabs or chunks of sandstone. Usually circular in shape, the single wall of the corbelled hut, with an average base thickness of approximately two feet six inches, curves slightly inward as it rises to the top, eventually leaving a top opening approximately eighteen inches in diameter. This opening is then closed by a single large, flat slab or four flat slabs with a fifth inserted to reduce the opening between them. A mass of rubble is usually piled on top of the slab or slabs to keep the slab firmly secured to the hut. The entrance to the hut is a low small one, approximately two feet in height and one and a half feet in width. To protect the occupants from wind, lions, and other wild animals, the opening is closed by a flat stone slab, pushed or rolled into position from the inside. Generally, corbelled huts are very small, with an internal base diameter of between five and seven feet and a height of four feet. The doorway rarely exceeds four feet in height and three feet in width.

The small size of the corbelled huts have caused much doubt about whether they were actually used as human dwelling places at all, in spite of extant evidence that proves so. The crucial point to recognize is that the rudimentary technology of corbelling in rough boulders imposes a severe limitation on how large such houses could be. To meet the need for more living space, a second type of corbelled hut was constructed using flat dolerite slabs. With a base diameter of nine feet and a height of six feet, the walls of these huts rise only slightly until they reach a height of four feet; they then curve more sharply inward to the extent that the corbelling will permit, leaving a relatively larger opening at the top that is covered with long slabs of dolerite. Rubble and broken ceramics are laid on top, creating a flattened-rooftop appearance. Sometimes, the corbelled hut can be expanded through the lengthening of one of its axes to create an oval extension that can reach an internal length of 16 feet or more.

The Tsoeneng, another Southern Sotho group, also built corbelled huts. Known as *sebopi,* these are built of mud rather than stone. They have a base diameter of eight feet and a height that ranges between five and seven feet. Made of a cone-shaped wall that curves slightly inward as it rises to the top, the Tsoeneng corbelled hut is crowned at the top with a central opening that is covered with a flat stone slab. A doorway, three to four feet or less in height, serves as the entrance. Corbelled mud huts are often decorated by smearing the inside and outside of walls with a mixture of clay and cow dung. Similar huts, used for grain storage, poultry raising, pigsties, and cooking are still being built among the Phuthi, Vunde, and the Ntande (a Xhosa group).[20]

The Dome-on-Cylinder Houses

According to Walton and Frescura, who have carried out extensive studies of Bantu architecture in South Africa, the next stage in the development of indigenous architecture in South Africa appears to be connected with the building of the dome-on-cylinder-houses. The dome-on-cylinder appear to be a graduation from the beehive dome. In the latter, the dome is placed directly on the ground; in the former, the beehive framework is placed on top of a cylindrical drum wall made up of timbers, woven saplings, mud, cow dung, or a combination of all or some of these materials. The dome-on-cylinder seems to have developed in response to a number of social and environmental contingencies. There was a need to prevent or minimize the hazard of fire by elevating the thatch off the ground. A higher cylindrical base fortified with mud and *daka* (*daga*) strengthened structural stability while protecting the hut wall from surface rainwater run-off. Increased population led to shortage of grass for construction, necessitating the use of alternative materials, especially mud. Finally the dome-on-cylinder hut, with its larger doorway and higher internal head room, provided greater comfort of entry and internal movement. Additionally, increased light and ventilation made it possible for windows to be more easily set in its sides, a feature especially attractive to those desiring a more sophisticated lifestyle.

The Cone-on-Cylinder Houses

The structural limitations of the dome-on-cylinder appear to have resulted in the development of the cone-on-cylinder huts, which, unlike the dome-on-cylinder, is not limited to the Zulu but widespread throughout much of South Africa. Widely known by its Afrikaans name, *rondavel,* it consists of a cylindrical wall topped by a conical thatch. The construction of its wall is structurally similar to that of the dome-on-cylinder wall, though its widespread provenance resulted in a wide variety of types. Generally the wall is constructed with a series of upright timber poles. These are closely spaced together and interwoven in a basket form with saplings. For a smoother and more integrated finish, the resultant cone-like structure is packed with earth and plastered with cow dung. In more modern times, it can be made of stones, sod, clay, burnt or sun-dried brick, concrete, or a mixture of two or more of these materials.

When the wall drum is constructed with solid materials such as mud or a mixture of mud, *daka,* and timber, the roof is usually built directly onto the wall. In other cases, where the walls are made of timbers or saplings only, it is difficult to build the cone roof in situ. In such cases, the roof is built separately on the ground, lifted into position, and fastened in various ways to the outer circle of posts making up the wall drum. The hut is sometimes enclosed by a veranda that can be opened or partly closed through a raised outer wall or kerb. The entire structure can be just one single room or it may be subdivided in a number of different ways, with each room performing specific or varied functions. In most cases, the conical roof is built with a central structural timber support to the apex that can be removed or retained with the completion of the roof structure and thatch covering. In some cases, with the increase in the diameter of the house, it is impossible to sustain the spanning of the roof timbers without a central timber support, which then assumes the added function of serving as the central pivot around which the internal division of the house is ordered and organized.

Cone-on-cylinder houses, Gauteng, 2002.

The cone-on-cylinder represents a major advancement on the dome-on-cylinder model. Its doorways are more stable and higher, rarely falling below 1,600 millimeters in height. Windows are widely used as ventilation openings that are initially left without shutters. Over time, more modern forms, such as embedded glass sheets, hinged timber shutters, and steel cottage frames have become regular features. Roof eaves have also proven an essential element of these houses, fulfilling their original function of keeping rainwater off the walls, but also in some cases becoming extended well beyond the wall to cover a veranda area to serve as a porch or multipurpose area. The cone-on-cylinder houses appear to have developed first among the Tswana, Venda, and other closely related peoples. Its widespread adoption and adaptation by the Pedi, Sotho, Swazi, and Zulu seems to be connected to the demographic upheavals associated with the *mfecane* during the first half of the nineteenth century and after. In all the places where it spread, a wide variety of types developed.

Among the Tswana, the cylindrical wall of mud and *daka* is surrounded by a circle of upright posts supporting the conical rooftop, which is built on the ground and lifted into position. The cylindrical wall itself plays no part in supporting the roof and, in most cases, a space exists between the top of the base wall and the roof. The Pedi and the Southern Sotho are known for building their cylinder walls entirely with stones. The Taung use turf blocks cut with sloping ends to construct their walls, which are then smeared with mud into which pebbles are stuck to create intricate designs.[21]

Modern Transformations in Rural Architecture: The Cone-on-Cube Houses

Though the cone-on-cylinder remains the most typical and the most widespread form of indigenous house in South Africa, the pressures of modern society have resulted in the transformation of rural architecture in response to the changing social, economic, demographic, and technological circumstances. Houses have thus been adapted to take in mass-produced furniture and fittings that are usually based on the straight line and the ninety-degree angle, while the demand of an ever-expanding population has led to the need for structures that are easily expandable. As in most rural societies, where domestic architecture represents centuries of evolution and adaptation and reflects sociocultural values and norms, there is a clear and understandable unwillingness to make radical departures from the basic traditional forms. Change, however, cannot be stopped entirely. Consequently, the circular- or spherical-shaped house forms began to give way, reluctantly, first to octagonal- and later hexagonal-shaped houses, while still retaining the conical rooftop. Structurally, the significance of the new adaptation of the cone-on-cylinder lies in its more functional floor plan, and its more efficient use of space to accommodate modern furnishings.

The next stage in the cone-on-cylinder evolution came with the development of the cone-on-cube houses. The major structural challenge posed by the cube form vis-à-vis the previous forms, was the need to thatch around a ninety-degree corner. Among the Xhosa, the attempt to resolve this problem led to the adoption of an ovate-oblong plan, with the structure having straight sides and rounded ends, giving the appearance of two cone-on-cylinder huts linked together by an extended thatched rectangular room or by two straight front and back walls. In other cases, three or four cone-on-cylinders may be linked together by walls to form the frame of a large and more extended house, with the central square section serving as the living room, while the corner cylinders serve as bedrooms or storerooms. It is not clear when the transition from the cone-on-cylinder to the cone-on-cube took place, but it does not appear to have antedated the 1830s, a period for which we have extant evidence showing that missionaries and Trekboer pioneers were building square-plan houses.

As more Africans moved to the cities in the wake of the discovery of diamonds and gold, partly under the influence of their European overlords and missionary teachers and partly in response to the realities of the structural and functional advantages of the cube house forms, they began to build houses with square and rectangular geometrical floor plans. The major structural advantage of the cube or rectangular form is that it is the most easily expandable of the forms so far discussed.[22]

Among the colored and Malay communities of South Africa, rectangular houses, structurally patterned after earlier European forms, were the common forms. Over the years, however, these houses developed their own individual character, as a result of creative social, technological, and environmental adaptations. A look at the houses in the Malay Quarter of Cape Town, shows the majority of them to be made up of simple rectangular, flat-roofed dwellings, usually embellished with molded parapets and cornices, spiral chimneys, and fan light–decorated doorways. The roofs are usually made of galvanized iron. The ready availability of corrugated iron roofs in the modern era, the purchase of which is made possible by the relative prosperity of Malay business people and of colored and other rural dwellers working in the mines and in industries and the relative scarcity of suitable thatching grass materials, has made the flat iron-roofed houses one of the dominant forms in the Karoo villages.

Common also in the North West and Free State and among rural Africans, the highveld flat-roofed houses marked a crowning stage in the development of rural architecture, in that the wall finally rose to a point where it could fully assert itself as the dominant element, with the roof becoming concealed and virtually invisible. On the other hand, for the colored and other fishermen living along the Cape coast, the preferred form of dwelling is the rectangular building constructed of mud, rubble, and reeds, plastered with clay or boards, with a thatched roof that frequently terminates in gables, with one end partly forming a hip to give a wolf-end appearance. As one moves eastward from the Cape to Mossel Bay and then to Plettenberg Bay and the Boland, the predominance of the rubble and mud becomes gradually replaced by the use of wattle and planks sometimes plastered with mud. Almost everywhere, the colored rural houses are marked by their massive stone chimneys, which initially served as open hearths and baking ovens but later became fitted with stoves to serve as kitchens.[23]

EUROPEAN ARCHITECTURE

Cape Dutch Style

The first building to be modeled in the European style was erected at the Cape in 1652 by Jan van Riebeeck. A wooden fort made with timbers imported from Holland, it could not withstand the harsh climate of the Cape and had to be replaced the following year by a second fort built with sod walls. Attempts to bring in bricks and other building supplies from Holland proved abortive and logistically cumbersome. The search for a local clay source by Riebeeck was successful, but the clay was of poor quality with a life span of only nine years. With no other readily accessible alternatives, the settlers began to use the clays. Initially the roofs of the houses and stores were all thatched with gabled ends that were either stepped or straight-sided, terminating in a small step or pediment. The main entrance was placed in the center of the long side, protected by another gable, instead of in the center of the short side, as it was then practiced in the Netherlands. The problem of fire and arson led by 1660 to the replacement of all Dutch East India Company's roofs with sloping pantile roofs, fastened to the building framework by battens cut from local plants.

By 1662, red brick-gabled buildings with gold-colored tile roofs, sprouted up all over the small Cape settlement. Cottages built with a mixture of sod, wattle, and daub and thatched with a heavy cluster of reeds also dotted the landscape. However, it soon became clear that this attempt by the settlers to replicate, with little or no modification, their European building forms in South Africa would not stand the test of time and weather. Repeatedly assailed by the storming rain and the tempestuous temperature of the South African southeast, the bricks began to corrode and hollow out, leaving only the projecting mortar joints, while the tile roofs also began to leak, leading to the collapse of some of the buildings. In response, the settlers turned to burning seashells in great quantities, to obtain lime plaster that they then used to protect the brick wall from further decay, thus covering much of the outer walls of the buildings with a coat of waterproof whitewash. Similarly, the tile roofs were covered with a plaster paint of black tar to seal off the leakages and protect them from the ravaging climatic elements. This was the beginning of what would become known as the Cape Dutch style, one of the most notable forms of South African architecture, with its white-walled and gabled homesteads.

Fashioned after the manor houses of contemporary Netherlands, these early Cape Dutch houses consist of a central hall (*voorhuis*) that serves as the main living room, from which radiate the other rooms, including the dining room (*gaanderij*) and a reception room. The *gaanderij* usually opened to the courtyard; beyond that were located the coach houses and servant quarters. The fear of fire led to the promulgation of a decree in 1736 that prohibited the use of thatch for roofing. Consequently, a tradition of flat-roof buildings developed at the Cape, with the roof being made of a layer of hard burnt, crushed brick spread on laths or timber boards, plastered with seashell lime plaster, waterproofed with tar or whale oil, and finished with clay tiles. Fram-

Cape Dutch house, Vergelegen Wine Farm, Western Cape. (Helen and Russell Mason)

ing the streets, often resting on a basement, with paved fronts and burnt brick steps, and decorated with exotic parapet framings and joinery, the houses usually consist of one or two stories, depending on the economic status of the owners. The first leaded windowpanes of coarse glass were introduced in 1663, though it was many years before their use became widespread.

Though a wide variety of colors were used, white was the most dominant for the exterior walls, while deep green featured prominently on the joinery. Adapting the houses to the heat of the summer months led to the use of thick external walls, boarded ceilings, clay tile floors and fairly dark interiors. Cape rural architecture varied widely, depending on local resources and building use. Among wine and wheat farmers who built long houses, the most typical were winged rectangular, L-, T-, U-, and H-shaped houses that still centered on a main hall just behind the front door. The building style preferred by the stock farmer was the tent-like, dwarf-walled *kappstylhuise,* with a steeply pitched thatched roof, consisting of one or two rooms. The arrival at the Cape in 1783, of L.M. Thibault, a Frenchman and the first of South Africa's professionally trained architects, led to the introduction of French neo-classical styles to South African public architecture. Among the many notable buildings in this tradition is the Masonic Lodge of Good Hope, first built between 1801 and 1803 and then rebuilt in 1892.[24]

British Advent and the Development of Synthetic Forms

The coming of British settlers in 1795 and British rule in 1806 inaugurated the era of Georgian and Regency styles. These carefully proportioned two-story, double-pile, rectangular brick houses and cottages had pitched roofs, hipped or gabled sides, back extensions, and often symmetrical front façades and veranda shades. Though this design had already been introduced prior to their advent, the British were largely responsible for popularizing building plans with halls or through-passages and rooms with precisely defined functions. The arrival of 4,000 British settlers in the Eastern Cape in 1820 further entrenched British influence, as the settlers strove successfully to create replicas of rural English houses with their rectangular, natural stone cottages enclosed by defensive walls. Several examples of such building forms can still be found in Grahamstown and Port Elizabeth, where many of the settlers later settled. Though the British settlers rejected many elements of local building traditions for practical and aesthetic reasons, they were compelled to adopt others. Dutch-speaking colonists in turn combined British styles with local forms. The result is a hybrid style of architecture that became a predominant feature of early nineteenth-century Cape building forms.[25]

With the northward migration of the *voortrekkers* in protest against the British rule at the Cape, the Cape Dutch style also extended into the interior. The city of Pietermaritzburg, founded in 1838, with its clay-plastered simple houses of wood and rushes and its many baroque-style public buildings is a byproduct of this movement. The arrival of nearly 5,000 British immigrants in Natal between 1849 and 1852, and their selection of Pietermaritzburg as the headquarters of their Natal province, further intensified the spread of British or English forms in the region. Using locally available materials, they erected wattle and daub structures, supported on termite-resistant mangrove poles, with lime-plastered and washed walls, and mud or anthill earth floors finished with a mixture of dung and ox blood. A distinctive feature of most of these houses is their hipped or pyramidal roofs and their long or encircling verandahs that are usually supported on timber posts. Creatively adapted to the subtropical climate of the Natal coastal region, and quite typical of British colonial architecture in India and Australia, the verandahs kept the walls cool, allowed easy airflow, gave the buildings a rustic and picturesque appearance, provided additional living spaces, and served as foyers for receptions and entertainment.

Durban was the site for the construction of some of the earliest and most beautiful Hindu temples in South Africa. Initially built with wattle and mud and later with wood and iron, these structures were fashioned in the contemporary colonial Victorian style. Axially planned and oriented east-west and bedecked with attractive and brightly colored cement-sculptured representations of deities, more than 70 of these temples survive as small but exuberant masterpieces of South African Hindu architecture.

The prosperity occasioned by the discovery of diamonds in Kimberley and of gold in the Witwatersrand, opened a new vista in the history of architecture in South Africa. The new materials of the industrial age, such as cast iron, corrugated iron, and cement came into the center stage, permitting a wide variety of building ventures. The architecture of the 1890s was characterized by increasing ornateness, in which gables, domes, dormer windows, spires, and finials proliferated, as architects and building engineers experimented with a blending of Flemish, Gothic, Baroque, Victorian, Arcade, Renaissance, Classical, and Neo-classical styles. The Eckstein Building and the Leander Mansion in Johannesburg, and the Raadzaal building in Bloemfontein, are remarkable examples of the eclectic but extraordinarily innovative architecture of these years.

THE ARCHITECTURAL ICONS: HERBERT BAKER, NORMAN EATON, AND LOUIS I. KAHN

The end of the second Anglo-Boer war brought a new wave of prosperity and rebuilding to all the ports and garrison towns of South Africa. New city halls were built in Cape Town, Durban, and Pietermaritzburg. The reconstruction of the Transvaal in the wake of the Anglo-Boer war brought into national prominence a hitherto relatively unknown architect, Herbert Baker, with his imperious outlook and his contagious fascination for classical architecture. Trained in the English art and crafts movement, noted for his use of local koppies stones for walls and shingles and warm-colored clay tiles for roofs, Baker dominated South African architecture during the early decades of the twentieth century. Among Baker's most notable designs are the Monument to the Honored Dead in Kimberley (1904–5); the Pretoria Railway Station (1908); and the sandstone Union Buildings complex (1910–13) situated on a hill overlooking Pretoria and built in an eclectic classical style that combined elements of Renaissance and Cape Dutch architecture.

Two of the first notable Afrikaner architects of the years following the second Anglo-Boer War were Wynand Hendrik Louw and Gerard Moerdijk, who adopted mixed historical styles in designing many Dutch Reformed Churches. Moerdijk's Voortrekker Monument (1936) is undoubtedly the most massive memorial in South Africa.

The work of Norman Eaton (1902–66) established him as the greatest artist among South African architects of the twentieth century. A student of Baker and Leith, he was a romantic rather than a rationalist. He made extensive use of local resources such as wood, stone, and thatch, and of handmade materials such as ceramic and brick. His organically structured buildings were fitted with marble-framed façades and bronze, over-hanging eaves, and sunshades between the windows of high buildings. The combination of these unique features revealed his great sensitivity to the needs of the people who would be inhabiting his buildings. Awed by the Egyptian Great Pyramid at Giza, he gradually became hypnotized by Africa, and worked assiduously till the end of his life to inject what he repeatedly described as the beautiful African quality into the most Western and most conservative architectural tradition on the African continent.[26] During the 1960s, architects trained in America—particularly at the University of Pennsylvania under Louis I. Kahn—dominated the South African building scene. Their structures are known for their strict geometric ordering and use of fair-faced brickwork and off-form concrete to achieve a synthesis of space, form, and materials to produce an integrated, powerful, and flexible style.[27]

With the end of apartheid, the ushering in of democratic governance, and the gaining of economic and political power by a rising number of black South Africans, the suitability of a continuing and noncritical embrace of alien and international modernist forms is increasingly being questioned, as the new black-dominated ruling elite begins to commission architects to design buildings that will symbolize their struggle and reflect the values of their African cultural identities. As vernacular architecture increasingly disappears and dominant Western-style structures—most imposingly represented by the *voortrekker* monument near Pretoria—are seen by the majority of the population as monuments to an oppressive and racist past, the need for a regionally adapted, climatically and topographically appropriate, visually and publicly accessible, aesthetically distinctive, and culturally relevant architecture cannot be overemphasized.[28]

NOTES

1. The major sources for the information on the rock art of the San are Alex R. Willcox, "Paleo-African Cultures: Prehistoric Art in Southern Africa," in *Encyclopedia of World Art* (New York: McGraw-Hill Book Company, 1966), xi, 37–53; Burchard Brentjes, *African Rock Art* (London: J.M. Dent & Sons Limited, 1965), 5–23; David Lewis-Williams, *Discovering Southern African Rock Art* (Cape Town: David Philip, 1990).

2. Willcox, "Paleo-African Cultures: Prehistoric Art in Southern Africa," 46–53; A.R. Willcox, *Drakensberg Bushmen and Their Art* (Winterton: Drakensberg Publications, 1990, 2nd rev. ed.); and R. Townley Johnson and Tim Maggs, *Major Rock Paintings of Southern Africa* (Cape Town: David Philip, 1992, 3rd rev. ed.).

3. Quoted in Monica Blackmun Visona, "Southern Africa," in Visona, Robin Poynor, Herbert M. Cole, and Michael D. Harris, et al., *A History of Art in Africa* (New York: Harry N. Adams, Inc., Publishers, 2000), 478. See also Vinnicombe,

People of the Eland: Rock Paintings of the Drakensberg Bushmen (Pietermaritzburg: University of Natal Press, 1976).

4. Anitra Nettleton, "Southern Africa: Free-Standing Wood Figures," *The Dictionary of Art* (New York: Grove Dictionaries Inc., 1996), vol. 1, 416.

5. Nettleton, "Southern Africa: Wood-carving," *The Dictionary of Art*, vol. 1, 414–17. See also E. Rankin, *Images of Wood: Aspects of the History of Sculpture in 20th-century South Africa* (Johannesburg, A. G., 1989, exh. Cat.).

6. Sandra Klopper, "Headrest (*isigqiki*)," in John Mack, *Africa: Arts and Culture* (Oxford: Oxford University Press, 2000), 172–73.

7. Anitra Nettleton, "Divining Bowl (*ndilo*)" in Mack, *Africa: Arts and Cultures,* 188–89 and "Venda," *Dictionary of Arts,* vol. 32, 154–55. See also her "The Figurative Woodcarving of the Shona and Venda," (unpublished Ph.D. thesis, Johannesburg: University of the Witwatersrand, 1984).

8. Lyn Wadley, "Water Bottle," in Mack, *Africa: Arts and Cultures,* 180–81. On domestic arts, see: Klopper, "Zulu," *Dictionary of Art,* vol. 33, 723–25 and Alex Zaloumis, *Zulu Tribal Art,* photographs by Ian Difford (Cape Town: Ama Zulu Publishers, 2000).

9. Margaret Shaw, "Material Culture," in W. D. Hammond-Tooke, *The Bantu-Speaking Peoples of Southern Africa* (London and Boston: Routledge and Kegan Paul, 1974), 116–17.

10. Nettleton, "Southern Africa: Pottery," *The Dictionary of Art,* vol. 1, 417–18 and A. C. Lawton, "Bantu Pottery of Southern Africa," *Anal of South African Museum,* 49, 1967, 1–440.

11. The major sources for the following summary history of painting and leading painters in South Africa are Hans Fransen, *Three Centuries of South African Art* (Johannesburg: Donker, 1982), 253–323; Lucy Alexander, "South Africa: Painting and Drawing," in *The Dictionary of Art,* vol. 1, 107–10; and Esme Berman, *The Story of South African Painting* (Cape Town: Balkema, 1975).

12. Fransen, *Three Centuries of South African Art,* 257–62.

13. Fransen, *Three Centuries of South African Art,* 285–89.

14. Fransen, *Three Centuries of South African Art,* 292–323; and Alexander, "South Africa: Painting and Drawing," in *The Dictionary of Art,* 107–10.

15. On Anreith and Wouw, see Fransen, *Three Centuries of South African Art,* 95–104, 325–29; and De Bosdari, *Anton Anreith, Africa's First Sculptor* (Cape Town: 1954).

16. For a fuller exploration of the careers and achievements of these and other pioneer modern African carvers and sculptors, and the major source for the discussion in this section, see Nettleton, "Home Is Where the Art Is: Six South African Rural Artists," *African Arts,* Winter 2000, 26–39, 93–94 and Elizabeth Rankin, "South Africa: Sculpture," *Dictionary of Art,* vol. 1, 111–13. See also Nettleton and Hammond-Tooke, eds., *African Art in South Africa: From Tradition to Township* (Johannesburg: Donker, 1989); and Visona, "Southern Africa," in Visona et al., *A History of Art,* 484–87.

17. Peter Magubane and Sandra Klopper, *African Renaissance* (Cape Town: Struik Publishers Ltd., 2000), 129–60; James Walton, "Ndebele," *Encyclopedia of Vernacu-*

lar Architecture of the World, Vol. 3: Cultures and Habitats, ed. Paul Oliver (Cambridge: Cambridge University Press, 1997), 2162–63.

18. On the architectural traditions of the Khoisans and related groups, see Franco Frescura, *Rural Shelter in Southern Africa, A Survey of the Architecture, House Forms and Construction of the Black Rural Peoples of Southern Africa* (Johannesburg: Ravan Press, 1981), 33–45 and J. Walton, *African Village* (Pretoria: Van Schaik, 1956).

19. On Zulu and Swazi architecture, see Walton, "Architecture: Vernacular," in *Standard Encyclopedia of Southern Africa* (Cape Town: Nasou Limited, 1970), vol. 1, 534–45.

20. On the corbelled houses, see Frescura, *Rural Shelter in Southern Africa,* 22–26 and Walton, "Architecture: Vernacular," 538–40.

21. On the dome and cone-on-cylinder houses, see: Frescura, *Rural Shelter in Southern Africa,* 45–74.

22. For Bantu architectural traditions, and the major sources for the discussion in this section, see: Frescura, *Rural Shelter in Southern Africa,* 33–84, a fascinating and richly illustrated exploration of African rural and indigenous house forms. See also Walton, "Architecture: Vernacular," 534–45.

23. On Cape Malay and "highveld" houses, see Fransen, *Three Centuries of South African Art,* 101–9 and Walton, *Homesteads and Villages of South Africa* (Pretoria: Van Schaik, 1965).

24. On Cape Dutch architecture, see C. De Bosdari, *Cape Dutch Houses and Farms: Their Architecture and History* (Cape Town: Balkema, 1964); Fransen, *Three Centuries of South African Art;* and Walton, *Old Cape Farmsteads* (Cape Town: Human & Rousseau, 1989). See also the entries on southern Africa architecture titled "Cape Dutch," "Colonial British," British Natal," and "Colonial: Cape," by Derek Japha and Vivian Japha in *Encyclopedia of Vernacular Architecture of the World, Vol. 3: Cultures and Habitats,* 2150–60.

25. On the history of the innovations and transformations effected in architectural forms in South Africa by the advent of the English during the last decades of the eighteenth century and after, see Rodney Harber, "South Africa: Architecture," in *The Dictionary of Arts,* vol. 32, 104–7; Francesco N. Arnoldi, "South Africa: Colonial and Modern Period," in *Encyclopedia of World Art,* vol. xiii, 144–47; R. Lewcock, *Early Nineteenth Century Architecture in South Africa: A Study of the Interaction of Two Cultures, 1795–1837* (Cape Town: Balkema, 1963); and G. E. Pearse, *Eighteenth Century Architecture in South Africa* (Cape Town: Balkema, 1968).

26. Clive M. Chipkin, *Johannesburg Style: Architecture and Society, 1880–1960s* (Cape Town: David Philip, 1993), 287–93.

27. On Baker, Leith, Eaton, and other notable architects of the early twentieth century, see Harber, "South Africa: Architecture," in *The Dictionary of Arts,* 104–7; Fransen, *Three Centuries of South African Art,* 209–51; D. E. Greig, *A Guide to Architecture in South Africa* (Cape Town: Timmins, 1971); and Chipkin, *Johannesburg Style: Architecture and Society, 1880–1960s,* 37–69, 81–137, 287–303.

28. For a perceptive articulation of the need for a new architecture for South Africa, see Sabine Marschall and Brian Kearney, *Architecture in the New South Africa: Opportunities for Relevance* (Pretoria: University of South Africa, 2000), 156–83.

7

Cuisine and Traditional Dress

A Culinary and Fashion Crossroad

With its intersecting races, peoples, and cultures, South Africa is a crossroad of many culinary traditions, dressing styles, and customs. Beginning with the indigenous Khoisan and Bantu-speaking peoples and extending through various groups of immigrants from inner Africa, Europe, Asia, and the Americas who came to settle permanently in the country, South Africa has witnessed the development of a wide variety of culinary and clothing traditions.

Khoisan Subsistence

Among the Khoisan, the earliest inhabitants of South Africa, subsistence appeared to have been based mainly on hunting and gathering, supplemented by fishing when possible. The gathering of insects, seashells, wild berries, and other fruits appeared to have supplied the bulk of the dietary needs, and was the sole preserve of women, though men also gathered when convenient or practicable. Hunting of the abundant wild game of the region provided a most valuable protein supplement, and was the sole prerogative of men. Cattle rearing and farming came later; both appear to have been connected in some way with the advent of iron-using, pot-making, food-planting, and cattle-rearing Bantu-speaking peoples, the vanguard of whom were already in the South African area by the thirteenth century.

BANTU CULINARY TRADITIONS

Milk and *Emasi*

Until the mid-eighteenth century milk was the most important food of the Bantu pastoralist.[1] His milk supply came from his cattle, his most valuable possession, which he rarely slaughtered for food. Only the sick, the old, and dying among the cattle suffered the fate of reduction to meat for the Bantu table. The pastoralist did trade his milk, and occasionally his cattle, to obtain valuable items such as game meat and fruits from hunter-gatherer Khoisan neighbors and, later, raw and manufactured metal and other wares from the Europeans who by the beginning of the sixteenth century became regular visitors and traders in the coastal areas of South Africa. Thus, for a long time, milk was the staple source of nutrition, imbibed fresh or soured. Sour milk (*emasi*) is a highly valued staple, due especially to the wide variety of its uses and applications. Souring the milk involves pouring it into a container, preferably a calabash gourd or a leather bottle with a stoppered hole at the bottom, and then leaving it until it curdles. The nature of the container can affect the taste of the final product. When the milk becomes thick enough the hole underneath the container is unstopped to allow the whey to drain out, ready to be drunk as it is and leaving the *emasi* or thick curds behind to be extracted with a wooden spoon and eaten as curds or converted into a wide variety of milk dishes and puddings.

As pastoralists, milk constitutes a major part of the Bantu diet. Milk comes mainly from cattle; goats and sheep are rarely milked. Fresh milk is not favored, except for infants, children, and the very old; instead, the preference is for soured milk or *emasi*. There are rules and taboos governing the eating of *emasi*. Generally one is permitted to eat *emasi* only from one's own clan, that is, from the home of a person having the same *sibongo* or clan name as one's mother. Eating *emasi* from the home of a family into which one can marry is thus strictly prohibited. While a girl can eat *emasi* from her parent's home, made from their herds' milk, all her life, she will not handle or eat *emasi* from her husband's home or herds until after the birth of her first child. In some cases, as part of the marriage gift, a man presents his daughter with a cow from among his herds, to milk for her own exclusive use. At the birth of her first child, she is freed from the taboo, as she receives permission from her husband to drink from his herds' milk, symbolized, in many cases, by his presenting her with the gift of a milch (milk) cow, *lipakelo,* from which she can now obtain her own milk for *emasi*. Girls and women are expected to avoid eating *emasi* while menstruating, though they can handle it while preparing food for men and other family members. After childbirth or miscarriage, a woman abstains from eating *emasi* for a month, and a widowed woman is expected to abandon it for life. While men consume *emasi* at the entrance to the cattle kraal, women are not supposed to eat *emasi* in public, but must consume it in the privacy of their huts.

Mealie

Though milk has remained an important food item, its primacy has been taken by the mealie or porridge made from maize (corn) or millet. Initially, millet, which is cultivated by women, was the principal crop and even today many still consider the mealie made from millet to be the most desirable, even after the introduction of American Indian corn or maize, which became more widespread with the advent of Europeans in the region. So central are millet and maize in the diet that a family without mealie is considered a starving one, the possession of other crops in abundance notwithstanding. Of the many ways of preparing millet or maize for food, two methods, both of them done by women, are most common. The first involves pounding or stomping the usually dry corn with a pestle in a mortar hollowed out of wood, stone, metal, or pottery, with a base or standing on a pedestal three to four feet high. The second method involves grinding the corn between two stones. The grinding or pounding continues until the desired degree of fineness or coarseness is achieved, a degree determined by the dish for which the ground corn is meant. For infants' food, the grain is transformed into a very fine powder, to prepare a very thin porridge known as *inembe* among the Swazi. Sometimes water is sprinkled on the dry corn to ensure easier grinding. Generally moist and fresh corn are either stamped or ground, while dry corn is either pounded or ground. Closely woven mats, baskets, leather strips, or leaves are often attached to the end of the grinding stone to catch the ground corn, while shallow baskets, cloth, or wire-net sieves are used to sift through the ground or stamped corn. Today, mechanical mills or grinding machines are available to facilitate a more efficient grinding of corn, though the two traditional methods have continued to be used, particularly in rural areas.

In the hands of the Bantu South Africans, mealie became a versatile food item. As the leading staple food, its uses are many and varied. To ensure freshness, the Swazi half-cook the newly harvested corn while still in its sheaves before storing it away on trees, to be taken and fully cooked when needed. Fully roasted kernels can survive in good eating condition for a long time and are favored food items to carry on a long journey or, as in the precolonial era, in times of warfare when cooking is particularly inconvenient. Mealie is cooked in many ways. Some, like the Zulu, prefer the dry, crumbly form. Most South Africans, however, prefer the less crumbly, smooth, thick porridge. This can be mixed with a wide variety of gravies, meats, vegetables, fruits, and other condiments to produce a variety of dishes. Among the finest of these is the Venda's King's Porridge or *koningpap,* prepared without salt from the finest of white mealie powder that has been soaked in water, pounded, and sifted many times. Among the side dishes that go with *koning-pap,* the most delicious are the roasted squares of beef and chicken cooked together in a clay pot with dried beans and stamped mealies. Green mealies and mashed peanuts are added to thicken the dish. *Umngqusho,* a concoction made with dried maize kernels, sugar beans, potatoes, butter, onions, chilies, and lemons, cooked together until tender, is said to be Nelson Mandela's favorite dish.[2] Among the Swazi, pumpkin mealie, known as *sidudu,* is a favorite meal. Among the Swazi, any thick porridge is called *sishwala,* while a very thick one is known as *ingwanqa.* A thin porridge made from either maize or millet is known as *lidishela;* the one made from millet alone is called *lijingi lemanti.*

Vegetables and Side Dishes

To enrich the porridge and satisfy the demands of different tastes and culinary appetites, many types of green vegetables are added and cooked with the pap or served as separate side dishes. Honey, herbs, and plant or fruit syrups are also added in different combinations for tastier mealie. Many government programs, through careful documentation and dissemination of information on the nutritional benefits of vegetable-rich diets, encourage men to eat vegetables as frequently as women and to stop regarding them as women's food.

Meat

Meat, though not usually from cattle, is a favorite delicacy of the Bantu and comes from three sources. The first group consists of domestic animals such as goats, sheep, chickens, and pigs. Unlike cattle, they have virtually no ritual restrictions barring their slaughter. The second source of meat supply consists of wild game, the hunting of which continues, in spite of official restrictions, though now on a very low scale. Rabbits and the wide variety of the ubiquitous South African deer and bucks are also favorite delicacies. Regulated slaughtering of game in the many private and public games reserves of South Africa has also made possible a wide range of game venison dishes, from crocodile and elephant to ostrich and eland stew. The third source is the much-valued cattle. These are killed only on very special religious, economic, and political occasions such as a marriage ceremony, a major ancestral ritual veneration and sacrifice, the festival of the first fruits led by the ruler, and the annual or periodic male or female initiation ceremonies.

Other sources of protein are small animals, as well as insects such as the locusts and grasshoppers, red and green caterpillars, and flying ants, roasted to a delicate crispness or prepared in other ways to serve as snacks or condiments. Eggs from chickens, and sometimes from ostriches, also supplement the diet. Fish meals, though not widespread, are prepared from dried fish by coastal and riverine groups, such as the Tsonga.

Though women and children are subjected to more food restrictions than men, a fat or full-figured woman is a major compliment to her husband, embodying his munificence; such a man has little difficulty attracting other women to marry into his household. Hospitality to strangers, most especially when they are unknown and indigent, is a highly valued custom. Children are taught very early that no behavior is more despicable than failure or reluctance to share whatever one has, especially meat, with others. Male visitors can be served separately or they may eat with the male head of the household. Women visitors eat with and assist the other women in preparing the meal. Cooking is done outside when the weather is good, which is usually the case. Typically each woman has her own kitchen, which houses her fireplace. Nevertheless, the use of kerosene stoves and gas and electric cookers has become widespread, not only in the urban centers, but also in the rural areas.

Cooking Utensils

A wide range of utensils are used, ranging from ostrich egg shells and carved wooden bowls to imported glass and china wares. For cooking, the most common utensil is the baked clay pot, of which a wide variety exist, designed for specific and distinct uses, such as the carrying and storage of water, brewing and storage of beer, cooking of porridge or relish, and the storage of dry beans and dehydrated vegetables, to mention just a few. Another versatile material can be found in the multishaped, hard, smooth-shelled fruits of the gourds, which in the skillful hands of the women become transformed into calabashes, dishes, scoops, ladles, flasks, cups, and urns used for a variety of functions in the home. Beside their other functions as medicinal receptacles and musical instruments (trumpets), ox horns are sometimes made into water flasks widely used by herd boys in the field. Shell utensils include snail shells, used as spoons to eat porridge; dried melon or pumpkin peels, used as spoons to eat thin porridge; and tortoise shells, used as porridge dishes by Pedi boys at cattle posts. Wooden utensils, carved almost exclusively by men, include conical jugs with handles; pronged stirring sticks; small or large rectangular or elliptical trays, with or without legs; small or large spoons used for eating and serving food; and a wide variety of deep or shallow, circular or concave serving dishes. Wicker utensils, woven by either or both men and women, include: the winnowing, circular, stout-brimmed back tray; the narrow beer strainer bulrush bag; grass and reed mats; and the different sizes and shapes of light and heavy-duty grass baskets. While all these materials continue to be used, nearly all of them have become tourist items or curios, ensuring their continuing production as a major source of income for the people of South Africa. Complementing and often replacing the traditional baked, carved, or woven utensils are imported or locally manufactured metal, glass, and enamel wares that have become the norm in virtually all South African homes, from the remotest village to the most urbanized center.

Beverages

There are two types of beverages: intoxicating and nonintoxicating. Both can be found in wide variety, and nearly all are made from fermented millet or mealie. Wheat introduced during the first half of the twentieth century is also widely used where available, though the preference remains with millet or sorghum. The Zulu produce at least four types of nonintoxicating beverages: *umcuku,* coarsely ground, boiled mealies fermented with beer screenings; *isibhebe,* thin mealie meal or kafir-corn porridge fermented with malted kafir-corn; *igwele,* crushed mealies or corn, mixed with boiled water and fermented with malted grain; and *amahewu,* porridge fermented with wheat flour. The Pedi use the term *metogo* to describe six varieties of their nonintoxicating fermented beverages. Served in the early hours of the morning or just before retiring for the night, these mildly alcoholic beverages are considered refreshing and highly nutritious, good for the belly, healthy to the body, useful as snacks for long journeys, and ideal as sustenance for hard work in the farms or mines. Among the many categories of intoxicating fermented beverages are the *bjalwa,* produced by the Pedi and the *utshwala,* brewed by the Swazi.

The Zulu and the Tsonga, who live in the palm belt of the Eastern Cape, tap the sap of the wine fruit and drink it fresh as a sweet, nonintoxicating drink or fermented as an intoxicating wine. Among the Tswana, honey mead is sometimes brewed into beer. Some seasonal fruits, like the marula (*Sclerocarya caffra*), and ripe prickly pears (*Opuntia megacantha*) are brewed into highly intoxicating drinks. Unlike the moderately to slightly intoxicating sorghum beers, fruit beers—with their high vitamin C content and their aromatic, champagne-like flavor—are desired more for their quick, highly intoxicating, aphrodisiac effect than for their nutritional value, of which they possess very little.

Among most South African groups, beer is not usually regarded as drink; instead it is considered food and an essential staple. Its high carbohydrate and yeast content make it a rich source of calories and vitamin B. During the winter grain harvest, many depend almost entirely on beverages, though young women and children are traditionally not expected to drink the most intoxicating types. In almost every case, women are responsible for the brewing of beer, even though men are the principal consumers, hence the saying among the Pedi: *Monna ke phafana ya bjalwa, mosadi ke moapei wa bjalwa* ("The man is a container for beer, though the woman brews it").[3] Though much beer is usually consumed, intoxication is not common. Beyond nutritional, medicinal, therapeutic, and narcotic uses, beer, most especially the millet and mealie varieties, plays very important social and ritual roles in the community. It is a visible and crucial part of major meals, family or communal feasts, birth or marriage celebrations, initiations, chieftaincy installations and other status transitions or rite of passage, social and religious ceremonies and festivals, ancestral spirit recall and sacrifices, and other rituals.

Modernization has had a major impact on beer production in South Africa. The introduction of imported liquors, which are often stronger in alcoholic content than traditional beverages, increased the incidence of intoxication and the use of beer as a soporific drowner of sorrows in the turbulent and alienating societies of apartheid South Africa. The mixing of maize meal and sorghum, with the addition of brown sugar to speed up the process of fermentation, has increased the alcoholic and intoxicating content while reducing the nutritional value of the beer. The economic deprivations (such as land shortage for herding or farming) and the demands (such as new taxes and fees) of colonial and postcolonial South Africa led to the depletion of men from the countryside as they moved in droves to the cities to seek work in the mines and industries. With the household prop gone, women were left alone to shoulder all the responsibilities of domestic production and caring for the children and the elderly, supported by occasional remittances from their men in the cities. In their loneliness, the women sought the company of other women in beer brewers' homes or in drinking establishments. The various traditional strictures placed on drinking by women began to fall by the wayside, as women themselves became the heads of the households and the principal players in the rural communities. Beer drinking among women, with all its debilitating and dulling consequences, became habitual. The official prohibition by the apartheid government against local beer brewing only resulted in the proliferation of illegal brewing and the widespread use of the legal but more intoxicating and thus more lethal imported liquor varieties. Some mission churches preached against alcoholic drinks, while members of the Separatist or African Initiated Churches were warned to avoid fermented drinks altogether. During the mid- to late 1990s, some Muslim groups created local and international sensations through a series of militant campaigns against widespread alcoholism and drug use in the increasingly more permissive society of postapartheid South Africa.

FOOD AND SETTLEMENT AT THE CAPE

A Refreshment Post: The Dutch and the Table Mountain

The establishment of the first European settlement at the Cape of Good Hope in 1652 was motivated principally by the need to ensure a regular supply of fresh food for the sailors and merchants in their long journeys from Europe across the Atlantic and Indian Oceans to and from Eastern destinations. The new settlement was neither meant to be permanent nor a colony; its sole purpose was to produce food and other provisions for passing European ships. Upon arrival at the Cape, the first site that greeted sailors was that of a flat-topped highland, shrouded in a white mist. Conscious of their mission to provide the seafarers with nourishment for their long journey to and from the East, these pioneer sailors and settlers called the landform Table Mountain and the even, white cloud covering it the Tablecloth. The bay at the foot of the mountain was tagged Table Bay. After erecting a fort, the first major task of the pioneers was the laying out of a vegetable garden, designed to experiment with growing produces of their Dutch homeland: sweet potatoes, pineapple, watermelon, pumpkin, gourd, cucumber, radish, vines, orange, lemon, and other fruits. While these were germinating, the pioneers resorted to eating many of the edible wild berries and other plants they found at the Cape. One of these, the yellow-flowered sorrel, was especially useful as a source of vitamin C. Chewing its root and stem or using them in cooking provided a good treatment for scurvy, the principal bane of the seafarers of this period. After a soldier died from eating wild almond, the settlers discovered that the lethal properties (prussic acid) of the almond could be neutralized by soaking the fruit in water before eating, or by roasting it in a way similar to that of the Khoisan.

After some initial weather blight and production disappointments, the Cape soon developed into a landscape of beautiful gardens that gave pleasure and nourishment to the settlers and their visitors, as well as to passing sailors and their passengers. The journal of Jan van Riebeeck, the Commander and leader of the first party to settle at the Cape, reveals that by the end of the first decade of settlement the Cape was producing in appreciable quantity and comparable qualities a wide variety of fruits and vegetables. Notable among these were spinach, lettuce, turnips, endives, red cabbage, yellow beet and beetroot, carrots and parsnips, cauliflower and cabbage, chervil, pumpkins, cucumbers, gourds, artichokes, watermelon, cantaloupes, fennel, and chilies. Different varieties of peas, beans, and other legumes were also grown. Fruits

Christmas dinner on the porch of a house overlooking the Table Mountain, Hout Bay, Western Cape, 1999. (Helen and Russell Mason)

grown with varying degrees of successes included citrus, bananas, olives, chestnuts, plum, apple, cherry, walnuts, quince, guavas, apricots, meddlers, and peaches. Also particularly successful was the attempt to grow grapes, a wide variety of which soon began to flourish at the Cape. In February 1659, the Cape pressed its own wine, laying the foundation for the South African wine industry that has shined and sputtered with varying vicissitudes of success and profitability up to the present time. Attempts made to cultivate grains and rice took some time before beginning to yield any fruits, compelling the settlers to depend on importation of rice and dry bread or ship's biscuits.

The demand for fresh meat had to be met through the rich fish and rock lobster supplies provided by the Cape waters. For awhile, the plentiful big game supply could not be converted into the delicacies that they would later become because of the inefficient and clumsy hunting and trapping methods of the settlers. Easily caught game such as porcupines, daisies, seagulls, penguins, and scalloped tortoise made their appearances on the Cape table. On discovering that penguin eggs were palatable, these pioneers made them part of their menu. After some initial difficulties, breeds of European cattle, sheep, pigs, hares, and goats began to be raised at the Cape, to supplement or even replace the insufficient and unreliable meat supply from the Khoisan, who were generally, for cultural and economic reasons, loathe to part with their stocks. With an average 6,000 sailors stopping at the Cape every year for food, drink, and other nourishment, cooking became an essential function of the new settlement. As a halfway house between Europe and the Far East, the Cape developed into a crossroad of culinary traditions to which the Dutch, French, Italian, British, Germans, and Malay contributed their cooking customs. Of these many culinary imprints, the earliest and certainly most pronounced is the Malay contribution.

Cape Malay Cooking

The term Malay is somewhat misleading. It refers not just to the people from Malaysia, but to an aggregate of groups and peoples from East Asia and the Middle East. Included in the category are Indians, Indonesians, Malayans, and others from Java, Sumatra, the East Indies, and the Middle East. The fact that the people from Malaysia constituted the majority and that nearly all of them spoke the Malay language and were Muslims resulted in the use of the common term Cape Malay. The Cape Malay are to be distinguished from the Cape colored, a later population resulting from sexual relations between white men and nonwhite women, namely Khoisan, Malay, and Africans. The Cape colored long identified with their European masters and paternal progenitors and adopted their cultures and religions, though the later did not wholeheartedly embrace them as kin. The Cape Malay, on the other hand, strove to retain their distinct identity, and kept tenaciously to their religion, language, and culinary customs. The culinary contribution described in this section refers to that made by the Cape Malay and not by the Cape colored.

The first group of Malay came to the Cape with the first settlers. The majority, though not all, began to arrive as slaves from Indonesia and Malaysia during the late seventeenth century. Described by one writer as kings of all slaves, they came to the Cape bringing their skills with them. Apart from being expert carpenters, tailors, musicians, gardeners, and fishermen, they were also excellent cooks. As the first gardeners, fishermen, vine keepers, and cooks for their Dutch masters, it became the lot of Malay men and women to define the nature and direction of culinary arts at the new settlement. In this endeavor, coming from a background noted for exotic cooking, they distinguished themselves, leaving an indelible imprint on Cape and South African cookery. To the Malay we owe the hot and spicy dishes of South Africa, as they were responsible for bringing with them to the Cape the many delectable spices of the East: turmeric, gira (cumin seed), cardamom, aniseed, barishap (fennel), bahia (star fennel), green and dried ginger, coriander, garlic, saffron, saltpetre, mussala, red pepper, mustard seed, the aromatic sari leaves, tamarind, and a wide variety of curry mixtures. In addition, they also converted locally available plants such as orange and lemon leaves, chutney, and dried apricots into seasoning agents. For anyone interested in experiencing the delights of Malay cooking, the best time to visit a Malay household is at the end of the 30-day Muslim Ramadan fast, which is usually followed immediately by the beginning of the Malay festival of Labaran with its great feast.

Born fishermen in a fisherman's paradise, and knowledgeable about preserving fish in a warm climate, the Malay made a lasting contribution to the practice of preserving and pickling fish and vegetables. This skill, even more than their expertise on other dishes, was what gave them a solid reputation and respect from the scurvy-scarred sailors of the Atlantic and the Indian Ocean worlds. In the hands of the Malay, the many ordinary fishes of the Cape such as the *maasbanker*, mackerel, galjoen, salmon, shad, *steenbras*, stumpnose, mullet, and stockfish were transformed into a wide assortment of delicious and popular dishes. With the abundance of fish supply at the Cape, the Malay had no problem keeping themselves busy; with the limited local demand for fish being met, they deployed their culinary arts toward preserving the bulk of their catch for export or for future use and sale. They developed two ways of preserving their fish. The first involves splitting the fish open, salting, braising, and drying it through smoking it or spreading it out to dry attached to lines and left dangling like laundry clothes in the sun. Dried snoek, the choicest of Cape fish, is the basis of *smoor-vis* or *gesmoorde vis*, two popular South African dishes. Salted and dried herring, *maasbankers*, grey mullet, and other smaller fishes, are known as *bokkems* (from the Dutch word, *bokking*, meaning herring or bloater), became a popular part of the diet, most especially of people too far away into the interior and beyond the reach of regular supplies of fresh fish.

With the battle against scurvy won, the Cape Malay developed other dishes, many of which are now among the best known national dishes of South Africa. The most notable of these are *bobotie, sosaties,* and *bredie.* There are as many ways of preparing each of these dishes as there are Malay homes in South Africa. The popularity of *bobotie,* a minced meat pie, has given it a sacramental quality as the national dish of South Africa. The basic ingredients for *bobotie* are minced lamb or beef, milk-soaked mashed bread, beaten eggs, butter, finely chopped onion, ground ginger, pounded almond (optional), garlic, curry powder or masala, and turmeric. Sugar or tamarind water can be added to the mixture for a particularly pleasant taste. The second great South African dish, *sosatie,* is formed from two Malay words: *sate,* which means spiced sauce, and *sesate,* which means meat on a skewer. Unlike the *bobotie,* which must be cooked and served at home, the *sosatie* is a more versatile treat. Well preserved in its marinade for days, it can be carried to and cooked anywhere, making it a particularly cherished outdoor meal. The third, if not the most, popular of the Cape Malay culinary gifts to South Africa is the *bredie,* a carefully flavored stew of meat and vegetables. The word *bredie* means spinach in Malagash, the language spoken by the neighboring island peoples of Madagascar, most of whom trace their distant origins to Indonesia, affirming again the dish's Eastern origin.

In addition, the Malay came up with a wide range of side dishes, salads, and condiments to accompany the main course. The most popular of these are *slaai,* a sliced or shredded vegetable dish; *sambal,* a grated and spiced cold fruits and vegetable dish; their many types of pickles known as *atjar.* Others include chutney sauce, made from heavily seasoned, cooked vegetables or fruits; *blatchangs,* a sauce made from a mixture of dry and pounded anchovies, vegetables, and sugar; *koesister,* spiced and plaited dough cake and one of the most fattening and most delicious pastries in the South African kitchen inventory; and *tameletje,* a caramelized sugar and vegetable sweet, much desired by children. In an international recipe book published by the United Nations in 1951, *bobotie* with yellow rice and raisins was selected as the representative South African dish; a clear testimony to the decisive role of the Malay in defining and developing a uniquely South African culinary tradition.

The French Huguenots and the Cape Wine Industry

Next in importance to the Malay is the French culinary influence at the Cape. The first group of French Huguenots arrived at the Cape in 1685, fleeing religious persecution in their homeland. Having left France before the eighteenth-century revolution in French cooking, living in scattered groups that made them vulnerable to easy assimilation by the Dutch, their impact at the Cape was a modest one. The French have been attributed with a variety of cooking practices: flavoring food delicately with herbs, using spices sparingly, and draining surplus fat from food. They also initiated in South Africa the practice of serving dishes in sequences beginning with the soup followed by the main course and concluded with the vegetable, fruit, or cake desert, instead of simultaneously. They also became famous for their sauces thickened with breadcrumbs. More importantly, coming from the world's most-renowned wine-making country, the Huguenots laid the foundation of South Africa's wine industry, for which the country soon became justly famous from the early eighteenth century. Made from the best of grapes, from Riesling, Sauvignon, and Clairette Blanche to Cabernet, Hermitage, Pontac, and Pinot

Diners at a restaurant in Pietermaritzburg, 2002.

varieties, the South African red and white wines rank among the most sought after by connoisseurs in different parts of the world. The distinctively fruity, purple-red Pinotage wine, developed exclusively in South Africa in 1925, has garnered in many international awards, most recently winning the gold medal at the 1997 Vin Expo Competition in France.[4]

Trekboer Staples and Specialities

In protest against the British advent, conquest, antislavery, and other policies, the Dutch settlers at the Cape migrated northward in the Great Trek. This northward push brought them into close contact with the African groups living in the interior. Far away from the Mediterranean climate of the Cape, they had to depend on different kinds of crops, fruits, and vegetables for their survival. Making virtue of necessity, they developed new culinary forms. They grew maize, which they called melie, and which the Africans soon adopted and called mealie. Mealie, which soon became a major staple of the African diet, became serviceable in the hands of the Trekboers, and their survival was in many ways connected with their ability to adapt creatively to this versatile crop in order to meet their dietary needs.

Dried fish meals, such as the *ingelegte vis* or the *gesmoorde snoek,* and the *moortjies* or *bokkems,* became both handy and serviceable in the wilderness of the interior. As for meat, the Trekboers, like the Africans, were reluctant to slaughter their limited stock of cattle for food; instead, they turned to hunting the abundant game of the South African veld, turning them into a wide variety of roasted or cooked venison dishes. Among the most popular of these is *boerewors,* a kind of farmer's sausage, made from mixed minced meats and deliciously spiced. Another is *biltong,* from two Afrikaans words, *bil* and *tong,* meaning buttock and tongue, since it is made of tongue-like strips of lean or cured beef, antelope, or ostrich meat, dried in the sun, and frozen until needed. *Potjiekos* refers to food such as venison, cubed lamb ribs, cooked in a *potjie* or a *drievoetpot,* a three-legged stand suspended over the fire. From the Africans the Trekboer pioneers learned to use scooped-out termite hills as bread ovens.[5]

TRADITIONAL AFRICAN DRESS

Originally all clothes were made from plants, animal skins, and brayed hides, but the advent of woven and manufactured cotton and other fabrics brought about far-reaching transformations in dressing materials and forms. For the African peoples and groups, dress makes and defines the person. A man or a woman's dress reveals immediately his or her age, sex, status, and ethnic group. While there is room for individual variation, what people wear is generally and carefully regulated by the society. Through dress, the man is differentiated from the woman, the boy from the girl, the married from the unmarried, the child from the toddler, the initiated from the novice, the adolescent from the young adult, the expectant mother from one still in search of pregnancy, the one who has born a child for her husband from the one whose womb is still cold and expecting, the commoners from the chiefs, the diviners from the others, and so on.

This regulation, in most cases, extends to the color of dress that one wears. Among the Zulu, for instance, white signifies purity, moral as well as sexual. As such, only a pubescent girl, because she is still technically a virgin, can wear a white cloth around her body; it is a taboo for a married woman to do so. White also represents beauty just as black represents defilement, resulting in the avoidance of black dress, except when mourning the death of a loved one. After a death and similar tragic occurrences, black medicine is prescribed to strengthen the bereaved and prevent further deaths. White medicine is simultaneously prepared to counter the untoward effects of the black medicine.

Using the Zulu-speaking people as a point of focus, while making references to other groups, the following sections will examine the nature and pattern of traditional dressing in South Africa. Before puberty, members of either sex wear very little. As infants and toddlers, the children go about naked, though a girdle, a string of beads or grass (*luqhotfo* in Swazi) may be worn around the waist, mainly for ornamental purposes. Usually the head is kept shaved, leaving only a small tuft, known as *isiguqa* (Zulu), in front. As the child nears the age of puberty, a piece of beadwork, three or more inches square, will be attached to the stringed girdle to cover the genital area. For a girl, this prepuce shield is known as *isigege* or *ubendle* when made from the leaves of the ubendle plant. Considered pure and innocent of sexual matters, girls can continue to go naked until they are well into their teenage years or, if they choose, they can wear, suspended from their shoulder, a white linen, the only color permissible to them at this age of ignorance.

Among the Swazi, a boy approaching the age of puberty is given a penile tip cover (*umncatfo*) fashioned from a special kind of calabash, wood, fruit shell, or even horn. As the boy approaches the age of puberty, a kilt of animal tails, or a coarsely made and untanned calf-skin buttock covering, *ibeshu,* cut into many twisted strips, would be given to him. At puberty, this is discarded for a properly tanned *umutsha,* presented to him by his father, consisting of a frontal covering of skin strips or tails (*isinene*) joined by a plant fiber or goat-skin cord to a back flap (*ibeshu*). Upon reaching puberty and as their breasts begin to bud, girls are permitted to take lovers, though they are not yet ready for full sexual intercourse or marriage. As she moves closer to the age of marriage, the girl exchanges her white garment for a red one, on which she can now wear both red and white beads. As she is now becoming exposed to sexual things, she is forbidden from wearing white, and she cannot yet wear spotted cloths, reserved exclusively for married women.

Thus, for women, the basic dress consists of aprons, cloaks, or skirts. The apron is often short and fringed with strings of beads or chords of rolled gazania leaves, as among the Southern Sotho. Initially the apron was made from skin, but now is made mostly from woven or manufactured fabrics. The style of the skirt also varies. Generally it consists of a large wrapper wound around the buttocks with the small apron hanging on top of it. The cloak can also be fashioned into a full skirt as among the Zulu and the Tsonga, or made up of two separate skin panels, linked or disconnected, but covering the woman's front and back sides. Breast covering was not always universal. Indeed, it was rare, since most women went bare-chested until well after their marriage. Where it was widely used, especially among the Xhosa, who were the first to come into direct contact with Europeans, breast covering appeared to have been an early concession to missionary influence and preaching against the immorality and indecency of such exposure. Basically the breast covering consists of a wrap tucked under the arm, tied at the back or around the neck; or a small piece of skin or beaded panel with fringes of beads attached and hanging loosely or tightly over the chest.

After her marriage a Zulu woman wears an *isidwaba* or *isiKhakha,* a kind of overlapping short leather skirt, tied to her waist by strings of animal skins, on top of which she wears her old preadolescent *isigege* ornament. Before the birth of her first child, and every time she is pregnant, the woman wears a brayed buckskin cloak (*isidiya* or *ingcayi*), sometimes fringed with brass ball ornaments (*ndonde*), tucked under her arms and tied at the back concealing both her abdomen as well as her breasts. A married woman must keep her breasts covered at all times, except when inside her kraal or homestead, but never in the presence of her father-in-law. When possible, her maternity apron is made of antelope skin, meant to give grace and strength to her baby. Whatever shape or form her cloth or blanket is, it can be of any color or combination of colors except white and pure red. On special and festive occasions, a woman wears a large leather gab (*ingubo*) or a profusely beaded cloth that drapes off from her shoulders to her knees and, depending on her status, covers her feet. For ladies of high rank this garment is adorned at the back by one or two extended strips extending for more than two yards beyond her feet and forming a Victorian-like lady's trailing train. The long trains worn by Ndebele women signify their married status. At night, the leather coat serves as a covering for the children with the hairy or beaded side facing outward.

Other than among some Xhosa groups, male nudity without either the penile sheath or prepuce cover is uncommon. Loin cloths (*emahiya* in Swazi) or aprons, usually wrapped around the waist, are common. Alone or on top of the loin wrapper, Swazi men superimpose two skin aprons, one in front (*amajobo*) and one at the back (*emabeba*), both like the *emahiya* tied on the right hip. It is considered improper for a man to venture beyond his kraal without his *amajobo,* which in some cases is large enough to wind around his entire waist. Among all the groups, usually little or nothing is worn above the waist, except during inclemental weather. To keep warm, men cover the top of their torsos with a skin cloak, called *sinokoti,* if made of antelope or cattle skin, and *siphuku,* when made of goat hide. In recent times, the skin cloak has been generally replaced by cloth or blanket draped over the right shoulder and under the left armpits. On becoming adults, Zulu men replace their adolescent *umutsha* with a larger one, consisting of a frontal apron made from the skin of a small animal and matched at the back side by a kilt of untwisted genet skin strips. Zulu men who have the means can acquire the *qubulo* dress used during the slow and stately *qubulo* dance that usually accompanies wedding ceremonies and the annual national festival of the first fruits. The dress is made up of three kilts of the *insimango* monkey tails, worn over the buttocks, above the hips, and over the shoulders, respectively. Unlike the Zulu and the Xhosa, both the Venda and the Sotho have dispensed with the penis sheath; instead they dress their bosom with a triangular skin apron, wound around the waist, with one point passing between the legs to be tied to the other two ends at the back, forming a most effective under garment and rendering the ubiquitous penis sheath obsolete.

Ceremonial Dresses and Costumes

Ceremonial dresses and costumes vary by gender, age, sometimes profession, and generally from group to group. Young boys going through the rites of initiation into adulthood wear elaborate costumes of palm leaf, grass, or other plants to conceal their identity and signify their liminal status. Bantwane and Pedi girls divest themselves of their everyday clothing before entering their initiation lodge to bring their childhood age to a symbolic close. The elaborate grass garments, rings, wrist bands, anklets, and other plant ornaments represent fertility and affirm their future roles as wives and mothers. Young Sotho girls going through the *bale* initiation school have their semi-nude bodies whitened with clay or powdered sandstone, and they ornament themselves with beaded masks, clay beads, rings of plaited and bound grass waist bands, and sheepskin or cloth aprons.

A Zulu bridal procession consists of the richly beaded bride and more than a dozen of her more lightly beaded maiden friends who escort her to the groom's father's kraal. An Ndebele bridal walk on the other hand, involves just two people: the bride, clad in her newly beaded gala blanket and ornaments that she made during her betrothal period, and the bride's maid, usually a niece or the eldest daughter of the eldest sister, who serves as the bride's chaperon to the groom's kraal. At her future home she is led into a matted enclosure in a hut, probably her hut-to-be. Here, shrouded from head to toe in her red blanket, she receives visitors and other well-wishers. With the conclusion of all the marriage ceremonials, the recently married lady can now wear, on special occasions, such as the circumcision of her son, her expertly designed, usually red, gala dress of sheepskin cloak, with its white, heavily beaded shoulder, front and back panels, and two-sided trailing train.

Warriors are also distinguished by the additional features to their everyday dress such as the headdress of crane feathers among the Xhosa, an assortment of colorful feathers among the Zulu, and ostrich and other feather attachments among the Ndebele and the Sotho. Diviners or Sangoma, who are predominantly women and thus usually attired in typical married women's dress, are unmistakable for their elaborate costumes and insignia which include dreadlock-beaded hair, chest bands of animal skins, snake skins, dry and inflated gall bladders of sacrificial animals, anklets and wristbands, and a switch of the sacred wildebeest or cow tail to match. Red, white, and black beads predominate in the Sangoma's attire as these are the colors generally associated with the ancestors with whom they maintain constant communication. In many places, the wearing of a leopard skin cloak is the exclusive preserve of royalty, and among the Xhosa the elephant tail is their insignia.[6]

Ornaments and Adornments

Among South African peoples, ornaments and adornments are not considered to be separate from dressing; rather, they are integral. Starting with the head, great attention is paid to how the hair is dressed, from childhood, through adolescence to adulthood. Different forms of hairstyle have developed: shaving the whole head except for a tuft in front (*isiguqa*); allowing the hair to grow into a thick mass (*isihiuthu*); twisting the hair into long pigtails of three strings each (*izinwele-ezalukiwe*); greasing and dressing the hair into long strings (*isiyendane*); and winding fiber around greased and stringed hair. Girls sometimes allow their hair to hang over their forehead to be decorated with beads (*isicelankobe*) or clipped and patted to form crisp and tiny curls over their head. Young men on the other hand will brush their hair into a standing mop above the head or dress the hair in ridges and relief rows to which they can attach various objects such as feathers and flowers. Crane feathers studded to the hair of a young Zulu man announce to maidens that he is on a courting mission, and the posy flower on his head is believed to contain elements capable of fostering amorous passion.

The dressing of hair with beads, especially by girls, creates rooms for stylistic expressions. As the young Zulu woman approaches marriage, she begins to wear the tall, ochred topknot hair style (*isicholo*) distinctive of a married woman. To construct this, the hair must first be plaited with grass to straighten it. Thereafter, using fiber-strings and a mixture of sour milk and red ochre, the hair in the center of the head is sewn together and greased, while the rest of the head is shaved. It has also become fashionable to leave a few strings of hair hanging over the eyes around which ornamental beads and brass rings are attached. Below the topknot or the upward flared headgear (before the birth of her first child and in the presence of her husband's male relations) a woman wears a colorfully decorated band of cloth, beads, or rushes, to indicate her respect for her husband and parents-in-laws. To lengthen the topknot, the hair will be undone and replaited periodically. First put up at her betrothal, the topknot cannot be cut until she is widowed. For a woman to cut her topknot outside of bereavement is to send a firm but insulting message to her husband that she wishes him dead. A great variety of topknots have developed, including detachable ones for those who work in the cities or cannot make them. The head of a young Ndebele woman is shaved completely, except for a few tufts, left for ornamental purpose and sometimes representing a current boyfriend.

In many places, married men decorate their heads with brightly colored feathers. Among the Zulu and the Swazi married men wear the head ring which is made from a circlet of fibre plant or root to which honeycomb black-wax is applied and then left to dry before being greased and polished with pebbles and leaves. As the symbol of his manhood, the man wears the ring at all times, removing it only for a period to mourn the death of his wife. To pull off a man's head ring or even take hold of it in a fit of rage is the greatest insult, an affront to his manhood, and a challenge to the authority of the chief who granted him the permission to wear it. Other headgear includes the often heavily beaded skin caps worn by Thembu and Xhosa women; the beaded knob worn over the forehead by married Bhaca women; the tall head knob of the Zulu woman that indicates many years of marriage; the beaded crown hoop worn by Pondo women to indicate marriage; the helmet-like coiffure headgear of married Ntwana women; and the brimmed or unbrimmed but sharply conical hats of the Southern Sotho.

Cosmetics used by the various groups vary, though the most common is fat, which gives the body a shining and healthy look. Among the Xhosa, Thembu, Sotho, Venda, and the Zulu, butter fat is mixed with red ochre to form a grease widely used for body beautification and for ritual anointing of individuals in liminal states. No Zulu young man will venture on a courting trip without first generously anointing himself with this grease and sprinkling his body with highly scented powder. A mixture of sour milk and red ochre, fat and aloe leaf ash, soot, charcoal, antimony, white and yellow ochre, and graphite are among the many other cosmetics used for both hair and body dressing. Only a few groups practice circumcision, and body scarification is not common. The Zulu are noted for piercing the ears of their children to confer on them wisdom and maturity. The Pondo, however, make patterned multiple small incisions on the faces of their children as an appeasement to ancestral spirits.

Before the introduction of glass beads, a wide variety of materials were used for body ornamentation. Notable among these were reeds, wood, and roots for necklaces and bangles; cowry and snail shells; claw, skin, bone and teeth of animals for strings, armlets, and headbands; and elephant tusk and horn for various ornaments. Metal objects, such as iron and copper, and even more significantly, brass and brass wire are serviceable in the fashioning of arm and leg bands and bangles. The first major source of beads to South Africa were the Swahili City States of East Africa, where the Arabs, and later the Portuguese, were trading. This explains why the use of beads was first established

A maiden dancer in her richly beaded attire, Gauteng, 2002.

in the northern part of southern Africa rather than in the southern region. Soon, however, European traders at the Cape began to import beads into the country, making them more widely available all over South Africa. Before long, beads became the single most important item of body and dress ornamentation among most of the African peoples of South Africa, who fashioned them into elaborate ornaments and wove or embroidered them into fascinating beadwork, skin, and cloth fabrics.

For everyday use as well as for festive occasions ornaments are made by both boys and girls, though girls' are often more elaborate. Among the most common are broad and narrow bands of beads of varying sizes, shapes, shades, and styles, to be worn around the forehead, neck, wrist, over the shoulders and breasts, around the waist, hips, and ankles, or hung like pendants and pigtails from the ear and hair. The multicolored, open-mesh, beaded collar is among the most impressive of the ornaments worn by Xhosa, Pedi, and Zulu women. In the hands of the Zulu and other South African groups, the beads were given voices with which they have continued to speak. Through beads, love messages are encrypted, sent, and decoded; the bead-work or forms worn by an individual immediately reveal his or her age, social and marital status, as well as ethnic or religious affiliation. Beadwork of different forms, shapes, sizes, patterns, and styles, are the most popular curio export from South Africa today. Their message of love, beauty, hope, joy, industry, diversity, and brotherhood is a universal one, striking many chords as it echoes far and wide. In many ways, for blacks and whites, citizens and tourists, the often exquisitely fashioned beadwork has become the unifying symbol of the new South Africa.

TRADITIONAL EUROPEAN DRESS

Fashion and Costume at the Cape and Beyond

The changing nature and forms of European dressing styles were followed closely in South Africa while allowing for local modifications. The difficulties of communication between the Cape and Europe ensured that the South African style was always a step or two behind those of Europe. A typical example of the dress of the first white settlers exists in an extant statue of Maria, the wife of Jan van Riebeeck, the leader of the first group of Europeans to settle at the Cape. In this portrait, she is presented as wearing a tight bodice, pointed in front and laced behind, decorated with slanting rows of braid or trimming converging at the waistline. Her accessories include a small cap and a cloth neck collar, edged with pillow lace sloping over from her neck to cover and hide her shoulders. These collars were often made from scarves or linen, and the neck opening, which was usually wide, could be V-shaped, circular, or square. The skirts, which were usually full and gathered or pleated at the waist, differed in color and material from the petticoat underneath. The hair was pulled straight backward and covered with a neckerchief or a lace-trimmed white cap while indoors or a close-fitting black cap for outdoor outings.

By Riebeeck's time, the typical coat for men was the military one, with its hip-length flaps, back and side slits, buttoned front, and wide-neck collar. Under this loose and sloppy long coat or its abbreviated (shortened to the waist to reveal more of the shirt) version, and in addition to their shirts, men had the choice of one of three types of breeches: the long full type, usually gathered in just below the knee into stocking-like bands and bows; the tubular, long, baggy, shorts-like breeches, unconfined at the knee, generally embroidered with golden or black rows of braid at the helm; and finally the divided skirt or kilt-like petticoat breeches, usually braced at the edges with ribbon loops and bunches. Men designed their hair to hang to the shoulders, while framing the face in curls. Hats were made of felt with pliable, broad rims, that were at times adorned with feathers or ribbons to complete the picture. Boys and girls were dressed like grown men and women respectively, and children of both sexes wore aprons. Servants followed the example of their mistresses, except that they often had to content themselves with castoffs that were usually a few steps out of fashion.

The Cape Malay men and women, both the free and servile, were noted for their colorful attires. Women treated their glossy black hair with coconut butter, brushing it backward into a bun that would be secured with a golden skewer, while leaving a kiss-curl on the cheek. Both men and women wore wooden sandals, known as *kaparrings,* while the men dressed their shaven heads with brightly colored kerchiefs, over which they often wore the pagoda-shaped cane hat, which came with their forebears from the East.

The late seventeenth century, which saw the arrival of the French Huguenots, also witnessed the advent of the collarless petticoat (usually blue), worn with tighter breeches that were fastened under the knees with buckles. These new garments, with linen cravat neckwear, the inevitable wig, and the ubiquitous three-cornered hats or tricorne remained the dominant fashion for much of the eighteenth century. Cape Malay women who, like the men constituted the bulk of the servile class, distinguished themselves as excellent embroiderers and knitters turning out impressive garments for their mistresses and their consorts.

The nineteenth century witnessed many changes, though simplicity in form and elegance in taste remained the most enduring features of fashion for the era. By the time the 1820 British settlers appeared in South Africa, the trouser had already made its appearance and become a dominant trend of the future. Overcoats with overlapping capes and choker collar neckties became fashionable. The *voortrekkers* who went northward from the Cape from the late 1830s onward took with them their jackets, trousers, shirts, neck cloths, waistcoats, and hats. Clothes made of moleskin, buckskin, and calfskin and hats made of straw or beaver's plush were not uncommon. The women took along their one-piece frocks, lined and full skirts, and multilayered petticoats. The poke-bonnet kappie became the most distinctive item of dress worn by *voortrekker* women during this period. Made of layers of silk and linen quilts, skillfully stitched together by hand, effectively shielding the face and the neck, it preserved the complexion of the wearer, besides protecting her face against the dust of the veld. Many of the dresses from this early period never survived, since people used them until they were completely worn out, but published extant portraits from the late nineteenth and early twentieth centuries show the characteristic fashion forms during this era.[7] By the mid-twentieth century, dresses became shorter, more brazen, less modest, and more revealing as improved communication and travel began to transform fashion from an expression of local culture into a global phenomenon of cross-cultural interaction.

The Spread of European Dress: Adoption and Adaptations

The advent and permanent settlement of Europeans in South Africa from the mid-seventeenth century resulted in far-reaching transformation in the social lives of the various African peoples with whom they would later come in direct contact. Probably in no other area of material culture is this transformation more dramatic and more evident than in dressing styles and forms. First, with the introduction of cotton fibers, Africans began to reproduce traditional styles in textiles instead of using tree bark, reeds, grass, hides, and beads. In some cases people continued to wear the skin costume under or over the newly introduced cotton clothes. In most cases, however, and in the face of missionary and other western influences in church and in schools, entirely new styles of dressing emerged.

The new styles were usually patterned after European forms, though with considerable rooms for local creativity and adaptations. Among the Cape Nguni, the Ndebele, and the Xhosa, the woolen blankets began to replace the cloaks for men, while their women adopted the plain cotton sheets and blankets, dying them in red, orange, or pale blue colors, and fashioning them into short skirts for girls, and ankle-length skirts for married women. Among the Pondo white was originally the sign of mourning, but after an unusually protracted mourning for an important chief the women developed a new taste for white and adopted the white cotton sheets dyed in pale blue to make it sparkling and whiter, as their ceremonial costume. Impressed by the snuggly fitting flared maternity smocks European hospitals gave their expectant African women, Ntwana and other women promptly adopted these maternity smocks as fashionable everyday dress for married women to symbolize fruitful womanhood. Under this ample gown, Ntwana women, especially in the rural areas, continued to wear their traditional spatulate goatskin back cloth and their cloth or beaded leather long apron.[8]

In the same vein, the Xhosa, the Thembu, and the Mpondo women also adopted the widely flaring European garment. On top of this they often add an assortment of ochred breast cloths, braided skirts, wrapping garbs, and (as

among the Xhosa) highly colorful turbans, providing for the beholder a strikingly gorgeous, dignified, and spectacular appearance. Smoother cloth dyed
in black or brown was the favorite choice of the Zulu to replace their skin
cloaks. The Venda and the Tsonga adopted the same cloth type but preferred
the striped patterns. South Sotho women retained their adopted nineteenth-
century full, ankle-length, gathered skirts, with their assortments of petticoats, blouses, and shawls. The Sotho woman, however, continued to wear
under her layers of cotton petticoats her short skirt made of twisted fiber,
which was her indispensable symbol of womanhood. Like their Xhosa counterparts, Sotho men took very enthusiastically to European woolen blankets.
First introduced by a German trader from Bali early in the nineteenth century, the woolen blanket remains one article of cloth that has remained in
fashion and in demand. The blanket cloak, most especially the multicolored,
vertically striped one, also became the favorite top garb of Ndebele women.
So intensive was the Sotho and the Ndebele demand for the woolen or Victoria blanket that Britain developed a highly profitable business and trade
weaving this pattern exclusively for the South African market.

The advent and popularity of European dressing styles, however, has not
meant an end to the wearing of traditional forms. The change has been more
dramatic and pronounced in the urban areas. Indeed so pervasive is this European impact that in the cities of South Africa the sight of people in traditional
garb is a rare occurrence, a trend not seen in other African countries such as
Ghana or Nigeria. In the rural areas, however, traditional forms, often in
modern adaptations, have managed to survive. In many places, the sustained
campaign against apartheid and European domination resulted in a renaissance of traditional forms, in rituals as well as in costumes. In one of his pre-
Rivonia trial court appearances in Pretoria, Nelson Mandela startled and
impressed the court audience when he appeared in court dressed in the full
traditional leopard regalia of a prince of the Xhosa-Thembu royal family. In
recent years, most especially since the end of apartheid and the onset of a new
democratic South Africa, the search for cultural authenticity has resulted in
the adoption by new generations of South African elite of popular dressing
styles from other African cultures. Asante *kente* dresses, Yoruba *agbada* (large
gown) and Hausa's *dansiki* have become costumes of choice among South
Africans of all colors.

Even more consequential and pervasive has been the adoption by Africans
of other more enduring European forms, such as shirts and trousers for men
and skirts, blouses, and gowns for women. With the suits or coats and ties,
these have become the most common everyday formal and informal dresses
for the majority of the South African populations. In the mines and indus-

tries, on the farms and the streets, in the rural and urban markets, and among all social and cultural groups, the overwhelming pervasiveness of these European forms cannot be denied. This ubiquitous establishment of European styles everywhere in the country, clearly qualifies them to be classified among South African traditional dressing forms. In the meantime, the renaissance of old indigenous styles, the invention of new forms, and the synthesis of traditional and modern to validate the emergence of a new society, continue unabated. In 2001, South Africa hosted the Miss World contest, signaling, among other things, its return to and reintegration into the vibrant, quickly changing, and interconnected world of international fashion.

NOTES

1. For a fuller discussion of the Bantu culinary traditions and the major sources for what follows, see Margaret Shaw, "Material Culture," in W. D. Hammond-Tooke, ed., *The Bantu-Speaking Peoples of Southern Africa* (London and Boston: Routledge and Kegan Paul, 1975), 99–101; P. J. Quin, *Foods and Feeding Habits of the Pedi with Special Reference to Identification, Classification, Preparation and Nutritive Value of the Respective Foods* (Johannesburg: Witwatersrand University Press, 1959); A. T. Bryant, *The Zulu People As They Were Before the White Man Came* (Pietermaritzburg: Shuter and Shooter, 1967), 264–95; Brian A. Marwick, *The Swazi: An Ethnographic Account of the Natives of the Swaziland Protectorate* (London: Frank Cass & Co. Ltd., 1966), 77–80; Eileen Jensen Krige, *The Social System of the Zulus* (Pietermaritzburg: Shuter and Shooter, 1965), 53–60, 383–87; and Vida Heard and Lesley Faull, *Cookery in Southern Africa: Traditional and Today* (Cape Town: Books of Africa, 1970), 471–83.

2. *Insight Guide: South Africa* (London: APA Publications, 2000), 110.

3. Quin, *Foods and Feeding Habits of the Pedi,* 255.

4. On the French Huguenots and the development of the wine industry at the Cape, see: Laurens van der Post, *First Catch Your Eland* (New York: William Morrow and Co. Inc., 1978); *African Cooking* (New York: Time-Life Books, 1970), 153–56; Renata Coetzee, *The South African Culinary Tradition* (Cape Town: C. Struick, 1977), 28–43. On the Pinotage wine industry, see: *Eyewitness Travel Guides: South Africa* (Cape Town: DK Publishing Ltd., 1999), 120–43.

5. For fuller discussions of the Dutch and Trekboer culinary contributions see: Post, *First Catch Your Eland,* 147–212; *African Cooking* (New York: Time-Life Books, 1970), 173–99; Renata Coetzee, *The South African Culinary Tradition,* 28–43. See also the notable and richly illustrated book of recipes by Myna Rosen and Lesley Loon, *South African Gourmet Food and Wine* (Pittsburgh, Pa.: Dorrance Publishing Co., Inc., 1997), which included several entries on traditional South African food. For a compendium of traditional recipes, see Hildagonda Duckitt, *Traditional South African Cookery* (New York: Hippocrene Books, 1996).

6. On African traditional dress forms and the major sources for the discussion in this section, see Barbara Tyrrell, *Tribal Peoples of Southern Africa* (Cape Town: T. V. Bulpin, 1976); Tyrrell, "Bantu Costume," *Standard Encyclopedia of Southern Africa,* vol. 2, 72–77; Shaw, "Material Culture," in Hammond-Tooke, ed., *The Bantu-Speaking Peoples,* 101–3; Bryant, *The Zulu People,* 132–73; Marwick, *The Swazi,* 84–86; Krige, *The Social System of the Zulus* (Pietermaritzburg: Shuter and Shooter, 1965) 370–82; and Sandra Klopper, "Zulu," in *Dictionary of Art,* vol. 33, 723–25.

7. Trudie Kestell, "Costume, Historical," in *Standard Encyclopedia of Southern Africa* (Cape Town: NASOU Limited, 1970), Vol. 3, 453. For additional information on the historical development of European dressing styles in South Africa, see two well-illustrated accounts: A. A. Telford, *Yesterday's Dress: A History of Costume in South Africa* (Cape Town: Purnell, 1972) and D. H. Strutt, *Fashion in South Africa, 1652–1900* (Cape Town: Balkema, 1975).

8. Tyrrell, *Tribal Peoples of Southern Africa,* 70–78, 165–74.

8

Gender Roles, Marriage, and Family

The institutions of kinship and marriage are at the core of South African culture. It is around them that the traditional social and political systems are structured. While the pressures of modernization associated with European colonialism, Christianity, Western education, industrialization, urbanization, and labor migration have resulted in major transformations, the institutions of kinship and marriage remain vital elements in the ordering of interpersonal and intergroup relations, the structure and management of social organization, and the definition of social identity and cultural consciousness among the peoples of South Africa. Kinship, based on the fundamental reality of biological descent, is the moral basis for the structuring of social relations and social organization. Through kinship, individuals and homesteads, irrespective of their spatial locations, became associated as relations, as members of the same clan, and as descendants of the same ancestor, now bound fundamentally together by the factors of blood, marriage, and adoption.[1]

MARRIAGE

Among the peoples of South Africa, marriage is the key institution around which the entire social structure revolves. Through marriage, kinship relations are established and reinforced. In its most basic function, marriage is directed at producing children, thus ensuring biological generation and genealogical continuity. In addition, through marriage the human needs for sexual expression, physical intimacy, psychological comfort, and social partnership are satisfied and contained. Among the Bantu-speaking peoples of South Africa, three basic rules are generally observed in regard to marriage.

First, while a woman may have only one husband at a time, a man may have more than one wife at any time if he so desires and has enough resources. Second, marriage involves a form of patrivirilocal residence in which the woman joins her husband after marriage, either at his homestead or at that of his father or brother. Third, marriage is not considered legal or consummated until after the transfer of the bridewealth or *lobola,* usually in the form of cattle, from the groom's family to the bride's.[2]

Choice of Marriage Partners

With its important function of linking families to families and lineages to lineages, and of connecting all these together within the wider social system, the choice of marriage partners is not made lightly. There are well-established and strictly followed rules determining who can marry who or not marry who and which clan one can marry into or marry from, usually based on lineage relations and cultural practices, rather than residential propinquity. Among the Nguni, clan exogamy is the rule, implying that any girl from one's father or mother's clan or with the same last name is strictly precluded from being considered a life partner. This means that marriage partners are usually strangers, not related and from a different descent group, who are from far-away or nearby wards. However, occasionally the chosen partner can be a former playmate, drawn from neighboring families not related directly by blood to one's own agnatic clans. On the other hand, among the Sotho and the Venda, the rules are different. Less emphasis is placed on exogamic relationship. Cross-cousin (mother's brother's daughter or father's sister's daughter) or parallel cousin (father's brother's daughter) marriages are the norm.

Almost everywhere in Africa, one's father's brother's daughters are described in kinship terminology as sisters; marriage to one's sister is regarded as being tantamount to incest. This makes the Sotho-Tswana, along with the Arab Bedouins, unique in Africa for the practice of parallel-cousin marriages. For the Sotho as well as for the Tswana, marrying within one's clan helps to keep the *bogadi* (bridewealth) in the family. Nevertheless, such marriages have far-reaching implications. The stability and longevity of these unions are enhanced by the fact that they involve two people who have known each other all their lives and have lived together and grown up in and within the same family. Divorcing one's sister is more difficult than divorcing a stranger. On the other hand, parallel-cousin marriages deny their practitioners the opportunity to use marriage as the basis for forming and consolidating new forms of social relations and alliances across clans and groups and with a wider social system. Cross-cousin marriages, where practiced, are not mandatory though they are expected. They are more flexible than parallel-cousin marriages since they involve taking marriage partners from descent groups other than one's own. In partrilineal societies, one's mother's brother's daughter and one's father's sister's daughter belong to other families different from one's own, and can thus qualify as one's marriage partners.[3]

Significance of the Bridewealth Exchange

The departure of a daughter from her family to become a wife in another creates a gap in the departing daughter's family. Filling this gap requires compensation from the groom's family for the loss of the daughter's presence, service, and productive labor. In some African societies this compensation is arranged through an exchange of sisters most especially from the groom's family to provide marriage partners for eligible young men in the bride's family. In other places and in cases where suitable sisters are not available for exchange, the groom and his brothers may perform other commensurate services for the bride's family. In virtually all South African societies, this compensation is expressed in the form of material compensation, or bridewealth transfer, known as *lobola* among the Nguni, and as *bogadi* among the Tswana. Traditionally, the *lobola* consists of cattle, usually not more than eight head, though more are expected from members of the royal family, other important dignitaries, and men of considerable means. While the practice of *lobola* has continued in rural areas, for contemporary urban dwellers of South Africa with limited or no access to cattle, *lobola* can be paid in cash. Calculated to reflect its equivalent value in cattle, such payment remains an expensive transaction for most urban workers, requiring the accumulation of months or years of earnings.

More than any other rites, the act of bridal wealth exchange is the vital element that legalizes the marriage, effectively transferring certain vital rights over the woman from her father or guardian to her husband and his family. The rights that are transferred can be grouped into two categories. In the first group are rights over the woman as a wife (rights *in uxorem*). These include rights of sexual access, now the exclusive preserve of her husband, his family, and whoever they may designate or permit. Also included in these rights is control over her labor and productive powers both domestically as well as in the fields. The second set of rights relate to a woman's procreative powers. These rights *in genetricem* give to the husband and his family legal control over all children born to the woman for as long as she is legally married to the man. This right can only be reversed through divorce, which usually involves the return of the bridewealth from the bride's family to the husband's. The centrality of cattle in legalizing marriage and in giving social status to the offspring of marriage is affirmed in the popular Nguni saying that "Cattle beget children," or as the Zulu says, children are "born through the cow."[4]

Marriage Forms and Conjugal Practices

The effectiveness of the transfer of ownership effected by cattle exchange is evident in the fact that no matter who the actual genitor or biological father of a woman's children is, only the woman's legal husband—whether dead or alive, virile or impotent—is regarded as the *pater* or social father of her children. Thus children born out of an adulterous relationship involving the woman belong to her legal husband. Her lover has no legal or social claim over the product of the illicit relationship, and can be forced to pay a fine for trespassing on the rights of another man or family. In the same vein, an impotent man can ask any of his kinsmen to have intercourse with his wife to ensure her procreation. The issue from that intercourse belongs to the husband who is regarded as their father. The brother's function is merely biological and purely on behalf of his disabled kinsman. It is also not forbidden for the family of a perennially absent migrant labor husband to welcome the birth of children born of an affair as a permissible way of ensuring the continuing productivity of the woman and of fulfilling an important obligation of the marriage.

It is important to note that in all these arrangements the emphasis is not on the individual but on the family. Marriage is first and foremost a union of two families, not just of two lovers, even though love and personal choice are not always ignored. The union of a man and a woman creates a new house within the family. Once created, the new house must not be allowed to die. To ensure this, different safeguards are put in place. The first major deterrent is the bridewealth, which will have to be returned to validate the dissolution of a marriage. The complication created by this requirement works to compel commitment to consolidating and preserving the union among all the members of the family to avoid a denuding of the family stock. Everything is done to make the woman welcome and comfortable by providing her with living quarters, a field or fields for farming, cattle for milking, and lifelong security and by ensuring that her sexual and procreative needs are taken care of, primarily by her husband, or by others when and where the husband is personally incapable of fulfilling his obligations in any of these areas.

In cases where a woman is found to be barren, her sister or another female relative from her family can be sent to put children in her womb, by conceiving for her sister's husband and producing children who will regard and call the barren woman their mother. In cases where the woman's family cannot send a substitute, they may be required to return the bridewealth to the husband's family, which will then be used to acquire a second wife who in turn will bear children for the barren woman to whom the children legally belong. Among the Zulu and the Swazi, no bridewealth is exchanged for the substitute woman if provided by the wife's family. Among the Lovedu and Southern Sotho, full bridewealth, though slightly lesser in amount, is required to consummate the second marriage. In a situation where the wife dies before producing issue for her husband's family, her family is obligated to send a substitute wife, most likely a sister of the deceased, "to set up the house that has fallen."[5] When, as among the Zulu, the deceased wife has given birth to more than two children, her family is no longer obligated to send a substitute or return the bridewealth unless they choose to since she is presumed to have fulfilled her procreative obligation. On the other hand, among the Southern Sotho and the Lovedu, the death of a married woman without any issue puts no obligation on her family to provide a substitute wife unless they so chose, and in that case they are entitled to a full bridewealth for the second woman. These measures are generally directed at ensuring the continuation of the union of families created by the marriage transfer, and they feature prominently in societies such as the Zulu's, the Tsonga's, and the Venda's. Among these groups, sororal polygyny (the marriage of one man to two or more sisters) is believed to be more resilient since sisters and cousins are believed to have a better chance of getting along more readily than unrelated wives. Each sister involved, of course, establishes her own house, is independent of the other wives, and is ranked according to her time of entry into the family, not according to her age in relation to her co-sister wives.

Similarly, the death of the man or husband need not bring an end to the marriage. In most cases, except among the Xhosa, the Thembu, and some Southern Sotho groups, a close relative of the deceased husband, usually a younger brother, a paternal nephew, or a son by another woman, assumes responsibility for providing full domestic, economic, and marital support for the woman. Of primary importance is the raising of the children for the deceased. Depending on the circumstances, the woman may remain in her husband's homestead where she is regularly visited and supported by the surrogate husband (*levir*) or she may move to his homestead. Whatever the situation, the children born of the new relationship belong to the deceased man and refer to him as their father (*pater*). In assuming these responsibilities, the *levir* ensures the continuance of the original marriage and affirms the principle that marriage consummated through the transfer of cattle is a union between two families rather than between two individuals. As such, the death of a spouse need not spell the end of this union of families. What is considered improper and therefore subject to prosecution is for the widow to leave her husband's family to live with a man not related to him or his family. For a woman who has already borne her husband many children or has passed her childbearing age, the levirate laws may not be enforced unless she so desires them to be for her own care. In such cases, the woman remains in the homestead of her husband, where she is cared for by either her eldest or youngest son, or any son taking over the homestead of his departed father.

In some cases, as among the Zulu, when a man of influence and property dies without leaving an heir or sometimes before marrying a betrothed woman, his full or half brother may find and marry the betrothed or a new woman in the dead man's name, bearing children in his name and thus raising an heir for him. The new woman becomes the basis for the creation of a new homestead. This homestead is named after the deceased and within it the new woman and her children are bestowed with all the rights and privileges that would have accrued to them had their father been alive. Known as *uku-vusa* among the Zulu and as *tsosa leina la mohu* (to raise the name of the deceased) among the Pedi, this type of marriage is very rare and occurs mainly among nobles and important dignitaries among whom the question of heirs and succession is of paramount importance.

Woman-to-woman marriage is another practice adopted by some South African societies to ensure the continuity of a house in the absence of sons or due to the death of the husband. Among the Southern Sotho an affluent but childless widow can marry a woman of her choice, thus bringing her into the family to provide a son and an heir to her husband and his property. A Lovedu widow with no son can use the cattle obtained through the marriage of her daughters to marry a wife, through whom she hopes to have a son and thus an heir to her deceased husband's house. The most elaborate form of woman-to-woman marriage is associated with the office of the Lovedu Rain Queen who, by virtue of her position as paramount ruler and her power as rain queen, receives many gifts of wives from her subjects and others in her kingdom and beyond who desire her favors. Many of these women are daughters of the queen's district headmen. Some of these women are in turn sent out as headmen of districts, as wives to district headmen, or to others in the kingdom deserving of the queen's favor. They fulfill a vital political function in establishing and cementing affinal ties and political linkages between the queen and her dependent districts and subject peoples and groups. Some of the women are, however, retained in the royal court, where they bear children for the queen. These children are, of course, fathered by men designated or permitted by her sovereign to carry out such conjugal tasks.

Among the Zulu, as among the Venda, daughters who succeed to the property of their fathers due to lack of sons may use the cattle so obtained to marry wives for themselves through whom they can raise a male heir to the house of their deceased fathers. Among the Lovedu and the Venda, women who have

Mothers and children, beading in front of their cone-on-cylinder house, Gauteng, 2002.

acquired wealth through trade or have become affluent through divination can use their wealth to marry wives in their own right. Though the children born through this marriage may take the name of the wealthy woman's husband, who is most probably their genitor, they belong with their mother to the house of the wealthy woman, the female-husband, and she exercises jural authority over them. In other cases, the female-husband designates a lover for her wife, usually among her deceased husband's or father's kinsmen, but the children born of the union belong to the female-husband and her deceased husband who continues to be regarded as the father (*pater*) to the children.[6]

Procedures and Ceremonies of Marriage

In virtually all South African societies, there is a clear distinction between biological fatherhood (genitor) and social fatherhood (*pater*). The *pater* is the one who gives the bridewealth for the woman, irrespective of who the genitor is. In the light of this principle, it is understandable how a woman can be the real or social father in a woman-to-woman marriage. The procedures for determining the amount of the bridewealth and how and when it is paid vary from group to group. Among the Nguni, the amount to be paid is subject to considerable negotiation. It need not be paid off before marriage, and in practice it is paid off in small installments over the course of several years after the marriage. Among most Sotho groups, such as the Pedi, bargaining over the bridewealth is unthinkable. The groom's family, often after some private consultations with the bride's family, offers what they think is fair or what they can afford, and whatever they offer must be transferred in full before marriage can take place. Marriage negotiations take different forms, though the first initiative is usually from the boy's parents; however, the parents of the girl can also start the process by taking the initiative as is frequently and generally done among the Xhosa. For Zulu royal families it is customary for the woman's family to take the first step in approaching the family of a suitable man on behalf of their daughters. An accepted practice among the Northern Nguni, known as *ukubaleka,* permits a girl, at the prompting of her lover or her father and often purely on her own initiative, to present herself at the homestead of the man she desires to marry.

How and when a marriage is considered consummated also varies from one group to the other. Two major forms and practices can be delineated. For the Sotho-Tswana and the Venda, the crucial element is the payment of the bridewealth. This ceremony takes place in the bride's father's home and is attended with much fanfare. The subsequent transfer of the bride to the home of her new husband receives little attention and is attended with practically no ritual ceremony.

On the other hand, among the Nguni the focus of attention is on the bride and her party as well as on her father's home, where the major ceremonies usually take place. The turning point in the marriage consummation is the transfer of the bride, an event attended with considerable ceremony and activity in contrast to the delivery of the bridewealth to her father, which usually occurs very much later and with little or no ritual emphasis. Among the Xhosa, the act of marriage involves a process called *ukuthwala,* in which the bride is kidnapped by the groom with the help of his friends. This can also be done where the bride's family is perceived to be dragging its feet in the marriage negotiation. Thereafter, the two families come together to negotiate the *lobola* to be paid to the bride's family. In the countdown toward marriage, it is the prerogative of a Nguni girl to select her lover and to visit his homestead for lovemaking while her family puts pressure on the groom's family to complete the payment of bridewealth. However, among the Sotho-Tswana it is the man or his father who chooses the bride and visits her for lovemaking in her parent's home, while his family pressures the bride's family to hasten and complete the process of her transfer.

The sharp contrast between the two groups can also be seen in the fact that among the Nguni, it is the groom's father who makes the main speech during the wedding ceremony, while among the Sotho-Tswana it is usually the bride's father who dominates the ceremony. The contrast is also evident in the carrying out of the major ritual element that consecrates the marriage contract: the killing of the ox and the use of its gall. Among the Nguni, the groom's father kills the ox while the bride is covered with the gall and dressed with gallbladder. Among the Sotho, the bride's father has the prerogative to sacrifice the ox and the groom is the one who is covered with gall.

The apparent contrast between the Nguni and the Sotho-Tswana can be seen as a by-product of the basic difference in their marriage systems. For the Sotho and the Venda, where cross-cousin marriage is the norm, the bride is always a kinswoman of the groom and thus well known to him and his family from childhood. Her movement to her husband's home is not usually as traumatic an event as that of an Nguni bride. For the Nguni cross-cousin marriage is strictly forbidden. The bride is usually a stranger, or at least has no known kinship relation to her husband. Though she is welcomed to her husband's home, she continues to be viewed with suspicion as a necessary outsider. To emphasize her nature as a stranger, she is made to observe certain rules of avoidance toward her husband's parents, most especially toward her father-in-law, for whom she constitutes a potential danger as a valid seducer since she has no blood kinship with him. She is not permitted to use any word that contains a syllable of her father-in-law's name. She must avoid being alone with him in the house and must never bare her breasts in his presence. A special goat must be sacrificed to rescind the taboo that bars her as a stranger from drinking sour milk from her husband's house. With this rite, begins the process of her being fully incorporated into the clan of her husband's family, qualifying her upon death to enter the status of an ancestress to her children.[7]

Stability and Resilience of Marriage

The stability of marriage and the rarity of divorce in these societies have drawn the attention of many scholars. Some have attributed this to the payment of bridewealth, the return of which would be required in the event of a divorce. The payment of bridewealth plays a vital role in the consummation of marriage relations. But it is a gross distortion to regard the exchange as a sale in a strict economic sense. Wives are not commodities. In addition to establishing rights over the wife, bridewealth exchange legalizes the status of the woman's children and their rights to inheritance in their father's house. By giving the bridewealth, the groom's family makes a symbolic statement of how valuable they consider the bride to be to them. Men are encouraged to treat their wives well, particularly in modern day South Africa, where in addition to losing their wives they could be forced to forfeit the return of their bridewealth if convicted of mistreatment, sexual deprivation, or other abuses of their partners.

In all these societies marriage is the vital rite of passage toward social maturity. It is the ultimate goal to which every man and every woman must strive to reach. It is the only acceptable and appropriate status that every adult male or female must attain to be viewed with respect and honor in the community. The full attainment of adulthood is achieved through marriage. To be unmarried is to be considered incapable of adult responsibilities. A state of perpetual singlehood is reserved only for the mentally and physically disabled. Neither barrenness nor impotence is considered a plausible excuse for not getting married, since the emphasis is not on the genitor but on the social father or mother of the children. Though there are machineries within all these societies for effecting divorce, they are rarely used. The combination of all these factors ensures first that a fall out, no matter how major, between the spouses is never permitted to bring about a break in the marriage contract, entered into by two families rather than individuals. Also all (including the spouses) work strenuously to ensure resolution and reconciliation, rather than dissolution of the relationship.

Marriage and House Systems

The homestead is the basic unit of settlement among virtually all South Africa's Bantu peoples. As a microcosm of the universe, the homestead is a self-contained social, self-sufficient economic, and self-controlled legal unit within the confines of which the individual experiences the major activities and cycles of life and existence. The principal responsibilities of procreation, nurture, and socialization of children, the planting of crops and raising of cattle, the making of utensils and the manufacturing of cloths, the establishment and maintenance of marital and kinship relations, the performance of the final rite of passage for the dead and the ritual veneration of the ancestors, and many other things besides are all played out around and within the homestead. Like the chief of the village or the king of the state, the homestead head is sovereign. Within his home he dispenses justice and has the prerogative over all affairs of life in relation to its members.

The Importance of Kin

Kinship relations provide the most fundamental basis for social interaction and wider association between individuals as well as between groups. Based crucially (though not necessarily) on ties of blood and marriage, kinship relations provide the foundation for important moral, religious, and jural rights and obligations. Though closely related, the terms kinship and descent are not synonymous and are rarely interchangeable. Kinship refers to the linking of people through biological descent and marriage. Descent, on the other hand, is a social aspect of kinship that refers exclusively to identification or connection through either the paternal or the maternal side of the family. Patrilineal descent, in which inheritance and group membership is traced from father to son, is the norm in all South African societies except among the Tsonga, for whom inheritance moves from brother to brother before reverting to the next generation of brothers. Three main types of kinship relations are patrilineal (agnatic), maternal (uterine), and marriage (affinine). Though biological relation is important in determining who is kin to whom, it is not an absolute requirement. People may define themselves as kin simply because they have been admitted into the family union by adoption, clientage, and other means of integration even when no biological or marital relations are involved. It is more important that they consider themselves or are accepted and perceived by others to be kin than the mere fact of biological identification. In this sense, kinship is primarily and functionally a system of social relationships.

In virtually all these societies the nuclear family, made up of father, mother, and children, is the basis of the kinship system, thus making the relationships between husband and wife, father and son, father and daughter, mother and son, mother and daughter, and son and daughter the most fundamental. The incest taboo, a nearly universal prohibition against sexual relations between parents and children or between siblings, underlines the importance of these ties as the most primary kinship relationships. However, beyond these primary or real kin, and unlike Western societies, the basic terms of kinship relations such as father, mother, brother, and daughter are applied more liberally and are not limited only to people within one's immediate nuclear family. Beside his or her biological father and mother, a man or a woman has, calls, and treats many other people within his or her extended family as father or mother. The most notable of these are his or her father's brother or sister and his or her mother's brother or sister. A man calls anyone within his extended family old enough to be his father his *father*, instead of uncle; and anyone old enough to be his mother is called and treated as *mother*, instead of aunt. This phenomenon of multiple fatherhood has always been seen as a source of bafflement for white South African employers who were always at a loss as to how a worker could be repeatedly taking time off to go and bury his father or mother.[8]

Similarly the phenomenon of multiple fatherhood and motherhood, renders the use of precise Western terms such as nephew and nieces redundant. If you call a man father, especially when he is not your biological father, all his children, who in the Western sense are your cousins, will become either your brothers or your sisters, and you will treat them as such, meaning no sexual or marital relations can occur between you and them, except with some exceptions among the Sotho. In the same vein and with the emphasis on the patrilineal principle, your father's brother's wife or wives would be regarded as your mother or mothers, and their children as your brothers or sisters. The incest taboo applies here as well, except in very exceptional cases such as among the Tswana, where such marriages do occur mainly in the royal family.

One's mother's brother is not, however, called father. He is known as *malume* or male mother, a term of endearment meant to capture the warm indulgent and sometimes joking relationship that exists between him and his nephews and nieces. Similarly his children are not regarded as brother or sister, but *mzala* (Nguni) or *motswala* (Sotho), terms meaning cross-cousin that ignore both age and gender. Among the Sotho and the Venda, marriage to one's mother's brother's daughter is the norm, and such a woman usually assumes the status of senior wife, irrespective of her position in the hierarchy of wives. Cross-cousin marriages of all types are prohibited among the Nguni and the Tsonga. Similarly, one's mother's sister is called and treated as mother, and one's father's sister is termed female father, a classification that gives her considerable respect, making her the family or ancestral priest among the Venda and the Sotho. The Venda also regards the female father as the most influential member of the family council.

Much importance is accorded to age in these societies. The older the person one has to deal with the greater the amount of respect one is expected to pay to them, irrespective of gender. Xhosa's terminology clearly distinguishes between one's elder brother, *mkhuluwa* (*khulu* or big), and one's younger brother, *umninawe*. No such clear-cut distinction is, however, made between sisters, who are lumped together as *dadewethu*. In dealing with one's father's generation, the Xhosa call their father's elder brother *bawomkhulu* (big father), and his younger brother *bawomcane* (little father). The ranking by age of siblings and parallel cousins in one's father's line is of crucial importance in a patrilineal society, since it involves the matter of succession to title and of property inheritance. In relation to one's maternal relations and cross-cousins, ranking by age is of little significance since succession to title and property is not involved.

Above and beyond the nuclear family, the patrilineal principle is the basis for the establishment of larger social groups such as clans and lineages. The emphasis on paternal identity does not mean that maternal kin are insignificant. Their role may be secondary, but it is not unimportant. Among the Lovedu, where cross-cousin marriages are encouraged, maternal kin play

Three generations of Ndebele women inside their family compound in Soweto in 2002. Note the beaded headband, beaded necklace, and the characteristic Ndebele-style breast or chest covering of the daughter, Nzini (second from left); the metallic neckrings, neck loop, and blanket cloak of the mother (first from right). (Jennifer Beard)

important roles in one's affairs. Nothing of major importance can take place without their presence and active participation. A man's father's sister exercises considerable influence over one's affairs, since the cattle obtained through her marriage would in all probability be used in contracting and securing one's marriage partner. Unlike the Tsonga, a man must treat his mother's brother with considerable respect, since he may end up being one's father-in-law. Among the Tsonga, the mother's brother offers regular sacrifices to the ancestors on behalf of his nephew's mother. While it is not unusual among the Nguni for the firstborn to be sent to his mother's people for upbringing, a boy is not expected to inherit anything from his mother's people, nor do they have any responsibility to provide part of his bridewealth cattle.

Beyond the bound and obligations of kinship, good neighborliness is highly valued. Neighbors, whether related or not, are often in close contact with one another and are expected to assist each other. A telling observation early in the twentieth century remains as true today as it had been for centuries: "Women are constantly dropping in to neighboring *imizi* (homesteads) to borrow a stamping-block, or beg tobacco. Always between neighboring *imizi* there are paths, well worn, and full of shadow-holding hollows, made by bare toes in the dust."⁹

Socialization and Growing Up

Among the Bantu, marriage is not considered fully consummated until the birth of at least one child. Childbearing is the most crucial function of the family. Without it the family cannot continue and the lineage has no future. The birth of a child confirms the bridewealth contract between the woman's family and that of her husband and validates her status as an adult and a complete woman. Beside providing emotional gratification for the parents, children are valued for a variety of practical reasons. From an early age, young girls serve as nursemaids to younger siblings and kin. They perform a wide variety of chores in the domestic spheres, thus providing invaluable services or relief to their mothers in the household. Girls also bring in cattle to the family at their marriage, and become the basis for the contracting of new relationships with other lineages and families. Similarly, boys herd cattle, sheep, and goats and as grown men assume full responsibility for the cares and security of their aged parents, in addition to ensuring the continuity of the lineage or descent group through childbearing and making regular sacrifices to the ancestral spirits. As a result of the importance attached to children, barrenness in a woman and impotence in a man are vigorously countered through the use of various medicines and formulae. As last resorts, the institutions of polygamy and of surrogate relationships ensure that no couple is left without an heir.

Special dolls, made from wood or beads, are used to promote fertility among many Sotho and Nguni groups. Preparations for the socialization and incorporation of the child begin from the time of conception. Once a woman is confirmed pregnant, she is expected to observe certain taboos and avoidances specifically to protect the child in the womb and ensure a comfortable pregnancy and successful delivery. The avoidances vary from group to group and even within groups. Southern Sotho women are enjoined to stay within their compound to avoid walking on bad paths prepared by malevolent forces, while Pedi women are forbidden from seeing corpses, looking at physical disabilities, and establishing contact with other pregnant and ritually impure women. Venda women are told to eschew hot food in order not to scald the growing child, while Zulu women, married or unmarried, are advised to avoid guinea-fowl, hare, rock rabbit, and swallows, which can cause their babies to have long, flat heads, long ears, or long teeth. As the pregnancy nears its end, among many of the groups (the Bhaca, Southern

Sotho, Venda, Pedi, and Tswana) the mother-to-be returns to her parents home, which serves as the venue for the delivery. This custom is especially observed for the birth of a first child.

Child delivery is women's affair in which older, postmenstrual women who are considered potentially and ritually pure play active and supervisory roles. Midwives and male herbalists are called in only in cases of complications. The cord is cut and the afterbirth buried secretly to ensure that witches have no access to use it to harm the newborn. The Tsonga describe the newborn to be not yet firm so rituals and medicinal incisions are applied to the baby to strengthen and protect it. The mother continues to observe the various ritual and food taboos, remaining in the hut with the child for between 6 and 10 days, depending on how long it takes for the cord to fall off. In the past, the birth of twins was not welcomed as they were considered to be unnatural and thus potentially dangerous. While the Xhosa kept their twins, the Sotho and the Venda usually killed them.

The reincorporation of the mother involves the performance of special ceremonies and rituals meant to return her and the birth hut to a state of cleanliness. Among the Xhosa, Mfengu, and Mpondo women this is achieved by brewing special beer. Among the Zulu, after the cleaning of the hut, the new mother is sprinkled and purified with *intelezi* medicine. The reincorporation process is consummated in a feast usually involving the killing and consumption of a sheep or a goat, whose hide becomes the carrying blanket for the child. The rites reincorporating the mother also mark the social birth of the child, his welcome and recognition as a new member of the lineage and group. Given a name, the child's introduction to the group is marked by feasting on beer and meat and by a special dance to celebrate its formal induction into its father's group.

On average, children are weaned at about three years, and full sexual intercourse is forbidden between the couple until this stage is passed. The institution of polygamy mitigates the inconvenience of this prohibition for the husband. It is not clear how women are expected to deal with their sexual needs during this period aside from concentrating on breastfeeding their babies. The introduction of modern methods of contraception appears to have contributed to leveling the playing field, at least as far as the women are concerned. Several methods are employed to take the child off the breast. A most common one involves the smearing of the nipples with some bitter-tasting substance—such as aloe juice, pipe oil, hot pepper or chili—that will no doubt turn the child off the breast. Unlike the other stages in the life cycle, weaning is not attended with much ritual. Both the Mpondo and the Zulu slaughter a goat to mark the transition, purify the mother, and permit the onset of sexual intercourse. The most elaborate ritual occurs among the

Tsonga, in which a doctor assigned to supervise the child from birth will treat the child with special medicine while formally taking his leave of the little patient on the day of weaning. Prior to its weaning, the child spends practically all its time with its mother. Carried by her on her back in a blanket or an animal skin, the child follows the mother literally to everywhere she goes, sharing her experiences as she brews the beer, pounds the grain, milks the cattle, hoes the field, beats the drum, and dances vigorously or violently to the deafening sound of the national dance drum and reed pipe playing.

Weaning sets the child free from the apron string of the mother, bringing the period of infantile dependency to an end, and providing the child with a necessary opportunity to grow socially and form wider social relationships. As one observer notes:

> For the next two to four years [the child] lives a relatively carefree, irresponsible life, with small jobs like chasing chickens and running errands being the only demands made on him. It is, however, a valuable period from the point of view of the child's socialization. This stage is important in that it lays the foundations for much of his future adult behavior, which will require his cooperation within a group of contemporaries. His peer group, watched over by those just a little older, lays down rules for acceptable conduct and is in a strong position to see that they are obeyed. Sanctions such as mockery and ostracism enable them to deal effectively with displays of temper, selfishness and poor sportsmanship.[10]

Few, if any, differences are evident in the daily lives of boys and girls up to the age of six. Thereafter, the interests and daily lives of the two sexes begin to diverge. Boys gradually adapt themselves to a life of livestock herding, which before long becomes a job, a hobby, and a passion. Among the Nguni, herding keeps the boys away from the homestead for much of the day, while among the Sotho it keeps them away for days in far-flung cattle posts. In addition, the boys keep themselves engaged through competitive dueling with sticks, playing games under the trees, and running errands for older folks. Through these activities, as well as through bullying, teasing, and threats of punishment and ostracism, the ethos of courage, self-discipline, respect for elders and constituted authorities, generosity, resourcefulness, as well as leadership and management skills are cultivated and inculcated in the boys. The endless, halcyon days spent together with the cattle in the veld give the boys the opportunity to acquire an intimate and useful knowledge of the wild, with all its flora and fauna. As scholars who studied pastoralism among the Lovedu discovered: "A herd boy walking along with you will give you the name and uses of almost every tree or shrub you pass in that rich bush veld environment, and once a boy of fifteen astonished us by being able to name over 200 specimens of plants from that area."[11]

The life of a girl does not change as dramatically as a boy's after age six. She also begins to expand her range of serviceable skills in the domestic spheres, usually by watching and imitating the actions of her mother and other adult females and serving as nursemaid to younger children. She also begins to learn how to better grind corn or maize, smear walls and floors, hoe, winnow, collect relishes and insects, make fires, cook, and generally to become adept at running a household by the onset of puberty.

Puberty marks a major change in the life of the child. Its signaling of the beginning of full sexuality with all its associations of fertility and adult accountability requires that it should be fully ritualized. Among the southern Bantu groups such as the Venda, Tsonga, Zulu, and Lovedu, the boy's first nocturnal emission is marked by his being treated with strengthening and protective medicine. The Zulu carries this further into an extensive ritual, the *thomba*, which involves the seclusion of the boy in a hut for a few days during which time he observes certain food taboos and avoids contact with women while receiving instructions on appropriate sexual behaviors. The rite concludes with the sacrifice of an animal to the ancestors, and with feasting, singing, dancing, and the giving of a new name to the boy. This is the name by which his peers will know and address him for the rest of his life. While older people can still call him by his boyhood name, it is tantamount to an insult for any of his peers and juniors to fail to acknowledge his new status by clinging on to his boyhood name. The annual puberty ceremony, *vhutamba vhutuka,* is a communal one consisting of six days of severe hardship, sexual instruction, and the inculcation of the ideals and norms of social customs and etiquette. Neither among the Venda, nor among the Zulu, do puberty rites involve circumcision.

At the onset of the first menstruation a girl, either alone or together with other girls undergoing the same transformation, will be covered with a blanket and secluded in a special hut. Venda and Zulu girls stay for approximately one week; Tsonga girls stay up to one month and can only be visited in the evening by the girls of her neighborhood who come to dance and sing with her. Subjected to different forms of hardships, such as sitting for hours in icy water, eating unpalatable meals, being pinched and teased, she receives considerable sexual instructions, such as how to lengthen the labia and avoid being pregnant while indulging in playful familiarities with boys. The rite usually concludes with a bath at the river, the smearing of the body with red ochre, and the receiving of a special funnel-shaped object (*thahu*) which she would henceforth tuck into her girdle at the back.[12]

KINSHIP AND MARRIAGE AMONG INDIANS

The Indian family is very similar to the African family in its focus on kinship and communal relations. However, it differs from African and European families in its greater emphasis on arranged marriage, joint family residency, the continuing resilience of caste in the choice of marriage partners, and its unequivocal disapproval of the practice of individuals living entirely on their own. As a rule, cross-cousin marriages are forbidden, except among some Tamil and Telegu Indians, where, until recently, a man was expected, though rarely compelled, to marry his sister's daughter. Monogamy is the rule, though polygamy is practiced among Muslims, while it is acceptable for a man to take another wife if his first wife is barren. Known as *kutum* or *kudumor,* the patrilineal extended family is the most important kinship unit among South African Indians. Headed by the eldest or ablest surviving patriarch, the *Bada* (The Big One), it is hierarchical in structure and made up of graded subunits who are bonded together by patrilineal descent and marriage ties. As in most of the African societies, age and sex define status and roles. Uncles, most especially paternal ones, and their wives are addressed as fathers and mothers and their children are regarded as brothers and sisters, with their relative age determining whether they are small or big. Couples who are childless are expected to receive a gift or gifts of babies from one or more of their married relatives who already have many children, and who give up all claims to their child, thereby enabling their childless kinsfolk to complete their family.

In her new home and as a mother and wife, the woman has primary responsibility for the continuing veneration of her husband's family deities, in addition to remaining connected with the deities of her paternal and maternal families. Though the child's strongest bond remains with the real mother, child upbringing is the mutual responsibility of all the women (and all the men) in the joint household. Only a bad mother would dote over her child or prevent other women willing and able from cuddling, suckling, disciplining, and indulging the child. Being a highly religious people, a series of life cycle rituals (*sanskara*) marks and validates a child's growth from conception to puberty, and thereafter from marriage to death.[13]

SOCIAL CHANGE

The foregoing, apparently neat discussion of traditional gender roles, marriage, and family forms should not leave anyone with the impression of a South African society that has existed in tranquility and social stability for centuries. In actual fact, the opposite is the case. By virtue of its strategic location, its geographical diversity, its turbulent history, and its internal and external relations South Africa has been a society in constant transformation. Whatever elements of indigenous culture survive did so in spite of or sometimes as a result of varied internal and external pressures of change. The discovery toward the end of the nineteenth century of extensive and extremely valuable deposits of minerals, most notably diamonds and gold, dramatically changed the fate of South Africa as well as those of its peoples. The mineral revolution resulted in industrialization, urbanization, and labor migration: three interrelated forces that unleashed a new era of socioeconomic change on South Africa.

To meet the manpower needs of mining and industrial capitalism, tens of thousands of people migrated from the rural areas to the new urban centers sprouting up around the mines such as Johannesburg, Pretoria, and Kimberley. Older thriving port cities and industrial centers such as Cape Town, Port Elizabeth, East London, and Durban also became magnets for rural migrants in search of economic opportunities unavailable in the dreary terrains of the country. To control the movement of Africans into and within the cities, an array of legislative and administrative measures were put in place, denying the migrants rights of residence in the major cities, all of which became white-only cities. Africans could only enter to work and had to leave to take up residence in one of the adjoining shantytowns sprawling around the cities, of which the most notable were Soweto, Alexandra, Sharpeville, and Sophiatown (later Meadowland) in the Johannesburg suburb. In the face of the harsh conditions and the dehumanizing gruesomeness of the apartheid system, these sprawling townships soon developed into thriving and throbbing authentic communities of black life and culture. Though some women also migrated, the majority of the migrants were men. Prohibited from bringing their wives and other members of the extended family into the cities, the development of a stable settled urban population of industrial workers was thereby inhibited. Consequently the migrants became men of two worlds as they shuttled periodically between their urban workplace and their rural homes.

Cut off—sometimes temporarily but often permanently—from their rural roots, migrant laborers were confronted with a life in the cities that posed new challenges and required new solutions. In most cases, the new urban worker found that he could no longer appeal to his extended network of family and kinship groups to deal with day-to-day problems and needs. Instead of the traditional elders and rulers, he now had the police and the court systems; instead of in-laws, age-grade compatriots, cousins and uncles, he had coworkers, fellow churchgoers, unrelated neighbors, and hostel or flat mates. As the new urban relationships began to replace the traditional ones or at least fulfill their functions, the nuclear family made up of the man, his wife, and children began to replace the extended family as the most basic unit of social or family organization.

Children growing up in the cities now have to be socialized through the Western, missionary, and other parochial school systems, instead of the traditional initiation schools. For enlightenment and entertainment, instead of the rejuvenating ecstasy of traditional ritual festivals and ceremonies, they must learn to dance to the new, dynamic, and multiethnic black city *marabi, kwela,* and *mbaqanga* dance and music styles or develop new tastes for modern theater and cinema. Domiciled in the city for much of the year and thus unable to participate in any meaningful way in the ritual and social lives of the rural communities, the African proletarians have developed new measures of personal prestige and social status based no longer on the number of one's cattle or wives but on Western education, occupation, and wealth. Permanently kept at the lowest rung of the economic ladder, with no prospect for upward or vertical labor mobility in a world dominated by whites, the aspiring African urban elite seized on his urban working experience with all its dangers, pains, and challenges as the essence of the transition ritual from adolescence to manhood, comparable in many respects to the rigor and challenges of the traditional initiation ceremonies. To successfully undertake the difficult journey from the rural to the urban center and survive time and again the rigors and the many hazards of the mines is to pass the true test of the attainment of manhood status.

The pressures of urbanization and modernization have also brought major changes in many aspects of sexuality and marriage. In the relatively open and anonymous society of the urban centers, many of the taboos connected with sexuality and marriage choice began to be violated or ignored. Generally or effectively shielded away from the watchful and censoring eyes of elders, young men and women in the urban areas became more proactive in exploring their sexuality by engaging in premarital or nonmarital sexual intercourse. This sexual freedom, of course, led to women becoming pregnant, giving birth out of wedlock, and living as single parents by choice and with pride: options that were and are still clearly unacceptable under the indigenous systems and in most rural African societies. The phenomenon of female-headed households, which may also include the offspring of unmarried daughters, is becoming common. Such an unattached woman (widowed, divorced, separated, or simply unmarried) can have one or several male lovers or consorts, some of whom may contribute to her financial support and that of her children. However, none of these largely transitory figures in the new family system have any legal rights over the woman or jural rights over her children, in spite of the qualifications of some of these men as biological fathers to the children.

With regard to the choice of marriage partners and in the absence of the kinship network and unlike the traditional system, the individual rather than his or her parents becomes the decisive factor in the choice. In most cases, parents are simply informed after the fact and sometimes after the wedding. Long established practices such as cross-cousin marriages become practically difficult to carry out, as urban dwellers become prone to marrying people they meet at work, church, the houses of friends, parties, credit associations (*stokfel*), a liquor and dance joint (*shebeen*), night clubs, and dozens of other hangouts in cities that have come to replace the kinship networks as venues of social interaction, group solidarity, and support for the urban dwellers.

In the supra-ethnic anonymity of the townships, interethnic, and sometimes interracial liaisons and marriages began to flourish. In some cases, instead of the traditional ceremonies of marriages, couples simply cohabit as husband and wife. In others, the relationship is consummated in a court or religious proceeding presided over by magistrates and priests, signifying the new sources of social affirmation and jural legitimacy: the modern state and the new religions of Christianity, Islam, Hinduism, Judaism, and others. Under the overarching influence of the state and of Christianity, polygamy began to give way to monogamy in the cities. *Lobola,* the exchange of cattle for a bride, could no longer be emphasized in the city with its cash economy. Cash is often offered and accepted in place of cattle, further reinforcing the recurrent criticism of *lobola* as the commodification of women.

The lure of the city, with its gold and diamonds, its sins and pleasures, and its totalitarian culture, does not mean that the migrant worker has totally severed his or her links with the rural areas and with his or her kinsfolk. While it is true that, for some, escape to the city means permanent closure to life in the rural areas, for many others urban life cannot cut their cultural umbilical cords to their rural communities and lineage groups. However long and apparently permanent their tenure in the city may seem, the majority of the migrants regard it as a temporary one. Some of the workers have attempted to recreate elements of their rural culture in their new urban shanty towns and locations. Others settle, as much as practicable, with members of their rural or ethnic groups. The majority maintains connections with the rural areas, which they visit once or twice a year. Denied full citizenship and residency rights in the cities (until recently), upon returning home and displaying and disbursing their acquired wealth, migrants have found a new sense of prestige, social standing, and group solidarity that is beyond their reach in the cities. Connection with the rural communities is maintained through regular remittances of earnings to wives and relatives left in the rural areas, a process of cash flow vital to the economic sustenance of the generally impoverished and overcrowded population of the erstwhile homelands.

Similarly, beginning with the rise of the Black Consciousness Movement of the 1970s, and as part of a concerted and an all-out strategy of resistance against the insidious attempts of the apartheid order to undermine the legitimacy of indigenous traditions, deliberate attempts began to be made to recapture and in some cases recreate the traditional values and customs of earlier generations. As part of the attempt to affirm the authenticity of African cultural heritage, and the African's pride in his or her identity as a black person, old ceremonies and rituals were revived or revitalized and new ones were created. Puberty, initiation, and marriage ceremonies that were in decline were revived and reinvigorated with new life and new meanings. In many cases they became even more elaborate, more ostentatious, more colorful, more picturesque, more publicized, and more consciously traditional than ever before. It became fashionable for young men and women born in and growing up in the cities to return to the rural areas and, when old enough, undergo the various rituals of puberty, initiation, and circumcision along with their rural age groups. Many more young people are also becoming apprenticed to receive training to qualify to practice as diviners and healers. Though most of the Western-educated elite would now readily resort to church and court proceedings to legalize their marriages, such ceremonies will usually be followed or preceded by the performance of the traditional wedding rituals, which in some cases still involve the payment of *lobola,* even if it is now in cash rather than cattle.[14]

The widespread adoption of Christianity has not precluded adherence to elements of indigenous traditions. For many converts God and the ancestors work together. Did not church traditions and the Bible itself enjoin respect for one's parents, even after their death? And what is the difference between the veneration of saints in the Catholic religion and ancestral veneration in African traditions? This blending is also evident in the continuing belief in the power of sorcery and witchcraft, and many Christians do not hesitate to seek the assistance of diviners and healers, who are perceived as coworkers with God and medical doctors in countering misfortune and healing the sick. While to the more radical Pentecostalists such synthesis smells like theological compromise of faith and true commitment, for many the two cultural and religious traditions are complementary. One of the reasons for the rapid growth of the African Independent Churches in the twentieth century, such as the Church of Nazareth or the Isaiah Shembe church among the Zulu, has been their blended quality, and particularly their successful attempt to combine Christian practices with elements of indigenous tradition. These incorporated traditions include ancestral worship, the wearing of distinctive beaded garments and animal skin head ties, the acceptance of polygamy, the emphasis on supernatural healings and miracles, the use of traditional musical instruments, and the promotion of active worship through songs and dance.[15]

THE CHANGING STATUS OF WOMEN

Traditionally in African societies, a woman occupies an ambiguous position. Through marriage she is brought into a new household: that of her husband. Through the payment of *lobola* in cattle, her husband and his family receive from her father the transfer of rights over her productive and reproductive rights. As a necessary but a subordinate outsider within her newly adopted homestead she is expected to live under the shadow and control of her husband and his extended family, whose present progress and future survival she is expected to continue to contribute to through her labor and productive powers. However, as the possessor of productive and reproductive powers, without which no homestead can survive, and around which every homestead revolves, the woman's subordination is a qualified one. By virtue of her labor power, she possesses a high degree of economic independence and autonomy, including real and major control over the agricultural process, obtaining and retaining access to her own productive land and the disposal of the yield of that land. No one (including her husband) can take away or tamper with her allotted piece of land or fields without her express permission. In case the land allotted to her by her husband's family is not enough for her agricultural needs, she may receive lands from her own people. But her children cannot inherit this additional land. It will revert back to her own people at her death or when she no longer needs to farm it.

Similarly, as natural custodians of fertility for the lineage, the woman enjoys considerable social prestige and influence within the homestead. A woman can also increase the wealth of her house by practicing as a diviner or engaging in craft making and commercial ventures. The ranking of wives in a homestead or in a polygamous setup is usually determined by the time a woman is married into the family rather than by her age; however, women of aristocratic background usually take precedence in seniority over other wives in the household unless they are also of comparable social standing.

Unlike in traditional African societies, women of European settler societies were more constrained in their social standing and public recognition. For settler women, the proper place was the domestic sphere of childbearing and rearing and cooking. Though many of these women were involved in some economic activities beyond the home, such involvements were considered to be the exception rather than the rule. The world of money and power and thus of greater value and prestige was considered to be the exclusive domain of men, a world that is not considered feminine and therefore naturally inappropriate for women. Whatever contributions (and they were considerable) settler women made to the domestic economy were accorded very little value and recognition since the emphasis remained on their role as reproducers rather than as producers. The Afrikaner ideology of *volksmoeder* or mother of the nation, which became a rallying point in the development of the Afrikaner nationalism and racial consciousness, only served to reinforce the prevailing settler gender ideology of female domesticity, now effectively harnessed to serve nationalist ends. The struggle by the white South African women for suffrage, during the early decades of the twentieth century, by demanding the admission of women into the heart of the political electoral system, was the first major blow to this consolidation of patriarchy. These suffragists saw no reason why the hands that rock the cradle and stir the stew should not cast the vote as well. Though the white women's struggle for electoral equality was dismissed by some of their husbands as a case of democracy gone mad, they eventually obtained suffrage.[16]

It was against this background of the dominant European gender ideology relegating women to the apparently less prestigious domestic sphere that Christianity came to South Africa. For the Christian missionaries, after converting the African woman their principal mandate was training her to assume her prescribed roles in the domestic sphere as a mother and a wife in her household or as a domestic servant in the house of her masters, who were invariably white. Missionary education for African women was education for domesticity.[17] Many of the women, however, rejected this missionary constraint on their traditional social autonomy and economic independence of action by adopting a blended approach that appropriated and mixed together elements of indigenous gender norms with settler and missionary ones, affirming their prerogatives in both the domestic sphere and the economic productive process.

Labor migration, the discovery of minerals, industrialization, and urbanization had far-reaching, disruptive effects on the African family, most especially related to the status of women. Rural South African communities became settlements of old men, children, and women. In this environment, women became principally responsible for the maintenance of the household, performing duties traditionally reserved for men as heads of households. In virtually all the rural African communities, women assumed full responsibility for every aspect of the household with the added weight of being single parents, even though the sociolegal system with its focus on male-headed nuclear family had long refused to accord women their recognition and rights as breadwinners. A World Bank report of 1994 showed that 29 percent of African households in South Africa are headed by women while the same was true of only 10 percent of white households.

However, many women also migrated to the cities, usually in defiance of both law and custom. Some did this in search of their husbands; others in search of economic opportunities to escape the grueling poverty that had become the lot of the rural African reserves or so-called homelands; and some to exchange the restrictions of the rural areas for the independence and adventure of the city. Many of these women ended up as domestic servants, working for whites, enduring the indignities of class and racial discrimination even in cases where they had developed real spatial intimacy with their madams and the children they were hired to raise.

For some of the women who would not buy into the Victorian ideal of domesticated motherhood, domestic servitude was not an option. Instead, with a high sense of initiative, self-reliance, and resourcefulness, they strove to create a new world of economic independence and autonomy free from the state, the church, and from African men by engaging in the controversial but profitable world of illicit beer brewing. As exquisite queens of the *shebeen* and the nightclubs, these women played a major role in the emerging and volatile urban black working class cultures of the locations and the shantytowns.

In the explosive and perennially unsettled conditions of the locations with a high ratio of men to women, flamboyant sexuality suddenly became fashionable in a way unthinkable in rural communities. Some of the migrant women sought to transform and commoditize sexual relations by turning to prostitution, which became a common though officially illegal trade. Among other factors, labor migration has also contributed to the rapid spread of HIV/AIDS in South Africa, especially among the African population. Deprived by law of the companionship of their wives for several months, many of the workers took lovers in the cities; others frequented prostitution houses, where unprotected sex was the norm. In the process, many of them became infected with HIV, which they in turn ignorantly took with them back to the rural areas during their annual or biannual brief visits to their rural families, turning the deadly disease into a rampaging and virulent epidemic.

In spite of the end of apartheid and the transition to a new democratic order, the challenges facing South African women of all races today are still many. With regard to the economy, women continue to suffer various forms of discrimination such as unequal pay for equal work and denial of pension, housing, and employment benefits. A World Bank report of 1994 indicated that 35.2 percent of women are unemployed compared to 25.7 percent of men. Though many of the apartheid laws that prevented women (especially black women) from moving to places where certain jobs were available are now gone, a number of social, economic, and domestic constraints continue to impede women's working mobility.

A 1994 SA Central Statistical Services survey shows that 78 percent of economically active persons are men, compared to 22 percent who are women. In mining and quarrying, men account for 94 percent of the workforce, while women account for less that 9 percent in transport, storage, and communication. It is only in the professional and administrative occupations that women account for close to or sometimes more than 50 percent of the workforce, making up 49 percent of technicians and associate professionals, and 63 percent of the clerical positions. The large number of women working as nurses and teachers ensures that women constitute 49 percent of the professional services. The discriminatory employment practices of the apartheid era ensured that by 1995, 85 percent of personnel in management positions were white males, 10 percent black males, 1.5 percent colored males, 1 percent Asian males, 2 percent white females, 0.6 percent black females, and 0.06 percent Asian females. In other categories, women constitute 5 percent of artisans and apprentices, 3 percent of registered engineers, and 9.6 percent of judges and magistrates. Though one third of black women in South Africa work in agriculture, 57 percent of these are classified as casual, part-time, and seasonal workers with little reward, no job security, and no benefits. Generally, white men have the best jobs and the best pay, at 3,000 Rands per month; while on the average, white women, at R1,000 per month, earn more than black men, at 300 Rands a month. Black women in formal jobs who earn less than black men are generally better off than black women eking out their livings in the usually dreary terrains of the former homelands and rural areas. On the whole women represent less than 7 percent of the R100,000–R299,999 income bracket.

With regard to politics and power, women were systematically kept by the ruling Afrikaner-dominated National Party from active participation in politics with the result that by 1985 only 2.8 percent of parliamentarians were women. The end of apartheid, however, dramatically changed this situation. The ANC, in recognition of the crucial roles played and the pains borne by women in the resistance movement against apartheid and racial oppression, made it mandatory that at least one-third of its electoral candidates be women. Thus, the first nonracial, nonsexist, democratic elections in South Africa in 1994 produced a 400-member National assembly with over 25 percent of them being women. As if to consolidate the new prominence given to women in national politics, both the first Speaker and the Deputy Speaker of Parliament were also women. At the local or rural level, unless specifically invited, women could not attend the meetings of the *kgotla,* the traditional community decision-making body. However, the absence of men and the increased responsibility and household leadership forced on women are combining to chip away at deeply entrenched patriarchal values and norms, and women are beginning to attend and speak in many of these meetings.

Until recently various marital regulations ensured the continuing subordination of women by defining them as legal minors to their husbands with regard to where and how to live and in relation to the custody of children in case of separation. New civil marriage laws passed in 1984, 1988, and 1993 abolished male marital powers, made women into legal adults, made both partners equals, and gave both parents equal guardianship rights over their children.

Women of all races are also dealing with a whole array of cultural and religious laws, sometimes benign but just as often restrictive, emanating from South African multireligious traditions. Though there are more Christian women than Christian men, unequal power relations remain a major concern, and source of tension. Both the Roman Catholic Church and the Anglican Church have remained opposed to the ordination of women, though the latter appear to be relenting. The African Independent or Initiated Churches, some of which were founded by women, have been more flexible in allowing women to play leadership roles in their movements. Members of the male Muslim clergy are advocating for the full adoption of the Sharia (Islamic Law), for Muslims, a move viewed with misgivings by both Muslim and other women's groups. Hindu women are also beginning to challenge the glorification of their roles as mothers and domestics, while calling for a return to the original and unadulterated Veda traditions that recognize the equality of women and men in all spheres of human activities, including playing visible public roles in the professional careers. In spite of traditional restrictions, Jewish women are also gaining inroads into some religious councils while some are beginning to question the Judaic laws that give to only husbands the exclusive legal rights to give or deny their wives divorce.

With regard to education and literacy, literacy rates are higher among men than women, among whites than blacks, and in urban areas than in rural areas. Black women are the least literate in the country. For instance, while 99 percent of white women over 15 years of age passed at least standard six, a third of all black women in the Transkei have no education at all. The legacies of inequality in expenditure and the poor standard of education dished out to blacks by the apartheid regime remain evident today in low literacy levels, low enrollments, lack of fully trained and qualified teachers, poor and inadequate facilities, high drop-out rates, and other ills that will take the new government of South Africa years of vigorous and sustained efforts, as well as enormous resources, to address and redress. Like other key institutions of South African society, the media is overwhelmingly controlled by men, though the appointment of Ivy Matsepe-Casaburri as the chairperson of the SABC in 1994 was seen by many as a first step in the right direction of bringing women into the control and decision-making spheres of the media. Many are also challenging the continuing media neglect of women's issues, except when portraying them as sex objects or in relation to their roles in the domestic spheres of family and health, and in connection with incidences of violence against women.

In the area of health, since 1994, the ANC-led government has taken steps to reform the historically and racially fragmented health care system through the adoption of a national health plan. Under this plan, children under six and pregnant women are entitled to free health care. The challenges here are daunting. There is one doctor for every 700 people in the cities, 1,900 persons in the rural areas, with the most critical shortage being in the former homelands, where there is only one doctor for every 10,000 to 30,000 people. To check the incidence of the high degree of low birth weight and malnutrition among South African children, a program of school-feeding is being implemented by local and national governments. The 1996 repeal of the Abortion and Sterilization Act of 1975 has given women unrestricted access to abortion up to 12 weeks of pregnancy and beyond 13 weeks in very unusual circumstances, though the lack of equipment and trained personnel continue to hamper access to safe abortions. Previously, between 200,000 and 300,000 illegal abortions were performed every year.

The subordinate position of women, their relative powerlessness to control how and with whom to engage in sexual activity or to compel men to wear condoms, and the prevalence of multiple partners among their migrant worker husbands, have rendered monogamous women particularly vulnerable to sexually transmitted diseases, most especially HIV/AIDS, which has become virulently pandemic among African women. The AIDS/HIV statistics for South Africa is staggering: 4.2 million people infected by the end of 1999, at the rate of 1,600 new infections per day; one in every five South Africans, aged between 15 and 49 carries the virus; 120,000 AIDS-related death a year, at the rate of 330 deaths a day. The figure for AIDS-related deaths is projected to rise to 500,000 annually by 2008.[18] In the wake of the rabid and lethal violence generated by apartheid and the struggle against it, violence against women, in the form of rape, sexual assault, abuse, child abuse, feminicide, and political violence have become endemic, requiring urgent response from the authorities. The government's initial questioning of the emphasis on unprotected sex as the main cause of HIV generated much controversy, but did little to arrest the pandemic. However, in 2000 the government launched the five-year HIV/AIDS/STD Strategic Plan for South Africa 2000–2005. This program of action was directed at mobilizing local,

A monument to the perils and the challenges of AIDS/HIV in South Africa, 2001. This is one of many such monuments and public billboards erected in different parts of the country directed at drawing attention to the seriousness of the epidemic and the urgency of the battle against the disease.

national, international, private, and public resources for a comprehensive campaign to combat HIV/AIDS, with a special focus on education and prevention measures.

This chronicle of major impediments and small gains should not, however, obscure the fact that since the late 1980s, women—most especially African, Asian, and colored women—have been making steady progress in the murky water of South African politics and society. More women are inching their way slowly up the civil service ladder than ever before; many more are qualifying as doctors and engineers; increased numbers are securing decent and respectable jobs; while more than a few are occupying management and leadership positions even in the face of continuing and pervasive male chauvinism. Beside effective mobilization and campaigning by the women themselves, one factor that has jump-started the train of progress for women has been the unequivocal political commitment of the ANC Mandela-Mbeki led government. The 1994 ANC Reconstruction and Development Program (RDP) White Paper recognized the subordinate position of most South African women and directed that the principle of gender equality should inform the implementation of the new government's agenda and programs.

The 1996 South African constitution specifically prohibits all forms of discriminations based on "race, gender, sex, pregnancy, marital status, ethnic or social origin, color, sexual orientation, age, disability, religion, conscience, belief, culture, language and birth." A December 1993 act abolished husbands' marital power, giving equality of management powers to both partners. That same year the Prevention of Family Violence Act 133 criminalized rape within marriage, while providing the battered spouse the right to use interdiction against the batterer. In 1998, Parliament passed the Employment Equity Act, which obliged any business with 50 or more workers to submit equity plans, as well as biannual progress reports on equity efforts. Two years later, Parliament passed into law the Promotion of Equality and Prevention of Unfair Discrimination Act of 2000.

Though the new constitution recognizes customary law, it stipulates that it can only be exercised within the limit permitted by the Bill of Rights and is subject to the constitution. Beginning with the 1983 Basic Conditions of Employment Act, and the 1991 amendments to the Mines and Works Act (27 of 1,956), a series of new laws were enacted to give women and nonwhites access to all works, to equalize opportunities between men and women, and to abolish unfair labor practices based on race and gender. In 2000, August 6 was institutionalized as South African Women's Day to commemorating the day in 1956 when South African black women organized their now famous protest march against the pass laws. The annual commemoration provides an occasion to focus the attention of the entire nation on celebrating the achievements and importance of South African women as well as addressing issues of importance to them in South Africa. Several nongovernmental organizations (NGOs) are active in South Africa working to disseminate information and assistance to the vast majority of the women in the rural areas who are still largely uninformed and unaffected by the substantial transformation in their legal status that has taken place since the early 1990s. Local and international NGOs and donor agencies are also active in health care; educational, economic, and social welfare; family planning; and other spheres of activity related to women.

NOTES

1. The major sources for the discussions on marriage, women, and kinship systems in this chapter are: Eleanor Preston-Whyte, "Kinship and Marriage," in David Hammond-Tooke, ed., *The Bantu-Speaking Peoples of Southern Africa* (London and Boston: Routledge and Kegan Paul, 1974), 177–210; Virginia van der Vliet, "Growing Up in Traditional Society," in Hammond-Tooke, ed., *The Bantu-Speaking Peoples,* 219–20; and Hammond-Tooke, *The Roots of Black South Africa* (Johannesburg:

Jonathan Ball Publishers, 1993), 101–47. For fuller information on specific ethnic groups, see Eileen Jensen Krige, *The Social System of the Zulus* (Pietermaritzburg: Shuter and Shooter, 1965), 23–158; A. T. Bryant, *The Zulu People as They Were Before the White Man Came* (Pietermaritzburg: Shuter and Shooter, 1967), 412–56; J. H. Soga, *The Ama-Xosa: Life and Customs* (Lovedale, 1932); and H. Kuckertz, *Creating Order: The Image of the Homestead in Mpondo Social Life* (Johannesburg, 1990).

2. Preston-Whyte, "Kinship and Marriage," 179.

3. Hammond-Tooke, *The Roots of Black South Africa,* 118–23 and Preston-Whyte, "Kinship and Marriage," 192–94.

4. On the centrality of the bridewealth transfer in the validation of the marriage transaction, see M. D. W. Jeffreys, "Lobolo is Child-Price," *African Studies,* 10, 4, 1951, 188; Adam Kuper, *Wives for Cattle* (London: Routledge and Kegan Paul, 1982); and Hammond-Tooke, *The Roots of Black South Africa,* 123–29.

5. E. J. Krige and J. D. Krige, *The Realm of the Rain Queen* (London: Oxford University Press, 1943), 159.

6. For a fuller examination of sororate, levirate, and women-to-women marriage practices in South African societies and the major sources for the discussion in this section, see Krige and Krige, *The Realm of the Rain Queen,* 159–77; Krige, "Property, cross-cousin marriage, and the family cycle among the Lobedu," in R. F. Gray and P. H. Gulliver, eds., *The Family Estate in Africa* (London: Routledge and Kegan Paul, 1964), 160–206; and Preston-Whyte, "Kinship and Marriage," 187–94.

7. Hammond-Tooke, *The Roots of Black South Africa,* 120–29 and Barbara Tyrrell, *Tribal Peoples of Southern Africa* (Cape Town: Books of Africa, 1968), 85–89, 117–24, 194–96.

8. Hammond-Tooke, *The Roots of Black South Africa,* 104.

9. Monica Hunter, *Reaction to Conquest* (London: Oxford University Press, 1936), 59, cited in Hammond-Tooke, *The Roots of Black South Africa,* 114.

10. Virginia van der Vliet, "Growing Up in Traditional Society," in Hammond-Tooke, ed., *The Bantu-Speaking Peoples,* 219–20.

11. Krige and Krige, *The Realm of the Rain Queen,* 108.

12. Krige, *The Social System of the Zulus,* 63; van der Vliet, "Growing Up in Traditional Society," in Hammond-Tooke, ed., *The Bantu-Speaking Peoples,* 219–20.

13. On marriage and family among the Indians of South Africa, see G. H. Calpin, *Indians in South Africa* (Pietermaritzburg: Shuter and Shooter, 1949); Hilda Kuper, *Indian People in Natal* (Westport, Conn.: Greenwood Press, 1974); and Fatima Meer, *Portrait of Indian South Africans* (Durban: Aron House, 1969).

14. Peter Magubane, *Vanishing Cultures of South Africa: Changing Customs in a Changing World* and Magubane and Sandra Klopper, *African Renaissance* (Cape Town: Struik Publishers, 2000). In an illuminating essay, Sandra Klopper shows how changes in dressing styles and labor migrancy have continued to mediate gender and power relations among the Zulu. See Klopper, "You need only one bull to cover fifty cows: Zulu Women and 'Traditional' Dress," in Stephen Clingman, ed., *Regions and Repertoires: Topics in South African Politics and Culture* (Braamfontein: Ravan Press, 1991), 147–77.

15. Jean Morris, *Speaking with Beads* (New York: Thames and Hudson, Inc., 1994), 61–73.

16. Cheryl Walker, "The Women's Suffrage Movement: The Politics of Gender, Race and Class," in Walker, ed., *Women and Gender in Southern Africa* (Cape Town: David Philip, 1990), 1990, 311–45, 378–80.

17. Jacklyn Cock, "Domestic Service and Education for Domesticity: The Incorporation of Xhosa Women into Colonial Society," in Walker, *Women and Gender,* 76–96.

18. For these sobering statistics, see: *South Africa Survey, 2000/01* (Johannesburg: South African Institute of Race Relations, 2001), 213–27.

9

Social Customs and Lifestyle

The multiracial, multilingual, and multicontinental origins of the nation we know as South Africa have produced a cultural tapestry woven from a wide variety of customs and lifestyles. Various rituals and ceremonies provide meaning and validity to life and existence for its many groups, peoples, and races. From birth to death, from home to school, from the farm to the market place, from pastureland to minefields, from shrines to mosques, from synagogues to churches, from the rural to the urban, and from the local to the national, life and activities are guided to varying degrees by a wide range of customs and ceremonies.

ORALITY, MYTHS, AND VALUES

A major feature of indigenous society in South Africa is the pervasive resilience of its oral culture. With the probable exception of artistic expressions in the forms of abstract and other paintings on rocks and caves, most notably by the Khoisan and other related groups, the technology of writing did not appear to have developed in South Africa until the advent of the Europeans. Oral cultures are neither inferior nor deficient compared to writing culture. The difference between the two is not necessarily in the quality of thoughts and ideas of one over the other, but rather in the nature of the technology for the preservation and transmission of those thoughts. Thus, in spite of the absence of the art of writing, the indigenous peoples of South Africa, like other peoples of the world, reflected on and theorized about the world around them. They thought about abstract and concrete matters, and wondered about the mysterious forces ostensibly operating around them. They formulated profound explanations about life and existence.

Out of this mental exercise there developed a wide array of concepts and ideas that found artistic and literary expressions in rock paintings and iconographies as well as in myths and legends, folklore and folktales, human and animal stories, rituals and ceremonies, norms and mores, lyrics and dramatic verse, riddles and proverbs, and praise poems and songs. Through these and other media, an encyclopedic knowledge about family, kinship, farming, pastoralism, trade and crafts, medicine and divination, government and politics, and responsibility and discipline have been systematically conceptualized, transmitted, and disseminated from one generation to the other. Through myths and legends, these different groups talk about the origins of things and chart the historical development of their peoples and societies. Through folktales, they transmit moral and didactic lessons for the young and the old. Through proverbs and riddles, they encapsulate the wisdom of the ages and of the ancestors for the living and the present. And through songs and praise poems, they celebrate their cultural heroes and commemorate significant events of the past to provide models and archetypes for the present and for posterity. Though the advent of European literary culture from the mid-seventeenth century provided an apparently more efficient alternative, orality has remained a dominant element of indigenous culture.

A strong sense of community permeates these groups. Thus, from childhood, the importance of kinship and of belonging to a shared communal and cultural identity are inculcated and highly valued. A high premium is placed on good social behavior; to be deficient in this most important area is to violate the norms of the civilized social order. It is to bring upon oneself the wrath of the ancestors, with all of its dire consequences in regard to ill health and other misfortune. For these groups, wealth, title, or position acquired through treachery, fraud, and injustice cannot last and will soon dissipate through the same means by which they were acquired. Since the most basic unit, the kinship group, is conceived as a moral community of people and families, no effort or sanction is spared to ensure that the individuals exhibit the highest form of commitment to good behavior. Personal and interpersonal tension as well as group and intergroup conflicts are promptly and diligently settled to forestall the disruption of the social order and to restore harmony between and betwixt the kinship groups.

A number of core values underlies these societies. As in most patriarchal societies, strong emphasis is placed on respect (Xhosa: *intlonipho*) for elders. As in all hierarchically structured societies, the young must respect the old and defer to them in all matters requiring the wisdom that is believed to come only with age and experience. Wives are expected to show deference to their husbands in the same way as commoners and councilors are expected to pay obeisance to their chiefs. In social and public gatherings, individuals must mingle, sit, drink, and eat only with members of their own age grades. A woman always found in the company of men, whether to drink beer or to socialize, is considered one of disreputable personality. In family or other communal gatherings, the younger must give up their seats to their seniors; it is a taboo for them to be seated while their elders are standing. From a very early age, children are exposed to the correct and acceptable etiquettes of social relations. Notable among these are unquestioning obedience to their parents and reticence in front of elders, who they must never interrupt or shout at, in order not to bring shame (*intloni*) to their parents. While occasional infringements by uninitiated children of these norms are not unusual and unexpected, violations by the initiated are viewed very seriously, since initiation into adulthood is generally expected to transform the initiate from the senselessness of childhood to the responsibility and maturity of adulthood. Similarly, while the parents usually punish breaches by children, violations by adults are left in the hands of the ancestors, whose supernatural censure and retribution is considered to be most dreadful. As a Xhosa saying has it, whoever plays the fool with the old people (*edlala ngabantu abadala nje*) will be visited by misfortune.

Another core value is fertility. Lovemaking and premarital sex are considered morally neutral, as long as they are voluntary and are within the limits imposed by custom, and do not result in conception. It is the procreative aspect of sexual intercourse that is considered sacred and can only be consummated within a marriage relationship. Adultery, most especially by women, is condemned while infidelity committed by men is generally ignored in this male-dominated society. A man must not permit himself to become too close to his wife to avoid being bewitched and thus controlled by her, a scenario that may imperil his commitment to his kinship group. Loyalty to one's kinsmen, unfailing solidarity with one's lineage group, and strong commitment to protecting its interests above all else are paramount responsibilities for which no sacrifice and measure can be too great. However, kinship solidarity is not a closed system; it is expected to be accommodative of relations with one's nonkinship neighbors in a society where neighborliness, whether of kin or otherwise, is an admirable virtue.

This openness is also useful in a society that is in demographic flux. As people began to move to the cities to live and to work, they found themselves living with people from outside their kinship or even ethnic groups. In times of crisis and of celebration, neighbors are more readily accessible and available to offer assistance and to share one's joy than kinsmen in distant places. A friend in need and at hand is better than a friend away and unseen. In all these societies, the virtue of generosity to one's kinsmen, to one's neighbors, and to others in need, and the importance of hospitality and generosity to strangers, are inculcated from childhood and continuously emphasized.[1]

CEREMONIES

Many ceremonies are celebrated by the peoples of South Africa. These ceremonies are associated with different aspects of their lives and are often expressive of the history, values, and dynamics of their culture. In spite of westernization and the effective penetration of Christianity, many of these traditional rituals have remained resilient, and in some cases are being imbued with new life and significance. Among the most notable are the ceremonies associated with marking the formal stages of transformation from youth to adulthood.

Life Transition Rituals: Initiation into Adulthood

Nearly all South African groups have developed various rituals and ceremonies to define, mark, and validate the various stages and processes of the transition of youth of both sexes from childhood or adolescence into mature members of society. Strictly speaking, the focus is not on physical maturity, except in a symbolic form; rather it is on social maturity. The age at which people are subjected to initiation varies from group to group. In some cases, the very young and the fairly matured can go through the rites together, most especially among groups such as the Lobedu, who hold initiation rites as infrequently as once every 12 to 15 years.

Among the Nguni, circumcision usually takes place in the late teens. Unlike among the Sotho, where initiation ceremonies are organized on a nationwide scale, Nguni rituals are arranged at the local level and often on a private basis. The processes and stages are fairly similar among the various groups. For a number of weeks before the beginning of the initiation schools, all the potential initiates spend time together: learning songs, as among the Lobedu; herding cattle, collecting firewood, cutting saplings, fashioning ropes to be used in the construction of the initiation lodge, learning songs, as among the Southern Sotho, and working for the chief, as among the Pedi. Wearing feather headdresses, painting themselves in ochre, and roaming and ravaging the countryside as a band of raiders, the boys live in a state of licentiousness intolerable at other times but permissible during this period signifying their final days of boyhood freedom.

Generally, the fathers in a local area who believe their sons are old enough to be circumcised initiate the process of initiation. After receiving permission from the chief, the fathers establish a wooden lodge or *ibhuma* to serve as the base of the circumcision school. Men build the frame of the hut, while the women—usually the mothers of the initiates—thatch it with grass. The service of a specialized circumciser to perform the actual circumcision is also engaged. Older boys, usually those most recently initiated, are recruited to serve as guardians to the novices. One of the fathers of the initiates, usually an individual of high rank, serves as the father of the school, over which he presides as master of ceremonies. The rough beehive-shaped circumcision hut (*ibhuma* or *isuthu*) is positioned a good distance from the settlement to signify the beginning of the separation of the initiates from the community and their liminal status. To emphasize this change in the status of the initiates, some groups such as the Pedi, Venda, and Tsonga shave the heads of the boys before they enter the *ibhuma*. Among the Xhosa, the initiates are led to the *ibhuma* by a group of skillful stick fighters. Among the Nguni and the Southern Sotho, the beginning rites are marked by the sacrifice of an uncastrated bull or ram at the home of the father of the lodge to alert and curry the blessings of the ancestors to the proceedings of transition and transformation taking place.

After a period of communal feasting, the elders admonish the boys to put away childish things, and to henceforth speak and conduct themselves with the dignity befitting men. Their old clothes, symbols of their childhood, are taken away. Stripped naked, they are led to the river, where the remaining relics or dirt of their childhood is washed away in purifying rites that set the stage for the actual circumcision at the river. As a mark of his new manliness, each boy is strictly exhorted not to flinch or cry, no matter how painfully intolerable the operation. Nothing can be more disgraceful than to fail the most important test of this most crucial rite of transition to manhood by crying out. The new adult life they are entering into, with all its pleasures and power, is full of pain and hardships, all of which must be borne with equanimity and great fortitude. Thus, as each boy is cut by the *ingcibi* he must exhibit great courage and endurance, two important attributes of manliness, by boldly addressing the circumciser and the onlookers, "I am a man," to which the later responds, "You are a man." To prevent the excised foreskins from falling into the hands of witches, they are buried in an anthill, where termites destroy them. The boys' wounds are then bound with the leaves of the *izichwe* plant, believed to contain healing and pain-relieving chemical properties. In recent years, the boys are made to take antibiotic drugs before and after the operation, while the *ingcibi* are directed to sterilize their operating spears after each cut to prevent the spread of HIV/AIDS and other infections.

Girls' Initiation Schools

Initiation schools (known as *intonjane* among the Xhosa) for girls are organized in similar ways to those of the boys, though with some significant differences. In some cases, the girls' initiation schools are closely associated with those of the boys. Among the Tswana, initiation schools for girls are formed shortly after those of the boys belonging to the same age grade are organized, with the two sharing the same name. Among the Lovedu, girls' initiation schools occur simultaneously with those of the boys, while Pedi girls' initiation schools begin immediately after the conclusion of those of the boys. Venda's *domba* is a combined initiation school for both girls and boys, while among the Kgaga, girls are initiated into age grades that run parallel to and are linked relationally with the equivalent boys' age grade throughout life.

The duration of the girls' initiations school vary from group to group, ranging from one month among the Tswana and Pedi, to a year among the Lovedu, and for as long as two years among the Venda. Unlike the men, the building of an initiation lodge is not indispensable, for there is very little emphasis on complete separation of the initiates from the community. In the same vein, while the women of the community dominate the proceedings at the Lovedu *byali* and the Venda *domba,* both men and women play active roles in the ceremonies. Girls' initiation rites do not involve actual circumcision, though there are traditions in nearly all of them suggestive of genital operations. Some of these rites include: instructions on how to expand the labia; the physical breaking of the hymen through the insertion of a finger; the making of a tiny cut above the clitoris, as among the Lovedu; the slight cutting and burning of the inside of the thigh as among the Tswana; and the pressing of a knife between the legs, to mimic circumcision, as among the Pedi. Though the girls, like the boys, are expected to observe certain taboos and undergo some training, they are not subjected to as much hardship as the boys.

Like the boys, the girls are also taught about communal rules and values; however, the focus of the formal instruction is more on the significance of the woman's role in the domestic spheres of marriage, childbearing, and farming. While for the man the emphasis is on the ethos of courage and endurance, for the woman the focus is on humility and submission. Among the Kgaga, the *baale* school involves the introduction of the girls to the terrifying and mysterious powers of the Bird or Senkokoyi, the communal spirit. It is Senkokoyi who presides over the operation of the *bogwera-baale,* and for whom regular dances and songs must be performed and in awe of which certain taboos, such as drunkenness, undue noise, and the beating of wives must be strictly avoided. Like the *bogwera,* Kgaga's *baale* brings all the girls to the capital of the chiefdom, bare-chested and attired in a skirt of grass for the ceremonies. Masked dancers, carved wooden models of animals, and other elaborately decorated objects (*digoma* or *dzingoma*) feature prominently in the ceremonies.

Instruction in sexual mores and practices also features prominently in the girls' initiation schools. While the practice of *metsha* or intra-crural intercourse is permitted, full intercourse and premarital pregnancy are frowned upon. Among the Venda, a girl who is examined at the end of the *domba* by the old women and found to be a *virgo intacta* is carried home triumphantly on the back of her mother and welcomed with much celebration, while a girl discovered to have been deflowered is spat upon and derided by members of her age group and the community at large. Among the Xhosa, a woman who becomes pregnant out of wedlock or before a bethrothal will be vigorously censured and runs the risk of being permanently consigned to the status of an *inkazana,* a free woman, ineligible for marriage or participation in the normal activities of her age group, available only for love affairs, usually with married men.

For both males and females, initiation ceremonies help the society to define the nature of the relations that should exist between the sexes and between age groups. By cutting across lineage, rank, and sexual boundaries, initiation rites become a powerful tool of sociocultural integration in the community. By providing the opportunity for the young to be formally introduced into and welcomed into the world of the adults, where they begin to assume new roles and new statuses, initiation rites provide the building blocks for guaranteeing the preservation, transmission, and survival of the norms and values of the society. As men and women advance in age they progress into new roles and responsibilities of enhanced authority, respect, and influence in both domestic and communal spheres that advanced age bring to the elderly and the experienced in these societies.

Khoisan Rites and Ceremonies

Food Avoidance Rites

Different rites and ceremonies are carried out by the Khoisan peoples. Among the most notable of these rites are those connected with food avoidance, pregnancy and childbirth, rain and hunting, menstruation and healing, as well as death and burial. Living in an environment not generally noted for

its abundance of food and water, the Khoisan developed a wide variety of rituals and rites to express their concern with food matters. Food features in
almost every rite, from hunting and healing to wedding and puberty rituals.
Over the years, a strong tradition of food avoidance has developed in which
many food items are avoided usually for one or more of three different reasons: the food has been proven by experience to be unhealthy; the old people
say the food should be avoided; and the food itself is naturally repugnant to
people.

Some creatures are tabooed for food because of their closeness to humans
such as cats, dogs, and mice, or because of their weird characteristics such as
monkeys, flamingos, and chameleons. Creatures such as vultures, hyenas, and
jackals, which regularly scavenge on human corpses, are also forbidden.
Young people, males or females, are expected to avoid eating ostriches and
ostrich eggs, gemsbok heads, cow and eland heads, red-crested korhaans,
giant bustards, puff adders, and the leguaan, the big lizard of the savanna.
Throats, eyes, tails, and fetuses of animals are to be avoided. Girls and young
women are to avoid eating blood, redwing partridges, warthogs, duikers, tor-
toises, and eland chests, as well as snouts and testicles. Boys avoid eating mar-
row, while men must avoid uterus consumption throughout their lives.

The practice of food avoidance has both social and physical value for the
society. It is designed to protect the observer from unwholesome and
unhealthy food, thus ensuring good health, strength, and survival. Some of
the foods are believed to possess actual potencies that can cause ill effects
when eaten. Among the identified ill effects are thinness, headaches, boils,
madness, bleeding, and nausea, to mention the most common. In many
cases, the food prescribed for avoidances are wholesome food, eaten by everyone except those required to avoid them and only during the required periods
of avoidance. For the San these are to be avoided because they possess certain
potencies and ingestion at certain crucial stages of life, such as childbirth or
lactation, might result in negative consequences.

Of the various consequences of violations, the most commonly cited is
thinness, an ill effect that usually elicits laughter and ridicule from others. On
the other hand, young men who obey the laws of food avoidance ensure their
agility, their strength, and vigor, and acquire the ability to endure the cold,
the hunger, and the thirst of hunting. Such men can go for days without eating, can run down an eland, and will obviously be the most enchanting to
women as the most fitting and virile to be successful mating partners. Girls
who fail to comply with the laws of food avoidance are routinely ridiculed,
dismissed as lazy, indulgent, and unfit to be marriage partners. Men avoid
such wayward girls like a plague since, by their violations, they are imperiling
their prospect of conception, successful childbirth, and upbringing.

But even more important is the social value of food avoidance. First it teaches restraint in eating, an important virtue in a society not noted for the overabundant food supply. From childhood, children are brought up not to desire or ask for food from other people. Greediness is roundly condemned as a despicable vice, unworthy of humans. Second, it inculcates the virtue of sharing, no matter how small the catch or the collection of the day might be. Hoarding one's kill for one's sole consumption or for members of one's own immediate family, especially when the catch is big enough to go round the band or village community, is a violation of customs considered extremely reproachable, and indeed unthinkable among the San people. To be generous in heart is to be human; to take food only for oneself reduces one to the level of the animals, just like lions take food only for themselves. Only the light-hearted and those whose bellies are like bags without openings think only of their appetite and of meeting their own needs at all costs. The philosophy of dog eat dog, common in some other societies, is not only alien to the San, but it is also considered patently inhuman. Satisfying one's hunger and quenching one's thirst, both legitimate concerns, must not be satisfied at the expense of the group. In a society dependent on hunting and gathering for its subsistence, where hunger and starvation are not distant menaces but ever-threatening realities, obedience to food taboos is a powerful symbolic affirmation of one's commitment to the rules and norms of society. As noted on the Nyae Nyae !Kung, a San group, "In obeying the rules of avoidances, a person demonstrates active, personal support of accepted customs, the social law, and shows that he is not 'too fond of food,' not 'light-hearted,' not lazy or indifferent to taking care of himself, to keeping himself strong—that he or she is, in all, a proper person."[2]

Hunting Rites

Hunting is an intricate art for which the San have over the years developed various skills. The most important rite in the life of a budding hunter is the rite of First Kill, carried out on the occasion of a boy's killing of his first big game of each sex, such as an antelope or a buffalo, animals that are large enough to feed an entire band. The most important aspect of this rite is the scarification, in the forms of vertical incisions on the body of the boy into which revitalizing, potent medicinal substances are rubbed. Seven scarifications, each ranging in number from 2 to 25 cuts, were made on different parts of the boy's body, with each directed to fulfill specific purposes, such as instilling vision, courage, and doggedness in the budding hunter to calming and trapping the animal being tracked. For the San this rite marks the transition from boyhood to hunter, from a state of nature to a state of culture. For the San, hunting is the crucial element of culture. So crucial is this rite of passage that a San boy may not marry until he has killed a big animal and the rite is performed.

Living in or around the usually hot and arid Kalahari Desert, the San see the sun as death-giving and the rain as life-giving. Rain is a rarity in the Kalahari; the main wet season is the summer, with its usually stormy, thunderclapping, lightning streaking rains. The turbulence not withstanding, the San welcome the rains as both life-giving and liberating, causing the food plants to grow and thus staving off the ever-present menace of starvation. Rain also frees the people from restrictions to their permanent water holes, enabling them to move around and visit friends and relatives in faraway, fertile areas. Some San healers are known to possess the power to make rain, though the practice does not appear to have been widespread.[3]

FESTIVALS AND PUBLIC HOLIDAYS

National and Religious Holidays

Officially South Africa has twelve public holidays. In chronological order they are: New Year's Day, January 1; Human Rights Day, March 21; Good Friday, the Friday before Easter Sunday; Family Day, the day after Easter Sunday; Freedom Day, April 27; Workers' Day, May 1; Youth Day, June 16; National Women's Day, August 9; Heritage Day, August 9; Heritage Day, September 24; Day of Reconciliation, December 16; Christmas Day, December 25; and Day of Goodwill, December 26. Some of these holidays like the New Year, Easter, Christmas, and Workers' Days are universal holidays with significance well beyond South Africa, though sometimes with local expressions, such as the Cape New Year Coon Carnivals. Others are peculiarly South African.

It is significant that unlike other new and modern nations of the world, no independence day is celebrated. South Africa obtained independence from British rule in 1910, but this was an independence that brought freedom and power only to the white minority. The black majority never fully accepted or acceded to 1910 as their year of independence; for many it was their year of formal subordination to white minority rule. For this majority, true liberation did not come until April 27, 1994, when the first nonracial, nonsexist, democratically elected government, headed by Nelson Mandela, came to power. The institutionalization of April 27 as Freedom Day is meant to commemorate this struggle of the South African peoples against apartheid and racist domination, and celebrate the eventual attainment of liberation and democracy. August 9 was the day in 1955 when several thousand women, led by Helen Joseph and Lilian Ngoyi, marched to protest against the mandatory carrying of passes by blacks in South Africa. August 9 was formally declared the National Women's Day in 2000, to commemorate the contributions of women to the struggle for freedom, equality, and justice in South Africa. It was meant, to borrow the words of a popular South African women's song, to "remember all our women" for their "jails," "campaigns," "fighting years," as well as for "their triumphs, and for their tears."[4]

Many of the public holidays that were celebrated during the colonial and apartheid era ceased to be national holidays, since most of them had significance only for the white minority population. Some of them were dedicated to remembering events that the black majority would rather forget, since they remind them of their colonial subjugation and dispossession. Among such holidays that have ceased to be national are: Founder's Day, April 6; Family Day, April 12; Ascension Day in May; Republic Day, May 31; and Kruger Day, October 10. Besides Easter and Christmas holidays, Workers' Day and the Day of Goodwill (December 26) also survived from the old order.

For the Afrikaner people the most significant holiday was the Day of the Vow, December 16. On that date in 1838 a small group of hardy and harried Calvinist trekkers confronted a Zulu *impi* (army battalion) at the banks of the Ncome River. Vastly outnumbered by their enemies, and besieged from all sides, almost certain their end had come, they called on their God, vowing to dedicate the day to him should he give them victory. The battle ended with the rout of the Zulu army, thanks to better strategy and superior weaponry on the part of the Boers. The river turned red with the blood of three thousand Zulu warriors, while the Trekboers escaped almost unscathed. Thus the river took on a new name, and the engagement entered into history as the Battle of the Blood River. Decades passed before the battle assumed legendary status, but once it did, from the 1920s onward thanks to the patriotic fervency of Afrikaner nationalists, Afrikaners began to commemorate that victory and the date associated with it as Geloftedag or Day of the Vow or Covenant.

In 1938, a symbolic trek from Cape Town to Pretoria was staged to mark the centenary of the Great Trek and to lay the foundation of the Voortrekker Monument. This ritual reenactment of the Great Trek was marked with religious fervor all over South Africa among Afrikaners who flocked to the outfitted ox-wagons with enthusiasm to touch them, anoint their bodies with grease from their wheels, and in some cases baptize their babies and conduct marriages near the wagons and in places made holy by the wagon's presence. The Voortrekker Monument took 11 years to build, and is the largest and the most imposing monument in the whole of southern Africa. At the center of the monument is a cenotaph. Every year, on December 16, exactly at noon, the sun shines through a strategically placed gap in the roof of the Monument to illuminate for visitors the words: "Ons Vir Jou Suid-Afrika (We For You

Voortrekker Monument, Pretoria, commemorating the Great Trek by Boer (Afrikaner) pioneers from the Cape to the interior during the 1830s, in protest against British domination at the Cape. Begun in 1938, the centenary of the Battle of the Blood River, the monument became a focus of Afrikaner nationalism. (Akin Akinade)

South Africa)." For the Afrikaners the Great Trek was the single most important episode of their history, and the Day of the Vow associated with it the most important day in their emergence as a distinct sociopolitical group in southern Africa. Most South Africans, especially non-Afrikaners, would rather not remember or commemorate the events associated with the Day of the Vow. In deference, however, to the deep feelings of the Afrikaners, the new government of South Africa retained December 16 as a national public holiday, but redesignated it as the Day of Reconciliation, thus giving it a larger significance and a more appropriate relevance to the challenges of contemporary South Africa. Of the widely celebrated ethno-religious festivals, among the most popular is the Cape Coon New Year celebration.[5]

The Cape Coon New Year Festival

Among the colored population, the most celebrated festival is the Cape Town Coon Carnival. Celebrated annually to mark the advent of the New Year, the origin of the Coon festival dates to the early colonial period and is directly connected with the musical and dancing activities of the slaves at the Cape. Then it was customary for the slaves to be given a holiday on New Year's Day, which they in turn transformed into a day of celebration, entertainment, feasting, visiting friends from house to house, wearing of fanciful attires, and reveling in music and dance. This tradition of New Year celebration continued after the emancipation of the slaves to the accompaniment of street parades and bands. Indeed, from the 1820s, street orchestras and singing societies became regular features of these performances. By the end of the nineteenth century these singing groups and bands began to be associated with particular sports clubs and were usually costumed in special attires distinguished by peculiar emblems. Every year, they competed with one another in songs, in dances, in parades, and in the wearing of colorful outfits, as they marched through the streets and suburbs of Cape Town.

The first attempt at organized celebration was on January 1, 1907 when the Green Point Cricket Club brought all the competitions and singing groups together in a grand competition at the Green Point Track stadium. This was repeated in 1908 and 1909, but was discontinued until 1920 and 1921 when Dr. A. Abdulrahman, the leader of the African People's Organization (APO), organized two successive Grand Carnivals on Green Point Track. The success of these Grand Carnivals brought other groups into the fray, leading to the regular organization of several Coon competitions by various groups and promoters in different parts of the city, every year, almost without exception, until the present.[6] The basic format of performance established for the Coon festival in the 1920s has continued with only very minor modifications.

The Cape Coon New Year festival is a crystallization of many elements, local and foreign. From the mid-nineteenth century onward, visiting sailors, actors, comedians, and musicians brought American Coon songs to the Cape. Groups like the Christy's Minstrels, from the USA, toured South Africa in 1862 with the African-American Orpheus McAdoo's Virginia Jubilee Singers, and spent approximately five years performing in South Africa between 1890 and 1898, were crucial in making the Coon Carnival, with its uniformed attires, its white- and black-painted faces, and its minstrel repertoire, the dominant element of the Cape Coon New Year festival. From the early 1900s and over the course of the next half-century, other elements, local and foreign, ranging from African American religious hymns to classical European musical forms and from Mexican Cattle Stampers to stilt dancers of West Indian inspirations, came to enrich the ongoing creolization of the Coon. Private groups such as the Matabele Warriors and the Zulu Warriors also jostled for recognition along with Christmas bands and Malay Choirs as they selectively adopted and innovatively adapted pop music to assume new significance in the Cape local environment. The social and political pressures associated with the formal institutionalization of apartheid led to the inclusion of songs in Afrikaans in the Coon Carnival repertoires from the 1940s. Other changes followed as dances disappeared and brass bands gradually replaced string bands.

For the colored population at the Cape, ex-slaves and free, with their diverse origins and tapestry of cultures, the Coon Carnival with its Creole elements provides a viable and vital means for strengthening social links and building a more cohesive Creole community. Living in a society where they were for centuries systematically oppressed, uniformly dehumanized, and discriminated against, the Coon provides a useful opportunity for this population to express and affirm their creative capacity as well as their essential humanity in the face of the racial ideology of inequality and alienation dominant in South Africa. Through the annual Coon festivals, the Cape colored are enabled to transcend, even if temporarily, their ambiguous and anomalous status in South African society by being linked socially and aesthetically with the international community. The latest musical forms—from rock, jazz, and soul to rap, disco, and techno—are creatively adopted to refashion a new identity, thereby affirming autonomy and modernity, two attributes denied to the colored population or contested in its own society. In spite of its apparent self-depreciating element, the Coon symbolizes the ambivalent position of the colored population in South African society: between and betwixt.

By looking beyond the confines of South Africa for inspiration and by glamorizing its mosaic of racial and cultural identities, the Coon is a subtle but definite rejection of the dual myths of white racial superiority and of racial purity over mixing in South African society. The persistence and continuing survival of the Coon Carnival, in spite of every effort by the authorities to suppress it through the restrictions and forced removal of the Group Areas Act and other apartheid measures, is indicative of the resilience of the colored community and the permanence of their claim to the possession of Cape Town. As Denis-Constant Martin aptly puts it, "the Coon was the locus of a brutal but disguised confrontation; he could not be a fighter; but he survived and with him survives, in the new South Africa, a discourse on one communal identity continuing to express pride in belonging to a group that survived all attempts at denying the humanity of its members, as well as anxieties regarding what the future has in store for them."[7]

SPORTS AND RECREATION

The climate of South Africa, with its moderate temperatures and lack of extreme weather variations makes it a friendly environment for outdoor

Picnicking on a sailboat, off Fourth Beach, Clifton, Western Cape. South Africans take much delight in their outdoor life, made possible by the country's amiable climate. (Helen and Russell Mason)

sports. Its physical environment—consisting of plain and mountainous regions, rivers, and adjacent oceans—has permitted the development of a wide variety of outdoor activities such as camping, hiking, rock-climbing, mountaineering, swimming, surfing, and waterskiing to name just the most common. However, for years, the remarkable talent and performances of South African sportsmen and women were overshadowed by the politics of apartheid.

From 1948 onward, a series of bills instituted racial differentiation in all areas of national and social life, from housing and education to sex and sport. Following the 1960 Sharpville massacre and the resultant clampdown on the resistance movement in South Africa in the 1960s, the international campaign against South African government policy of apartheid took a dramatic turn. Every avenue was utilized to put pressure on the pariah state by ostracizing them from the international community. In 1969 South Africa was expelled from the Olympic Games, and even the continued diplomatic support of Britain could not stop its expulsion from the Commonwealth of Nations and the Commonwealth Games. Athletes with South African nationalities were barred from major international competitions, while athletes of other nations began to boycott events in or organized by South Africa or in which South African athletes were taking part.

For budding and promising young athletes, the denied opportunity to test their talents was heartbreaking. To break out of this politicization of sport, a few athletes changed nationalities and moved to other countries. One of these was Zola Bud, who was whisked away to Britain in 1984 and naturalized in order to enable her to compete in the 1991 Olympics in Barcelona. Though her much expected victory failed to materialize and the gold medal eluded her due to a disastrous track collision with her American rival, Mary Decker, this brave Afrikaner from Bloemfontein went on to distinguish herself in other international events through her world record performances on the track. Similarly, through high-powered stick and carrot diplomacy, South Africa also attempted to lure sport teams from sympathetic nations to tour South Africa in defiance of the international sanctions. Cricket teams from England and rugby teams from New Zealand received widespread condemnation in the world press, and were greeted everywhere in South Africa with huge protests. For instance in 1990 an English cricket team led by Mike Gatting cancelled its tour of South Africa in the face of strong local opposition and widespread protest that greeted it everywhere it went. However, the ascension of F. W. de Klerk and his adoption of a series of measures that officially abrogated apartheid in all areas of national life set the stage for the readmission of South Africa to international competition. In July 1991, after 21 years of isolation, South Africa was readmitted to the International Olympic Committee (IOC). Its team of 125 members participated in the next Olympics in Barcelona and came back with two silver medals. In 1996, at the Atlanta Olympics, the South African runner, Josiah Thugwane, in a stunning performance, won the gold medal in the most Olympian of events, the marathon, while his countryman, Penny Heyns, outswarmed all the favorites, striking gold twice in both the 100 meters and 200 meters breaststroke. In golf, Ernie Els, who won the U.S. Open in 1994 and 1997 and led the World Matchplay tournament for three years, was ranked in 2003 as among the top three golfers in the world.[8]

The Most Popular Sport: Soccer

Poll after poll taken in 2001 showed that soccer, known as football in South Africa as in much of the world outside North America, is the most popular sport in South Africa, especially among the black population. The first soccer club appears to have been established in Pietermaritzburg around 1879. In 1882 the first football association was established, made up of four teams: Pietermaritzburg County, Natal Wasps, Durban Alpha, and Umgeni

Stars. As more clubs appeared in other parts of South Africa, the Football Association of South Africa emerged 10 years later.

Several amateur and professional clubs and groups are engaged in the organization of soccer competitions between schools, communities, clubs, and provinces, from the local to the national levels. Many professional series sponsored by big corporations, such as SA Breweries, have become part of the annual national sport festivals. Leading clubs such as the Iwisa Kaiser Chiefs, the Jomo Midas Cosmos, Orlando Pirates, and Moroko Swallows compete for championship in the major series such as the Castle League, the Mainstay League, the BP Top 8, the Ohlssons Challenge, and the Cosafa Cup. Soccer City, located halfway between Johannesburg and Soweto, is a grand showpiece of the South African passion for the most popular game on the planet. The South African Women's Association was established in 1974 to promote women's soccer and organize competitions between the various women's soccer clubs especially at provincial and national levels. With the ending of sport sanctions, South Africa has thrust itself into the mainstream of world soccer, playing with several African countries from Zambia and Zimbabwe to Cameroon and Nigeria. In 1996, the national team, nicknamed Bafana Bafana (Zulu phrase meaning the boys, the boys), won the African Nations Cup trophy. In both 1998 and 2002, it qualified to represent Africa at the World Cup Finals in France as well as in Japan and South Korea.

The National Winter Sport: Rugby

If soccer is the most popular sport, arguably the most controversial game and the one generally identified with South Africa in the outside world is rugby. This is the national winter sport. Introduced, it would seem, by Canon G. Ogilvie, headmaster of the Diocesan College in Cape Town, who arrived from England in 1858, the first organized game was played between regiments of the military and civilians on the Green Point Common in Cape Town in August 1862. Rugby lovers formed the first club, Hamilton Rugby Football Club in Cape Town in 1875. This was followed by other clubs, namely the Villagers in 1875, the Buffaloes in 1877, and the Rugby Club of Stellensbosch in 1880. Stellensburg and its university soon developed into the most important nursery of South African rugby, supplying nearly 25 percent of all the players who have represented the country in the carrying code sport.

South Africa played host to its first international touring side with the visit of a British team captained by Bill Maclagan in 1891. A second British side came in 1896. So rooted had the game become, that during the Anglo-Boer war, the two sides agreed to a one-day cease-fire to allow a rugby match to be played between the teams of the opposing forces in the afternoon of April 29,

1902. Four years after the war, the first South African team went on a tour of Britain, where they adopted the name Springbokken at the request of the London press. This and subsequent tours enabled the Sprinboks to perfect their art; thereafter for the next 50 years they dominated the game on a world scale, garnering an impressive record and never losing a test series to any country.

Rugby players compete for honors at various levels and categories in the society. The most important competition is for the Currie Cup. First presented by a British touring side in 1891, the cup is presented annually to the best provincial team. First won by the Griqualand West team in 1891, in the last two decades the Western Province (1982–86) and the Northern Transvaal (1987–88) have between them dominated the Currie Cup championship, as they have also dominated the Lion Club knock-out competition, which was introduced in 1983. Their impressive record notwithstanding, political pressures emanating from the global campaign against apartheid resulted in censure for the Springboks and sport sanctions because they were perceived to be representatives of the apartheid state. The Springboks, who until recently were a white-only team, were banned from touring many countries while tours by foreign teams dwindled to a trickle. The formal ending of apartheid and the progressive deracialization of sport led to the re-admission of South Africa into international competitions in 1992. Three years later, the Springboks defeated the New Zealanders and were crowned as the 1995 world champions.

Cricket: The Premier National Summer Sport

As rugby is the principal national winter sport, so cricket is the premier national summer sport. Like rugby, cricket also appears to have been first introduced by regiments of British soldiers following their occupation of the Cape in 1795. The first competition was played between a team of army officers and civilians from the Cape. The first club, the Port Elizabeth Cricket Club, was formed in 1845. Another 30 years lapsed before the first inter-town competition was organized for the Champion Bat, which was won by King William's Town in 1875. An English team, C. Aubrey Smith, became the first international side to tour South Africa in 1888–89, playing and winning its two test matches in Cape Town and Port Elizabeth. Though South Africa's record in cricket is not as sterling as in rugby, a few South African players have distinguished themselves in the sport. One of the most notable among these is Graeme Pollock, reputedly among the greatest left-handed batsmen to grace the sport. Others include Barry Richards, Eddie Barlow, Mike Proctor, and Clive Rice, to mention just a few.

Cricket at Club Wanderers on a Sunday afternoon at Amaleurs. (Jane Davis)

Like rugby, cricket also came under political pressures during the 1970s and 1980s as the international campaigns against the apartheid state intensified. Temporary relief came during the 1980s only by way of a series of rebel tours by teams from England, Australia, Sri Lanka, and the West Indies, who were lured into touring the pariah state through deft diplomacy by the apartheid state struggling to break out of its growing worldwide isolation. The end of apartheid once again brought South African cricket teams back to the world sport, gaining admission into the International Cricket Conference (ICC), to which it had been denied membership for many years. After losing to Australia in the 1999 ICC final, South Africa reemerged in January 2003 and was rated by the ICC as the leading cricket nation in the world.[9]

NOTES

1. W. D. Hammond-Tooke, "World-View II: A System of Action," in Hammond-Tooke, ed., *The Bantu-Speaking Peoples of Southern Africa* (London and Boston: Routledge and Kegan Paul Ltd., 1974), 359–63 and Hammond-Tooke, *The Roots of Black South Africa* (Johannesburg: Jonathan Ball Publishers, 1993), 97–99.

2. Lorna J. Marshall, *Nyae Nyae !Kung Beliefs and Rites* (Cambridge, Mass.: Peabody Museum of Archaeology and Ethnology, 1999), 93.

3. Marshall, *Nyae Nyae !Kung Beliefs and Rites,* 143–62.

4. See Hilda Bernstein, *For Their Triumphs & For Their Tears: Women in Apartheid South Africa* (London: International Defence and Aid Fund for Southern Africa, 1985).

5. On the enduring memory of the Great Trek in South African, and most especially Afrikaner folk history, see A. F. Jaarsveld, "A Historical Mirror of Blood River," in A. Kong and H. Keane, eds., *The Meaning of History* (Johannesburg: UNISA, 1980); E. A. Walker, *The Great Trek* (London: Black, 1948); and Duncan Guy, *The Very Best of Johannesburg and Surrounds* (Cape Town: Struik Publishers, 2000), 74–77.

6. The discussion of the Cape Coon Festival in this chapter is based on: Denis-Constant Martin, "Cape Town Coon Carnival," in Sarah Nuttall and Cheryl-Ann Michael, *Senses of Culture: South African Culture Studies* (Oxford: Oxford University Press, 2000), 363–79 and Martin, *The New Year in Cape Town: A History of the Coon Carnival* (Cape Town: David Philip, 1998). For a video presentation, see Martin, *The Cape Minstrels* (Meudon: CNRS Audiovisual, 1995), a video VHS PAL, color, 28'.

7. Martin, "Cape Town Coon Carnival," 379.

8. On the checkered history of sports and politics in South Africa during the apartheid era, and the major sources for the discussion in this section, see *South Africa, 1989–90: Official Yearbook of the Republic of South Africa* (Pretoria: Bureau for Information, Department of Foreign Affairs, 1989/90), 677–702; *South Africa, 1993: Official Yearbook of the Republic of South Africa* (Pretoria: South African Publication Service, 1993), 267–82; *South Africa Yearbook, 2001/2002* (Pretoria: GCIS, 2001), 507–17; John Nauright, *Sport, Cultures and Identities in South Africa* (London and Washington, D.C.: Leicester University Press, 1997); and David R. Black and John Nauright, *Rugby and the South African Nation* (Manchester and New York: Manchester University Press).

9. On cricket in South Africa, see C. Bryden, *Story of South African Cricket, 1990–1996* (Cape Town: Inter-African Publishers, 1997) and J. Winch, *Cricket in Southern Africa: Two Hundred Years of Achievement and Records* (Rosettenville, Johannesburg: Windsor, 1997).

10

Performing Arts and Cinema

Music and dance are important features of all South African societies. Both are intricately and inextricably linked together in the life and cultures of the peoples of South Africa. From the indigenous praise poems and classical church hymns to modern jazz and industrial rhythms, music permeates the daily lives of the South African people. For the rulers of the indigenous people, music is perceived as the symbol of political power.

Among the means through which kings maintain and express their power is the institution of royal musicians, permanently retained or regularly hired to eulogize and verbally affirm the ruler's power, potency, and legitimacy. The heterogeneity of South African society has led to the emergence of a wide variety of musical traditions. Three and one-half centuries of European commerce, conquest, and domination have dramatically transformed, though not supplanted, the indigenous musical traditions in addition to producing new musical forms. Like every musical tradition, South African musical forms are in many ways reflective of the historical and cultural experiences of its peoples. Its tumultuous history can be seen in its turbulent and variegated musical forms. A study of South African music is a cynosure of South African history and society. In this chapter, we will examine the varieties of South African music; their historical evolution and current forms; musical instruments and their uses; the connections between music and dance, music and society, and music and politics; the emergence of popular music; and the internationalization of South African music.

INDIGENOUS MUSIC

Khoisan

As the first indigenous people of southern Africa, the Khoisan and their musical forms have had a major impact on the musical cultures of those who later came to settle in the country. Like most nomadic and pastoral peoples, the Khoisan embraced music as an important part of daily life. Over the years, utilizing the resources of their arid environment, they developed a wide variety of musical bows, of which the most notable was the *gora*. This stringed instrument could be made to produce different tones by the player forcefully inhaling and exhaling over a feather, which connects the string to one end of the bow. The *gora* is a favorite of the cattle herders, who use it as much for their own entertainment as they do to harry their herds. From the Khoisan the *gora* spread to the Tswana, who called it *lesiba* (feather), before passing it on to the Sotho, who retained the Tswana term *lesiba* for the instrument. Early in the nineteenth century, the Xhosa adopted the instrument as well as its Khoisan name before passing it on to the Zulu well before the middle of the nineteenth century. Another bow was the short-braced mouth bow played by men. The playing of the longer bow, *kha:s* is the prerogative of women. The *kha:s* is usually played seated, with the woman securing the lower end of the instrument with one foot, resting the center on a hollow object meant to serve as a resonator, while the upper end is supported by her face or chin. Other instruments include the single-note flutes, usually about 15 inches long, fashioned from particularly suited reeds and roots. The raising or lowering of a plug inserted at the bottom of the pipe allows the player to modify the pitch and thus produce different tones. During important communal dances the flutes are played in ensembles with each man producing different sounds and tones to create a melody in concert. Men and women dance in separate concentric circles, though which sex dances on the inside and outside varies from one group to the other. To make the drums, which early European visitors called *rommelpot*, the Khoikhoi place hides over their ceramic pots.

The San

In spite of the precariousness usually associated with a hunting-gathering culture, the San developed a musical tradition that came to play an important role in their daily existence. Their music was meant for self-expression, dealing with everyday issues such as hunting, fishing, and foraging while their quivering trance dances were meant to serve as curative rituals. Like the Khoikhoi, San used the bow most frequently. The most common were the long bows, usually stopped at the end to produce two fundamental tones that can in turn be separated at intervals by a second or third minor or major tones. With one end of the bow on the ground and the other end in the mouth, the player resonates the bow to produce or modify tones by changing the shape of the mouth. A variety of overtones can also be produced by holding a gourd against the bow, while moving it in contact with the player's bare chest.

Even more fascinating is the San tradition of the group bow. Its name, *kambulumbumba,* indicates that this instrument was probably originally adopted and adapted from the Bantu. Fairly complex but highly versatile, the group bow is played by at least three players. Playing at different sections of the bow, depending on the song, the players use short sticks and sometimes gourds to produce steady or irregular triple or duple rhythms that in combination end up producing a harmony of tones and overtones vital to the hunting, curative, and other dances of the San. To match the expressive variety of the group bow, the San developed a vocal, multipart musical tradition that permitted singers to sing individual variants of the same basic song. In addition, the San used palm leaf ribbon to fashion their own form of mouth-resonated musical bow.

The antiquity and variety of the musical bow and playing style in southern Africa is shown by a San rock painting showing a single player playing seven bows lined up on the ground. Other instruments include the *kuma,* a raft zither, and *bavugu,* a type of stamping tube, made from the assembling together with wax of three gourds or orange-shaped resonators that are beat against the upper thigh and tapped spasmodically by hand. Played mainly by women, who are often reluctant to display it to the predominantly male researchers, the *bavugu* is probably associated with fertility rituals. Unlike other responsorial singing in other parts of Africa, the San soloists interweave their songs without directly responding to each other. Similarly, unlike other parts of Africa, the Khoikhoi and the San yodel as they sing.[1]

BANTU MUSICAL TRADITIONS

General Features

For many South African people, the presence of metered rhythm is the most important indicator of music. Thus, drumming without any vocal expression is considered to be music, provided the beat is rhythmical. Songs that have no rhythm are considered unqualified to be described as singing. As with other African peoples, the music of South Africa is also noted for the pervasiveness of the polyrhythms. Another common trait is the impact of linguistic tones on musical forms, though tonality is not as dominant in the languages of South Africa as it is in those of West Africa. The musical bow is more prevalent in southern Africa than it is in other parts of the continent. Though musical traditions varied from one group to the other and even within groups, centuries of intergroup and intercultural relations and exchanges have resulted in considerable overlapping, making the boundaries of musical traditions less distinct and fairly porous. This section will examine the peculiarities as well as the commonalities of these musical traditions.

Among the Nguni choral singing is the most dominant form. With the focus being on vocal polyphony, very little emphasis is placed on drum or percussion ensembles. Instead, open voice singing, "like the lowing of cattle,"[2] in which dancers sing their own dance music without the aid of any instrument, is the norm. However, over the years and partly in response to various pressures and influences, a number of instruments have become part of the musical paraphernalia of the Nguni people. In addition to ankle rattles and hand clapping, war shields are used percussively by warriors, while ox hides are beaten during initiation ceremonies, especially for Xhosa boys. Similarly, among the Zulu, the friction drum and the double-headed drum are used to mark girls' puberty rituals. Medicine men are known to have used different types of drums in the past, while in recent years, drums and wooden clappers have become part of the musical ensembles of some of the neotraditional performances, such as the modern *ingoma* dance of the Zulu. A prominent principle of Nguni choral dance song is nonsimultaneous entry of voice parts. Their polyphonic vocal interactions become quite intricate, with different voice parts having different starting points and, thus, overlapping with one another without ultimately achieving a final combined resolution. An important feature of Nguni music is the tonality shift or tonality contrast which is expressed among Xhosa women and girls through a form of overtone singing (*umngqokolo*) in which singing in a low fundamental tone is interspersed with different overtones as the singer shapes and reshapes her mouth to isolate and bring out different overtones.[3]

Among the Nguni, there are no professional musicians. The Zulu *imbongi*, the court praise poet comes very close to qualifying, but his *izibongo* (praise poetry)—in spite of its melodic delivery—is not regarded as vocal music. Praise poetry often appears as choral recitation and may sound, in ears atoned to Western music, like a type of praise song, but it generally lacks the regular meter that for the Zulu defines *ukuhlabela* (singing). Music and dance are so inextricably linked in the life of the Nguni people that it is impossible to analyze or understand one without the other. The unity of music and dance is usually demonstrated through the blending of rhythmic singing with simultaneous actions or body movements on the part of the singers themselves as they clap their hands, sway their bodies, shake their buttocks, move their steps, stamp their feet, hit their ox-hide shields with spears, or wield their other weapons or regalia in perfect unison.

The Sotho and the Tswana share the tradition of choral singing for which the Nguni have become famous. However, a major distinction between them is the inclusion of praise singing in virtually all elements of Sotho-Tswana music. Praise singing, recalling, celebrating, and extolling past historical events or the lives and deeds of great men and notable families often accompanies or sometimes interrupts choral singing. The quicker rhythms and fast pace of Sotho-Tswana languages have enabled the development of a rapid, almost recitative praise song performance style for which Sotho-Tswana choreography is noted. In addition, the Sotho-Tswana vocal music is primarily pentatonic and responsorial. Unlike the Nguni polyphonic style, the Sotho call-and-response forms do not often overlap. Led by leaders adept at manipulating words, the group response is usually static, while the individual call remains flexible.

Among the notable Sotho vocal performances are the *mohohelo* and *moko-rotlo* songs performed by men in L-shaped regimental formation, as they stamp their feet in periodic rhythmic patterns while simultaneously raising and lowering knobkerry sticks in motion with their dance movement. Among Sotho women, the *mokgibo* knee dance-song is most prominent. Ululating and handclapping while kneeling in a semicircle formation, the women perform an elaborate dance movement involving the raising and lowering of the knees and a call-and-response singing of praise songs. The *diphotha* song is another synchronized step dance performed by men in gumboots that they strike together and slap rhythmically with their hands. The *lialolo* and *met-jekong* call-and-response dance-songs are the specialties of Sotho girls, often accompanied by clapping and other simple movements, while Sotho boys are noted for their deep bass melodic renderings of the *lengae* initiation songs.[4]

Among the Venda as among the Nguni, music is determined by rhythm. Thus the art of speaking (*u amba*), reciting praises (*u renda*), or narrating stories (*u anetshela*) does not qualify as singing (*u imba*) since they usually lack conscious cultivation of rhythms. However, when accompanied by an instrument (a single note blown on a stopped pipe or a horn even though it may have no rhythm) speaking is acceptable as music because the performer is said to make the instrument cry. Giving musical instruments the name *zwilidzo* directly likens them to things that are made to cry. In Venda parlance, a soloist is said to plant (*sima*) his song, while the chorus thunders in response (*bvumela*); the dance leader (*maluselo*) shows the step or a leg (*sumbedza mulenzhe*) while the followers pour it out (*shela mulenzhe*) after him. Communal dances are usually circular and counterclockwise, mimicking the formation of a cattle kraal (*danga*). Teamwork in dancing, especially during communal rituals, is especially emphasized. Different individual styles are also valued, such as *u tanga,* in which old women and notable people dance in stately style and on special occasions; *u pembela* refers to an excited dance meant to conclude an initiation ritual or chieftaincy installation, and *u dabela* refers to a dance in which a new initiate dances in the opposite direction to the rest of the group to indicate his or her graduation from the initiation school.

Though patterns are not isolated, music is perceived as repetitions of basic patterns in which loud and soft music, high and low tones, as well as male and female voices, are distinguished. Performers are judged for their vigor, energy, agility, and dexterity. To pull off a great performance is to sing until one nearly bursts one's diaphragm, to dance until one's foot digs a hole in the ground, to leap until one's head can touch the clouds, or to jump so high that three men can crawl under one. It is not uncommon, and it is indeed welcomed, during the heat of performances for skin drums to break from vigorous pounding, for leg-rattles to disintegrate during excited dancing, for xylophone leather chords to break due to hard playing, and for voices to become hoarse as intense excitement reaches a feverish pitch.[5]

MUSIC AND SOCIETY

Music plays an important role in the traditional life of the peoples of South Africa. The songs and the dances are usually functional. They regulate activities, enliven social events, and guide behavior and conduct. This is clearly exemplified by the Tswana, who classify their vocal music in relation to the function that specific types of music performed in different social institutions on different occasions. One category of music is associated with boys' initiation ritual (*moama*), during the course of which the initiates commit to memory special songs taught by an elderly musician specialist (*nake*). Similarly, music and dance also feature prominently in the girls' puberty school (*boyale*). One such dance is the *radikgaratlane,* in which a masked woman disguised as a deity and attired with clay horns becomes a symbol of fertility. The puberty school is concluded with an all-night ceremonial dance (*thojane*) after which each girl is declared ready for marriage. Thereafter, the family of each girl will receive her with the special songs of return known as *megolokwane*.

Tswana communal musical festivals follow a calendrical cycle associated with the agricultural season. The period between autumn and spring is a time of clearing, sowing, and weeding; though it is a time of low musical activity, there are a few common exceptions: work songs, fireside story songs taught to children by women, and songs sung lustily by women in the fields as they chase birds off the crops. The postharvest summer season involves an explosion of musical performances, excited songs, and vigorous dances amidst beer drinking and other merriments. A similar seasonal regimen is followed by the Venda; girls usually begin to practice their *tshigonbela* dance toward the end of the weeding season, when the muddy soil of the raining season has turned to hard clay suitable for dancing. Circumcision schools and other communal dances are held mainly during the period of rest between harvest and planting.

In combination, music and dance provide the basis for the organization of orderly social interactions among individuals and between groups. Among the Nguni choral dance music is an informative, educative, and regulatory expression of new ideas, opinions, and even criticism of constituted authorities. In many cases, each performance is directly associated with particular ceremonies, rituals, or groups, and the performance is meaningless and even dangerous or forbidden when separated from its specific context. An example of this would be the annual royal *incwala* ceremony of the Swazi. Meant to celebrate the power and potency of the Swazi priest-king, the *Ingwenyama* or Lion, the *incwala* involves a mass demonstration of Swazi national solidarity through a series of solemn but dramatic displays of choral dance music and other performances, many of which cannot be sung at any other time. Through music, a ruler demonstrates his or her authority and consolidates relationships and alliances. Among the Venda a ruler periodically dispatches musical expeditions or dance-teams (*mabepha*) to reinforce his ties with allies, consolidate and confirm his dominance of conquered groups, extract tributes from subordinates, and strengthen the bonds between his people and other groups.

Among the Venda and the Nguni, there are at least 16 musical styles, each with its own distinctive rhythm, number of singers, specific instrument, and definite body movement. Within each division, there are several other subdivisions. For instance, within the category of initiation songs there are 70 songs of one type and 30 songs of another representative of an initiation subdivision. However, these songs and even the subdivisions are not static and are constantly refined with the addition of new words and new lines. New songs are also created regularly.

Great composers are respected and often well rewarded for their dancing skills as well as for their facility with words and creativity as song and music generators. For the Venda, music is part of an oral tradition transmitted from one generation to another. Every Venda child is expected to possess at least a rudimentary knowledge of music and dance. To become a master-singer or master-performer later in life is more a function of choice, effort, and experience than one of mental or physiological competence. Even the deaf are expected to sing, and those with other disabilities, such as dwarfism or a hunched back, are known to have excelled in choral performances. Though there are families noted for producing lines of exceptional musicians, birth alone is not considered sufficient or even necessary to the cultivation of musical talent. Even among families or groups devoted to the production of musicians as a means of maintaining group solidarity and performative rituals, only the few able to devote the required time and effort usually emerge as exceptional musicians. There is no formal musical training. Children learn and improve their skills by watching and imitating the singing and dancing of peers and adults. Regular participation in communal music and dance provide every Venda child with an opportunity to begin to acquire the basic choral dance skills.[6]

MUSICAL INSTRUMENTS

The Musical Bow

The peoples of South Africa use a wide variety of instruments. The most dominant of these is the musical bow, a distinctive musical feature of southern Africa. The musical bow appears to have its origin in the hunting bow if the similarity in workmanship and style are studied closely. Typically a musical bow consists of one string fastened to the two ends of a curved stick. The pulling, plucking, scraping, tapping, or striking of the string causes it to vibrate, producing the sound that translates into music. Different forms of contact with the string result in different kinds of vibration that in turn produce different types of musical tones.

Musical bows are constructed to enable them to produce two or more fundamental tones. In the brace bow, the string is linked to the bow in one or more places along its length, causing the string to vibrate in different ways that produce more than one fundamental tone. Stopping a vibrating string with one or more fingers or with other objects can achieve similar effects. Striking the string at different points will also elicit different tones. The Zulu's *umakhweyana* bow, which is braced at the center, is believed to have been adopted from their Tsonga neighbors to the north. In the same group is the Tsonga's *dende,* a braced-gourd resonated bow, and their *tshizambi,* a friction bow that also appears to have been adapted from the Tsonga. Depending on its design, a bow usually resonates in different ways, usually through the use of a calabash or other hollow objects or the player's mouth to amplify the sounds and vary the tones. A mouth bow has part of the bow inserted in the player's mouth, enabling him or her to produce different overtones by varying mouth and throat movement. In the case of a gourd bow, a gourd is attached to or held against the bow. By moving or rubbing the gourd against his or her body, and thus varying the amount of air resonating in the gourd, the player is able to produce different overtones.

Bows are usually made from solid wood, bamboo, or cane, and strings can be fashioned from twisted horse or cow's tail hair, sinew, shredded leather, or (in recent years) brass or copper wire. Strikers are made of thin wood, straw, reed, or grass. The calabash resonators are made from small- or medium-size gourds and, in recent years, from cylindrical tins. They are usually insulated from the bow rod with pads made from fiber or, in recent times, from twisted cloths or cushions. Among the Xhosa the shaft of the bow is known as *injikwe*, the string as *usinga*, the calabash resonator as *uselwa*, and the beater as *umcinga*. The calabash resonator bow is one of the most widely used instruments in South Africa, though it appears not to have been used by the Khoisan until recently. It is known among the Tswana as *segwana* and among the Sotho as *sekgapa*, two terms meaning calabash that indicate their focus on the instrument's resonating quality. Known as *ligubu*, it is the classical instrument played by Swazi men. Women are the key players of calabash resonators among the Zulu, Sotho, Pondo, Thembu, and Xhosa. There are no specialist players, though it is not uncommon for men to make instruments for the women who are the principal players. The second category of calabash resonator bows features strings braced or tied back by a loop of sinew or fiber cords at the center of the string and directly secured to the calabash at the center of the bow. These instruments vary in size, with those played by men being larger than those played by women.[7]

Rattles

Dancing is a central feature of the social life of the peoples of South Africa. To facilitate the process of the dancing art a variety of rattles have been designed. One common type of rattle is made from springbok ears that have been dried, filled with ostrich eggshell pieces, and sewn together. When attached to the dancers' legs and in motion, the rattles produce a pleasant musical sound for the enjoyment of both the dancers and the audience. Another type of dancing-rattle is made from empty cocoons filled with small pebbles or hard seeds and strung together on two cords of fiber. An example of this type of rattle is the Herero *ozohahi*, which is tied around the ankle of the performer and used only during the *outjina* or women's dance. During this dance, men are not permitted to wear the rattle and can only serve as spectators. Other rattles are made from hollow shells of fruits, such as the Venda's *mutshakatha*, made from small, globular fruits. With their interior removed, the fruits' outer shells harden and are filled with stones. Threaded together four or five to each stick, they are secured to pads of cloth tied to the dancer's legs. Rattles are also shaped into little boxes made from palm leaf, like the Zulu's *amafohlwane,* or the Tsonga's leg-rattles called *fowa,* worn by the convalescent for protection from the perspiration emitted by those who have had sexual relations and considered inimical to quick recovery.

Drums

Drums also feature in the musical accoutrements of the Bantu people. One of the earliest appears to have been the Xhosa's *ingqongqo.* A dried hide is fastened to poles stuck into the ground and beaten, mainly by women to accompany the *abakweta* dances and songs of boy initiates during a circumcision school. The hide comes from a bull donated by a prominent man and father of one of the initiates that is killed specially for the *abakweta* dance. The flesh of the bull is not eaten, and the skin is destroyed at the end of the initiation ceremonies. Similar to this is the *ikawu,* a multicolored ox-hide shield. Sewn close to the top of the shield is a small piece of skin with a hole designed to receive and hold a knob-stick, as well as a small or large *assegai* (spear). The *ikawu* is beaten with a knob-stick and played at the *abakweta* dances as well as during the *isijadu,* which is a communal festival of boys and girls who gather together at night to sing and chant for their own enjoyment. The *ikawu* appears to have evolved from the use of shields—common weapons of war in the region—as ceremonial drums.

A number of resonator drums were also developed or adopted by the Bantu people. One of these is the Swazi's *intambula,* a name most probably derived from the Portuguese *tambor.* Made of untrimmed and dried goatskin and stretched temporarily over a clay beer pot (*imbiza*), it is used in the concluding rituals associated with the initiation of a diviner and, at times, in rituals of exorcism. Another is the Zulu's *ingungu* drum, similar in shape to the *intambula* but vastly different in make and function. It is made of goatskin that has been cleaned of its hairs, turned inside out, and permanently laced with strips of hide to a black clay pot. Playing it involves placing a smoothed piece of reed vertically on the drum and vibrating it with both hands. The drum responds to the reed's vibration with a roaring sound of surprising power. Among the Zulu the *ingungu* is played to announce the onset of a girl's first menstruation. The Zulu proverb, *ingungu yaleyo ntombi kayakali* ("the menstruation drum of that girl does not sound well"), is meant to ridicule a girl who has had too much experience with young men.

A more common type of resonator drum is the Venda's *murumbu,* made of an ox-hide pegged wet to a professionally carved piece of soft wood approximately 24 inches in length and 10 to 12 inches in the top diameter. Shaped like the carved *khamelo* or wooden jug, it has large handles and is held between the legs while in use. Whereas the milk jug is closed at the base, the drum remains open. The *murumbu* is played by women who elicit different sounds and rhythms by striking the center of the drum with flat palms or tapping its rim with their fingers. Similar drums exist among the Pedi, Tswana, Venda, and Sotho. The Venda's single-headed *ngoma* drum, made of a hemispheric resonator carved out of a single solid wood, is closely related to these groups. Used to accompany certain dances of the girls' *vhushu* menstruation ceremonies, it is also beaten to warn men not to trespass into the ritual space occupied by the women, who are usually naked. The drum is also used to summon initiates to the *domba,* the ceremony at which young people are taught everything pertaining to sex and marriage. Sex matters are called *dzingoma* or drums. In this category there is also the Tsonga's *muntshintshi* big drum, into which no one must ever look. Traditionally it was used to summon warriors to the capital at the approach of war and to announce major fatalities. It is also featured in various choral performances such as the *nkino* harvest celebratory dance. Another of the Tsonga's drums is the *mantshomane,* which is shaped like a tambourine, played by women, and associated with witchcraft. The *mantshomane* also generates hypnotic and frenzied performances used for exorcism. Finally, there is the Zulu's *isigudu* drum, which appears to have been modeled from the European military bass drum with all its accoutrements included.

Xylophone

Among the earliest and the most elaborate musical instruments of South Africa is the resonated xylophone. This instrument is generally referred to as *marimba,* and the most prominent is the Venda's *mbila.* There are at least three varieties: the 11- to 18-key pentatonic or hexatonic lamellophone or *mbila tshipai;* the 21-key xylophone or *mbila mutondo;* and the 27-key lamellophone or *mbila dzamadeza.* Each instrument is usually made up of between 11 and 27 slabs of wood stretched by means of two bark cords over a wooden frame. At the end of each wooden slab a cucumber-shaped calabash is securely lashed. These are usually graduated so as to produce different and distinctive sound pitches. The slab, when struck by a leather or rubber-covered, knobbed beating stick, resonates into the calabash in a clear and powerful tone, producing a harmonious and rhythmical sound comparable to that produced by European organs. In the *mbila* class is the *sansa* instrument, made of fire-tempered iron tongues fastened across a wooden slab by two bridges of thick iron wire. Placed inside a calabash resonator it is played with the thumbs.

Performing on the street with indigenous instruments. Note especially the traditional feather-studded leather garb attires, worn by the performers. (Jane Davis)

Horns and Flutes

The rich fauna of South Africa also made available ample resources for the making of different types of wind instruments made from animal horns. The most common and the most versatile are made from antelope horns, both large and small. In places where the game population has been exhausted from overhunting, ox horns are used instead. Among the Venda the *phalaphala* is used for different ceremonial purposes. A communal rather than an individual instrument, it was traditionally played by men and belonged to the kraal, where it was used in the past to summon warriors for battle. Similarly, at the appearance of Sirius, the morning star, the first man to sight it would climb to the top of a high hill and blow the *phalaphala*, to announce the beginning of the harvest season. Such a man would be rewarded by the ruler with the present of a cow. Horn trumpets are also made from the horns of other animals such as koodoo and gemsbok.

Among the first musical instruments of South Africa to be described by European travelers were the flutes of reeds played by a performing band, with each player responsible for playing a single note. As early as 1497, Vasco da Gama reported being welcomed by a band of Cape San performing on four or five flutes of reeds. In 1661, Peter van Meerhoff, a European visitor to the Cape, witnessed a Nama hollow-reed-flute ensemble made up of between one and two hundred flute players who danced in a circle, led by a master who directed the performance from the center with a long stick in his hand. Van Meerhoff compared the sound of the reed-flutes to that of several trumpets being played together.

From the San, the tradition of reed-flute ensembles appears to have spread to other groups. Among the Venda, a complete set of reed-flutes is known as *mutubu*, the flute pipes are made from bamboo plants grown in a secret grove in eastern Venda country; the reed band is led by the *molugwane*, who plays the lead flute or *pala* and is responsible for the care of the flutes. Each player plays a particular flute. When not in use all the reed flutes are kept together in a bag and stored in a special hut, which also houses all the key musical instruments belonging to the kraal. Along with the *ngoma* and the *murumbu* drums, the reed flute plays a central role in the *tshikona,* the national dance of the Venda people. The ensemble also features in other dances including puberty and rainmaking rituals.

EUROPEAN MUSICAL TRADITIONS

The Church and Early Musical Development

When Europeans arrived in South Africa, beginning with the Dutch settlers in 1652, they brought with them their European musical traditions. Continuing contact with Europe, the use of the Genevan Psalter and other church hymnals, and the periodic musical displays by military bands combined to keep the European and in particular Dutch musical traditions alive among the new settlers at the Cape. Over the next two hundred years, many migrated from the Cape into the interior, well beyond the reach of direct contact with Europe and visiting Europeans. As these white settler communities became more populous and more consolidated, variations in or deviations from European musical forms began to emerge.

Until the end of the nineteenth century, the dominant musical forms were those provided by the church, military bands, and other amateur groups. Professionalism did not become important in the South African musical scene until after 1900. Religious music associated with the Calvinist Dutch Reformed Church was prominent for these settlers. The church, for a number of reasons, discouraged the cultivation of secular music among the Dutch settlers. Instead the focus was on training the young to sing the psalms. The first organ was built in South Africa in 1737, and for a long time thereafter many churches could not afford to buy one. Choral singing thus remained the dominant musical form. Using free improvisatory style, settlers creatively adopted and adapted religious texts, popular songs, or folk songs to create new melodies that were collectively called *liederwysies*. The advent and political dominance of the British from the mid-nineteenth century onward began the process of Anglicization to which Dutch religious music was as vulnerable as other aspects of life in South Africa. The concerted efforts made by the Dutch Reformed Church to counter this religious aspect of the British onslaught yielded few results as less orthodox gospel hymns, such as those of Sankey and Moody, spread rapidly among the European population, infecting the colored community which hitherto had followed the Dutch way.

Secular Music

In spite of its best efforts, the church was unable to stop secular music at the Cape. To enliven their daily and social lives, the settlers established or encouraged the establishment of slave musical bands to entertain dinner guests and to put on dance shows. In the taverns, banquet halls, and parks of Cape Town—South Africa's Mother City—as well as on country estates, slave musicians had opportunities to display their talents to the delight of their masters, guests, and audiences. By 1676 a slave orchestra was organized by the Dutch governor of the Cape. Other performances were pioneered by military bands, who played at weddings and other special occasions. The first major performance of note was given in 1781 by a visiting French mercenary troop band. Their impressive performance of Beaumarchais's *Le barbier de Sevelle* (The Barber of Seville) contributed to the galvanization of musical interests that culminated in the building of the African Theater in 1801 at the Cape by its new British rulers. Musical plays and comic operas were staged at the new theater, as local and visiting groups competed to satisfy the musical needs and aesthetic tastes of their mainly European audience.

By the closing decades of the nineteenth century, local professional touring companies were jostling with visiting overseas opera companies to minister to the musical desires of the constantly increasing European population and their increasingly diverse communities in South Africa. The professionalization of musical art was further accelerated by the establishment in Cape Town, in 1893, of an opera house. The following year, the University of the Cape of Good Hope inaugurated the first major, professional musical qualifying examination system in the country. The Cape Town Municipal Orchestra staged its first concert in 1914 under the conductorship of Theophil Wendt. With its growing popularity and increased membership it changed its name to Cape Town Symphony Orchestra (SO) in 1968.

Since its establishment in 1936, and more than any other single institution, the South African Broadcasting Corporation (SABC) has contributed immensely to the promotion of modern musical arts in South Africa. Between 1966 and 1977, when Anton Hartman headed its musical department, the SABC granted many commissions to and organized several competitions for composers, young performers, dancers, and school choirs. Its well-equipped music studio was made available for budding artists to record their talents. Its regular offering and broadcast of music courses, illustrated lectures, indigenous African music, and the performances of the national troupe, the National, stimulated discussion and generated widespread interest in the musical arts. In 1963 the Performing Arts Council for each of the four South African provinces was established. Each province had its own ballet, drama, opera, music, and technical section and it was this provincial network that kept the performing arts traditions alive in South Africa during the dark days of apartheid when the nation was cut off from the outside world by economic sanctions and cultural boycotts. During these decades, South Africans were forced to turn increasingly inward to rely solely on the nation's resources and people to keep the performing arts alive and functioning.

Afrikaner and Cape Malay Folk Music

Beginning with the establishment of the Dutch settlement in 1652, a tradition of folksong developed and flourished among the Boer settlers, their Cape colored progeny, and the Cape Malay. The Cape Malay were among the earliest settlers in South Africa, with some of them arriving with the Dutch in 1652. They brought with them elements of their Asian homeland music, though much of these appeared to have disappeared or become assimilated into the Afrikaner folksong tradition, which the Cape Malay adopted, preserved, transformed, and transmitted from one generation to another. To them has been attributed the development, survival, and preservation of many Afrikaans folksongs. Among their contribution to the South African musical tradition are the *ghommaliedjie* and the *moppie* dancing songs. The *ghommaliedjie* is sung between verses of Dutch songs, while the *moppie* is a short humorous song of a derisive nature. The popular Cape Malay *chalifa* sword dance with its tambourine step dances, prayer chants, mock sword fight, fake cuts, and false blood letting combines religious themes of self-sacrifice and unflinching dedication with social themes of group solidarity and conflict resolution. The *pudjies* is an antiphonal responsorial religious singing between an imam and the members of his congregation. *Boeremusiek* is the basic traditional Afrikaner folk music. It developed as an amateur adaptation of nineteenth-century European dance music, with influences coming from the slave and freed slaves dance orchestra performances of the eighteenth and early nineteenth century. Its basic ensemble, *boeremusiek,* consists of concertina, guitar, violin, trumpets, drums, and other instruments.

DEVELOPMENT OF POPULAR MUSIC

The variegated music of South Africa is a direct by-product of the heterogeneous nature of South African society as well as the historical and cultural diversity of its peoples. Over the centuries, several influences combined to produce a cosmopolitan musical culture. Beginning with its first peoples, the San, primordial ideas of music, dance, and performative rituals changed hands between the aboriginal San and the Khoikhoi. These two in turn transmitted many of their choral dance musical traditions and melodic instruments to the initially nomadic Bantu-speaking peoples. The slaves from India, Malaysia, and Madagascar, who formed slave choral orchestras, westernized traditional musical instruments, and performed westernized versions of Afro-Islamic-Asiatic music, also contributed to the creation of a hybrid musical tradition at the Cape. Scholars are still working to unravel the nature and extent of Indonesian musical influence on southern Africa.

Another pivotal influence came from the Christian missionaries who brought European hymnology and choral forms to the South African scene in the early nineteenth century. The first Bantu group to confront the European invaders were the Xhosa. Under the double onslaught of European military incursion and land dispossession and the Zulu-instigated *mfecane* military implosion, many Xhosa fled as refugees to the Cape colony, where most of them soon adopted Christianity. One of these early converts, Ntsikana, soon emerged as a visionary Xhosa prophet. He advocated a synthesis of Christian and African religious beliefs and practices. He composed several Afro-Christian hymns, of which the most popular was his *Ulo Tixo Mkulu* (Thou, Great God). His congregation performed and thus orally popularized many of these songs. Christian congregational singing was a major hit among Africans already used to communal musical performances.

Makwaya

Other African leaders, like Tiyo Soga, the first ordained black minister in South Africa, responded positively by adapting many western melodies to indigenous African texts. Others, like John Knox Bokwe of Lovedale, a notable Xhosa composer and Presbyterian minister, were determined to preserve the poetic beauty and intelligibility of the Xhosa language from the destruction threatened by uninformed adoption of European hymnology. Bokwe espoused an ideology of cultural revitalization and Africanism, which led him to pioneer a new South African choral style. Known as *makwaya* (choir), the new style was a creative blending of African and European choral forms. Others who followed in Bokwe's steps are Benjamin Tyamzashe, A. A. Khumalo, Hamilton Maisa, Reuben Caluza, Joshua Mohapeloa, Michael Moerane, and Enoch Sontonga. In 1897, Sontonga, then a teacher in Johannesburg, composed *Nkosi sikelel'-iAfrika* (God Bless Africa) which, with the addition of more stanzas by S. E. K. Mqhayi and its popularization by Caluza's Ohlange Institute Choir, became the anthem of the African National Congress in 1925. Its stirring affirmation of African pride and greatness, and its melancholic yearning and rhythmic melody resulted in its adoption as national anthem by many central and southern African countries after 1960, following independence. *Makwaya* dominated the South African popular music scene during the late nineteenth and the early twentieth centuries. It featured prominently in choral activities associated with the churches, civil and political organizations, trade union meetings, wedding parties, and school and community concerts.

Concurrent with the *makwaya* movement, and certainly a part of it, were influences emanating from the United States. Many of the leading South African black elite were educated in or had visited the United States. They were familiar with and admired the ideas and works of Booker T. Washington, Marcus Garvey, and other black American leaders. Through the missionary work of the African Methodist Episcopal Church, based in Philadelphia, Negro spirituals and other Afro-Western musical forms were spreading to South Africa, where they began to shock the local Christians into realizing the tremendous potential of Afro-Christian hymnology. The decisive point came with the tours of the Orpheus "Bill" McAdoo's Virginia Jubilee Singers through Cape Town and other cities during the 1880s and 1890s. The stunning performances of this and other black American troupes created widespread sensation among blacks and whites in South Africa.

The Jubilee Singers gave the oppressed people of South Africa a powerful vision of black pride and African dignity that reverberated with far-reaching consequences in the years to come. For those privileged to experience their minstrelsy style performance, the Jubilee Singers offered music as an instrument of sociopolitical liberation. Within weeks of the Jubilee Singers' departure, several amateur music companies modeled after the McAdoo's troupe sprang up in the urban centers of South Africa. In Cape Town, the periodic Cape Coon Carnival, involving colored men marching through the streets in American minstrel costume, was instituted. In Kimberley, the Diamond

Minstrels and the Philharmonic Society began to render many previously neglected traditional African folk songs into *makwaya* forms.

In 1891 and 1893, the recently formed South African Native Choir embarked on tours of Britain and the United States as emissaries of the colonized, determined to use music to advocate for a new relationship of equality and mutual respect between the colonized and the colonizer, and an era of enlightened self-rule. The tours ended in a fiasco and did not appear to have achieved either of the intended purposes of raising funds or securing a promise of better treatment for blacks in colonial South Africa. But their mission was well articulated in their first interview with the English press when a member of the troupe presented the vision of the singers thus: "Let us be in Africa even as we are in England. Here we are treated as men and women. Yonder we are but as cattle. But in Africa, as in England, we are human. Can you not make your people at the Cape as kind and just as your people here?"[8]

Mining, Migrants, and Music

In 1867 diamonds were discovered in South Africa. Eight years later, gold deposits that turned out to be the largest concentration of the precious metal anywhere in the world were also discovered. By the end of the century, Kimberley and Johannesburg developed as two of the most populous urban centers in Africa, both of them teaming with capitalists, industrialists, miners, and others who had come to stake their claims and to make a fortune or at least a living in the newly opened and boisterous mines of South Africa. The progressive loss of land to European colonizers combined with other pressures (including the need to pay taxes) impelled Africans to migrate by the thousands to seek work in the mines. Leaving their families and traditional bases behind, migrants were forced to become creative in their new environment in order not to lose whatever sense of cultural or group identity they had brought along with them. Their traditional rituals and associated musical forms had to be adapted to the new challenges and possibilities of their new urban settings. In their innovations, they created new genres of dance, music, and oral poetry by blending traditional and modern forms, values, and experiences. Xhosa migrants, for instance, deployed their traditional praise songs to entertain themselves as well as to flatter and satirize their mining supervisors, while apostrophizing their chiefs, themselves, and their urban and working experiences and adventures.

Isicatamiya

The Zulu adapted their traditional courting songs to modern instruments to explore the uncertainties and fickleness of modern friendship and romantic love. As members of two worlds where values and realities are radically different, Zulu migrant workers turned to traditional music to make sense of or resolve the contradictions of their anomalous positions as translators or mediators between worlds. In the hands of these migrants, the Zulu hybrid choral dance music, *ingoma busuku* night music, was transformed into a step dance musical form known as *isicatamiya* (Zulu: a stalking approach) to denote the stealthy and synchronized movements of arms, torsos, and bodies characteristic of its performance. Among the leading exponents of *isicatamiya* was Solomon Linda and his Original Evening Birds. Linda's hit song, "Mbube 'Lion,'" remained for many years the signature tune for this form of Zulu choral music. Another is the Durban-based Ladysmith Black Mambazo (meaning the black axe of Ladysmith) whose performance tours made this genre of South African popular music famous worldwide. Their unaccompanied, meaning noninstrumental, performance, powerfully sonorous vocalization, and vigorous body movement in traditional Zulu military style have given the group considerable authenticity, making them one of the largest record-selling and audience pulling groups in South Africa and around the world.[9]

Sefela

One of the most creative transformations in traditional musical forms has taken place among the Basotho migrants, thousands of whom have labored in the backbreaking works of the Kimberley diamond and Johannesburg gold mines since the late nineteenth century. In the hands of these migrants, the recitative musical praise poetry of the Basotho people, known as *lithoko*, has been transformed into a new and rich genre of choral or sung oral poetry with the simple but revealing name *sefela* (a song) or *lifela* in plural. Disengaged from their traditional rural communities and grafted by necessity into the exploitative world of European industrial capitalism, the migrants were racially alienated from participation in this new world's social and political spaces. Through music they were able to create a sphere of personal autonomy and cultural creativity simultaneously critical and celebratory of their challenging material conditions. Out of the crucible of migrant labor they developed a choral form, which helped them in resolving the contradictions of their anomalous standing as mediators between worlds: traditional and modern, African and European, rural and urban, agrarian and industrial.

Through *lifela*, they redefined themselves as modern heroes prepared like the heroes of the old to sacrifice everything to achieve greatness (The Great Shaka Zulu never married, nor did members of his fearsome regiments permit themselves to be encumbered by marriage or sexual love, both of which they eschewed until their discharge from the army). Through *lifela*, migrant labor is conceptualized and presented as the modern form of initiation through which innocent and raw young men gain not only the money to obtain *bohali* (bridewealth) and cattle, but also achieve a sense of adulthood having experienced and survived the discipline, regimentation, hardship, and dangers of working in the hostile, alien, health-crushing environments of the mines. In the maw of the mines, owned and ruled mindlessly and ruthlessly by the modern cannibals (the mine owners) who have grown fat and rich by living off the workers' labor, sweat, and blood, *sefela* becomes the means of retrieving, reinterpreting, and reasserting the authenticity and validity of traditional social values. With evocative metaphor, piercing imagery, and imaginative originality, *sefela* becomes in the hands of the *likheleke* (the eloquent one) a veritable and powerful means of heroic self-definition: "self-realization, status achievement, and social commentary within a system of values they themselves have partly formulated."[10]

Marabi and Mbaqanda Styles

In spite of the government's best efforts to keep the new cities like Kimberley and Johannesburg white-only through customary and legal segregation, Africans could not be kept out. Unable to gain property, land, or residential rights in the cities, the majority of the Africans had to content themselves with living in adjacent shantytowns such as Soweto, Orlando, Alexander, and Sophia which in official parlance were described as locations, a word meant to emphasize their illegality and temporality.

Wherever they found themselves, however, Africans developed new forms of values and communities of cultures for themselves. Central to this new culture and the soul of it was a new form of urban choreography. Canteens, taverns, dance halls, street joints, and house parties were the places of music and dancing to which male and female migrants turned as a means of dealing with the social anomy and cultural disorientation of life in these new and westernizing urban centers. Musical performances became the means for personal self-discovery, collective self-definition, and for fashioning new patterns of interpersonal relationships and group identities in the heterogeneous but naturally alienating worlds of the new metropolis. The most prominent site for the new cultural efflorescence was the *shebeen*. This was usually an unlicensed bar located in a private residence where patrons gathered to buy and drink illegally brewed beer and listen to or perform neotraditional dance music. Over the decades the *shebeen* remained the heart throb of South Africa's black city music and popular culture, attracting different kinds of patrons, permitting the constellation of different categories of class, ethnic, occupational and other group formations, as they caroused together to the sounds of guitar, harps, violins, banjos, ox-hide or rubber tin drums, and other neotraditional instruments.

To satisfy the entertainment needs of a diverse clientele, performers creatively blended elements from Afrikaner folk music, American ragtime and jazz, and indigenous vocalization and rhythm to fashion a hybrid music, dance form, and social occasion, known as *marabi*. Noted for its incorporative flexibility, lively danceability, and inclusive purpose, *marabi* is a distinctive South African jazz variant that is simultaneously and harmoniously indigenous, urbanized, African, and modern. The *kwela* penny whistle and guitar musical forms popularized during the 1950s by the likes of Spokes Mashiyane and Lemmy "Special" Mabaso are variants of this choral form. Another variant is *famo,* a wild and risqué form of *marabi,* developed among Basotho migrants in Johannesburg, who in turn popularized it in the towns and villages of the Orange Free State and Lesotho. Closely related to *marabi,* but denuded of its American melodic elements and suffused with more elements of indigenous musical idiom and rhythmic motif is *mbaqanda* (a Zulu term for a stiff homemade cornbread), a fully developed South African jazz form. Big jazz dance bands like the Jazz Maniacs and vocal quartets like the Manhattan Brothers have been important international proponents of this form.[11]

During the 1980s and 1990s the *mbaqanda* style underwent major musical reformulations that grounded it even more fully in indigenous choreography in the hands of more traditionalized groups such as Mahlathini and his Mahottella Queens, who further internationalized this distinctively South African musical form. Born in the Alexandra township, near Johannesburg, in 1937, Mahlathini began his musical career with the Alexandra Black Manbaza, a group that had a major influence on Joseph Tshabalala, who would later form the Ladysmith Black Mambazo. Though unknown to white record-buyers, Mahlathini was a hit among blacks in the townships during the sixties and the seventies. His powerful and eloquent vocal style gave him the title Lion of Soweto. His invitation and appearance (along with his Queens) in 1989 at the Waza Afrika Festival in New York and at the Nelson Mandela Concert at Wembley in London brought world fame to him, his *mbaqanga* township pop, and his Queens (Nobesutho Mbabu, Hilda Tlaubatla, and Mildred Mangula). Though Mahlathini died in 1999, the Queens continue their regular world tours and their vibrating, storming, relentlessly aggressive bottom-shaking, breast-flaunting, foot-stomping, torso-gyrating performance style.

As the struggle against apartheid intensified from the 1960s onward, an ideology of cultural nationalism impelled many musicians to become increasingly and positively disposed toward more indigenized musical forms and practices as a strategy of sociopolitical liberation and African authenticity. Groups like Philip Thabane's Malombo Jazz adopted many indigenous musical instruments and choral styles. Another was the Juluka band of Anglo-Jewish Jonathan Clegg and Zulu Sipho Mchunu, whose blend of Zulu, American, and other choral forms attempted to bridge the cultural and racial chasms. Others like the Soweto String Quartet, created an extraordinary hybrid of musical traditions, that placed their first album, Zebra Crossing, on platinum in 1996. That same year, the theatrical reggae star, Lucky Dube, with his Bob Marley style, received the World Music Award for Best Selling African recording artist.

Another artist of note is Dollar Brand. Born in 1934 of Basuto/San parents, he played with many groups before forming his Jazz Epistles in 1960. After a tour of Europe, during the course of which he met and was inspired by the African-American jazz musician Duke Ellington, the Dollar Brand Trio moved to America in 1965 where over the subsequent decades he gained widespread recognition and won several awards. His 1976 song, *Mannenberg Is Where It's At,* a jazz classic, with its profoundly evocative lyric, is widely regarded in many circles as the finest example of South African musical composition.[12] Another musician forced to flee South Africa and seek fame, freedom, and recognition abroad was Hugh Masekela, whose early ambition was to become a soccer star rather than a musical player. However, his trumpet-playing musical talent eventually won out, especially after he received the gift of a trumpet from the famous African American jazz player, Louis Armstrong. In 1959, he left South Africa to study music in Britain and the United States. His 1968 composition and recording, *Grazing in the Grass,* reached number one on the American charts where it stayed among the top 20 for nine weeks selling four million copies. After 32 years in exile, and with scores of songs, dozens of albums, and worldwide fame in the saddle, Masekela, the godfather of South African jazz, returned to a rousing welcome in South Africa in 1991.

Margaret Singana and the Ipi Tombi Musical

The first black South African musician to break through the color line and achieve international fame comparable to that of musicians in exile was Margaret Singana. Born in the Cape Province, she came to Johannesburg to work as a domestic servant. Her employers, discovering the musical talent of their little maid from Queenstown, asked her to perform for their guests at parties while secretly recording her songs and waxing them into records without her knowledge or consent. Though very few noticed these recording, Margaret eventually came into the public limelight when she landed a chorus part in Alan Paton's *Sponono* musical, which played in New York in 1964, and a lead part in the highly controversial but sensational *Ipi Tombi* musical, which opened in South Africa in 1974. Margaret's magnificent rendering of three of the singles, namely *Ipi Tombi, The Warrior,* and the showstopper song, *Mama Thembu's Wedding,* adapted from a traditional Sotho wedding song called "Kiloyena," took the white audience by storm, literally taking over the white record market.

Though a huge success with white audiences, South African blacks and other critics remain justifiably critical of *Ipi Tombi*. They dismissed the musical as another efficient government propaganda tool to promote tribalism, justify the homeland policy, and perpetuate the lie of black people being happy-go-lucky, childlike, skin-and-feather-clad-clowns who sing naturally and rhythmically and are satisfied with their lot. Nevertheless the show went on a world tour, where an estimated six million people, from Australia to France, Israel to the United States, and from Zimbabwe to Nigeria, saw it. As the world and, most especially, the white markets lapped up her music, Singana became a household name, and the first crossover (selling to both blacks and whites) singer-record seller in South Africa. In 1974 she was signed to Satbel and Jo'burg Records under the management of Patric van Blerk, the Potchesfstroom-born producer, songwriter, record-label owner, and visionary, who further stimulated and stirred her budding talent to worldwide fame. Singana's stunning performances in London caused the British trade publication, *Music Week,* to vote her Star of the Year successively in1976 and 1977. In the United States, she received a Grammy Award nomination in 1977 in the best new female vocalist category. In 1978, her highly sophisticated and evocative single, *I Never Loved a Man,* sold over 100,000 copies and secured for her a platinum disc. Despite the fact that Radio 5 declared the song the top record of 1977 and Margaret the top South African artist of the year, and that the SABC PRO described Singana as "the voice of the century," she was denied the Sarie Award for the top female artist by the SABC, which everyone had expected her to win hands down. Very few in the music industry had any doubt that the politics of apartheid had everything to do with this denial.[13]

Miriam Makeba, Brenda Fassie, and Kwaito Style

Among the most recent genres to emerge on the South African scene is the distinctively African urban popular dance balladry beat known as bubblegum or Soweto soul. The leading exponents of this genre are Miriam Makeba, Sipho Mabuse, Yvonne Chaka Chaka, the Boomshaka quartets, Rebecca Malope, and Brenda Fassie. Born in Nelspruit, in 1934, Miriam Makeba worked as a domestic servant while singing with various groups such as the Manhattan Brothers and the Skylarks until her participation in the musical *King Kong* took her to London in 1959 and revealed her choral talents to the world. Thereafter and for nearly four decades, Makeba dominated the scene as the most famous exiled South African musician, waxing dozens of records and performing before sold out audiences in Europe and the Americas. Her strong and dynamic performances, her eclectic taste, her incisive antiapartheid protest songs and her creative blending of a wide range of musical styles— from Indonesian lullaby to West Indian and Israeli folk music as well as Xhosa and Zulu songs—established for this songstress or songbird a solid reputation as the mother of modern South African music and a favorite in the night club, television, and concert hall circuits in Europe and in the United States.[14]

In more recent years, the crown for the most sensational South African pop star belongs to Brenda Fassie, the bad girl of South African pop. Born in 1964, her mother—who was expecting a boy and thus had no girl's name in store— named her after the U.S. country singer, Brenda Lee. Brenda Fassie has lived up to her name. By the age of five she was already earning money singing for tourists. Her teenage single, *Weekend Special,* made it to the charts and received international airplay. Fassie's wildly outrageous and high-pitched delivery style has given her the title of Queen of Kwaito. A musical and a dance form, *kwaito* is a cultural movement with its own fashion and lifestyle. A pulsating pop style developed in the townships during the early 1990s, *kwaito* (literally: these guys are hot) is a creative blending of American hip-hop, British garage, Jamaican reggae, and traditional African percussion and *toyi-toyi* (protest) chants. It is South Africa's latest and best selling sensation. *kwaito's* popularity is a direct function of the genre's ability to effectively contextualize its lyrics within South Africa's conditions and thus turn itself into a vocal and vibrating instrument of social and political commentary. As the true exemplar of the new genre, Fassie's lyrics innovatively fuse traditional and modern themes while confronting and addressing some of the most complex sociocultural issues that Africans are grappling with in the new and changing South Africa. Dubbed, albeit admiringly, by *Time* Magazine as "the bad girl of South African pop" and the "Madonna of the township, Fassie remains defiant, outspoken, resolute, and determined. With tongue-in-cheek, Fassie, who turned 36 in 2001, said recently during a visit to America: "I'm getting old: I realize how beautiful it is to be African.... Musically, sexually, I'm the best."[15]

Singing in a Troubled Society: The Pains and Gains of Music and Musicians in South Africa

The catalogue of South African music and musicians is an endless one. Over the last one hundred years the country has produced a wide range of musical talents who, through a creative blending of indigenous and foreign choral styles, developed several new and dynamic musical forms. Of all the different forms of media communication, music may be the most influential. More than any other media, it has tremendous potential to reach across the boundaries of race, class, gender, literacy, and political convictions. As Hugh Masekela said: "Music is the key. We sing about everything in South Africa, there's nothing we don't sing about. And when we sing, the boere [Afrikaner masters] listen. It's the only time they listen."[16] In the fractured and troubled society of apartheid South Africa, music has been in the forefront of the struggle for freedom, equality, and human dignity.

However, for the musicians and their fans it has not been an easy ride. Continuously harassed by the apartheid state security operatives, denied access to a proper audience, restricted in territorial reach by the Group Area Acts, compelled to sing only songs considered acceptable, discriminated against and denied airplay time by the state-controlled radio and television services, and buffeted by the duplicity and scavenging exploitation of scoundrel producers, many of these musicians remained unflappable and undaunted.[17]

Rather than submit to the apartheid state, many of these groups chose instead to die by disbanding. Some of these, who remained outspoken about apartheid, could see no hope or future for themselves in the pariah state that was then South Africa. Feeling the relentless pressures of the apartheid state crushing their talents and threatening their very lives, many followed the path of exile, joining the ever-swelling ranks of the South African musical talents and bands on the run. As sons and daughters of Africa, these exiles remained connected through their music and in their souls with their South African roots, the source of their inspiration and the subject of their harmonious and beautiful longings. Through music they spoke of freedom. They celebrated mother Africa. They protested against the perversion of justice, the loss of their land, and the oppression of their people. In eloquently powerful lyrics they looked forward with unflagging hope to the day when South Africa shall be free. This passionate longing and belief in the inevitable triumph of good over evil, of freedom over slavery remained a powerful force linking the hounded musicians at home with those on the run abroad, looking forward to the day when the moonless and starless nights would give way to the dawn in which all would join hands together to finally sing the song and celebrate the advent of freedom.

Music in the New South Africa

After many years of relentless and costly struggle the dark and starless nights are over. In February 1990, Mandela walked out of Victor Verster

Prison, soon to become South Africa's first democratically elected president in 1994. A new South Africa was born. With freedom now in the saddle, it is time to build and weave a new society characterized by justice, equality, and fraternity. The exiles are still streaming home. Some of them, like Makeba and Masekela, returned as triumphant freedom fighters to a heroine's or hero's welcome. South Africa's music and musicians are presently experiencing a new lease on life, a resurgent vibrancy as they bring their comforting, healing, and unifying powers to bear upon the numerous and daunting challenges confronting the new society. Just as they did in the dark days of apartheid, either from within the confines of South Africa or in exile, musicians and their music prepared the ground for and ultimately worked to bring about the demise of apartheid and the creation of a nonracial and democratic society. As South Africa enters a new era of freedom, openness, justice, and democracy, let us join them in celebrating the miracle of transformation from a twentieth-century pariah to one of the most respected, dynamic, and vibrant states of the twenty-first century as we visit and dance to say to them: Let the music play on.

Theater and Cinema

There are two theatrical traditions in South Africa. The most studied of these is the European tradition, which began in the mid-seventeenth century with performances by mercenary troops passing through or stationed at the Cape. The building in 1801 of the African Theater in Cape Town provided a formal venue for the staging of plays, musicals, dances, and other experimental performances of European origin by various amateur theater groups and companies that began to be established in different parts of the colony, particularly after the establishment of the first indigenous English company by Sefton Parry in 1853. From 1900 onward, Afrikaans amateur theater was rejuvenated by the performances of plays by Melt Brink, J. H. de Waal, and Longenhoven, whose 1913 presentation of his *Die Hoop van Suid-Afrika* inaugurated a new era in Afrikaans theater art. Many theaters located in virtually all the major urban centers of South Africa are used for opera, ballet, drama, dances, and film production, as well as musical performances.

The 1,000-seat 1820 Monument Theater in Grahamstown, which opened in 1974, is noted for its annual winter national festival of the arts that has become South Africa's most celebrated cultural event. It attracts amateur and professional artists of every race, from within and outside South Africa, to perform and compete in various categories from music, drama, and dances, to poetry, fine arts, and literature. The Klein Karoo Nasionale Kunstefees held every March at Oudtshoorn, in the Western Cape, provides opportunities for

South Africa, 1993: Official Yearbook, 251–60; J. Fletcher, *Story of Theatre in South Africa: A Guide to Its History from 1780–1930* (Cape Town: Vlaeberg, 1994); T. Hauptfeisch, *Theatre and Society in South Africa: Some Reflections in a Fractured Mirror* (Pretoria: Van Schaik, 1997); R. M. Kavanagh, *Theatre and Cultural Struggle in South Africa* (London: ZED Books, 1985); P. Larlham, *Black Theatre, Dance, and Ritual in South Africa* (Ann Arbor, Mich.: UMI Research Press, 1985).

performances in drama, cabaret, and music, presented mainly, though not exclusively, in Afrikaans. Art Alive, held annually in September in Johannesburg, is an international festival for the performing arts in dance, music, drama, and performance poetry.

Over the years, three forms of black theater developed. The first, which is almost wholly commercial in inspiration, consists of plays written by whites and performed by blacks. A notable example of these is *Ipi Tombi,* which received rave reviews and successful runs within and outside South Africa, but which was widely criticized as lacking in African cultural authenticity. The second category consists of black plays cast in European moulds, often written by whites, performed by blacks or mixed casts, but with considerable empathy for black themes and sociocultural sensibilities. The plays of Athol Fugard constitute the most notable examples of this form. The third type consists of plays and performances inspired by black themes, written, directed, and performed almost entirely by black actors. This vigorous and dynamic form, with its occasional crudity and frequent disregard for orthodox literary conventions, is considered to be the truly African theater.

The final years of apartheid and after have seen the emergence of a new hybrid tradition that attempts to fuse elements of African and European traditional forms by placing emphasis on ritual and symbolic forms, maintaining a strong musical base, integrating a strong narrative element and dancing culture, and requiring spectators' active engagement with its performative expressions. The political repression and sociocultural alienation of the apartheid years banned racially mixed productions and resulted in the isolation of South Africa, but this insularity often led to considerable indigenous creativity and inventiveness. As the population converged on the cities, new people-oriented theaters and theater groups emerged to channel township musicals into veritable means of entertainment and artistic experimentations to cater to the needs of urban communities and of workers. The tense social and political climate, which combined with the ideas of the nationalist groups like the Black Consciousness Movement to transpose daily events and social concerns into the theatrical stage, resulted in the emergence of a protest theater. The new or alternative theater was entertaining, populist, urban, multilingual, multicultural, and political. Its versatile and creative synthesis of African and European forms and its diversity of styles and forms—ranging from classical to rock music, from cabaret and dance-drama to children's theater and satire, from social protest to political commentary—marked the first, furtive attempts to fashion an authentic South African theatrical and cultural identity.

Until the late 1980s, the South African film industry experienced only spasmodic growth. This was due first to its dependency on European and

American film products; second, its failure to reflect accurately the experiences of every group and culture within the country; and, third, its continuous control and manipulations through subsidies by the apartheid state government. The emergence of an alternative film industry from the mid-1980s and the end of apartheid from the early 1990s inaugurated a new era of film production and film culture in the country. Darryl Roodt's *A Place of Weeping* was the first film sharply criticizing apartheid to be permitted by the censorship committee of the Directorate of Publications to be shown on the South African film circuit. With its population and literary culture, South Africa is a major market for film producers and distributors. Hundreds of foreign films are screened every year in the country's more than 500 theaters. The largest film distributor in the country is Ster-Kinekor with its circuit of 157 four-wall cinemas and 49 drive-ins. Next in importance is the New Metro Theater with 52 conventional theaters. The freedom that came with the end of apartheid and the postapartheid state requirement that local television broadcasts should have a large local content have resulted in a boom in the local film industry. The local film industry's contribution to the economy in 2000 was close to 1.4 billion Rands.[18]

NOTES

1. On Khoisan musical traditions, and the major sources for the discussion in this section, see Percical R. Kirby, *The Musical Instruments of the Native Races of South Africa* (Johannesburg: Witwatersrand University Press, 1965), 1–53, 71–94, 135–92; John E. Kaemmer, "Southern Africa: An Introduction," *The Garland Encyclopedia of World Music, Volume 1: Africa,* ed. Ruth M. Stone (New York and London: Garland Publishing, Inc., 1998), 700–705; David K. Rycroft, "Khoikhoi Music," *The New Grove Dictionary of Music and Musicians,* edited by Stanley Sadie (London: Macmillan, 2001), vol. 13, 571–74.

2. Hugh Tracey, *Ngoma: An Introduction to Music for Southern Africa* (New York: Longman, 1948), 46.

3. David Dargie, "Umngqokolo: Xhosa Overtone Singing and the Song Nondel'ekhaya," *African Music,* 7 (1) 1991, 32–47.

4. Y. Huskisson, "A Note on the Music of the Sotho," *South African Music Encyclopedia,* ii, edited by J.P. Malan (Cape Town: Oxford University Press, 1982), 375–76 and G.F. Barz, "South Africa, Indigenous Music: Sotho Music," *The New Grove Dictionary of Music and Musicians,* vol. 24, 77–90. See also Robin Wells, *An Introduction to the Music of the Basotho* (Morija, Lesotho: Morija Archives, 1994).

5. For these dramatic descriptions with references to the vigor and virtuosity of the Venda performer, see John Blacking and Jaco Kruger, "South Africa, Indigenous Music: Venda Music," in *The New Grove Dictionary of Music and Musicians,* vol. 24, 78–85. For further exploration of Venda music, see J. Blacking, "Songs, Dances, Mimes and Symbolism of Venda Girls' Initiation Schools," *African Studies,* xxviii,

1969, 1–35, 69–118 and J. Kruger, "Singing Psalms with Owls: A Venda 20th-century Musical History, Part 1: Tshigombela," *Journal of African Music,* vii, 4, 1999, 122–46.

6. For a fuller examination of the connections between music and society among the indigenous peoples of South Africa, and the major source for this section, see the various contributions by David K. Rycroft, Angela Impey, Gregory F. Barz, John Blacking, Jaco Kruger, and C.T.D. Marivate, "South Africa: Indigenous Music," in *The New Grove Dictionary of Music and Musicians,* vol. 24, 72–93. See also J. Blacking, "The Role of Music in the Culture of the Venda," in M. Kolinski, ed., *Studies in Ethnomusicology* (New York: Folkways Records and Service Corp., 1965), 20–53; S. Moitse, *The Ethnomusicology of the Basotho* (Morija, Lesotho: Morija Archives, 1994); and Joseph Rosemary, "Zulu Women's Music," *African Music,* 6, 3, 1983, 53–89.

7. Kirby, *Musical Instruments,* 177–245.

8. Viet Erlmann, "Africa Civilized, Africa Uncivilized: Local Culture, World System, and South African Music," *Journal of Southern African Studies,* 20, 7, 1994, 165–79.

9. On *isicatamiya,* see David Coplan, *In Township Tonight: South African Black City Music and Theatre* (London and New York: Longman, 1985), 65–73.

10. Coplan, *In Township Tonight,* 19. For a fuller exploration of *sefela,* see Coplan's fascinating and pulsating study of Basotho migrant songs: *In the Time of the Cannibals: The Word Music of South Africa's Basotho Migrants* (Chicago and London: The University of Chicago Press, 1994). On Zulu migrant workers' songs, see Erlmann, "'Singing Brings Joy to the Distressed': The Early Social History of Zulu Migrant Workers' Choral Music," in Erlmann, *African Stars,* 156–74.

11. On Mbaqanda and its multiple expressions, see Coplan, *In Township Tonight,* 161–82 and "Popular Music in South Africa," 767–80.

12. Garth Chilvers and Tom Jasiukowicz, *History of Contemporary Music of South Africa* (Johannesburg: Toga Publication Company, 1994), 150.

13. See Muff Anderson, *Music in the Mix* (Johannesburg: Ravan Press, 1981), 98–101, 163–65; Chilver and Jasiukowicz, *History,* 118.

14. On Miriam Makeba see M. Makeba with J. Hall, *Makeba: My Story* (New York: New American Library, 1987) and "Miriam Makeba: The Power and the Passion," *The Reggae and African Beat,* vii, 2, 1988, 16–20. On Makeba's sensational debut on the American musical stage, see: "With a Touch of Zulu," *Newsweek,* January 25, 1960; "Good to My Ear," *TIME,* February 1, 1960; and "Xhosa Songstress," *New York Times Magazine,* February 28, 1960.

15. See "The Madonna of the Townships: Brenda Fassie, the Bad Girl of South African Pop, Finally Gets Her Shot at Musical (and Media) Stardom in America," *TIME,* Special Issue "Music Goes Global," Fall 2001, 64–66.

16. Anderson, *Music in the Mix,* 121.

17. For the story of the struggle, the travails, the triumphs of all these and other South African musicians and musical groups, see Muff Anderson, *Music in the Mix,* 108–79; and Chilver and Jasiukowicz, *History.*

18. On the film and theater industries in South Africa, and the major sources for the discussion in this section, see *South Africa, 1989–90: Official Yearbook,* 587–98;

Glossary

abakhwetha (Xhosa). initiates

abathakathi (Zulu/Xhosa). witchcraft or sorcery

agbada (Yoruba, West Africa). flowing large gown

amahewu. a nonintoxicating beverage, made from porridge fermented with wheat flour

Arya Samaj. a Neo-Hinduist movement started in Bombay in 1875, which came to define the nature and practice of Hinduism in South Africa

atjar. many types of pickles

baale (Kgaga). girls' initiation school held at the capital of the chiefdom

Bada (Hindi: The Big One). Partriarchal head of the Indian joint-family

Bantu (people). a term used by the apartheid government to designate all black South Africans; Africans consider the term derogatory, most especially when used in reference to the people rather than to their languages

bavugu. a stamping tube-like musical instrument played mainly by women

bawomcane (Xhosa: little father). term used to address one's father's younger brother

bawomkhulu (Xhosa: big father). term used to call one's father's elder brother

biesies (Khoisan). the thinner and harder reeds used for making mats

biltong. sun-dried salted strips of boneless meat

bjalwa (Pedi).   intoxicating fermented beverages

blatchangs.   a sauce made from a mixture of dry and pounded anchovies, vegetables and sugar

bobotie.   richly spiced curried minced meat pie

bodika.   initiation school

boeremusiek.   Afrikaner traditional dance music

boerewors.   deliciously spiced mixed minced meat farmer's sausage

bogadi (Sotho).   bridewealth

bogwera (North Sotho and Tswana: friendship).   supplementary initiation schools organized a year or two after the *bodika*

boyale (Tswana).   girls' puberty initiation school

bredie (Afrikaans).   a carefully flavored and thickened stew of meat and vegetables

Broederbond (Afrikaans: brother and bond).   an Afrikaner secret society

chalifa (Cape Malay).   sword dance

dadewethu (Xhosa).   sisters

daga (daka).   a mixture of mud and cow dung, used as a plastering substance for walls

dansiki (Hausa, West Africa).   long gown, usually worn by men

dende (Tsonga).   a braced-gourd resonated bow

dertigers.   Afrikaner poets of the 1930s

dimo (Sotho).   half-human, half-beast, and often deformed monsters of folk tales

diphotha (Sotho).   synchronized step-dance song performed by men

domba (Venda).   a huge initiation drum; a combined initiation school for both girls and boys

emabeba (Swazi).   back skin apron tied on the right hip, worn alone or with an *emajobo* or on top of a loin cloth

emahiya (Swazi).   loin cloths or aprons, usually wrapped around the waist

emajobo (Swazi).   front skin apron tied on the right hip, worn alone or on top of a loin wrapper

emasi.   sour milk

gaanderij.   the dining room of early Cape Dutch houses which usually opens to the courtyard

//gagwasi.   spirit of the dead or ancestral spirits

ghommaliedjie (Afrikaans). dancing song

gora (Khoisan). stringed musical bow instrument, known as *lesiba* among the Tswana and the Sotho

ibeshu (Zulu). a kilt of animal tails, or a coarsely made and untanned calf-skin buttock covering, cut into many twisted strips, worn by a boy as he approaches the age of puberty

ibhuma. the rough beehive-shaped circumcision hut (also known as *isuthu*)

igwele. a nonintoxicating beverage, made from crushed mealies or corn, mixed with boiled water, and fermented with malted grain

ikawu (Xhosa). a multicolored ox-hide shield

ikhankatha (Xhosa). instructor at initiation rites

imbongi (Zulu). court praise-poet

incwala. Swazi annual national royal ceremony

inembe (Swazi). a very thin porridge infants' food, made from mealie grain transformed into a very fine powder

ingcibi. circumciser

ingelegte vis. dried fish meals, such as the *gesmoorde snoek,* and the *moortjies* or *bokkems*

ingoma busuku (Zulu: night music). hybrid choral dance music

ingubo (Zulu). a large leather gab, or profusely beaded cloth worn by a married woman on special and festive occasions

ingungu (Zulu). resonator drum

ingwanqa (Swazi). a very thick porridge

ingwenya. literally, crocodile, but used to describe large monoxylous doors carved exclusively for chiefs among the Venda

inkazana (Xhosa). a free woman

intambula (Swazi). resonator drums made of untrimmed and dried goatskin and stretched temporarily over a clay beer-pot (*imbiza*)

intlonipho (Xhosa). respect, most especially for elders

intonjane (Xhosa). initiation schools for girls

isangoma (Zulu). diviner or *ngaka* among the Sotho-Tswana

isibhebe. a nonintoxicating beverage

isicatamiya (Zulu: a stalking approach). a step dance musical form

isicelankobe (Zulu). hair decorated with beads and hanging over the forehead, usually of girls

isicholo (Zulu).   the tall, ochred topknot hair-dress distinctive of a married woman

isidiya or inGcayi (Zulu).   a brayed buckskin cloak

isidwaba or isiKhakha (Zulu).   a form of overlapping short leather skirt

isigege (Zulu).   a prepuce beaded shield, attached to a stringed girdle and worn by a girl approaching the age of puberty to cover the genital area

isiguqa (Zulu).   a small tuft of hair left in front after the entire head has been shaved

isihiuthu (Zulu).   hair grown into a thick mass

isiyendane (Zulu).   hair greased and dressed into long strings

izibongo.   Zulu royal praise poetry

izintambo (Zulu).   grass ropes used for building huts

izintungo (Zulu).   framework of beehive huts made of tree or plant saplings and into which grass is woven or attached by reeds or ropes

izinwele-ezalukiwe (Zulu).   hair twisted into long pigtails of three strings each

/Kaggen or cagn (San).   creator god and trickster

kambulumbumba (San).   group bow musical stringed instrument

karoo (Khoikhoi).   the arid plateau or semidesert regions

kente (Asante, West Africa).   colorfully patterned strip-woven dresses

kgotla (Sotho).   the meeting of the traditional community decision-making body

kha:s (Khoisan).   long braced musical bow stringed instrument played by women

koesister (Afrikaans).   a spiced and plaited dough cake

koningpap.   porridge prepared without salt from the finest of white mealie powder that had been soaked in water, pounded, and sifted many times

kraal (Afrikaans).   a cattle enclosure; a cluster of houses occupied by one family or lineage; an African settlement or village

kuma.   a raft zither musical instrument

kutum or kudumor (Hindi).   the patrilineal extended family unit

kwaito **(literally: these guys are hot).**   a hybrid popular music and dance form

lialolo/metjekong (Sotho).   call-and-response dance-songs performed by girls

lidishela (Swazi). a thin porridge made from either maize or millet

liederwysies (Afrikaans). folk songs resulting from popular adaptations of religious texts

lifala or libopi (Tswana and Southern Sotho groups). beehive-shaped corbelled stone huts, built from boulders

ligubu (Swazi). calabash resonator, played by men

lijingi lemanti (Swazi). a thin porridge made from millet

lipakelo. a milking cow presented by a man to his daughter as part of her marriage gift

lithoko. the recitative musical praise poetry of the Basotho people

lobola (Zulu). bridewealth

luqhotfo (Swazi). a girdle, a string of beads or grass won around the waist, by infants and toddlers, mainly for ornamental purposes

mabepha (Venda). musical expeditions or dance-teams

makwaya (Xhosa). choir

malume (male mother). a term of endearment used to describe one's mother's brother

mantshomane (Tsonga). tambourine-shaped drums, played by women, and associated with witchcraft

marabi. a hybrid music, dance form, and social occasion; a distinctive South African jazz variant

marimba. resonated xylophone like the Venda's *mbila*

matano (Venda). carved wooden figures used during women initiation rituals

matjiesgoed. thick and soft reeds used for making mats, found mainly in riverbeds and swamps

mbaqanda (Zulu: stiff homemade cornbread). a fully developed and indigenized South African jazz form

mbila (Venda). resonated xylophone

mealie. porridge made from maize or millet

metogo (pedi). nonintoxicating fermented beverages

mfecane (Nguni: crushing). the sociopolitical upheaval and transformation associated with Shaka Zulu (d. 1828)

mkhuluwa (Xhosa: *khulu or* big). elder brother

mohohelo/mokorotlo (Sotho). vocal performances by men in L-shaped regimental formation

mokgibo (Sotho).   knee dance-songs by women

moppie (Afrikaans).   dancing song

motaba (Venda).   a complete set of reed-flute pipes made from bamboo plants

murumbu (Venda).   ox-hide resonator drum played by women

mzala (Nguni) or motswala (Sotho).   terms meaning cross-cousin, used to describe one's mother's brother's children

ngoma.   drum

num (San).   medicine, healing potency, energy, power, special skill

phalaphala (Venda).   horn flute used for different communal ceremonial purposes

potjiekos.   venison, cubed lamb ribs, cooked in a three-legged *potjie* or a *drievoetpot* suspended over an open wood fire

qubulo.   dress used during the slow and stately *qubulo* dance that usually accompanies wedding ceremonies and the annual national festival of the first fruits

sambal.   a grated and spiced cold fruits and vegetable dish

sangoma.   diviners

sanskara (Hindi).   life cycle rituals, marking the series of transitions from conception to birth, to puberty and to death

sebopi (Sotho).   corbelled huts built of mud instead of stones

sefela (Sotho: a song).   a genre of choral or sung oral poetry; *lifela* in plural

sestigers.   Afrikaner literary writers of the 1960s

shebeen.   an establishment where illicit home-brewed liquor is sold, usually run by black women (shebeen queen), a vibrant joint for the efflorescence of popular culture among African urban workers and dwellers

sidudu (Swazi).   pumpkin mealie

sinokoti.   a male skin cloak made of antelope or cattle skins

siphuku.   a male cloak made from goat hide

sishwala (Swazi).   any thick porridge

slaai.   a sliced or shredded vegetable dish

sosati.   richly spiced meat on a skewer

tameletje.   a caramelized sugar and vegetable sweet

thangu (Venda).   divining tablet

thomba.   rite of seclusion during boy's initiation ceremony

Tshikona.   the national dance of the Venda people

tshoa (Khoisan).   rite performed to mark the end of food avoidance

ukuthwala (Xhosa).   bride kidnapping by the groom, with the help of his friends

umcuku (Zulu).   a nonintoxicating beverage, made from coarsely ground boiled mealies fermented with beer screenings

umncatfo (Swazi).   a penile tip cover fashioned from a special kind of calabash, wood, fruit shell, or even horn, and worn by a boy approaching the age of puberty

umninawe (Xhosa).   younger brother

umutsha.   a frontal covering of tanned skin strips or tails joined to a back flap, presented to a boy by his father to mark his transition into puberty

utshwala (Swazi).   intoxicating fermented drink

veld.   country, the South African landscape, grazing or farming land

vhutamba vhutuka (Venda).   annual puberty ceremony

voorhuis (Afrikaans).   the central hall of early Cape Dutch houses

voortrekkers (Afrikaans).   Boer pioneers, members of the Great Trek parties of the 1830s

Bibliographical Essay

SOUTH AFRICA may be the most researched and the most written on country in Africa. The policy and practice of apartheid and the sustained nationalistic struggle against it both within and outside the country kept South Africa in the limelight of world news for much of the twentieth century. A major consequence of these has been a plethora of writings of various genres by many scholars in many disciplines. Much of this literature, however, is focused on modern South Africa, most especially on apartheid, its historical origins, its formulation, implementation, its devastating consequences on the African peoples of South Africa, resistance against this racialist ideology, and its eventual demise. We thus know more about modern South Africa, the history of its white people who had dominated its politics, economy, society, and educational system, than about its indigenous African peoples, who had suffered over three centuries of varying degrees of European domination, dispossession, and dehumanization, and whose history, culture, and civilization were systematically assaulted, maligned, denied, and even suppressed. Thus, in spite of an abundance of literature, the coverage is uneven and the picture incomplete. We know more about the history than about the culture, about politics than about the people. The closing decades of the twentieth century which witnessed the end of apartheid and democratic transformation and gave power to the powerless, had also given voice to the hitherto voiceless, and visibility to the hitherto invisible, resulting in a new resurgence of literary and intellectual activities, directed at redressing the imbalance and remedying the deficiency in the scholarships of the past.

This brief essay will not attempt to cite all that has been published on South Africa in the last few decades. Space will not permit such an undertaking. Instead the focus will be on works consulted in the course of this writing and others considered relevant and valuable for those interested in deeper explorations of the issues we have examined in very highly compressed forms in this book. More specialized and micro treatments of these issues can be found in journals such as *Africa, African Arts, African Studies, Bantu Studies, Journal of African History, Journal of Modern African Studies, Journal of Southern African Studies, Journal of Theology for South Africa, Religion in Southern Africa,* the *South African Historical Journals,* to mention the most prominent. Among the many valuable periodicals, magazines, and newspapers, published in South Africa, are: *Bona, Cape Times, Drum, Mail and Guardian, Sowetan, The Star,* and *You.* In addition, many commercial films, as well as several public and private documentaries have been produced on the South African crisis and society. Notable among these are *Cry, the Beloved Country, The Lost World of the Kalahari, The Gods Must Be Crazy, Cry Freedom* [on Steve Biko], *The Search for Sandra Lane, Shaka Zulu, A Dry White Season, Sarafina, Facing the Truth* (on the Truth and Reconciliation Commission (TRC) of South Africa) with Bill Moyer, and a host of others on Nelson Mandela and the end of apartheid in South Africa.

GENERAL

On culture and customs in Africa in general and on South Africa in particular, see Molefi Kete Asante and Kariumu Welsh Asante, eds., *African Culture: The Rhythms of Unity* (Westport, Conn.: Greenwood, 1985); William R. Bascom and J. Herskovits, eds., *Continuity and Change in African Cultures* (Chicago: University of Chicago Press, 1959); Toyin Falola, ed., *Africa: Culture and Society* (Durham: Carolina Academic Press, 2000); David Hammond-Tooke, ed., *The Bantu-Speaking Peoples of Southern Africa* (London and Boston: Routledge and Kegan Paul, 1974); Hammond-Tooke, *The Roots of Black South Africa* (Johannesburg: Jonathan Ball Publishers, 1993); Peter Magubane, *Vanishing Cultures of South Africa* (Cape Town: Struik Publishers, 1998); Richard Olaniyan, *African History and Culture* (Ikeja and Essex: Longman, 1982); Kwesi Wirendu, *Philosophy and an African Culture* (Cambridge: Cambridge University Press, 1980). Christopher Saunder's *Historical Dictionary of South Africa,* 2nd ed. (1999), provides a quick vignette of the major players and issues of the South African past and is available online. Jean Branford, *A Dictionary of South African English* (Cape Town: Oxford University Press, 1978), is a valuable introduction to the South African variant of the English language. On bibliography, the best place to begin is Reuben and Naomi Musiker, *Southern African*

Bibliography (Lanham, Md., and London: The Scarecrow Press, 1996), 64–218, which provides a most comprehensive bibliography on South Africa for works published between 1945 and 1995.

INTRODUCTION

For a general introduction to the geography of South Africa, see Roddy Fox and Kate Rowntree, eds., *The Geography of South Africa in a Changing World* (Oxford: Oxford University Press, 2000); A. Lemon, ed., *The Geography of Change in South Africa* (Chichester: Wiley & Sons, 1995); A. Lester, *From Colonization to Democracy: A New Historical Geography of South Africa* (London: I. B. Tauris, 1996); M. Meadows, *Biogeography and Ecosystems of South Africa* (Cape Town: Juta, 1985); R. A. Preston-Whyte and P. D. Tyson, *The Atmosphere and Weather of Southern Africa* (Cape Town: Oxford University Press, 1989); Christian Rogerson and Jeffrey McCarthy, eds., *Geography in a Changing South Africa: Progress and Prospects* (Cape Town: Oxford University Press, 1992); D. M. Smith, ed., *The Apartheid City and Beyond: Urbanization and Social Change in South Africa* (London: Routledge, 1992) and J. H. Wellington, *Southern Africa: A Geographical Study* (Cambridge: Cambridge University Press, 1955), 2 vols. For maps and atlases see: A. J. Christopher, *Atlas of Apartheid* (Johannesburg: Witwatersrand University Press, 1994); I. Griffiths, *Atlas of African Affairs* (Johannesburg: Witwatersrand University Press, 1994); *New RSA Atlas* (Maskew Miller Longman, 2002); *Reader's Digest Atlas of Southern Africa* (Cape Town: Reader's Digest Association, 1995). On environmental issues, see: J. Clarke, *Back to Earth: South Africa's Environmental Challenges* (Halfway House: Southern Books, 1991); B. R. Davies and J. Day, *Vanishing Waters* (Cape Town: University of Cape Town Press, 1998); R. F. Fuggle and M. A. Rabie, *Environmental Management in South Africa* (Cape Town: Juta, 1992); Jacklyn Cock and Eddie Koch, eds., *Going Green: People, Politics and the Environment in South Africa* (Cape Town: Oxford University Press, 1991); Eddie Koch, et al., *Water, Waste and Wildlife: The Politics of Ecology in South Africa* (Johannesburg: Penguin, 1990); and Mamphela Ramphele, ed., *Restoring the Land: Environment and Change in Post-Apartheid South Africa* (London: Panos, 1991). On the flora and fauna, see: Auriol Batten, *Flowers of Southern Africa* (Halfway House: Southern Books, 1988); Hans Grobler, et al., *Predators of Southern Africa* (Johannesburg: Macmillan, 1984); D. Hey, *Wildlife Heritage of South Africa* (Cape Town: Oxford University Press, 1966); Liz McMahon and Michael Fraser, *Between Two Shores: Flora and Fauna of the Cape of Good Hope* (Cape Town: David Philip, 1994); and *Southern Africa: Spectacular World of Wildlife* (Cape Town: Reader's Digest Association, 1993). On population groups and languages, very little has been published on the indigenous groups and their languages. Much more has, however, been published on the Afrikaners, the Cape colored, Indians, and Jews. For the Afrikaners, see: W. A. de Klerk, *The Puritans in Africa: A History of Afrikanerdom* (Harmondsworth: Penguin, 1975); Vernon A. February, *The Afrikaners of South Africa* (London: Kegan Paul, 1989); and J. A. Templin, *Ideology on a Frontier: The Theological Foundation of Afrikaner Nationalism, 1652–1910* (Westport, Conn.: Greenwood Press, 1984). On the Cape Malays, see F. R. Bradlow and M. Cairns, *The Early Cape Muslims: A Study of Their Mosques, Genealogy and Origins* (Cape Town: Balkema, 1978) and I. D. Du Plessis, *The Cape Malays: History, Religion, Traditions, Folk Tales. The Malay Quarter* (Cape Town: Balkema, 1972). For the colored people, see: Roy H. Du Pre, *Separate but Unequal: The 'Coloured People' of South Africa: A Political History* (Johannesburg: Jonathan Ball, 1994); Wilmot James, et al., eds., *Now That We Are Free: Coloured Communities in a Democratic South Africa* (Boulder and London: Lynne Rienner Publishers, 1996); and Chris Schoeman, *District Six: The Spirit of Kanala* (Cape Town: Human and Rousseau, 1993). On Indians see: S. Bhana and J. B. Brain, *Setting Down Roots: Indian Migrants in South Africa 1860–1911* (Johannesburg: Witwatersrand University Press, 1989); Bill Freund, *Insiders and Outsiders: The Indian Working Class of Durban, 1910–90* (Durban: University of Natal Press, 1994); and Hilda Kuper, *Indian People in Natal* (Pietermaritzburg: Natal University Press, 1960). On Jews, Zionism, and anti-Semitism, see: Mendel Kaplan and Marian Robertson, eds., *Founders and Followers: Johannesburg Jewry 1887–1915* (Cape Town: Vlaeberg Publishers, 1991); G. Saron, *The Jews of South Africa: An Illustrated History to 1953* (Johannesburg: South African Jewish Board of Deputies, 2001); and Milton Shain, *The Roots of Antisemitism in South Africa* (Virginia: University Press of Virginia, 1994).

HISTORY AND SOCIETY

On the history, the three standard general, comprehensive, and excellent texts are: Rodney Davenport and Christopher Saunders, *South Africa: A Modern History* (New York: St. Martins, 2000); Leonard Thompson, *A History of South Africa* (New Haven: Yale University Press, 1996); and the richly illustrated *Reader's Digest Illustrated History of South Africa,* 3rd ed. (Cape Town: Reader's Digest Association, 1994). Other shorter but equally excellent introductions are J. D. Omer Cooper, *History of Southern Africa,* 2nd ed. (Portsmouth: Heinemann, 1994); Robert Ross, *A Concise History of South Africa* (Cambridge: Cambridge University Press, 1999); Roger B. Beck, *The History of South Africa* (Westport, Conn.: Greenwood Press, 2000); and

Nigel Worden, *The Making of Modern South Africa* (Oxford and Malden, Mass.: Oxford University Press, 2000). William Beinart's *Twentieth-century South Africa* (New York: Oxford University Press, 1994), provides a stimulating introduction to the present century. On the history of Black South Africans, most especially before the twentieth century, see: Peter Delius, *The Land Belongs to Us: The Pedi Polity, the Boers and the British in the Nineteenth Century Transvaal* (Berkeley: University of California Press, 1984); Jeff Guy, *The Destruction of the Zulu Kingdom* (London: Longman, 1979); P. Maylam, *A History of the African People of South Africa: From the Early Iron Age to the 1970's* (New York: St. Martin's Press, 1986); J. D. Omer Cooper, *The Zulu Aftermath: A Nineteenth Century Revolution in Bantu Africa* (Evanston: Northwestern University Press, 1966); J. B. Peires, *The House of Phalo: A History of the Xhosa People in the Days of Their Independence* (Berkeley: University of California Press, 1982); Les Switzer, *Power and Resistance in an African Society: The Ciskei Xhosa and the Making of South Africa* (Madison: University of Wisconsin Press, 1993); and Stephen Taylor, *Shaka's Children: A History of the Zulu People* (London: HarperCollins, 1994). On Cape colonial history, see the excellent collection by Richard Elphick and Herman Gillomee, eds., *The Shaping of South African Society, 1652–1840* (Middletown, Conn.: Wesleyan University Press, 1988). On specific issues and groups, see Jonathan Crush and Charles Ambler, eds., *Liquor and Labor in Southern Africa* (Athens: Ohio University Press, 1992); Elphick, *Khoikhoi and the Founding of White South Africa* (Athens, Ohio: Ohio University Press, 1986); A. Grant, *The Huguenots* (Cape Town: Maskew Miller Longman, 1988); W. Beinart and C. Bundy, eds., *Hidden Struggles in Rural South Africa: Politics and Popular Movements in the Transkei and Eastern Cape, 1800–1930* (Johannesburg: Ravan Press, 1987). On slavery at the Cape, see Robert Ross, *Cape of Torments: Slavery and Resistance in South Africa* (London: Routledge and Kegan Paul, 1983); Robert C. Shell, *Children of Bondage: A Social History of the Slave Society at the Cape of Good Hope* (Hanover and London: Wesleyan University Press, 1995); and N. Worden, *Slavery in Dutch South Africa* (Cambridge: Cambridge University Press, 1985). On mining capitalism and urbanization, see: Lawrence Hughes, *Johannesburg: The Cosmopolitan City* (Johannesburg: Delta Books, 1983); N. A. Mandy, *A City Divided: Johannesburg and Soweto* (Johannesburg: Macmillan, 1984); T. Dunbar Moodie and Vivienne Ndatshe, *Going For Gold: Men, Mines and Migrancy* (Johannesburg: Witwatersrand University Press, 1994); B. Roberts, *Kimberley: Turbulent City* (Cape Town: David Philip, 1985); Robert V. Turrel, *Capital and Labour on the Kimberley Diamond Mines, 1871–1890* (Cambridge: Cambridge University Press, 1987); Charles van Onselen, *Studies in the Social and Economic History of the Wit-*

watersrand, 1886–1994: Volume 1, New Babylon; Volume II, New Nineveh (London: Longman, 1982); and William H. Worger, *South Africa's City of Diamonds: Mine Workers and Monopoly Capitalism in Kimberley, 1867–1895* (New Haven: Yale University Press, 1987). The South African or Anglo-Boer War is one of the most researched and most written about subjects in the southern African historiography. Among the most valuable are: Thomas Pekenham, *The Boer War* (New York: Random House, 1979); Bill Nasson, *Abraham Essau's War: A Black South African in the Cape, 1899–1902* (Cambridge: Cambridge University Press, 1991); Lian Smith, *The Origins of the South African War, 1899–1902* (New York: Longman, 1996); P. Warwick, *Black People and the South African War, 1899–1902* (London: Longman, 1983). On the origins, consequences, and demise of apartheid, see: Brian Lapping, *Apartheid: A History* (New York: George Braziller, 1989); Saul Dubow, *Racial Segregation and the Origins of Apartheid in South Africa, 1919–1936* (London: Macmillan, 1989); George M. Frederickson, *Black Liberation: A Comparative History of Black Ideologies in the United States and South Africa* (New York: Oxford University Press, 1995); R. W. Johnson and Lawrence Schlemmer, *Launching Democracy in South Africa: The First Open Election, April 1994* (New Haven: Yale University Press, 1996); Tom Lodge, *Black Politics in South Africa since 1945* (New York: Longman, 1993); Martin Murray, *The Revolution Deferred: The Painful Birth of Post-Apartheid South Africa* (New York: Verso, 1994); Julian May, ed., *Poverty and Inequality in South Africa: Meeting the Challenge* (Cape Town: David Philip, 2000); Dan O'Meara, *Forty Lost Years: The Apartheid State and the Politics of the National Party, 1948–1994* (Johannesburg: Ravan Press, 1995); Allister Sparks, *Tomorrow Is Another Country: The Inside Story of South Africa's Road to Change* (Chicago: University of Chicago Press, 1996); Leroy Vail, ed., *The Creation of Tribalism in Southern Africa* (Berkeley: University of California Press, 1989); Peter Walsh, *The Rise of Nationalism in South Africa: The African National Congress, 1912–1952* (London: Hurst, 1970). Among the useful biographies and autobiographies are: F. W. de Klerk, *The Last Trek—A New Beginning: The Autobiography* (New York: St. Martin's Press, 1999); Emma Gilbey, *The Lady: The Life and Times of Winnie Mandela* (London: Vintage, 1994); Ellen Kuzwayo, *Call Me Woman* (London: The Woman's Press, 1985); Albet Luthuli, *Let My People Go: An Autobiography* (Johannesburg: Collins, 1962); Rian Malan, *My Traitor's Heart* (New York: Vintage Press, 1990); Nelson Mandela, *Long Walk to Freedom: The Autobiography of Nelson Mandela* (London: Little Brown & Company, 1994); Winnie Mandela, *Part of Soul went with Him* (New York: Norton, 1985); Ezekiel Mphahlele, *Down Second Avenue* (Berlin: Seven Seas, 1959); Mamphela Ramphele, *My Life* (Cape Town: David Philip, 1995); Anthony Sampson,

Nelson Mandela: The Authorized Biography (New York: Harper Collins, 1999); Leonard Thompson, *Survival in Two Worlds: Moshoeshoe of Lesotho, 1786–1870* (Oxford: Claredon Press, 1975); Charles van Onselen, *The Seed in Mine: The Life of Kas Maine, a South African Sharecropper, 1894–1985* (Cape Town: David Philip, 1996); and Robert I. Rotberg, *The Founder: Cecil Rhodes and the Pursuit of Power* (New York: Oxford University Press, 1988). On the Truth and Reconciliation Commission, see: Alex Boraine, *A Country Unmasked* (Oxford: Oxford University Press, 2000); Lyn S. Graybill, *Truth & Reconciliation in South Africa: Miracle or Model?* (Boulder: Lynne Rienner, 2002); Desmond Tutu, *No Future without Forgiveness* (London: Rider Books, 1999); and the compelling account by the South African poet and writer, Antjie Krog, *Country of My Skull* (Johannesburg: Random House, 1998). The five-volume *Report of the Truth and Reconciliation Commission of South Africa* (Cape Town: Juta, 1998) is available in print, on CD-ROM, as well as on the World Wide Web at http://www.polity.org.za /govdocs/commissions/1998/trc/index.htm.

RELIGIONS

The best single volume brief introduction to the history and practice of religions in South Africa is David Chidester, *Religions of South Africa* (London: Routledge, 1992). On African traditional religion see John W. Argyle and Eleanor Preston-White, eds., *Social System and Tradition in Southern Africa* (Cape Town: Oxford University Press, 1978); Alan Barnard, "Structure and Fluidity in Khoisan Religious Ideas," *Journal of Religion in Africa* 18 (1988): 216–36; T. Beidelman, "Swazi Royal Ritual," *Africa* 36 (1966): 373–405; Axel Iver Berglund, *Zulu Thought-Patterns and Symbolism* (London: C. Hurst, 1976; W. D. Hammond-Tooke, "Do the South-eastern Bantu Worship Their Ancestors?," in Argyle and Preston-Whyte, eds., *Social System and Tradition*, 134–49; *Boundaries and Belief: The Structure of a Sotho Worldview* (Johannesburg: Witwatersrand University Press, 1981); *Rituals and Medicines: Indigenous Healing in South Africa* (Johannesburg: A. D. Donker, 1989); Irving Hexham, "Lord of the Sky, King of the Earth: Zulu Traditional Religion and Belief in the Sky God," *Sciences Religieuses/Studies in Religion* 10 (1981): 273–78; Janet Hogson, *The God of the Xhosa* (Cape Town: Oxford University Press, 1982); H. Kuckertz, ed., *Ancestor Religion in Southern Africa* (Cacadu: Lumko Missiological Institute, 1981); J. D. Lewis-Williams, *Believing and Seeing: Symbolic Meanings in Southern San Rock Paintings* (London: Academic Press, 1981); Lorna Marshall, "!Kung Bushmen Religious Beliefs," *Africa*, 32, 1962, 221–52; Harriet Ngubane, *Body and Mind in Zulu Medicine* (London: Academic Press, 1977); Gabriel Setiloane, *The Image of God among the Sotho – Tswana* (Rotterdam: A. A. Balkema, 1976); M. G. Whisson and M. West, eds., *Religion and Social Change in Southern Africa* (Cape Town: David Philip, 1975). On Islam, Hinduism and Judaism, see: A. Davids, *The Mosques of Bo-Kaap: A Social History of Islam at the Cape* (Athlone, Cape: South African Institute of Arabic and Islamic Research, 1980); Chris Greyling, "Shech Yusuf, The Founder of Islam in South Africa," *Religion in Southern Africa* 1 (1980): 9–22; Jocelyn Hellig, "South African Judaism: An Expression of Conservative Traditionalism," *Judaism* 35 (1986): 232–42; "The Religious Expressions of South African Jewry," *Religion in Southern Africa* 8, 2 (1987): 3–17; and C. Kuppusami, *Religions, Practices and Customs of South African Indians* (Durban: Sunray, 1983). On Christianity, see the recent collection by Richard Elphick and Rodney Davenport, eds., *Christianity in South Africa: A Political, Social, and Cultural History* (Berkeley: University of California Press, 1997). Other useful studies are: J. B. Brain, *The Catholic Church in the Transvaal* (Johannesburg: Missionary Oblates of Mary Immaculate, 1990); D. N. Brigg and J. Wing, *The Harvest and the Hope: The Story of Congregationalism in Southern Africa* (Johannesburg: United Congregational Church of South Africa, 1970); *By Taking Heed: The History of Baptists in Southern Africa, 1820–1977* (Roodepoort: Baptist Publishing House, 1983); Hans W. Florin, *Lutherans in South Africa* (Durban: Lutheran Publishing Co., 1967); and Peter Hinchliff, *The Anglican Church in South Africa* (London: Darton, Longman, & Todd, 1963). On African Initiated or Independent Churches, see: J. M. Chirenje, *Ethiopianism and Afro-Americans in Southern Africa, 1883–1916* (Baton Rouge: Louisiana State University Press, 1987); A. Dubb, *A Community of the Saved: An African Revivalist Church in the Eastern Cape* (Johannesburg: Witwatersrand University Press, 1976); Louise Kretzchmar, *The Quest for a Black Theology in South Africa* (Johannesburg: Ravan Press, 1985); and B. G. M. Sundkler, *Bantu Prophets in South Africa* (London: Oxford University Press, 1948). On Pentecostalism, see the splendid introduction by: Allan Anderson, *Bazalwane: African Pentecostals in South Africa* (Pretoria: University of South Africa, 1992). On religion and politics, see: David Chidester, *Shots in the Streets: Violence and Religion in South Africa* (Cape Town: Oxford University Press, 1992); Martin Prozesky, ed., *Christianity in South Africa* (London: Macmillan, 1989); Jean Comaroff and John Comaroff, *Of Revelation and Revolution: Christianity, Colonialism and Consciousness in South Africa* (Chicago: University of Chicago Press, 1991); Cosmos Desmond, *Christians or Capitalists? Christianity and Politics in South Africa* (London: Bowerdean Press, 1978); J. W. De Gruchy, *The Church Struggle in South Africa* (Grand Rapids, Mich.: Wm. B. Eerdmans, 1987); Z. Mbali, *The Churches and Racism: A Black South African Perspective* (N.p: SCM Press, 1987); K. Nurnberger, *Power and Beliefs in South Africa*

(Pretoria: University of South Africa, 1988); and Charles Villa-Vicencio, *Trapped in Apartheid: A Socio-Theological History of the English-Speaking Churches* (Cape Town: David Philip, 1988).

LITERATURE

An excellent single-volume introduction to South African literature is Michael Chapman, *Southern African Literature* (London and New York: Longman, 1996). Other useful critical studies are: David Adey, et al., eds., *Companion to South African English Literature* (Johannesburg: Donker, 1986); Jaccques Alvares-Pereyre, *The Poetry of Commitment,* translated by Clive Wake (London: Heinemann, 1984); Ursula Barnett, *A Vision of Order: A Study of Black South African Literature in English (1914–1980)* (Amherst: University of Massachusetts Press, 1983); Duncan Brown and Bruno van Dyck, eds., *Exchanges: South African Writing in Transition* (Pietermaritzburg: University of Natal Press, 1991); Michael Chapman, et al., eds. *Perspectives on South African English Literature* (Johannesburg: Donker, 1992); Vernon February, *Mind Your Colour: The 'Coloured' Stereotype in South African Literature* (New York: Routledge, 1991); Stephen R. Gray, *Southern African Literature: An Introduction* (New York: Harper & Row, 1979); Matthew Krause, ed., *The Invisible Ghetto: Lesbian and Gay Writings from South Africa* (Johannesburg: Cosaw, 1993); Don McLennan, *Perspectives on South African Fiction* (Johannesburg: Donker, 1980); Njabulo S. Ndebele, *Rediscovery of the Ordinary: Essays on South African Literature and Culture* (Johannesburg: Cosaw Publishing, 1991); Jeff Opland, *Xhosa Oral Poetry: Aspects of a Black South African Traditions* (Cambridge: Cambridge University Press, 1983); Martin Trump, ed., *Rendering Things Visible: Essays on South African Literary Culture* (Athens: Ohio University Press, 1990); P. A. Shava, *People's Voice: Black South African Writing in the Twentieth Century* (Athens: Ohio University Press, 1989); Michael Chapman, *South African English Poetry: A Modern Perspective* (Johannesburg: Donker, 1984); M. Van Wyk Smith, *Grounds of Contest: A Survey of South African English Literature* (Kenwyn, South Africa: Juta, 1990); Michael Wade, *White on Black in South Africa: A Study of English-Language Descriptions of Skin Colour* (New York: St. Martin's Press, 1993); and Jane Watts, *Black Writers from South Africa: Towards a Discourse of Liberation* (New York: St. Martin's Press, 1989); Landeg White and Tim Couzens, eds., *Literature and Society in South Africa* (Harlow: Longman, 1984). For collections of short stories, an especially accessible and popular genre among black writers, see: Robin Malan, compiler, *Being Here: Modern Short Stories from Southern Africa* (Cape Town: David Philip, 1994); *The Best of South African Short Stories* (Cape Town: Reader's Digest Association, 1991); Martin Trump and Jean

Marquard, ed., *A Century of South African Short Stories* (Johannesburg: Donker, 1981); Michael Chapman, ed., *Drum Decades: Stories from the 1950's* (Pietermaritzburg: University of Natal Press, 1989); Chinua Achebe and C. L. Innes, eds., *The Heinemann Book of Contemporary African Short Stories* (Oxford: Heinemann, 1992); Stephen Gray, *Penguin Book of Cotemporary South African Short Stories* (Johannesburg: Penguin Books, 1993); Annemarie van Nickerk, ed., *Raising the Blinds: A Century of South African Women's Stories* (Johannesburg: Donker, 1990); Norman Hodge, ed., *To Kill a Man's Pride and Other Short Stories from South Africa* (Johannesburg: Ravan Press, 1984); and David Adey, ed., *Under the Southern Cross: Short Stories from South Africa* (Johannesburg: Donker, 1982). Notable anthologies of poetry include: Michael Chapman and Achman Dangor, eds., *Voices from Within* (Johannesburg: Donker, 1982) [Black South African Poetry]; Tim Couzens and Essop Patel, eds., *The Return of the Amasi Bird: Black South African Poetry (1891–1981)* (Johannesburg: Ravan Press, 1991); Stephen Gray, *Modern South African Poetry* (Johannesburg: Donker, 1984); Liz Gunner and Mafika Gwala, eds., *Musho: Zulu Popular Praises* (Johannesburg: Witwatersrand University Press, 1984); Cecily Lockett, *Breaking the Silence: A Century of South African Women's Poetry* (Johannesburg: Donker, 1990); Robin Malan, ed., *New Outridgings: Contemporary South African Verse* (Cape Town: Oxford University Press, 1993); Andries Walter Oliphant, *Essential Things: An Anthology of New South African Poetry* (Johannesburg: Congress of South African Writers, 1992); Jeff Opland, ed., *Words That Circle Words: A Choice of South African Oral Poetry* (Johannesburg: Donker, 1992). For children and juvenile literature, see: Rita V. Hirsch, ed., *A Day Like Any Other: Stories, Poetry and Art by Street Children in South Africa* (Johannesburg: Cosaw, 1993); Elwyn Jenkins, *Children of the Sun: Selected Writers and Themes in South African Children's Literature* (Johannesburg: Ravan Press, 1993); and Robin Malan, ed., *Explorings: A Collection of Poems for the Young People of Southern Africa* (Cape Town: David Philip, 1988).

MEDIA

For general treatment of the media, see Keyan Tomaselli, et al., ed., *Addressing the Nation: Studies on the South African Media* (Durban: Richard Lyon, 1986). On the press, see Jennifer Crwys-Williams, *South African Despatches: Two Centuries of the Best in South African Journalism* (Rivonia, Sandton: Ashanti Publishers, 1989); Wessel De Kock, *A Manner of Speaking: The Origins of the Press in South Africa* (Cape Town: Saayman and Weber, 1982); Gordon S. Jackson, *Breaking Story: The South African Press* (Boulder: Westview Press, 1993); Joel Mervis, *The Fourth Estate: A Newspaper Story*

(Johannesburg: Jonathan Ball, 1991); G. Shaw, *Some Beginnings: The Cape Times (1876–1910)* (Cape Town: Oxford University Press, 1975); Keyan Tomaselli, Ruth Tomaselli, and John Muller, eds., *The Press in South Africa* (New York: St. Martin's Press, 1987); and D. H. Varley, *A Short History of the Newspaper Press in South Africa, 1652–1952* (Cape Town: Nasionale Pers, 1952). On broadcasting, the most comprehensive is Keyan Tomaselli and Ruth Tomaselli, eds., *Currents of Power: State Broadcasting in South Africa* (Bellville: Anthropos, 1989). See also R. Fardon and G. Furness, eds., *African Broadcast Cultures: Radio in Transition* (Cape Town: David Philip, 2000); R. Gerber and R. Braun, *New Connections: Telecommunications in a Changing South Africa* (Rondebosch: University of Cape Town Press, 1998); Thelma Gutsche, *History and Social Significance of Motion Pictures in South Africa, 1895–1940* (Cape Town: Timmins, 1972) and E. Rosenthal, *You Have Been Listening: The Early History of Radio in South Africa* (Cape Town: Purnell, 1974). On press, politics and apartheid, see: Morris Broughton, *Press and Politics of South Africa* (Cape Town: Purnell, 1961); Chenhamo C. Chimutengwende, *South Africa: The Press and the Politics of Liberation* (London: Barbican, 1978); J. Duncan and M. Seleoane, eds., *Media and Democracy in South Africa* (Pretoria: Human Sciences Research Council and FXI, 1998); Anthony C. Giffard and William A. Hachten, *The Press and Apartheid: Repression and Propaganda in South Africa* (Madison: University of Wisconsin Press, 1984), published in South Africa by Macmillan, under the title: *Total Onslaught: South African Press under Attack;* Joseph Harker, ed., *Legacy of Apartheid* (London: Guardian Newspapers, 1994); Shaun Johnson, *Strange Days Indeed* (London: Bantam Press, 1993); Eric Louw, *South African Media Policy: Debates of the 1990's* (Durban: Center for Cultural and Media Studies, University of Natal, 1993); I. Manoim, *You Have Been Warned: The First Ten Years of the Mail and Guardian* (London: Viking, 1996); Christopher Merrett, *A Culture of Censorship: Secrecy and Intellectual Repression in South Africa* (Pietermaritzburg: University of Natal Press, 1994); Kenneth Owens, *These Times: A Decade of South African Politics* (Johannesburg: Jonathan Ball, 1992); Richard Pollak, *Up against apartheid: The Role and Plight of the Press in South Africa* (Carbondale: Southern Illinois University Press, 1981); Elaine Potter, *The Press as Opposition: The Political Role of South African Newspapers* (London: Chatto & Windus, 1975); Leo Radista, *Prisoners of a Dream. The South African Mirage: Historical Essay on The Denton Hearings* (Johannesburg: Ashanti Publishers, 1989); S. Stein, *Who Killed Mr. Drum?* (Cape Town: Mayibuye Books, 1999), a history of the *Drum* newspaper; Keyan Tomaselli, ed., *The Cinema of Apartheid: Race and Class in South African Film* (Bergvlei: Random Century SA, 1989); and Harvey Tyson, *Editors under Fire* (Sandton: Random House, 1993). On the alternative or resistance press, see: M. Botha and A. H. van Aswegan, *Images of South Africa: The Rise of the Alternative Film* (Pretoria: Human Sciences Research Council, 1992); William Finnegan, *Dateline Soweto: Travels with Black South African Reporters* (New York: Harper & Row, 1988); Les Switzer, ed., *South Africa's Alternative Press: Voices of Protest and Resistance, 1880s–1960s* (Cambridge: Cambridge University Press, 1997); Les Switzer and Mohamed Adhikari, eds., *South Africa's Resistance Press: Alternative Voices in the Last Generation under Apartheid* (Athens: Ohio University Center for International Studies, 2000); and Keyan G. Tomaselli and Eric Louw, eds., *Alternative Press in South Africa: Studies in the South African Media* (Bellville: Anthropos, 1991).

ART AND ARCHITECTURE

On prehistoric rock art of the San and related groups, see W. W. Battiss, *The Artists of the Rocks* (Pretoria: Red Fawn Press, 1949); C. K. Cooke, *Rock Art of Southern Africa* (Cape Town: Books of Africa, 1969); Thomas A. Dawson, *Rock Engravings of Southern Africa* (Johannesburg: Witwatersrand University Press, 1992); Thomas A. Dawson, eds., *Contested Images: Diversity in Southern African Rock Art Research* (Johannesburg: University of Witwatersrand Press, 1994); Townley R. Johnson and Tim Maggs, *Major Rock Paintings of Southern Africa,* 3rd ed. (Cape Town: Philip, 1992); N. Lee and B. Woodhouse, *Art on the Rocks of Southern Africa* (Cape Town: Purnell, 1970); David Lewis-Williams, *Discovering Southern African Rock Art* (Cape Town: David Philip, 1990); David Lewis-Williams and Thomas Dawson, *Images of Power: Understanding Bushman Rock Art* (Halfway House: Southern Book Publishers, 1989); Jalmar Ruder and Ione Ruder, *The Hunter and His Art: A Survey of Rock Art in Southern Africa* (Cape Town: Struik, 1970); P. Vinnicombe, *People of the Eland: Rock Paintings of the Drakensberg Bushmen as a Reflection of Their Life and Thought* (Pietermaritzburg: University of Natal Press, 1976); and A. R. Wilcox, *Drakensberg Bushmen and Their Art* (Winterton: Drakensberg Publications, 1990). On the art of the African peoples, see the valuable contributions in Anitra Nettleton and W. D. Hammond-Tooke, eds., *African Art in South Africa: From Tradition to Township* (Johannesburg: Donker, 1989). Other useful studies are: E. J. De Jager, *Contemporary African Art in South Africa* (Cape Town: Struik, 1973); De Jager, "Five South African Artists," *African Arts* 11, January 1978, 250–55; N. Dubow, "Art and Protest," *Leadership,* South Africa 5, 6, 1986: 60–65; R. Levinsohn, *Art and Craft of Southern Africa: Treasures in Transition* (Johannesburg: Delta Books, 1984); Anitra Nettleton, "Home Is Where the Art Is: Six South African Rural Artists," *African Arts,* Winter 2000, 26–39, 93–94; U. Scholz, *Phafa-Nyika: Contemporary Black Art in South Africa with Special Reference to the Transvaal*

(Pretoria: History of Art Archives, University of Pretoria, 1980); Monica Blackman Visona, "Southern Africa," in Visona, et al., *A History of Art in Africa* (New York: Harry N. Abrams, Inc., Publishers, 2001), 472–97; and Gavin Yagin, *The Art of the African Township* (London: Thames & Hudson, 1988). On beadwork, see: H. S. Schoeman, "A preliminary report on traditional beadwork in the Mkhwanzi area of the Mtunzini district Zululand," Part I, *African Studies* 27(2), 1968, 57–81; Part II, *African Studies* 27(3), 1968, 107–33; R. G. Twala, "Beads as Regulating the Social Life of the Zulu and Swazi," *African Studies,* 10(3), 1958, 113–23. Hans Fransen, *Three Centuries of South African Art: Fine Art, Architecture, Applied Arts* (Johannesburg: Donker, 1982), provides the most comprehensive panoramic coverage of the history of South African art, most especially its Western and European dimensions. On European and modern South African art generally, see Esme Berman, *Art and Artists of South Africa: An Illustrated Biographical Dictionary and Historical Survey of Painters and Graphic Artists since 1875,* rev. ed. (Halfway House, Transvaal: Southern Book Publishers, 1992); Berman, *Painting in South Africa* (Halfway House: Southern Book Publishers, 1993); *Contemporary South African Art: The Gencor Collection* (Johannesburg: Jonathan Ball, 1997); Frieda Harmsen, *Looking at South African Art* (Pretoria: Van Schaik, 1993); F. Herreman, ed., *Liberated Voices: Contemporary Art from South Africa* (New York: Museum for African Art, 1999); Grania Ogilvie and Carol Graff, *Dictionary of South African Painters and Sculptors* (Johannesburg: Everard Read Gallery, 1988); Celestine J. Pretorius, *The History of Folk Art in South Africa* (Cape Town: Vlaeberg, 1993); Elizabeth Rankin, *Images of Metal: Post-War Sculptures and Assemblages in South Africa* (Johannesburg: Witwatersrand University Press, 1994); Murray Schoonraad and Elzabe Schooraad, *Companion to South African Cartoonists* (Johannesburg: Donker, 1990). On resistance art see: South African History Archive, Poster Book Collection, *Images of Defiance: South African Resistance Posters of the 1980's* (Johannesburg: Ravan Press, 1991 and Sue Williamson, *Resistance Art in South Africa* (New York: St. Martin's Press, 1990).

On indigenous African architecture, see the valuable and richly illustrated study by Franco Frescura, *Rural Shelter in Southern Africa: A Survey of the Architecture, House Forms and Constructional Methods of the Black Rural Peoples of Southern Africa* (Johannesburg: Ravan Press, 1981). Other shorter but useful explorations include: *Standard Encyclopedia of Southern Africa* (Cape Town: Nasou Limited, 1970) vol. 1; Gary Van Wyk, *African Painted Houses: Bashoto Dwellings of South Africa* (New York: Harry N. Adams, 1998). On Cape Dutch, British colonial and other European architectural expressions in South Africa, see: C. de Bosdari, *Cape Dutch Houses and Farms: Their Architecture and History* (Cape Town: Balkema, 1964); M. A. Cook and

H. Fransen, *The Old Buildings of the Cape* (Cape Town: Balkema, 1981); Roger C. Fisher, Schalk Le Roux, and Maré Estelle, *Architecture of the Transvaal* (Pretoria: University of South Africa, 1998); David Goldblatt and Margaret Courtney-Clark, *Famous Cape Dutch Homesteads,* text by James Ambrose Brown (Cape Town: Struik, 1981); D. E. Greig, *A Guide to Architecture in South Africa* (Cape Town: Timmins, 1971); R. Lewcock, *Early Nineteenth Century Architecture in South Africa: A Study of the Interaction of Two Cultures, 1795–1837* (Cape Town: Balkema, 1963); Sabine Marschall and Brian Kearney, *Opportunities for Relevance: Architecture in the New South Africa* (Pretoria: University of South Africa Press, 2000); C. Muwanga, *South Africa: A Guide to Recent Architecture* (London: Ellipses, 1998); A. M. Oberholzer et al., *The Cape House and Its Interior* (Stellensbosch: Stellensbosch Museum, 1985); G. E. Pearse, *Eighteenth Century Architecture in South Africa* (Cape Town: Balkema, 1968); D. Picton-Seymour, *Historical Buildings in South Africa* (Cape Town: Struikhof, 1989); Pamela Strauss, *Africa Style in South Africa: Pondokkies, Khayas and Castles,* photographs by John Curtis and Pamela Straus (Johannesburg: Jonathan Ball, 1994); Graham Viney and Alain Proust, *Colonial Houses of South Africa* (Cape Town: Struik Winchester, 1987); James Walton, *Homesteads and Villages of South Africa,* 2nd ed. (Pretoria: Van Schaik, 1967); and Walton, *Old Cape Farmsteads* (Cape Town: Human & Rousseau, 1989). For the life histories and careers of notable individual artists and architects, see: C. De Bosdari, Anton Anreith, *Africa's First Sculptor* (Cape Town: 1954); N. Dubow, *Irma Stern* (Cape Town: C. Struik, 1974); D. E. Greig, *Herbert Baker in South Africa* (Cape Town: Purnell, 1970); C. Harrop-Allin, *Norman Eaton, Architect* (Cape Town: C. Struik, 1975); and F. F. Haenggi, *Lucas Sithole* (Johannesburg: gallery 21, 1979).

CUISINE AND COSTUMES

Precious little has been written on the culinary customs of the indigenous peoples of South Africa. Two very comprehensive, albeit dated, explorations are: P. J. Quin, *Food and Feeding Habits of the Pedi* (Johannesburg: Witwatersrand University Press, 1959) and Sonya M. Jones, "A Study of Swazi Nutrition: Report of the Swaziland Nutrition Survey 1961–62 for the Swaziland Administration," unpublished manuscript, Institute for Social Research, University of Natal, Durban, 1963, 193 (I found and used a copy on deposit at the Library of the University of Natal, Pietermaritzburg, SA, June 2002). Other useful, albeit dated, studies include: E. H. Aston, "A Sociological Sketch of Sotho Diet," *Transaction of the Royal Society of South Africa* 27, 2, 1939–40: 147–214; A. T. Bryant, *The Zulu People As They Were Before the White Man Came* (Pietermaritzburg: Shuter and Shooter, 1967), 264–371;

and B. P. Thompson, "Two Studies in African Nutrition," *Rhodes Livingstone Papers* 24, 1954: 1–57. On South African cooking generally, and most especially Cape cooking and its Malays' expressions, the best place to begin are the works of Louis C. Leipoldt and Laurens van der Post, two well-known South African writers, whose love for food and cooking led them to write highly eloquent books on the subject enthralling to read not only as valuable guides to cooking but as fascinating works of literature: Leipoldt, *Leipoldt's Cape Cookery* (Cape Town: W. J. Flesch, 1976); van der Post, *First Catch Your Eland* (New York: William Morrow and Company, Inc., 1978); and *African Cooking* (New York: Time-Life Books, 1970). For Cape Malay cooking, see: Hilder Gerber, *Traditional Cookery of the Cape Malays* (Amsterdam and Cape Town: A. A. Balkema, 1957). For an illuminating historical survey of the development of Cape Cookery, see: Renata Coetzee, *The South African Culinary Tradition: The Origins of South Africa's Culinary Arts during the 17th and 18th Centuries, and 167 Authentic Recipes of This Period* (Cape Town: C. Struik, 1977). Other valuable works on South African Cooking, with numerous recipes, are: Hilary Biller and John Peacock, *Tastes: Thoughts on South African Cuisine* (Halfway House: Zebra Press, 1998); Renata Cetzee, *FUNA: Food from Africa* (Durban: Butterworths, 1982); Hildagonda Duckitt, *Traditional South African Cookery*, rev. ed. (New York: Hippocrene Books, 1996); Vida Heard and Leslie Faull, *Cookery in Southern Africa: Traditional and Today* (Cape Town: Books of Africa, 1970); Mimi Jardin, *Cooking the Portuguese Way in South Africa* (Sandton, SA: Penguin Books, 2000); Eve Palmer, *Return to Camdeboo: A Century's Karoo Foods and Flavours* (Cape Town: Tafelberg, 1992); D. J. Van Zyl, *The Woman's Value Book of Traditional South African Cooking* (Cape Town: Human and Rousseau, 1985); and Peter Veldsman, *Flavours of South Africa* (Cape Town: Tafelberg, 1999). On the traditional dress of the various African groups, very little has been published in recent years; the most useful sources are therefore quite dated. Barbara Tyrell's *Tribal Peoples of Southern Africa* (Cape Town: Books of Africa, 1968), with its richly illustrated exploration of "tribal dress" is a must read for anyone with keen interest in the vanishing cultures of South Africa. Other valuable sources are: A. T. Bryant, *The Zulu People* (Pietermaritzburg: Shuter and Shooter, 1967), 132–73 and E. Krige, *The Social System of the Zulu* (Pietermaritzburg: Shuter and Shooter, 1965), 370–82. For a recent but illuminating exploration of the resilience of traditional forms in the face of modernization, see Sandra Klopper, "You Need Only One Bull to Cover Fifty Cows: Zulu Women and 'Traditional' Dress," in Stephen Clingman, ed., *Regions and Repertoires: Topics in South African Politics and Culture* (Braamfontein: Ravan Press, 1991), 147–77. On ornaments, beads, and body adornments, see: Frank Jolles, "Traditional Zulu Beadwork of the Mzinga Area," *African Arts,*

January 1993, 42–53, 101; Carolee G. Kennedy, "Prestige Ornaments: The Use of Brass in the Zulu Kingdom," *African Arts,* Autumn 1994, 50–55, 94–95; Jean Morris and Eleanor Preston-Whyte, *Speaking with Beads: Zulu Arts from Southern Africa* (New York: Thames and Hudson, 1994); and Peter Magubane and Sandra Klopper, *Dress and Adornment* (Cape Town: Struik Publishers, 2001). On European traditional dress forms in South Africa, see: Trudie Kestell, "Costume, Historical," in *Standard Encyclopedia of Southern Africa,* Vol. 3, 449–54; D.H. Strutt, *Fashion in South Africa, 1652–1900* (Cape Town: Balkema, 1975); and A.A. Telford, *Yesterday's Dress: A History of Costume in South Africa* (Cape Town: Purnell, 1972).

Gender Roles, Marriage, and Family

The subject of women has received considerable attention in South African studies. Among the issues that have been examined are the impacts of colonization, Christianization, industrialization, mining capitalism, labor migrancy, urbanization, and apartheid on women and their changing status under apartheid and modernization. On women in indigenous South African societies, see Jeff Guy, "Women in Precapitalist South African Society," in Shula Marks and Anthony Atmore, eds., *Economy and Society in Pre-Industrial South Africa* (London: Longman, 1980); and C.N. Quinta, *Women in Southern Africa* (Johannesburg: Skotaville, 1987). On women and apartheid, see Jane Barrett, ed., *South African Women Speak* (New York: Grove Press, 1986); Susan Bazilli, *Putting Women on the Agenda* (Johannesburg: Ravan Press, 1991); Hilda Bernstein, *For Their Triumphs and for Their Tears: Women in Apartheid South Africa* (London: International Defence and Aid Fund for Southern Africa, 1985); J. Goodwin, *Cry Amandla: South African Women and the Question of Power* (New York: Africana Publishing Company, 1984); R.E. Lapchick and S. Urdang, *Oppression and Resistance: The Struggle of Women in Southern Africa* (Westport, Conn.: Greenwood Press, 1982); Margaret Lessing, ed., *South African Women Today* (Cape Town: Maskew Miller Longman, 1994); Bata Lipman, *We Make Freedom: Women in South Africa* (London: Routledge Kegan Paul and Pandora Press, 1984); C. Obbo, *African Women: Their Struggle for Independence* (Johannesburg: Ravan Press, 1981); Sean Redding, "Witchcraft, Women, and Taxes in the Transkei, South Africa, 1930–1963," in Catherine Higgs et al., eds., *Stepping Forward: Black Women in Africa and the Americas* (Athens: Ohio University Press, 2002), 87–99. Diana E.H. Russell, *Lives of Courage: Women for a New South Africa* (New York: Basic Books, 1989); Barbara Schreiner, ed., *A Snake with Ice Water: Prison Writings by South African Women* (Fordsburg: Congress of South African Writers, 1992); Kathryn Spink, *Black Sash: The*

Beginnings of a Bridge in South Africa (London: Methuen, 1991); N. Van Vuuren, *Women against Apartheid: The Fight for Freedom in South Africa, 1920–1975* (Palo Alto: California R & E Research Association, 1979); Cherryl Walker, *Women and Resistance in South Africa,* 2nd ed. (New York: Monthly Review Press, 1991); Walker, ed., *Women and Gender in Southern Africa to 1945* (London: James Currey, 1991); and Julia C. Wells, *We Now Demand: The History of Women's Resistance to Pass Laws in South Africa* (Johannesburg: Witwatersrand University Press, 1993). On women in the industries, see: Iris Berger, *Threads of Solidarity: Women in South African Industry, 1900–1980* (London: James Currey, 1992); Bill Freund, *Insiders and Outsiders: The Indian Working Class of Durban, 1910–1990* (London: Heinemann, 1990); Fatima Meer, ed., *Black-Women-Worker,* 2nd ed. (Durban: Mediba Publishers, 1991); Belinda Bozzoli and Mmantho Nkotsoe, *Women of Phokeng: Consciousness, Life Strategy and Migrancy in South Africa, 1900–1983* (Portsmouth, N.H.: Heinemann, 1991); Fatima Meer, *Factory and Family: The Divided Lives of South Africa's Women Workers* (Durban: University of Natal, Institute for Black Research, 1985); Meer et al., *Patriarchs, Race, and Class: South Africa's Women Industrial Workers* (Durban: Institute for Black Research, 1986). On the institution of domestic servants, see: Jacklyn Cock, *Maids and Madams: A Study in the Politics of Exploitation,* rev. ed. (London: Women's Press, 1989) and Suzanne Gordon, *A Talent for Tomorrow: Life Stories of South African Servants* (Johannesburg: Ravan Press, 1985). On women, violence and the justice system, see: Alice Armstrong, *Women and the Law in Southern Africa* (Harare: Zimbabwe Publishing House, 1987); Binaifer Nowrejee and Bronwen Manby, *Violence against Women in South Africa: State Response to Domestic Violence and Rape* (London: Human Rights Watch, 1996); Julie Stewart and Alice Armstrong, eds., *Legal Situation of Women in Southern Africa* (Harare: University of Zimbabwe Publications, 1990); L. Vetten, ed., *Man Shoots Wife: A Pilot Study Detailing Intimate Femicide in Gauteng, South Africa* (Gauteng: POWA, 1995). On marriage and family, see: Anthony Bannister, *Bushmen: A Changing Way of Life* (Cape Town: Struik, 1991); S. Burman and E. Preston-Whyte, eds., *Questionable Issue: Illegitimacy in South Africa* (Cape Town: Oxford University Press, 1992); Mark Gevisser and Edwin Cameron, eds., *Defiant Desire: Gay and Lesbian Lives in South Africa* (Johannesburg: Ravan Press, 1994); Eileen J. Krige, *Essays on African Marriage in Southern Africa,* 2nd ed. (Pietermaritzburg: University of Natal Press, 1981); and B. Tyrrell, *Tribal Peoples of Southern Africa* (Cape Town: Books of Africa, 1968). On the challenges ahead for women in postapartheid South Africa, see: UWC Gender Equity Unit and SARDC-WIDSAA, *Beyond Inequalities: Women in South Africa* (Bellville, South Africa and Harare, Zimbabwe: University of

Western Cape, Gender Equity Unit & Southern African Research and Documentation Center, 1997). See also Patricia Romero, *Profiles in Diversity: Women in the New South Africa* (East Lansing: Michigan State University Press, 1998).

SOCIAL CUSTOMS AND LIFESTYLES

For cultural, aesthetic, and exotic reasons, social customs may be one of the most researched topic in South African studies. On the Khoisan and related groups, see Anthony Bannister, *Bushmen: A Changing Way of Life* (Cape Town: Struik, 1991); Alan Barnard, *Hunters and Herders of Southern Africa: A Comparative Ethnography* (Cambridge: Cambridge University Press, 1992); A. Smith, et al., *The Bushmen of Southern African: A Foraging Society in Transition* (Cape Town: David Philip, 2000); H. P. Steyn, *Vanished Lifestyles: The Early Cape Khoi and San* (Pretoria: Unibook, 1990); Lorna J. Marshall, *Nyae Nyae !Kung: Beliefs and Rites* (Cambridge: Peabody Museum Monograph, Harvard University, 1999). Among the most valuable studies on the Bantu-speaking peoples of South Africa are: John Argyle and Eleanor Preston-Whyte, eds., *Social System and Tradition in Southern Africa: Essays in Honour of Eileen Krige* (Cape Town: Oxford University Press, 1978); W. Bozongwana, *Ndebele Religion and Customs* (Gweru: Mambo, 1990); Jean Comaroff, *Body of Power, Spirit of Resistance: The Culture and History of South African People* (Chicago: The University of Chicago Press, 1985); W. D. Hammond-Tooke, *The Roots of Black South Africa* (Johannesburg: Jonathan Ball, 1993); Hammond-Tooke, ed., *The Bantu-Speaking Peoples of Southern Africa* (London: Routledge & Kegan Paul, 1974); R. M. Kavanagh, *Making People's Theatre* (Johannesburg: Witwatersrand University Press, 1997); E. J. Krige, *The Social System of the Zulu,* rev. ed. (Pietermaritzburg: Shooter and Shuter, 1988); Peter Magubane, *Vanishing Cultures of South Africa: Changing Customs in a Changing World* (Cape Town: Struik Publishers, 1998); and Magubane and Sandra Klopper, *African Renaissance* (Cape Town: Struik Publishers, 2000). On urbanization and social change, see: T. Hauptfleisch, *Theatre and Society in South Africa: Some Reflections in a Fractured Mirror* (Pretoria: Van Schaik, 1997); N. Mathiane, *Beyond the Headlines: Truths of Soweto Life* (Bergvlei: Southern Book Publishers, 1990); Sarah Nuttall and Cheryl-Ann Michael, eds., *Senses of Culture: South African Culture Studies* (Oxford: Oxford University Press, 2000); David Smith, ed., *Living under Apartheid: Aspects of Urbanization and Social Change in South Africa* (Winchester, Mass.: Allen & Unwin, 1986); and H. W. Van Der Merwe and C. J. Groenewald, *Occupational and Social Change among the Coloured People in South Africa* (Cape Town: Juta, 1977). On sport, recreation, and tourism see: I. Alfred, *Lifting the Covers: The Inside*

Story of South African Cricket (Cape Town: Spearhead, 2001); L. Burke, et al., *The Complete South African Guide to Sports Nutrition* (Cape Town: Oxford University Press, 1998); S. Derwent, *Guide to Cultural Tourism in South Africa* (Cape Town: Struik, 1999); *EyeWitness Travel Guides: South Africa* (Cape Town: DK Publishing, Inc., 1999); E. Griffiths, *Bidding for Glory: Why South Africa Lost the Olympic and World Cup Bids, and How to Win Next Time* (Johannesburg: Jonathan Ball, 2000); A. Grundelingh et al., *Beyond the Try-line: Rugby and SA Society* (Randburg: Ravan Press, 1995); Duncan Guy, *The Very Best of Johannesburg and Surrounds* (Cape Town: Struik, 2000); *Insight Guide: South Africa* (London: Insight Guide/APA Publications, 2000); and J. Nauright, *Sport, Cultures and Identities in South Africa* (Cape Town: David Philip, 1998).

PERFORMING ARTS AND CINEMA

On African music generally, see Alan P. Merriam, *African Music in Perspective* (New York: Garland Publishing, 1982); John Miller Chernoff, *African Rhythm and African Sensibility: Aesthetics and Social Action in African Musical Idioms* (Chicago: University of Chicago Press, 1979; Ronnie Graham, ed., *Stern's Guide to Contemporary African Music* (London: Pluto Press, 1988); Graham, ed., *Stern's Guide to Contemporary African Music, vol. 2: The World of African Music* (London: Pluto Press, 1992). On the indigenous musical traditions of the Khoisan and the Bantu-speaking peoples, see: John Blacking, "Movement, Dance, Music, and the Venda girls' Initiation Cycle," in Paul Spencer, ed., *Society and the Dance* (Cambridge: Cambridge University Press, 1985); Rosemary Joseph, "Zulu Women's Bow Songs: Ruminations on Love," *Bulletin of the School of Oriental and African Studies,* 50, 1, 1987, 90–119; T. F. Johnston, "Notes on the Music of the Tswana," *South African Music Encyclopedia,* ii, edited by J. P. Malan, 376–81; John E. Kaemmer, "Southern Africa: An Introduction," in *Garland Encyclopedia of World Music, vol. 1: Africa* (New York: Garland Press, 1998), 700–721; Daniel Kunene, *Heroic Poetry of the Basotho* (Oxford: Clarendon, 1971); Z. B. Molefe and M. A. Mzileni, *A Common Hunger to Sing: A Tribute to South Africa's Black Women of Song, 1950 to 1990* (Cape Town: Kwela Books, 1997); David Rycroft, "Hottentot Music," *The New Grove Dictionary of Music and Musicians,* edited by Stanley Sadie (London: Macmillan, 1980); "Stylistic Evidence in Nguni Song," in K. P. Wachsmann, ed., *Essays on Music and History in Africa* (Evanston: Northwestern University Press, 1971); Elkin Sithole, "Ngoma Music among the Zulu," in John Blacking and J. Keali'inohomoku, *The Performing Arts: Music and Dance* (The Hague: Mouton, 1979); "South Africa: Indigenous Music," in *The Garland Encyclopedia of World Music,*

72–93 (contributions by David K. Rycroft, Angela Impey, Gregory F. Barz, John Blacking, Jaco Kruger, and C. T. D. Marivate); Leroy Vail and Landeg White, *Power and Praise Poem: Southern African Voices in History* (Charlottesville: University Press of Virginia, 1991); Robin Wells, *An Introduction to the Music of the Basotho* (Morija, Lesotho: Morija Archives, 1994). The classic work on indigenous musical instruments remains Percival R. Kirby, *The Musical Instruments of the Native Races of South Africa,* 2nd ed. (Johannesburg: Witwatersrand University Press, 1965). On the Xhosa see: D. Dargie, *Xhosa Music: Its Techniques and Instruments, with a Collection of Songs: With Cassette* (Cape Town: David Philip, 1988) and Dargie, *Xhosa Zionist Church Music* (Bergvlei, South Africa: Hodder & Stoughton Educational, 1987). For a fairly comprehensive history of South African music, three surveys are most valuable: Muff Anderson, *Music in the Mix* (Johannesburg: Ravan Press, 1981); Garth Chilvers and Tom Jasuikowicz, *History of Contemporary Music in South Africa* (Johannesburg: Toga, 1994); and J. P. Malan, ed., *South African Music Encyclopedia,* 4 volumes (Cape Town: Oxford University Press, 1979, 1982, 1984, and 1986). On European musical traditions see Caroline Mears and James May, "South Africa: European Art Music," in *The New Grove Dictionary of Music and Musicians,* vol. 24, 87–91; J. J. A. van der Walt, "Afrikaans Church and Mission Music," *South African Music Encyclopedia,* ed. J. P. Malan (Cape Town: Oxford University Press, 1979–86); and J. Bouws, "Music," *Standard Encyclopedia of Southern Africa,* ed. D. J. Potgieter, viii (Cape Town: NASOU, 1970–76). On ballet, see Marina Grut, *The History of Ballet in South Africa* (Cape Town: Human & Rousseau, 1981). More than any other genre of South African music, popular music has been the focus of many fascinating studies. Notable among these are: Christopher Ballatine, *Marabi Nights: Early South African Jazz and Vandeville* (Johannesburg: Ravan Press, 1993); Basil Breakey, *Beyond the Blues: Township Jazz of the '60s and '70s* (Cape Town: David Philip, 1994); David B. Coplan, *In Township Tonight! South Africa's Black City Music and Theatre* (London and New York: Longman, 1985); Coplan, *In the Time of Cannibals: The Word Music of South Africa's Basotho Migrants* (Chicago: The University of Chicago Press, 1994); Veit Erlmann, *African Stars: Studies in Black South African Performance* (Chicago and London: The University of Chicago Press, 1991); Erlmann (with an introduction by Joseph Shabalala), *Nightsong: Performance, Power and Practice in South Africa* (Chicago and London: The University of Chicago Press, 1996); Yvonne Huskisson, *Black Composers of Southern Africa* (Pretoria: Human Sciences Research Council, 1992); and Helen Q. Kivnick, *Where Is the Way: Song and Struggle in South Africa* (New York: Viking Penguin, 1990).

Index

About the Author

FUNSO AFOLAYAN is Associate Professor of History at the University of New Hampshire, Durham.